THE HASKINS SOCIETY JOURNAL
STUDIES IN MEDIEVAL HISTORY

The Charles Homer Haskins Society
Officers and Councilors for 2023

Officers
Jennifer Paxton, President
Laura Gathagan, Vice-President for North America
Emily Winkler, Vice-President for UK
Hirokazu Tsurushima, Vice-President for Japan
Thomas J.H. McCarthy, Executive Secretary
Austin Mason, Treasurer
Joanna Drell, Conference Director
Steven Isaac, Associate Conference Director
William North, Editor of the *Haskins Society Journal*
Laura Wangerin, Associate Editor of the *Haskins Society Journal*
Amy Livingston, Editor of Haskins Society Book Series

Councilors
Scott G. Bruce
Charlotte Cartwright
Katie Hodges-Kluck
Charlie Rozier

THE HASKINS SOCIETY JOURNAL

STUDIES IN MEDIEVAL HISTORY

EDITED BY WILLIAM NORTH AND LAURA E. WANGERIN

Volume 34
2023

THE BOYDELL PRESS

© Contributors 2024

All Rights Reserved. Except as permitted under current legislation
no part of this work may be photocopied, stored in a retrieval system,
published, performed in public, adapted, broadcast,
transmitted, recorded or reproduced in any form or by any means,
without the prior permission of the copyright owner

First published 2024
The Boydell Press, Woodbridge

ISBN 978-1-83765-042-2

ISSN 0963-4959

The Boydell Press is an imprint of Boydell & Brewer Ltd
PO Box 9, Woodbridge, Suffolk IP12 3DF, UK
and of Boydell & Brewer Inc.
668 Mt Hope Avenue, Rochester, NY 14620-2731, USA
website: www.boydellandbrewer.com

A CIP catalogue record for this book is available
from the British Library

The publisher has no responsibility for the continued existence or accuracy of
URLs for external or third-party internet websites referred to in this book, and
does not guarantee that any content on such websites is, or will remain, accurate
or appropriate

Please note that some of the discussion in this book addresses sensitive material,
including racism (chapter 12) and mention of rape and violence (chapter 8).

Contents

List of Illustrations		vii
Editors' Note		viii
Abbreviations		ix
1	Reading the Greek Fathers in Latin in Pre-Conquest England *Scott G. Bruce*	1
2	Journey to the South: The Travels of William of Malmesbury in the Mid-1130s *Ming Liu*	15
3	Kings in the Cloister: Contemporary Reception of Aelred of Rievaulx's Royal Biographies *W. Tanner Smoot*	31
4	Heretics, Miracles, and Cistercian Preachers: The Influence of Henry of Marcy on Herbert of Clairvaux's *Liber visionum et miraculorum Clarevallensium* *Emmie Rose Price-Goodfellow*	51
5	Some Problems of the Peace: Angels in America (and Angevin England) *Simon Yarrow*	69
6	Purgatory Revisited *Carl Watkins*	91
7	The Exemplary Knighting of Geoffrey Plantagenet: A Historiographical and Documentary Reappraisal *Arnaud Montreuil*	109
8	The Repentance of Geoffroy de Milly: Anger, Penance, and the Limits of Sovereign Authority in Thirteenth-Century France *Anne E. Lester*	127
9	The Politics of Witnessing: *Enquêtes* as a Technique of Power in Thirteenth-Century France *Richard E. Barton*	153

10 Taking It on Trust? Writing about Officials in the Medieval
   Italian Communes   201
   Frances Andrews

11 Following Her Star: Evelyn Faye Wilson, *The Stella Maris
   of John of Garland*, and Making a Career in Medieval Studies
   in America   235
   William Chester Jordan

12 The Life, Scholarship and Legacy of Bennett David Hill,
   1934–2005   249
   Randall Todd Pippenger

Illustrations

2. *Ming Liu*, Journey to the South: The Travels of William of Malmesbury in the Mid-1130s

Map

2.1 The Travel Route of William of Malmesbury along the Main Roads   23

10. *Frances Andrews*, Taking it on Trust? Writing about Officials in the Medieval Italian Communes

Figure

10.1 Anonymous, Cover of the account book for July to December 1343 produced by the Cistercian treasurer, Don Simone di Ser Vanni, monacho di San Galgano, Siena, Treasury of the Biccherna (Metropolitan Museum of Art, New York, NY; Item no. 10.203.3)   202

12. *Randall Todd Pippenger*, The Life, Scholarship and Legacy of Bennett David Hill, 1934–2005

Figure

12.1 Bennett David Hill, 1960   264

Full credit details are provided in the captions to the images in the text. The editors, contributors and publisher are grateful to all the institutions and persons for permission to reproduce the materials in which they hold copyright. Every effort has been made to trace the copyright holders; apologies are offered for any omission, and the publisher will be pleased to add any necessary acknowledgment in subsequent editions.

Editors' Note

This volume of the *Haskins Society Journal* includes papers read at the Annual Conference of the Haskins Society before the pandemic at University of North Carleton, Raleigh-Durham; those hosted online in 2020 and 2021; and the hybrid conference hosted in 2022 at the University of Richmond. It contains scholarship pursued under often challenging research and writing conditions resulting from the COVID-19 pandemic. This volume presents the Bethell Prize Essays for 2021 (judged by Dr Hugh Thomas) and 2022 (judged by Dr Frances Andrews), as well as the C. Warren Hollister Memorial Essays for 2021 and 2022. The Editors would like to offer thanks to the contributors, anonymous reviewers, and Caroline Palmer and the excellent staff at Boydell & Brewer Ltd for their help, good spirits, and patience during the production of this volume.

The *Haskins Society Journal* is an international refereed journal, and its contents are not limited to papers read at the Society's own conference or at the sessions which it sponsors at Leeds, Kalamazoo, or other venues. Papers on topics in the many fields and periods of the medieval past to which Charles Homer Haskins contributed, including but not limited to Anglo-Saxon, Viking, Norman, and Angevin history as well as the history of the neighboring peoples and territories, are welcome from any scholar. Authors intending to submit are asked to consult the Society's website (www.haskinssociety.org) or write to the Editor (Dr William North, Department of History, Carleton College; email: wnorth@carleton.edu) or Associate Editor (Dr Laura Wangerin, Department of History, Seton Hall University; email: laura.wangerin@shu.edu).

William North, Editor
Laura Wangerin, Associate Editor

Abbreviations

AASS	*Acta Sanctorum (67 vols, Antwerp/Brussels/Paris 1643–1884)*
AHR	*American Historical Review*
ANS	*Anglo-Norman Studies* (formerly *Proceedings of the Battle Conference on Anglo-Norman Studies)*
ASC	Anglo-Saxon Chronicle; normally cited from *Two of the Saxon Chronicles Parallel,* ed. Charles Plummer (2 vols, Oxford, 1892–9), with year and MS
ASE	*Anglo-Saxon England*
Bede, *EH*	Bede, *Ecclesiastical History of the English People,* ed. and trans. B. Colgrave and R.A.B. Mynors (Oxford, rev. edn, 1991)
Bk of Fees	*Liber feodorum: the Book of Fees, commonly called Testa de Nevill* (3 vols, London, 1920–31)
BL	British Library, London
Bracton	*Bracton on the Laws and Customs of England,* ed. and trans. Samuel E. Thorne (4 vols, Cambridge, MA, 1968–77)
Bracton's Note Book	*Bracton's Note Book: a Collection of Cases decided in the King's Courts during the Reign of Henry the Third,* ed. F.W. Maitland (3 vols, London, 1887)
CCM	*Cahiers de Civilisation Médiévale*
Cal. Chart. R.	*Calendar of the Charter Rolls, 1226–1516* (6 vols, London, 1903–27)
Cal. Docs. France, ed. Round	*Calendar of Documents preserved in France illustrative of the History of Great Britain and Ireland, I: A.D. 918–1206,* ed. J.H. Round (London, 1899)
Cal. Lib. R.	*Calendar of the Liberate Rolls preserved in the Public Record Office* (6 vols, London, 1916–64)
Cal. Pat.	*Calendar of the Patent Rolls preserved in the Public Record Office* (London, 1891 and in progress)
Camb. Hist. Jnl	*Cambridge Historical Journal*

Abbreviations

CCCM	*Corpus Christianorum, continuatio mediaevalis* (Turnhout, 1971–)
CCSL	*Corpus Christianorum, series latina* (Turnhout, 1953–)
CSEL	*Corpus Scriptorum Ecclesiasticorum Latinorum* (Vienna, 1866–)
Close R.	*Close Rolls of the Reign of Henry III preserved in the Public Record Office* (14 vols, London, 1902–38)
Complete Peerage	G.E. C[okayne], *The Complete Peerage of England, Scotland, Ireland, Great Britain, and the United Kingdom, Extant, Extinct, and Dormant,* new edn by V. Gibbs and others (12 vols in 13, London, 1910–59)
Cur. Reg. R.	*Curia Regis Rolls preserved in the Public Record Office* (17 vols, in progress, London, 1922–)
DB	*Domesday Book, seu liber censualis Wilhelmi primi regis Angliae* [ed. Abraham Farley] (2 vols, London, 1783)
DNB	*Dictionary of National Biography*, ed. Leslie Stephen and Stephen Lee
Dudo, *History*	Eric Christiansen, trans., *Dudo of St Quentin: History of the Normans* (Woodbridge, 1998)
EcHR	*Economic History Review*
EHD	*English Historical Documents, I: c. 500–1042*, ed. Dorothy Whitelock (2nd edn, London, 1979); *II: 1042–1189*, ed. David C. Douglas and George W. Greenaway (2nd edn, London, 1981); *III: 1189–1327*, ed. Harry Rothwell (London, 1975)
EHR	*English Historical Review*
EME	*Early Medieval Europe*
EYC	*Early Yorkshire Charters*, ed. W. Farrer and C.T. Clay (13 vols: vols i–iii, Edinburgh, 1914–16; index to vols I–iii, and vols iv–xii, Yorkshire Archaeological Soc. Record Ser. Extra Ser. 1–10 [1935–65])
FSI	*Fonti per la Storia d'Italia*
Gesta Stephani	*Gesta Stephani*, ed. K.R. Potter and revised R.H.C. Davis (Oxford, 1976)
Glanvill	*The Treatise on the Laws and Customs of the Realm of England commonly called Glanvill*, ed. and trans. G.D.G. Hall with guide to further reading by M.T. Clanchy (Oxford, rev. ed. 1993)
GND, ed. van Houts	*The Gesta Normannum Ducum of William of Jumièges, Orderic Vitalis, and Robert of Torigni*, ed. and trans. Elisabeth M.C. van Houts (2 vols, Oxford, 1992–5)

Henry of Huntingdon, *Historia*	Henry, Archdeacon of Huntingdon, *Historia Anglorum: the History of the English People,* ed. and trans. Diana Greenway (Oxford, 1996)
Hist. Res.	*Historical Research* (formerly *Bulletin of the Institute of Historical Research*)
HSJ	*Haskins Society Journal*
JEH	*Journal of Ecclesiastical History*
JMH	*Journal of Medieval History*
John of Worcester, *Chronicle*	*The Chronicle of John of Worcester*, ed. and trans. R.R. Darlington, P. McGurk, and J. Bray (3 vols, Oxford, 1995–)
MGH	Monumenta Germaniae Historica
AA	*Auctores Antiquissimi*
Epp.	*Epistolae*
LdL	*Libelli de Lite*
SS	*Scriptores in folio*
SSRG	*Scriptores Rerum Germanicarum, separatim editi*
SSRG, n.s.	*Scriptores Rerum Germanicarum, nova series*
MS/MSS	manuscript/manuscripts
NA	The National Archives, Kew, London
OV	*The Ecclesiastical History of Orderic Vitalis*, ed. Marjorie Chibnall (6 vols, Oxford, 1969–80)
PP	*Past & Present*
PBA	*Proceedings of the British Academy*
Pipe R.	*The Great Roll of the Pipe* (Pipe Roll Society), with regnal year
PL	*Patrologia latina cursus completus*, ed. J.-P. Migne (221 vols, Paris, 1844–64)
Rec. Com.	Record Commissioners
Recueil, ed. Fauroux	*Recueil des actes des ducs de Normandie de 911 à 1066,* ed. M. Fauroux (Caen, 1961)
Regesta	*Regesta regum Anglo-Normannorum, 1066–1154,* ed. H.W.C. Davis and others (4 vols, Oxford, 1913–69
RHC	*Recueil des Historiens des Croisade*
Doc. Arm.	*Documents arménienes* (2 vols, Paris, 1869–1906)
Gr.	*Historiens Grecs* (2 vols, Paris, 1875–81)
Lois	*Lois* (2 vols, Paris, 1841–3)
Occid.	*Historiens Occidentaux* (5 vols in 6, 1844–95)
Or.	*Historiens Orientaux* (5 vols, Paris, 1872–1906)
RIS	*Rerum Italicarum Scriptores*

Rot. de Lib.	*Rotuli de liberate ac de misis et praestitis, regnante Johanne,* ed. T.D. Hardy (London, 1844)
Rot. Hund.	*Rotuli hundredorum temp. Hen. III & Edw. I*, ed. W. Illingworth and J. Caley (2 vols, London, 1812–18)
Rot. Litt. Claus.	*Rotuli litterarum clausarum in turri Londinensi asservati, 1204–27,* ed. T.D. Hardy (2 vols, London, 1833–44)
Rot. Litt. Pat.	*Rotuli litterarum patentium in Turri Londinensi asservati (1201–16),* ed. T.D. Hardy (London, 1835)
RS	Rolls Series
Sawyer, *Charters*	P.H. Sawyer, *Anglo-Saxon Charters: an Annotated List and Bibliography* (London, 1968), with charter number
s.a. (no italics)	*sub anno/annis* [under the year/-s]
ser.	Series
Settimane	*Settimane di Studio del Centro Italiano di Studi sull'Alto Medioevo*
Soc.	Society
Stubbs, *Charters*	*Select Charters and Other Illustrations of English Constitutional History from the Earliest Times to the Reign of Edward the First,* ed. William Stubbs (9th edn, revised H.W.C. Davis, Oxford, 1913)
s.v. (no italics)	*sub verbo*
Symeon, *Opera*	*Symeonis monachi opera omnia,* ed. Thomas Arnold, RS 75 (2 vols, London, 1882–5)
TRHS	*Transactions of the Royal Historical Society*
Univ.	University
unpub.	Unpublished
VCH	*The Victoria History of the Counties of England* (in progress), with name of county
William of Malmesbury, *GP*	William of Malmesbury, *Gesta Pontificum Anglorum,* ed. and trans. R.M. Thomson and M. Winterbottom (2 vols, Oxford, 2007)
William of Malmesbury, *GR*	William of Malmesbury, *Gesta regum Anglorum,* ed. and trans. R.A.B. Mynors, R.M. Thomson, and M. Winterbottom (2 vols, Oxford, 1998–9)
William of Malmesbury, *HN*	William of Malmesbury, *Historia novella,* ed. K.R. Potter and E. King (Oxford, 1998)
William of Poitiers, *Gesta*	William of Poitiers, *The Gesta Gvillelmi of William of Poitiers,* ed. and trans. R.H.C. Davis and M. Chibnall (Oxford, 1998)

I

Reading the Greek Fathers in Latin in Pre-Conquest England[1]

Scott G. Bruce

The acquisition of proficiency in Greek did not come easily in pre-Conquest England.[2] Far removed from the linguistic currents of the Mediterranean Sea and lacking the resources available to Latin Christian scholars of an earlier age, the Venerable Bede (672–735) labored for long hours alone to wring meaning from the single Greek manuscript at his disposal: the so-called 'Laudian Acts', a copy of the Acts of the Apostles with parallel Greek and Latin texts produced in Sardinia in the decades around 600 and brought from Italy to Northumbria a century later by either Benedict Biscop or Ceolfrith.[3] Lacking both teachers who were native Greek speakers and specialized instruments of reference to facilitate his understanding of Greek grammar and syntax, Bede's progress was slow, but over many years he seems to have advanced from a passive student unable

---

[1] I am grateful for the opportunity to have presented this paper at the 2022 meeting of The Haskins Society at the University of Richmond (28–30 October 2022) and at the 42nd Annual Medieval Studies Conference at Fordham University, entitled 'Lost & Found: The Legacies of Greek Culture in the Global Middle Ages' (4–5 March 2023). This contribution is part of the first phase of the 'Lost Patriarchs Project', a research initiative funded by a National Endowment for the Humanities Fellowship 2020–21 (FEL-267928).
  The following abbreviations are used in this article: ALL = Michael Lapidge, *Anglo-Latin Literature 600–899* (London and Rio Grande, OH, 1996); CLA = Ellis Avery Lowe, *Codices Latini Antiquiores: A Paleographical Guide to Latin Manuscripts Prior to the Ninth Century* (11 vols and supplement, Oxford, 1934–71); and HE = Bede, *Historia Ecclesiastica*, ed. and trans. Bertram Colgrave and R.A.B. Mynors, in *Bede's Ecclesiastical History of the English People* (Oxford, 1969) (cited by book, chapter, and page number).

[2] For a masterful survey of the reception of Greek language and literature in medieval Europe, see Walter Berschin, *Greek Letters and the Latin Middle Ages: From Jerome to Nicholas of Cusa*, trans. Jerold C. Frakes (Washington, DC, 1988), esp. 99–101 on pre-Conquest England.

[3] Oxford, Bodleian Library, MS Laud Grec. 25 = CLA, vol. 2, 37 (no. 251); and Bernhard Bischoff, *Katalog der festländischen Handschriften des neunten Jahrhunderts (mit Ausnahme der wisigotischen)* (4 vols, Wiesbaden, 1998–2017), ii, 267 (no. 3812a). For what follows, see Kevin M. Lynch, 'The Venerable Bede's Knowledge of Greek', *Traditio* 39 (1983), 432–9.

to decipher a passage of the New Testament without a Latin crib to an active reader able to deduce the forms and meanings of Greek nouns and verbs. Two of Bede's eighth-century hagiographers singled out this aspect of his learning for praise, but he produced no heirs to his ambition to become a competent reader of Greek, and no English scholar would rival his proficiency until the thirteenth century.[4]

With a hint of melancholy, Bede knew that he had already missed the golden age of Greek learning in Christian England. It had flourished a generation previously at the school of Canterbury, inspired by the arrival of Archbishop Theodore of Tarsus on 27 May 669.[5] A native of Greek-speaking Cilicia in Asia Minor, Theodore was a student in Antioch until the successive Persian and Arab invasions of Syria made him a refugee, first in Constantinople and later in Rome at the monastery of Cilician monks located *ad aquas Salvias*. There his learning earned him the attention of a succession of Roman pontiffs, most notably Pope Vitalian, who in 667 appointed Theodore to fill the vacant see of Canterbury. Since Theodore was not a native westerner, Vitalian took the precaution of sending with him a handler, a bilingual North African prelate named Hadrian, who had been the abbot of a monastery in Campania (near Naples).[6] Together Theodore and Hadrian founded a school in Canterbury, where they expounded on the literal meaning of the Old and New Testaments, as well as works of Latin patristics, Christian history, hagiography, and more.[7] The surviving portions of their biblical commentaries and the lecture notes of their students preserved in early medieval glossaries provide valuable insight into the use of Greek in their teaching.[8] As Michael Lapidge has shown, Theodore and Hadrian in all likelihood lectured on the New Testament Vulgate with a copy of the Greek text in hand for comparative reference and sometimes spoke in Greek as they

---

[4] *Brevis commemoratione de venerabili Beda* 2 (BHL 1071), PL 90, col. 37: Et cum in Latine erudiretur lingua, Graecae quoque peritiam non mediocriter percepit; and *Vita venerabilis Bedae* (BHL 1069), PL 90, col. 46: Cumque Latinae aeque ut vernaculae linguae in qua natus est percepisset notitiam, Graecae quoque non parva ex parte attigit scientiam. On the study of Greek in thirteenth-century England with a focus on the industry of Robert Grosseteste (c. 1168–1253) and Roger Bacon (1215–92), see Berschin, *Greek Letters and the Latin Middle Ages*, 249–55.

[5] On the life and work of Theodore, see Bernhard Bischoff and Michael Lapidge, *Biblical Commentaries from the Canterbury School of Theodore and Hadrian* (Cambridge, 1994), 5–81; and Michael Lapidge, 'The Career of Archbishop Theodore', in *Archbishop Theodore: Commemorative Studies on his Life and Influence* (Cambridge, 1995), 1–29, reprinted in ALL, 93–121.

[6] On the career of Hadrian, see Bischoff and Lapidge, *Biblical Commentaries from the Canterbury School*, 82–132.

[7] For what follows, see Michael Lapidge, 'The School of Theodore and Hadrian', *Anglo-Saxon England* 15 (1986), 45–72, reprinted in ALL, 141–68; and more generally Bischoff and Lapidge, *Biblical Commentaries from the Canterbury School*, 133–89.

[8] Bischoff and Lapidge, *Biblical Commentaries from the Canterbury School*, 190–274. On the so-called 'Leiden Glossary', which was produced around 800 CE at St Gall and based on an insular exemplar, see now *Canterbury Glosses from the School of Theodore and Hadrian: The Leiden Glossary*, ed. Michael Lapidge (2 vols, Leiden, 2023).

taught.⁹ In his *Ecclesiastical History of the English People*, Bede provided an idealized portrait of the impact of these Greek-speaking teachers on their early English pupils:

And because both of them were extremely learned in sacred and secular literature, they attracted a crowd of students into whose minds they daily poured the streams of wholesome learning. They gave their hearers instruction not only in the holy Scripture but also in the art of metre, astronomy, and ecclesiastical computation. As evidence of this, some of their students still survive who know Latin and Greek just as well as their native tongue. Never have there been such happy times since the English first came to Britain...[10]

'Never have there been such happy times.' There was thus a well-documented efflorescence of interest in Greek language and learning in late seventh-century Canterbury. It did not last, however. The most celebrated student of this school, Aldhelm of Malmesbury, betrayed little knowledge of Greek in the entire corpus of his written work.[11] It is telling that no direct evidence of the impact of this school survives in the textual or material record beyond Bede's nostalgic report.

While there were very few scholars who could read a Greek text in pre-Conquest England, this did not diminish interest in the rich tradition of eastern patristics produced in late antiquity. The history of the reception of Christian Greek writings in western Europe is still in its infancy.[12] Fortunately, studies of the earliest English manuscripts and the contents of insular libraries allow us to investigate the availability of these kinds of texts in pre-Conquest England.[13] Like their counterparts in Europe, early English readers encountered Greek patristics exclusively in Latin translations made in the fourth, fifth, and sixth centuries. The first part of this essay surveys the works of the eastern fathers

---

9   Michael Lapidge, 'The Study of Greek at the School of Canterbury in the Seventh Century', in *The Sacred Nectar of the Greeks: The Study of Greek in the West in the Early Middle Ages*, ed. Michael W. Herren (London, 1992), 162–94, reprinted in ALL, 123–39.
10 HE 4.2, 332–5: Et quia litteris sacris simul et saecularibus, ut diximus, abundanter ambo errant instructi, congregata discipulorum caterua scientiae salutaris cotidie flumina inrigandis eorum cordibus emanabant, ita ut etiam metricae artis, astronomiae et arithmeticae ecclesiasticae disciplinam inter sacrorum apicum uolumina suis auditoribus contraderent. Indicio est quod usque hodie supersunt de eorum discipulis, qui Latinam Graecamque linguam aeque ut propriam in qua nati sunt norunt. Neque umquam prorsus, ex quo Brittaniam petierunt Angli, feliciora fuere tempora...
11 Berschin, *Greek Letters and the Latin Middle Ages*, 99–100.
12 Albert Siegmund, *Die Überlieferung der griechischen christlichen Literatur in der lateinischen Kirche bis zum zwölften Jahrhundert* (Munich, 1949), 49–138, provided the most extensive treatment of this topic in the twentieth century. For a new initiative to survey and catalogue works of Greek patristics in medieval Europe, see Scott G. Bruce, 'The Lost Patriarchs Project: Recovering the Greek Fathers in the Medieval Latin Tradition', *Religion Compass* 14 (2020), 1–8.
13 Lapidge, *The Anglo-Saxon Library* (Oxford, 2006); and Helmut Gneuss and Michael Lapidge, *Anglo-Saxon Manuscripts: A Bibliographical Handlist of Manuscripts and Manuscript Fragments Written or Owned in England up to 1100* (Toronto, 2014) have been indispensable resources for this inquiry.

rendered into Latin in late antiquity. It then charts the reception history of these translations in the early medieval west and identifies three Greek authors whose work was especially prized in Latin reading communities: Origen of Alexandria, Eusebius of Caesarea, and John Chrysostom. The second part of the essay turns to England, whither pilgrims and prelates conveyed manuscripts of translated eastern patristics for the new abbeys of the north. The evidence of surviving books and library catalogues both from England and from missionary zones on the Continent provides a valuable index of the Greek Christian fathers known to early English readers and the specific works available to them in translation. Lastly, the essay considers the evidence for the diverse ways in which Latin translations of works by Origen, Eusebius, and John Chrysostom were deployed by exegetes, teachers, and preachers in the centuries leading up to the Conquest.

Reading the Greek Fathers in Latin in Early Medieval Europe

The translation of the Greek Fathers began in earnest at the end of the fourth century, when the wayward friends Jerome of Stridon and Rufinus of Aquileia became rivals in their ambition to render the exegetical works of the third-century theologian Origen of Alexandria into Latin, a medium better suited for intellectuals in Rome and elsewhere at a time when Greek learning was on the wane in the western provinces and for wider dissemination among the clergy of the Latin West.[14] Of the two, Jerome had a longer history of engagement with Origen's work, but he only translated thirty-seven of his homilies on Isaiah, Jeremiah, and Ezekiel and two of his homilies on the Song of Songs before other projects captured his attention.[15]

In contrast, Rufinus came late to the enterprise of translating Greek patristics into Latin, but he did so with an almost manic industry during the last decade of his life.[16] The result was a staggering corpus of translated materials that provided

---

[14] For older, but still useful, accounts of the contentious relationship between Jerome and Rufinus, see Francis X. Murphy, *Rufinus of Aquileia (345–411): His Life and Works* (Washington, DC, 1945), *passim*; and J.N.D. Kelly, *Jerome: His Life, Writings, and Controversies* (London, 1975), esp. 243–58. For a succinct summary of the controversies surrounding their translation efforts, see now Richard A. Layton, 'Reception of Origen in the Fourth Century', in *The Oxford Handbook of Origen*, ed. Ronald E. Heine and Karen Jo Torjesen (Oxford, 2022), 445–60 at 452–56. The classic account of the controversy caused by Origen's legacy in the decades around 400 remains Elizabeth Clark, *The Origenist Controversy: The Cultural Construction of an Early Christian Debate* (Princeton, NJ, 1992).

[15] Kelly, *Jerome*, 75–9. On Jerome's emulation of Origen and indebtedness to his exegetical scholarship, see Mark Vessey, 'Jerome's Origen: The Making of a Christian Literary Persona', *Studia Patristica* 28 (1993), 135–45; and, most recently, Andrew Cain, *Jerome's Commentaries on the Pauline Epistles and the Architecture of Exegetical Authority* (Oxford, 2021), 161–94.

[16] For what follows, see Caroline P. Hammond, 'The Last Ten Years of Rufinus' Life and the Date of his Move South from Aquileia', *Journal of Theological Studies* 29 (1977), 372–429, reprinted in Caroline P. Hammond, *Origeniana et Rufiniana* (Freiburg, 1996), no. IV.

generations of Latin readers in western Europe with a veritable library of biblical exegesis, apologetic literature, homilies, and sacred history of Christian Greek origin. These texts included a collection of Basil the Great's homilies as well as his *Rule for Monks*, Pamphilius' *Apology for Origen*, Gregory of Nazianzos' homilies, the *Sentences of Sextus*, the anonymous *History of the Monks of Egypt*, and Eusebius's *Ecclesiastical History* (for which Rufinus composed a Latin continuation from the death of Constantine in 337 to the death of Theodosius the Great in 395). Rufinus spent most of his time and energy, however, on the writings of Origen, rendering into Latin his sprawling books of exegesis on Genesis, Exodus, Leviticus, Numbers, Judges, and the Song of Songs, as well as his commentary on Paul's Letter to the Romans. He also made available in Latin translation Origen's ill-fated treatise *On First Principles*, a work of experimental theology that contributed to the Alexandrian teacher's condemnation as a heretic.[17]

While the immediate reception of the Latin translations made by Jerome and Rufinus is difficult to evaluate, it is clear that their body of work was vital to the educational program envisioned in the second half of the sixth century by Cassiodorus (d. 585) at the abbey of Vivarium in Calabria.[18] Assembling an *équipe* of bilingual monks well-equipped with Greek manuscripts collected from Constantinople and North Africa, Cassiodorus set out to translate into Latin any works of Greek Christian learning that might prove to be beneficial to religious communities in the west. Thanks to the labors of Jerome and Rufinus, he already had in hand an impressive collection of Latin translations of biblical exegesis and Christian history written by a host of Greek fathers.[19] With substantial resources and manpower at his disposal, Cassiodorus amplified the cultural inheritance left by these late antique translators.

As described in the *Institutions of Divine and Secular Learning*, a treatise that would become one of the most important touchstones for monastic pedagogy in medieval Europe, Vivarium was a veritable hive of bookish industry. Throughout the first section on the topic of Christian learning, Cassiodorus presented the lineaments of a course of study that paired books of the Bible with the commentaries of the ancient fathers. When he could not find an appropriate commentary in Latin, Cassiodorus reported on the translation work undertaken by his monks from the Greek to fill in the *lacuna*. For example, in the absence of a commentary on the Acts of the Apostles by a Latin authority, he noted that he had discovered a Greek commentary on this book by John Chrysostom, which 'my friends, with the Lord's aid, have translated in two volumes of fifty-five

---

[17] On the utility and readership of Origen's translated works in the Latin West, see Scott G. Bruce, 'Origen Issues: The Reception of a Renegade Greek Theologian in Early Medieval Europe', *Journal of Medieval Latin* 33 (2023), 267–303.
[18] For what follows, see James J. O'Donnell, *Cassiodorus* (Berkeley, CA, 1979), 177–222.
[19] Cassiodorus, *Institutiones divinarum et secularium litterarum* 1.1–17, ed. R.A.B. Mynors (Oxford, 1937), 11–57; English translation: Cassiodorus, *Institutions of Divine and Secular Learning, On the Soul*, trans. James W. Halporn (Liverpool, 2004), 111–51.

sermons'.[20] In this way, the enterprise of Cassiodorus increased the number of Greek patristic texts available to Latin reading communities in the west.

The earliest medieval manuscripts provide a valuable, though impressionistic, index of the reception of this corpus of translations before the Carolingian period.[21] Among the nearly two thousand codices and associated fragments written in Latin and produced in western Europe before or around the year 800, there survive over 100 copies of individual works of eastern patristics and ecclesiastical history translated from Greek into Latin in late antiquity.[22] These early exemplars allow us to make inferences about the reading habits and tastes of western monastic communities, including their preferences for particular Christian Greek authors and genres. Among the dozens of doctrinal, devotional, and historical works of Greek origin circulating in early medieval Europe, the scriptural commentaries of Origen of Alexandria (c. 185–254) were by far the most popular among Latin readers.[23] Any doubts surrounding his orthodoxy did little to diminish the utility of his exegetical writings on the Old Testament. His commentaries on the Pentateuch were by far his most sought-after work in western reading communities. Before the Carolingian period, his sixteen homilies on Genesis survived in five copies; his thirteen homilies on Exodus in three copies, and his sixteen homilies on Leviticus in six copies. His commentary on Paul's letter to the Romans found an audience in western abbeys as well; the four earliest manuscripts preserving this work date between the fifth and eighth centuries.

---

[20] Cassiodorus, *Institutiones* 1.9.1: 'Sed in Actibus Apostolorum sancti Iohannis, episcopi Constantinopolitani, in Graeco sermone commenta repperimus; quae amici nostri in duobus codicibus LV omeliis iuvante Domino transtulerunt,' ed. Mynors, p. 33; trans. Halporn, p. 131.

[21] For what follows, see Scott G. Bruce, '*Veterum vestigia patrum*: The Greek Patriarchs in the Manuscript Culture of Early Medieval Europe', *The Downside Review* 139 (2021), 6–23; and Scott G. Bruce and Benjamin A. Bertrand, '*Ex sanctorum patrum certissimis testimoniis*: Reading the Greek Fathers in Latin in Early Medieval Monasteries', *Journal of Medieval Monastic Studies* 11 (2022), 9–34.

[22] The information supporting this analysis is found in Ellis Avery Lowe, *Codices Latini Antiquiores: A Paleographical Guide to Latin Manuscripts Prior to the Ninth Century* (11 vols and supplement, Oxford, 1934–71), which provides a comprehensive list of all extant Latin manuscripts or fragments thereof written on soft material (vellum and papyrus) before the year 800. There have been two updates to CLA: Bernard Bischoff and Virginia Brown, 'Addenda to *Codices latini antiquiores*', *Mediaeval Studies* 47 (1985), 317–66; and Bernard Bischoff, Virginia Brown, and James J. John, 'Addenda to *Codices latini antiquiores* (II)', *Mediaeval Studies* 54 (1993), 286–307. For an overview of Lowe's achievement, see Julian Brown, 'E.A. Lowe and *Codices Latini Antiquiores*', *Scrittura e Civiltà* 1 (1977), 177–97.

[23] The evidence presented in the following paragraph has been laid out more fully in Bruce, '*Veterum vestigia patrum*', 8–9; and Bruce and Bernard, '*Ex sanctorum patrum certissimis testimoniis*', 23–6. More generally on the reception of Origen among Latin readers, see Henri de Lubac, *Medieval Exegesis, Volume 1: The Four Senses of Scripture*, trans. Mark Sebanc (Edinburgh, 1998), 161–224; and Bruce, 'Origen Issues'. A recent collection of essays on Origen's influence (*The Oxford Handbook of Origen*, ed. Heine and Torjesen) contains no contribution on his reception between Augustine and Erasmus, a startling omission.

On the heels of Origen were two Greek patriarchs whose works nearly rivaled his in popularity in early medieval Europe. The first was the church historian Eusebius of Caesarea (c. 260–339/340), whose sprawling *Ecclesiastical History* as translated and amplified by Rufinus survived in eleven early manuscripts, making it the most widely copied work of Christian Greek provenance in Latin translation before the year 800.[24] Alongside Flavius Josephus' *Antiquities of the Jews*, which Cassiodorus had recommended to Christian readers because it provided a narrative of the ancient past inflected and informed by the Hebrew scriptures, Eusebius' *Ecclesiastical History* was essential reading for monastic communities because it 'strived to attach all events to the providential guidance of the Creator'.[25] Following Origen and Eusebius was John Chrysostom (340/350–407), whose name was attached to biblical commentaries and ascetic treatises in no fewer than eighteen early Latin manuscripts.[26] His most popular work in Latin, which circulated under the title *On the Reparation of a Fallen Man*, was in fact two separate works on a related theme: the need for repentance and a return to virtue for those who had abandoned the religious life. To be sure, early medieval readers favored other eastern authors as well, though on a lesser scale. Devotional and homiletical works by Basil of Caesarea, Theodore of Mopsuestia, Ephrem the Syrian, and Gregory of Nazianzos were read in some western communities, as were anonymous works of eastern origin like the second-century *Shepherd of Hermas*, but these texts did not have the same appeal among Latin readers as those composed by Origen, Eusebius, and John Chrysostom.[27]

Eastern Patristic Authors Known in Pre-Conquest England

The choices of a handful of translators from Rufinus to Cassiodorus created the initial fund of Greek patristic texts available to Latin readers in the early medieval west, but as we have seen, the reception history of some eastern authors was more robust than that of others. The availability of these favored authors in Merovingian Europe had a direct impact on their reception in early medieval England. European codices first arrived in Kent during the Gregorian mission, when Augustine and his companions brought with them 'very many manuscripts'

---

[24] Bruce, '*Veterum vestigia patrum*', 9.
[25] Cassiodorus, *Institutiones* 1.17: 'Necesse est ut sensus legentium rebus caelestibus semper erudiant, quando nihil ad fortuitos casus, nihil ad deorum potestates infirmas, ut gentiles fecerunt, sed arbitrio Creatoris applicare veraciter universa contendunt,' ed. Mynors, 55; trans. Halporn, 149. On Cassiodorus's endorsement of Josephus as an historian appropriate for Christian readers, see Scott G. Bruce, 'The Redemption of Flavius Josephus in the Medieval Latin Tradition', in *Litterarum dulces fructus: Studies in Honour of Michael Herren on his 80th Birthday*, ed. Scott G. Bruce (Turnhout, 2021), 53–69.
[26] Bruce, '*Veterum vestigia patrum*', 10; and Bruce and Bertrand, '*Ex sanctorum patrum certissimis testimoniis*', 20–1.
[27] Bruce, '*Veterum vestigia patrum*', 10–11; and Bruce and Bertrand, '*Ex sanctorum patrum certissimis testimoniis*', 17–23.

(*codices plurimos*) to aid them in their evangelical efforts.[28] Throughout the seventh and eighth centuries, pilgrim traffic between England and Italy resulted in the transport of many individual books and, in some cases, entire libraries from the Mediterranean to the far north.[29] Benedict Biscop (c. 629–90) alone made no fewer than six trips to Rome, where he acquired dozens of manuscripts for new monastic communities in Northumbria at Monkwearmouth (founded around 673) and Jarrow (founded around 681). A generation later, Bede claimed that Abbot Ceolfrith (c. 642–716) managed to double the number of books initially provided for these foundations by Benedict, again from resources on the Continent. Likewise, the school founded in the late seventh century at Canterbury by Theodore and Hadrian would have relied almost exclusively on manuscripts imported from Europe, including a Greek New Testament and perhaps a copy of the Septuagint as well. While none of the volumes associated with these communities have survived, it is clear that in general the earliest English abbeys 'were in the first instance stocked with books from Mediterranean libraries'.[30]

Two kinds of sources allow us to chart the availability of Latin translations of Greek patristics in pre-Conquest England: a handful of manuscripts and a few library booklists. The manuscript evidence for the reception history of this tradition before 1066 is very thin, but nonetheless suggests that early English monks took their cues from their European counterparts when it came to their acquisition of Greek patristics in Latin translation. To judge from the small number of surviving codices, Origen, Eusebius, and John Chrysostom were the favored eastern fathers both in England and in missionary centers on the Continent in the early Middle Ages. Origen's homilies on the book of Numbers as translated by Rufinus survives in two copies with early English ties.[31] The earliest is a later eighth-century manuscript written, according to E.A. Lowe, at an English scriptorium 'on the Continent, probably in Germany, but hardly in Würzburg', where the book resided from the ninth century onwards.[32] When Bishop Hunbert of Würzburg wrote to Abbot Rabanus Maurus of Fulda in the 830s to request copies of biblical commentaries, he may have been referring to this manuscript when he told the abbot: 'We already have Origen' (*habemus Origenem*).[33] The second example is a codex of Jerome's commentary on the psalms that includes excerpts of Origen's commentary on Numbers, which was produced at Winchester in the middle of the tenth century.[34]

---

[28] HE 1.29, 104–05.
[29] For what follows, see Lapidge, *The Anglo-Saxon Library*, 22–30.
[30] Lapidge, *The Anglo-Saxon Library*, 29.
[31] Lapidge, *The Anglo-Saxon Library*, 322–3 (Origen).
[32] Würzburg, Universitätsbibliothek, M. p. th. f. 27 = CLA, vol. 9, p. 48 (no. 1407); and Hans Thurn, *Die Pergamenthandschriften der ehemaligen Dombibliothek* (Wiesbaden, 1984), 18–19, who dates the manuscript to the '2. Hälfte 8. Jh'. (p. 18).
[33] This letter has been edited among Rabanus's correspondence: *Epistola* 26, ed. E. Dümmler, MGH, *Epp.* 5 (Berlin, 1899), 439–40 at 440.
[34] London, British Library, Royal 4. A. xiv = Gneuss and Lapidge, *Anglo-Saxon Manuscripts*, 375 (no. 455).

Reading the Greek Fathers in Latin in Pre-Conquest England 9

The manuscript evidence for works by Eusebius and John Chrysostom in pre-Conquest England is also thin, but slightly more robust than that for Origen. Rufinus' Latin translation of Eusebius' *Ecclesiastical History* survives in whole or in part in four manuscripts of English provenance copied before the turn of the first millennium.[35] Some of these manuscripts preserved the entirety of this massive work, like the earliest insular exemplar, a seventh-century codex produced by English scribes in Ireland or Northumbria, while others included only excerpts, like the ninth-century patristic miscellany from Bury St Edmunds that concluded with a snippet from the last book of the *History*.[36] There is also fleeting evidence that writings on the ascetic life by John Chrystostom were also current in early medieval England.[37] These works circulated in Latin as part of the so-called Wilmart collection, a corpus of thirty-eight sermons originally composed by Chrystostom or attributed to him and named after André Wilmart, the scholar who brought them to light in 1918.[38] Fragments of an eighth-century Northumbrian codex salvaged from the bindings of a book owned by the monastery of Beyenburg near Werden included samples of three Latin Chrysostom texts from the Wilmart collection.[39] The original manuscript may have accompanied the missionary saint Liudger (742–809) from York, where he studied under Alcuin between 767 and 781, to Werden, where he founded an abbey around 800.[40] Two sermons from the Wilmart collection also appear in Bodley 516, a ninth-century patristic miscellany produced on the Continent, but likely in England by the eleventh century, when a scribe added an Old English cryptogram to the manuscript.[41] There is no evidence for knowledge of any other works by John Chrysostom in Latin in England until the later eleventh century.

The evidence provided by surviving booklists is likewise meagre. There are only six known inventories of scholarly books owned by individuals or

---

35 Lapidge, *The Anglo-Saxon Library*, 302 (Eusebius of Caesarea).
36 See, for example, Cambridge, Corpus Christi College 192; Cambridge, Pembroke College 108; and Worcester, Cathedral Library Q.21 = Gneuss and Lapidge, *Anglo-Saxon Manuscripts*, 75–6 (no. 61), 132–3 (no. 137), and 550 (no. 768).
37 Lapidge, *The Anglo-Saxon Library*, 316–17 (John Chrysostom).
38 André Wilmart, 'La collection des 38 homélies latines de saint Jean Chrysostome', *Journal of Theological Studies* 19 (1918), 305–27.
39 Düsseldorf, Universitäts- und Landesbibliothek, Fragm. K 1: B 215 + K 2: C 118 + K 15: 009 + K19: Z 8/8 + M.Th.u.Sch. 29a (Ink.) Bd. 4 (pastedowns) = CLA, vol. 8, p. 46 (no. 1187) = Gneuss and Lapidge, *Anglo-Saxon Manuscripts*, pp. 586–87 (no. 819), with Klaus Zechiel-Eckes, 'Vom *armarium* in York in den Düsseldorfer Tresor: Zur Rekonstruktion einer Liudger-Handschrift aus dem mittleren 8. Jahrhundert', *Deutsches Archiv für Erforschung des Mittelalters* 58 (2002), 193–203; and Klaus Zechiel-Eckes, *Katalog der frühmittelalterlichen Fragmente der Universitäts- und Landesbibliothek Düsseldorf: Vom beginnenden achten bis zum ausgehenden neunten Jahrhundert* (Wiesbaden, 2003), 27–8.
40 Rolf H. Bremmer, Jr, 'The Anglo-Saxon Continental Mission and the Transfer of Encyclopedic Knowledge', in *Foundations of Learning: The Transfer of Encyclopaedic Knowledge in the Early Middle Ages*, ed. Rolf H. Bremmer and Kees Dekker (Paris, 2007), 19–50 at 23–9 (no. 4).
41 Thomas N. Hall and Michael Norris, 'The Chrysostom Texts in Bodley 516', *Journal of Ecclesiastical History* 62 (2011), 161–75 at 165–8.

institutions produced in England and dated before or around the time of the Norman Conquest.[42] In total, they list almost two hundred individual volumes. Only one of these lists, a robust catalogue of sixty books possibly made in Peterborough around the year 1100, makes any mention of patristic works of Greek origin. There are, in fact, four relevant titles on the Peterborough list: first, a copy of Eusebius' widely read *Ecclesiastical History* (*Ecclesiastica historia Eusebii Cesaris*); second, a treatise entitled *On the Distinctiveness of Clerics*, here falsely attributed to Origen (*Origenis de singularitate clericorum*) and likely an original Latin composition rather than the translation of a Greek work; third, a dialogue between Basil and John (*Dialogus Basilii et Johannis*), a Latin translation of John Chrysostom's treatise *On the Priesthood* (*De sacerdotio*), which was presented as a dialogue between John and an interlocutor named Basil; and fourth, the text called the *Apologiticus* attributed to Gregory Nazianzos (*Gregorii Nazanzeni Apologiticus*), which was Rufinus' translation of Gregory's second oration: *Liber apologeticus de fuga*.[43]

There are also three short booklists that survive from early English missionary zones in eighth-century Germany, which together contain a total seventy-six books.[44] Only one of these inventories – from the abbey of Fulda – provides any references to Greek patristics, and it is frustratingly opaque. The Fulda inventory includes an unnamed text attributed to Basil the Great (*Sancti Basilii*) and another by Ephrem the Syrian (*Liber sancti Effrem*). In both cases, the texts are unidentified and unknowable. If the Basil text in question was his rule for monks, then the inventory may have been describing Basel, Universitätsbibliothek, F. III 15c, a Carolingian manuscript from Fulda that preserves a copy of Rufinus' translation of this influential handbook.[45] The identity of the Ephrem text is an even greater mystery, however, because several of his treatises were available in Latin translation and many anonymous works circulated under his name.[46] Moreover, there is no further evidence of any knowledge of his works in Latin in pre-Conquest England.[47]

Lost Patriarchs at Work

While surviving manuscripts and booklists provide some indication of the works by Greek fathers available in Latin to early English readers, we must turn to other kinds of evidence to delineate with greater clarity the function

---

[42] Lapidge, *The Anglo-Saxon Library*, 133–47.
[43] Lapidge, *The Anglo-Saxon Library*, 143–7.
[44] Lapidge, *The Anglo-Saxon Library*, 148–54.
[45] Basel, Universitätsbibliothek, F. III 15c, fols 28–41 = CLA, vol. 7, p. 3 (no. 846) = Bischoff, *Katalog der festländischen Handschriften*, vol. 1, p. 61 (no. 275), with Lapidge, *The Anglo-Saxon Library*, 152.
[46] *Clavis Patrum Latinorum*, ed. Eligius Dekkers, 3rd ed. (Turnhout, 1995), 373–6, *s.v.* Ephraem Latinus (nos 1143–52).
[47] On the reception of the Latin Ephrem corpus in early medieval Europe more generally, see David Ganz, 'Knowledge of Ephraim's Writings in the Merovingian and Carolingian Age', *Hugoye: Journal of Syriac Studies* 2 (1999), 37–46; and Scott G. Bruce, "From Nisibis to the North: The Latin Sermons Attributed to Ephrem the Syrian," forthcoming.

of translated Greek patristics in early medieval England. Copies of eastern Christian texts in Latin translation did not migrate from Europe to English monastic centers by accident. As Michael Lapidge has argued, the contents of pre-Conquest libraries exhibited a 'functional bias' that reflected pragmatic choices on the part of reading communities to copy and preserve those texts that were deemed most useful to the monks who read them.[48] Three branches of Christian teaching guided their choices with respect to the acquisition of Greek patristics in Latin. According to the evidence provided by direct citation and indirect reference to eastern authorities, early English scholars were particularly interested in textual resources that informed their interpretation of the Bible, enriched classroom instruction, and supported the preaching of the faith in their communities.

Repeated references to eastern Christian authors by scholars like Bede underscore the value of their writings for his scholarship, particularly in his works of scriptural exegesis. We know from Bede that the libraries of Monkwearmouth and Jarrow comprised manuscripts imported from the Continent by Benedict Biscop and Ceolfrith during their multiple trips to Rome in the late seventh century.[49] Unfortunately, no manuscript of a Christian Greek author survives from these Northumbrian scriptoria, and there are no early medieval booklists to turn to for hints about their book holdings. Despite this dearth of information, we can nonetheless delineate the horizons of the eastern patristic resources at Bede's disposal from the citations to Greek fathers in his works.[50] Over the course of his career, during which he authored seventy or so treatises, histories, and biblical commentaries, Bede quoted directly from thirteen different works of Greek origin written by six separate authors as well as two anonymous texts. The works of eastern patristics at his disposal included Athanasius' *Life of Anthony* as translated by Evagrius; Didymus the Blind's treatise on the Holy Spirit as translated by Jerome; Eusebius of Caesarea's *Chronicon* and *Onomasticon*, both translated by Jerome, as well as his *Ecclesiastical History* as translated and extended by Rufinus; Gregory of Nazianzos' fourth oration; John Chrysostom's *Homily on the Date of Christmas*; the *Shepherd of Hermas*, and pseudo-Clement's *Recognitions*. The most outstanding feature of the library at Bede's disposal, however, was its collection of biblical commentaries and homilies by Origen, which may have been the largest assemblage of the Alexandrian teacher's work before the great Carolingian libraries of the ninth century.[51] In his exegetical writings, Bede made reference to no fewer than six separate texts by Origen:

---

[48] Lapidge, *The Anglo-Saxon Library*, 129.
[49] On the history of this library and its holdings, now completely lost, see Lapidge, *The Anglo-Saxon Library*, 34–7.
[50] For what follows, see Lapidge, *The Anglo-Saxon Library*, 191–228.
[51] Lapidge, *The Anglo-Saxon Library*, 220–1. On the transmission of Origen's works to pre-Conquest England, see Caroline Bammel, 'Insular Manuscripts of Origen in the Carolingian Empire', in *France and the British Isles in the Middle Ages and Renaissance: Essays by Members of Girton College, Cambridge, in Memory of Ruth Morgan*, ed. G. Jondorf and D.N. Dumville (Woodbridge, 1991), 5–16, reprinted in Caroline Bammel, *Origeniana et Rufiniana*, no. IX.

his thirteen homilies on Exodus, sixteen homilies on Leviticus as well as those on the Book of Kings, all translated by Rufinus; the two homilies on the Song of Songs translated by Jerome as well as the commentary on the Song of Songs translated by Rufinus; and lastly an anonymous Latin translation of Origen's commentary on the Gospel of Matthew. Bede deployed the Alexandrian master's interpretations without any self-consciousness regarding his status as a heretic in the eastern church.[52] While he betrayed no knowledge of Origen's notorious treatise *On First Principles* – it seems to have been unknown in pre-Conquest England – he would surely have been aware of the controversies surrounding its rendering into Latin by Rufinus from Jerome's invective-laden letters on the subject.[53]

The value of patristic Greek texts in translation extended to their use as tools for classroom instruction, even when that instruction had little to do with the Christian content of the text in question. The so-called 'Leiden Glossary' preserves the notes of late seventh-century students at the school of Theodore and Hadrian at Canterbury, who recorded the lessons of their teachers as they explicated biblical and patristic texts word-by-word.[54] Three batches of these glosses derive from their teaching on Rufinus' Latin translation of Eusebius' *Ecclesiastical History*.[55] These sets of glosses reveal that this influential work of Christian history also served as a repository of information on medical knowledge, the reckoning of time, and Mediterranean geography.[56] Moreover, Rufinus was also particularly useful for introducing students to the meaning of the Greek loan-words that he frequently employed in his translation. For example, in the third book of the *Ecclesiastical History* Rufinus rendered into Latin some passages that Eusebius had excerpted from Josephus' *Jewish War*, which described the horrific conditions of famine suffered by the Jews when the Romans laid siege to Jerusalem during the First Jewish-Roman War (66–73 CE). In their final famished desperation, the people of Jerusalem had allegedly tortured one another to find the last morsels of edible food: 'I shudder to relate what happened; by these [torments] they forced the wretched to confess to a bit of bread or a very small measure of flour.'[57] Rufinus employed the Greek loan-word *cyathus* (κύαθος) to describe the size of this measure of flour (*cyathi*

---

[52] On the condemnation of Origen's teaching at the Synod of Constantinople (543) and the Second Council of Constantinople (553), see most recently the studies and translated sources collected in *Verurteilung des Origenes: Kaiser Justinian und das Konzil von Konstantinopel 553*, ed. Alfons Fürst and Thomas R. Karmann (Munster, 2020).

[53] On the reception of Origen's *On First Principles* in the early medieval west, see Bruce, 'Origen Issues', 290–6.

[54] On the Leiden Glossary, see note 8 above.

[55] *Canterbury Glosses*, ed. Lapidge, ii, 331–69 (no. IV), 370–80 (no. V), and 526–615 (no. XXXV).

[56] Michael Lapidge, 'Rufinus at the School of Canterbury', in *La tradition vive: Mélanges d'histoire des textes en l'honneur de Louis Holtz*, ed. Pierre Lardet (Turnhout, 2003), 119–29 at 122.

[57] Rufinus, *Historia Ecclesiastica* 3.6: 'Horresco quae gesta sunt referens, ad confessionem per haec unius panis aut cyathi farinae miseros perurgebant', ed. Theodor Mommsen, in *Eusebius Werke II: Die Kirchengeschichte* (3 vols, Leipzig, 1903–09), i, 203.

farinae). Attentive readers of Horace and Pliny may have recognized this Greek loan-word for 'ladle', which lent its name to an Attic unit of measurement ('ladleful') the equivalent of about 1/12th of a pint or slightly more less than 1/5th of a cup.[58] This unusual term drew the eye of one of the Canterbury teachers, who qualified its meaning in Latin as 'a very small measure' (*mensum minutum*).[59]

Lastly, early English preachers sometimes drew from the well of eastern Christian wisdom when they prepared sermons for their audiences, both lay and monastic. While the reception history of the Latin translations of writings attributed to John Chrysostom in pre-Conquest England is sketchy at best, the available evidence points to the fact that a robust collection of sermons written by him or attributed to him circulated in northern England by the time of Bede.[60] As Rosalind Love has shown, the Northumbrian scholar knew at least six of these sermons, which he quoted verbatim or paraphrased in several of his biblical commentaries and treatises.[61] Likewise, as noted above, fragments of an eighth-century manuscript produced in Northumbria but brought to Germany around the year 800 preserved three Chrysostom sermons in Latin.[62] While the evidence is meagre, the currency of the Latin tradition of the archbishop's sermons in pre-Conquest England was strong enough that a tenth-century scholar translated a portion of at least one of them – a homily on Hebrews – into Old English.[63] By means of this vernacular rendering, an early English preacher on the cusp of the new millennium voiced in an alien tongue the centuries-old eloquence of a late antique Greek archbishop to relay his timeless warnings about the laziness of women and the sins of gluttony.

In conclusion, while translators from Rufinus to Cassiodorus provided western readers with a veritable library of eastern Christian patristics, three of these Greek authors rose to prominence in Latin reading communities: Origen of Alexandria, Eusebius of Caesarea, and John Chrystostom. Taking their cue from their European contacts, the abbots of pre-Conquest abbeys stocked their libraries with texts not only by these popular authors, but also by other lesser luminaries whose work shone some eastern light on the teachings of the church.

---

[58] For examples of its use in Roman literature, see Horace, *Od.* 3.8.13 and 3.19.12; and Pliny, *Nat.* 10.50. For the definition of the Greek word, see Henry Liddel and Robert Scott, *A Greek-English Lexicon* (9th ed., Oxford, 1940), *s.v.* κυαθος. The presence of this loan-word in early medieval glossaries may account for its later currency in Anglo-Latin sources: *Dictionary of Medieval Latin from British Sources*, ed. R.K. Ashdowne, D.R. Howlett, and R.E. Latham (3 vols, Oxford, 2018), i, 727, *s.v.* cyathus.

[59] *Canterbury Glosses*, ed. Lapidge, ii, 370–1 (no. V.1: 'cyati. mensum minutum').

[60] Hall and Norris, 'The Chrysostom Texts in Bodley 516', 173: '[T]he circumstantial evidence does encourage one to suspect that a reasonably full version of the Wilmart collection was indeed circulating in Northumbria in the early eighth century.'

[61] Rosalind Love, 'Bede and John Chrysostom', *Journal of Medieval Latin* 17 (2007), 72–86.

[62] See note 39, above.

[63] *Vercelli Homily 7*, ed. D. G. Scragg, in *The Vercelli Homilies and Related Texts* (Oxford, 1992), 134–7, with Samantha Zacher, 'The Source of Vercelli VII: An Address to Women', in *New Readings on the Vercelli Book*, ed. Samantha Zacher and Andy Orchard (Toronto, 2009), 98–149.

They were, indeed, a regular feature of learning in early English monasteries. As we have seen, the presence and use of these Christian Greek authorities in pre-Conquest England is painstaking to reconstruct, surviving mainly in manuscript fragments, as titles on booklists, and in citations of their writings in exegetical, historical, and homiletical works produced in northern reading communities. Yet all this evidence attests to the enduring value of the Greek patristic tradition in the farthest outposts of early medieval Christendom. After the initial rush to stock early English monastic foundations with the books necessary for their missionary and pastoral agendas, however, the copying of works by the Greek fathers in Latin translation died down until the late eleventh century, when we see a renewed interest in collecting both Latin and Greek patristic texts throughout the abbeys of Anglo-Norman England.[64]

---

[64] On this trend, see Teresa Webber, 'The Patristic Content of English Book Collections in the Eleventh Century: Towards a Continental Perspective', in *Of the Making of Books: Medieval Manuscripts, their Scribes and Readers: Essays Presented to M.B. Parkes*, ed. P.R. Robinson and Rivkah Zim (Aldershot, 1997), 191–205.

2

Journey to the South: The Travels of William of Malmesbury in the Mid-1130s

Ming Liu

William of Malmesbury has long been regarded as a well-travelled historian, and modern scholars have placed a great deal of emphasis on his personal travels as the basis for his narratives in his works, especially his *Gesta Pontificum Anglorum* (hereafter the *GP*). Antonia Gransden believed that William had used 'personal observation' and 'tireless sightseeing' to get the evidence for his historical writing.[1] Likewise, Sarah Wright has stressed William's focus on eye-witnessing and has suggested that the *GP* should be read as an itinerary.[2] In his commentary on the *GP*, Rodney Thomson provided a long list of the places which William certainly or probably had visited: Athelney, Bangor, Bath, Bayeux, Bruton, Bury, Canterbury, Carlisle, Chester, Chichester, Corfe, Coventry, Crowland, Durham, Ely, Exeter, Glastonbury, Hereford, Hexham, Lewes, London, Milton, Muchelney, Oxford, Ramsey, Reading, Rochester, Shaftesbury, Sherborne, Soham, Tavistock, Thorney, Winchester, Worcester, and York.[3] Although William Kynan-Wilson and Stanislav Mereminskiy have articulated some doubts over William's travels in northern England, the fact that William travelled widely is still the general consensus.[4]

The details of William's itinerary, however, are not clear in the previous research. Questions need answers; for example, when and why did William visit certain places? It is usually assumed that he travelled to collect information and

---

[1] Antonia Gransden, 'Realistic Observation in Twelfth-Century England', *Speculum* 47 (1972), 29–51 at 34; Antonia Gransden, *Historical Writing in England c. 550–c. 1307* (Abingdon, 2008 [1974]), 174.
[2] Sarah Breckenridge Wright, 'The Soil's Holy Bodies: The Art of Chorography in William of Malmesbury's *Gesta Pontificum Anglorum*', *Studies in Philology* 111 (2014), 652–79 at 664–5.
[3] William of Malmesbury, *GP*, ii, xli–xliii.
[4] William Kynan-Wilson, '*Mira Romanorum artifitia*: William of Malmesbury and the Romano-British Remains at Carlisle', *Essays in Medieval Studies* 28 (2012), 35–49; Stanislav Mereminskiy, 'William of Malmesbury and Durham: The Circulation of Historical Knowledge in Early Twelfth-Century England', in *Discovering William of Malmesbury*, ed. Rodney M. Thomson, Emily Dolmans, and Emily A. Winkler (Woodbridge, 2017), 107–16.

materials for his writings, but was this his only or most important motivation? This essay does not aim to clarify the details of every itinerary throughout William's life, but, instead, traces one of his journeys in the mid-1130s. I will use the evidence from the different versions of his *GP* and *Gesta Regum Anglorum* (hereafter the *GR*) to argue that he took a trip across southern England probably in early 1136, visiting places including Winchester, Milton, Muchelney, Sherborne, Doulting, Corfe, and Wareham.[5] Moreover, I will suggest that, although this journey provided him with new information for his writings, his primary impetus was to defend the liberty of Malmesbury Abbey against Roger bishop of Salisbury, who had taken over the abbey since the 1120s.

Previous research has not paid much attention to the slight differences between the versions of William's *GR* and *GP*, but he constantly revised these two works throughout his life.[6] The changes in his narratives and the shifts in tone between the versions very likely reflect the fact that he had found new information during that period, and this may help to determine the date of his journeys. We shall start with the **C** and **B** versions of the *GR*. As Thomson and Winterbottom notes, they both include an alteration which involves the death of Robert Curthose, so they should be dated after February 1134, the date of Robert's death.[7] Since the **C** version had been disseminated by around 1135 and the *GR* did not allude to William's writing of the *Historia Novella* (hereafter the *HN*) which he started in 1140, the **B** version was probably finished between 1135 and 1140, probably closer to the mid-1130s, leaving a short interval between **C** and **B**.[8] This means that compared to **C**, the **B** version's new information was very likely to have been collected by William in the mid-1130s.

---

5   See Map 1.
6   According to Rodney Thomson and Michael Winterbottom, the *GR* mainly has four versions, **T**, **A**, **C**, and **B**, in chronological order. The last two versions were made after February 1134. On these versions and their chronology, see William of Malmesbury, *GR*, ii, xvii–xxxiv. For the *GP*, they adjusted Hamilton's view that there were two recensions, arguing instead for an ongoing process of revision with different stages until his death. See William of Malmesbury, *GP*, i, xi–xxv. Hamilton's suggestion can be found in *Willelmi Malmesbiriensis Monachi De Gestis Pontificum Anglorum Libri Quinque*, ed. N.E.S.A. Hamilton (London, 1870), viii–xxvi.
7   William of Malmesbury, *GR*, ii, xxv. For the alteration that mentioned Robert's death, see William of Malmesbury, *GR*, i, 706. On the date of Robert's death, see William M. Aird, *Robert Curthose, Duke of Normandy (c. 1050–1134)* (Woodbridge, 2008), 276–81.
8   Thomson and Winterbottom believed that these two versions were finished soon after 1134. See William of Malmesbury, *GR*, ii, 397. For the dating of the **C** version, see Paul Antony Hayward, 'The Importance of Being Ambiguous: Innuendo and Legerdemain in William of Malmesbury's *Gesta Regum* and *Gesta Pontifcum Anglorum*', *ANS* 33 (2011), 75–102 at 78; Jaakko Tahkokallio, *The Anglo-Norman Historical Canon: Publishing and Manuscript Culture* (Cambridge, 2019), 27. For the dating of the *HN*, see William of Malmesbury, *HN*, xxxi. The dating of the **B** version between 1135 and 1140 was also suggested by William Stubbs, see *De Gestis Regum Anglorum Libri Quinque & Historiae Novellae Libri Tres*, ed. William Stubbs (2 vols, London, 1887–9), i, xxxi. Thomson and Winterbottom thought that William's following sentence at the end of the *GR* – 'in altero erit idem uitae qui scripturae terminus' (the writing of the other will end only with life itself) – was referring to the *HN*, but as Hayward noticed, this reference was meant

Bearing this in mind, we might suggest that William had new information or changed his tone in the **B** version, concerning three places as follows:

a) Winchester: William omitted the words 'ut aiunt' (as they say) when he was referring to King Æthelstan's sword which was still preserved in the royal treasures.[9] As Thomson and Winterbottom suggested, this might mean that William had viewed the royal treasures at Winchester by the time of this redaction.[10]

b) Milton: William inserted a letter describing several relics sent from Rodbod provost of Dol Cathedral, Brittany to King Æthelstan.[11] He also copied this letter into the margins of folio 93v of his autograph of the *GP* (Oxford, Magdalen College, MS lat. 172, fols 1–104; hereafter the Magdalen manuscript), where he added that he found it from the archive at Milton: 'Haec epistola inventa est in scrinio apud Mideltun-ense cenobium, quod idem rex a fundamento fecit, et ubi reliquias sancti Samsonis posuit.' (This letter was found in the archive at the monastery at Milton, which the king [i. e. Æthelstan] built from the foundations, and where he placed the relics of St Samson.)[12]

c) Muchelney: William added some new information related to the monastery of Muchelney, mentioning that he had read the muniments of the church: 'sicut in cartis eiusdem aecclesiae legi, rex Ethelstanus aecclesiam Miclaniensem sancto Petro excelsiorem fecit, multis redditibus habitatores consolatus' (as I have read in the muniments of the church, King Æthelstan raised the church of Muchelney to greater heights in honour of St Peter, helping those who dwelt there with many rents).[13]

It is noteworthy that these changes are all related to King Æthelstan.[14] It is even more interesting that their contexts in the *GR* all involve St Aldhelm or Malmesbury Abbey directly or indirectly.[15] First, Æthelstan's sword is a witness

---

to be the *Chronicles*, see William of Malmesbury, *GR*, ii, 399; Paul Antony Hayward, 'William of Malmesbury as a Cantor-Historian', in *Medieval Cantors and Their Craft: Music, Liturgy and the Shaping of History, 800–1500*, ed. Katie Ann-Marie Bugyis, A.B. Kraebel, and Margot E. Fassler (York, 2017), 222–39 at 225–6. The lack of references to the *HN* may mean that the **B** version had been finished a couple of years before 1140.

[9] The words before the **B** version can be seen in William of Malmesbury, *GR*, i, 208–209: '…ensem, qui hodieque pro miraculo in thesauro regum seruatur. Est sane, ut aiunt, una parte sectilis, nec umquam auri aut argenti receptibilis.' (The sword, which is still preserved among the royal treasures as evidence of the miracle. It is, they say, chased on one side, but can never be inlaid with either gold or silver.)

[10] William of Malmesbury, *GR*, ii, 116.

[11] William of Malmesbury, *GR*, i, Appendix I: Additions of **B** and **C**, 820–3.

[12] Oxford, Magdalen College, MS lat. 172, fols 1–104 at 93v; William of Malmesbury, *GP*, i, 598–9. The Magdalen manuscript was a working copy of the first draft of the *GP* just after mid-1125, and was continuously revised probably until William's death. See William of Malmesbury, *GP*, i, xii.

[13] William of Malmesbury, *GR*, i, Appendix I: Additions of **B** and **C**, 824–825.

[14] Thomson and Winterbottom also noticed this, but only used it to prove that the **B** version of the *GR* is later than **C**, see William of Malmesbury, *GR*, ii, xxviii–xxix.

[15] This is understandable, because King Æthelstan was the most significant pre-Conquest

to the miracle of St Aldhelm, who made it reappear in its scabbard during the battle of *Brunanburh*.[16] Second, after copying the letter found at Milton, William continued to write that the relics of St Paternus, which had been mentioned in it, were entrusted by Æthelstan to Malmesbury, while those of the other saints were preserved at Milton.[17] Third, the position of William's addition concerning Muchelney is just before Chapter 140 in the main text, in which he told readers that Æthelstan's body was buried at Malmesbury with many gifts and relics.[18] In fact, Æthelstan's preference for the monastery of Malmesbury had already been shown in Chapters 136 and 137 in the original text, where William copied a charter which recorded such favor.[19] The blood relationship between St Aldhelm and Æthelstan is also particularly emphasized by the **B** version.[20] This raises an interesting possibility that William travelled to Winchester,

---

benefactor of Malmesbury Abbey, and William was probably trying to defend the rights of his abbey by interpretating and redacting his sources about the king. See Sarah Foot, *Æthelstan: The First King of England* (New Haven, CT, 2011), 187–91; Matthew Firth, 'Constructing a King: William of Malmesbury and the Life of Æthelstan', *Journal of the Australian Early Medieval Association* 13 (2017), 69–92.

[16] William of Malmesbury, *GR*, i, 208–09: 'Quocirca, cum omnia formidinis et ceci tumultus plena essent, inclamato Deo et sancto Aldelmo reductaque ad uaginam manu inuenit ensem, qui hodieque pro miraculo in thesauro regum seruatur.' (At this moment of universal fear and blind confusion, he called upon God and St Aldhelm, reached again to his scabbard, and there found the sword, which is still preserved among the royal treasures as evidence of the miracle.) Also see Foot, *Æthelstan*, 182–3.

[17] William of Malmesbury, *GR*, i, Appendix I: Additions of **B** and **C**, 822–3: Ceterum rex reliquias beati Paterni Malmesberiae, reliquorum Mideltune commendauit, quo loci monasterium a fundamentis procuderat. (For the rest, the king [i.e. Æthelstan] entrusted the relics of St Paternus to Malmesbury, and those of the other saints to Milton, a place where he had established a monastery from its foundations.)

[18] William of Malmesbury, *GR*, i, 228–9: Exuuiae triumphales Malmesberiam delatae et sub altari tumulatae. Portata ante corpus multa in argento et auro donaria, simul et sanctorum reliquiae de transmarina Britannia emptae. (His remains were borne in state to Malmesbury, and buried beneath the high altar. Many gifts from him in silver and gold were carried before the body, and many relics of saints, bought in Brittany.) For the king's death and association with Malmesbury Abbey, see Foot, *Æthelstan*, 186–200.

[19] William of Malmesbury, *GR*, i, 222–5: Nam quia Malmesberiam corpora cognatorum deferri et ad caput sepulchri sancti Aldelmi tumulari iusserat, ita locum illum coluit in posterum ut nichil desiderabilius, nichil haberet sanctius. Multa ibi largitus predia cartis quoque confirmauit, in quarum una post donationem subiecit:... (For the king, having ordered that the bodies of his kinsmen should be taken to Malmesbury and buried there at the head of St Aldhelm's tomb, had such a veneration for the place thereafter that he thought nowhere more desirable or more sacred. He gave it many estates and confirmed them with charters, in one of which after making the gift he continues as follows:...) The charter (S 436), which William copied both here and in c. 250 in his *GP*, is a conflation of S 415 and 434–5. The conflation is believed to be the work of William himself. See William of Malmesbury, *GP*, ii, 298; *Asser's Life of Alfred: Together with the Annals of Saint Neots Erroneously Ascribed to Asser*, ed. William Henry Stevenson (Oxford, 1959 [1904]), 246, note 4; *Charters of Malmesbury Abbey*, ed. S.E. Kelly (Oxford, 2005), 226–7.

[20] For example, only the **B** version added such an emphasis in the narration of the sword miracle as a reason why Æthelstan called upon St Aldhelm, see William of Malmesbury, *GR*, i, 208–09: 'erat enim ei ex antiquis progenitoribus consanguineus' (for he was related to him by blood a long way back).

Milton, and Muchelney in the mid-1130s in order to find more information about St Aldhelm and his own monastery, and the new information about King Æthelstan is just one result of these travels.[21]

Considering the *GP* was also under revision at the same time, we can reasonably conjecture that such a hunt for materials concerning Aldhelm and Malmesbury Abbey in the mid-1130s also bore other fruit in the *GP*, apart from the letter from Rodbod that William found at Milton, and which appeared in the revised text of both *GR* and *GP*. One problem with the *GP* is the lack of medieval copies of the fifth book, which focuses on Aldhelm and the history of William's own monastery. The existence of only one entire medieval copy, which is in the Magdalen manuscript, means that the changes made by William can only be vaguely dated after 1125, when he finished his original text in the autograph, instead of indicating a more precise date in most cases.[22] However, several corrections and supplements in the fifth book of the *GP* may result from William's travels in the mid-1130s as well, involving the following places:

a) Sherborne: William mentioned that he had seen the church built by St Aldhelm at Sherborne in an insertion between lines made some time after 1125: 'habuitque sedem Scireburniae, ubi et aecclesiam, quam ego quoque uidi, mirifice construxit' (His seat he established at Sherborne, where he built the remarkable church which I have myself seen).[23]

b) Corfe and Wareham: in the original Chapter 217 of the *GP*, William offered a great deal of detailed information on the church built by St Aldhelm close to the coast of south Dorset, but he later added a sentence at the end of this chapter, emphasizing its closeness to Corfe Castle and Wareham: 'Locus est in Dorsatensi pago duobus milibus a mari disparatus, iuxta Werham, ubi et Corf castellum pelago prominet' (The place is in Dorset, two miles from the sea, near Wareham, where Corfe Castle also stands).[24] The church described by William is believed to be in the position of the present St George's Church, Langton Matravers, on the Isle of Purbeck.[25]

c) Doulting: in his corrections to Chapter 228 in the fifth book of the *GP*, William provided more information about the church of Doulting where Aldhelm had died, together with the testimony from the locals:[26]

---

[21] Although William might have learned the information from correspondence or in other ways, his travelling to these places is a more likely scenario, considering his use of words in the evidence of (a), (b) and (c). Moreover, the evidence which follows makes the likelihood even stronger.

[22] Another manuscript, London, BL, Cotton MS Claudius A V, fols 129v–133v (hereafter the Cotton manuscript), only preserves an abbreviation of the fifth book of the *GP*.

[23] William of Malmesbury, *GP*, i, 566–7. This supplement is in the middle of folio 89r of the Magdalen manuscript which does not indicate the exact place it should be inserted. Unfortunately, this chapter is not included in the abbreviation of the Cotton manuscript.

[24] William of Malmesbury, *GP*, i, 548–9.

[25] E. Dudley C. Jackson and Eric G.M. Fletcher, 'Aldhelm's Church Near Wareham', *Journal of the British Archaeological Association* 26 (1963), 1–5.

[26] Oxford, Magdalen College, MS lat. 172, fol. 89v; London, BL, Cotton MS Claudius

Domus obitus eius conscia [*main text of the Magdalen manuscript and the abbreviation of the Cotton manuscript*] in aecclesiam mutata.	[*supplement in the Magdalen manuscript*] lignea erat aecclesia, in quam se ultimum spirans inferri iussit, ut ibi potissimum efflaret, sicut incolae hodie per succiduas generationes asseuerant.
(The building where he died [*main text of the Magdalen manuscript and the abbreviation of the Cotton manuscript*] was changed into a church.)	[*supplement in the Magdalen manuscript*] was a wooden church, to which he had himself carried as he was breathing his last, so that he could die there and nowhere else; this is what the locals even today affirm, for the story had come down the ages.)

William's tone also became more definite when he was referring to the stone there which had witnessed Aldhelm's death:[27]

[*main text of the Magdalen manuscript and the abbreviation of the Cotton manuscript, the latter without 'esse'*] Fertur in eadem aecclesia lapis esse, cui Sanctus acclinis morbo decubuerat.	[*after correction in the Magdalen manuscript*] Constat in eadem aecclesia lapidem esse, cui Sanctus moriens insederat.

A V, fol. 133r; William of Malmesbury, *GP*, i, 572–3.

[27] Oxford, Magdalen College, MS lat. 172, fol. 90r; London, BL, Cotton MS Claudius A V, fol. 133r; William of Malmesbury, *GP*, i, 572–3.

[main text of the Magdalen manuscript and the abbreviation of the Cotton manuscript]	[after correction in the Magdalen manuscript]
(The stone is said to be in the same church, leaning to which the saint had died for sickness.)	(It is a fact that in this church there is a stone on which the saint sat when he was dying.)

For (d) and (e), the two pieces of evidence bear the risk of being supplemented only from William's memory of his early visits before 1125 at those places, but the new information and change of tone when he was describing St Aldhelm's death at Doulting almost certainly resulted from his latest observation after 1125.[28] More interestingly, unlike the insertions in (d) and (e) which can only be vaguely dated after 1125, William certainly made the changes in (f) after the making of the so-called β-recension of the *GP*, from which the Cotton manuscript descended.[29] Since the β-recension must have been made before later revisions in the Magdalen manuscript were copied into another manuscript, Oxford, All

---

[28] Evidence shows that William was very likely to have already visited these places before 1125. He seemed to have seen Bishop Wulfsige's staff and other tokens at Sherborne, which was recorded in the original text of the Magdalen manuscript, suggesting a date before 1125. See William of Malmesbury, *GP*, i, 282–3: 'Seruatur ibi adhuc baculus eius et quaedam alia pontifices insignia, mediocritatis et humilitatis eius uiuum, ut ita dicam, simulacrum preferentia.' (His staff and some other tokens of his rank are preserved at Sherborne to this day, and provide, so to speak, a living image of his humility and his desire to avoid extremes.) He also heard a priest taking about the good qualities of Bishop Ælfwold of Sherborne (d. 1058) probably at Sherborne before 1125. See William of Malmesbury, *GP*, i, 282–3: 'Audiui ego bonae fidei presbiterum et iam canis sparsum bona eius lacrimabili gaudio referentem.' (I have heard a reliable priest, his hair now flecked with white, weeping with joy to tell good things of him.) For Corfe and Wareham, his detailed information about Aldhelm's church at Langton Matravers and related local miracles in the original text of the Magdalen manuscript suggests his early visits, and he would have had occasion to pass by Corfe and Wareham on his way to that church considering their locations (see Map 1). See William of Malmesbury, *GP*, i, 548–9: Eius domus maceriae adhuc superstites caelo patuli tacto uacant, nisi quod quiddam super altare prominent, quod a feditate uolucrum sacratum lapidem tueatur. (The walls of the building are still there, roofless and open to the sky, except that there is a projection above the altar to protect the hallowed stone from defilement by birds.) Finally, for Doulting, in the text of the Magdalen manuscript before revisions, William narrated that he had seen the stone crosses erected to mark the funeral procession of St Aldhelm every seven miles from Doulting to Malmesbury, which indicates his visit before 1125. See William of Malmesbury, *GP*, i, 574–5: Manent omnes cruces, nec ulla earum uetustatis sensit iniuriam, uocanturque biscepstane, id est lapides episcopi; quarum unam in claustro monachorum in promptu est uidere. (The crosses all still stand, and not one of them has felt the ravages of time. They are called *Biscepstane*, that is Bishop's Stones; and one of them can readily be seen in the monks' cloister.)

[29] β is a lost copy of the Magdalen manuscript at some point after 1125 which is believed to contain William's early revisions. From it descended the Cotton manuscript and another manuscript, London, BL, Harley MS 3641, fols 1r–95r. See William of Malmesbury, *GP*, i, xiii.

Souls College, MS 34, fols 1–93 (hereafter the All Souls manuscript), whose main text was made between 1130 and 1140, a more likely date for the changes in (f) is after 1130, simultaneously with, or after, the making of the All Souls manuscript.[30] This means that the date of William's latest visit at Doulting was at least close to the mid-1130s, or perhaps even during that period.

On the basis of the textual changes alone, it is hard to determine whether William's journey to Doulting really happened in the mid-1130s, and we cannot even confirm that he did visit Sherborne, Corfe, and Wareham after 1125, let alone in the mid-1130s. However, if we start to look at the map and compare their locations with Milton and Muchelney, things seem much clearer.

If William was travelling from Malmesbury to Muchelney in the mid-1130s, he probably used the famous Fosse Way, which runs near Malmesbury from Cirencester to Bath, and then stretches to Ilchester, a place close to Muchelney.[31] Since Doulting is near the midpoint of this route between Bath and Ilchester, he would have passed this place on his way to Muchelney, especially as this was a spot of great importance, since St Aldhelm died there. After visiting Muchelney, if William continued his trip to Milton, he may have used the Roman road running from Ilchester to Dorchester, and then taken the route heading towards Badbury Rings.[32] Milton is to the north of this road, and Wareham and Corfe are not far to the south. More interestingly, Sherborne is also located near the Ilchester–Dorchester road. This suggests that William may have visited these places together around the same time. In addition, the Badbury Rings–Dorchester route stretches north-eastward to Salisbury, where another road directly leads to Winchester.[33]

I propose that William probably visited all these places during one journey, thereby saving time and money, rather than travelling to only one place each time. He is supposed to have had some travel plans before his journey, and the road system would have allowed him easily to visit them one by one. Although he is thought to have visited at least some of these places before 1125 when he finished the original texts of both *GR* and *GP*, he may well have travelled there again, visits that would have refreshed his memory and allowed him to add the supplements as shown in (d) and (e). Just as at Aldhelm's church near Corfe and Wareham, the wealth of local miracles about the saint would have encouraged William to visit.[34] Therefore, it can be more confidently suggested

---

[30] For the dating of the main text of the All Souls manuscript, see William of Malmesbury, *GP*, i, xviii.

[31] For the Foss Way between Ilchester, Bath and Cirencester, see Margary, *Roman Roads in Britain*, 125–7, 141–3, and his map II; Christopher Taylor, *Roads and Tracks of Britain* (London, 1979), 188.

[32] For the road mentioned here, see Margary, *Roman Roads in Britain*, 108–12, and his map II; Taylor, *Roads and Tracks of Britain*, 67 and 82.

[33] Margary, *Roman Roads in Britain*, 100–01, 104–05; Taylor, *Roads and Tracks of Britain*, 47, 66 and 77.

[34] Just before his addition about the church's location near Corfe and Wareham, William particularly emphasized the great number of Aldhelm's miracles at the place, which,

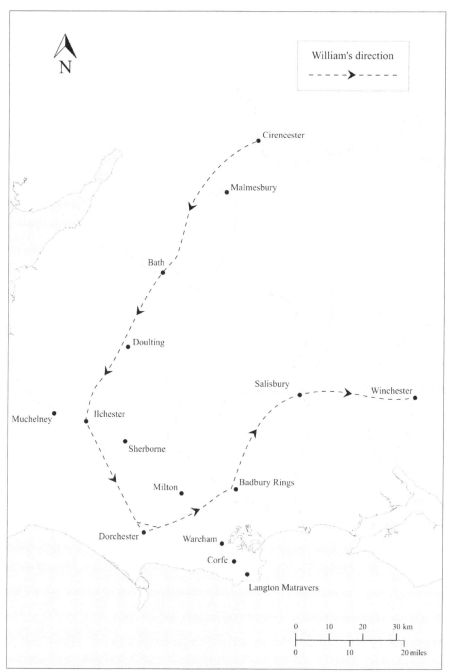

Map 2.1. The travel route of William of Malmesbury along the main roads. The main roads depicted in this map are based on Ivan Margary's valuable research of Roman Roads in Britain; see Ivan D. Margary, *Roman Roads in Britain* (London, 1967 [1955]), 82–188. I am grateful for Mr Yuhua Qiu's help in making this map.

that William took a long journey in the mid-1130s across southern England in order to collect more information about St Aldhelm and his own monastery, visiting places including Doulting, Muchelney, Sherborne, Milton, Wareham, Corfe, and Winchester, probably in this order. More places related to St Aldhelm and Malmesbury Abbey may have been included in his journey, but these places above are more clearly reflected by his writings.

Then, one question needs to be asked: why is the date of this journey in the mid-1130s? It is reasonable to think that William's interest in St Aldhelm was closely related to his concern over the liberty of his own abbey. The abbey's problems began in 1118, a miserable year for the monks of Malmesbury, for not only had their prestigious patron King Henry I's wife, Queen Matilda of Scotland, died, but also their abbot Eadwulf was dismissed for a reason that remains unclear.[35] After Abbot Eadwulf's dismissal, Roger, bishop of Salisbury, had acquired the abbey by 1125, probably intending it as a second cathedral priory in his diocese; his possession was first confirmed by Pope Honorius II on 1 January 1126, then by King Henry I on 8 September 1131.[36]

---

he seems to think, raised the prestige of Malmesbury because it possessed the saint's body itself. See William of Malmesbury, *GP*, i, 548–9: Copia signorum eo quot annis ad festum eius inuitat populum, frequentaturque ibi et munerum oblatio et sanitatum exhibitio, quanta nec in loco ubi sacratissima eius adorantur ossa: Deo, credo, per haec innuente satis superque sufficere debere Meldunensibus corporis eius gloriam, modo ceteris non inuideant uirtutum eius presentiam. (The number of miracles attracts the locals to the place every year on Aldhelm's feast day, and there is much giving of offerings and much healing, more even than at the hallowed place of his burial. My belief is that this is God's way of showing that the monks of *Meldunum* should be quite satisfied with the prestige of possessing his body, without begrudging others their local miracles.)

35 *Annales Monasterii de Wintonia*, in *Annales Monastici*, ed. Henry Richards Luard (5 vols, London, 1864–9), ii, 45: Hoc anno [1118] ... Matildis regina mortua est et sepulta in Westmonasterio. Edulfus abbatiam Malmesberiae sine causa amisit. (In this year [1118] ... Queen Matilda was dead and buried at Westminster. Eadwulf lost the abbacy of Malmesbury without reason.) Probably Eadwulf was dismissed shortly before the queen's death, since the two dedication letters of the *GR* referred to her only fault as leaving their church without a shepherd; see William of Malmesbury, *GR*, i, 4–5: Hoc solum in habundantia totius bonitatis superfuit, quod absque pastore gregem aecclesiae nostrae liquerit (One thing alone was wanting in this abundant goodness: she left our church a flock without a shepherd); William of Malmesbury, *GR*, i, 6–7: Maxime uero, cum de uita eius nil aliud reprehendi possit nisi quod ipsam aecclesiam sine rectore dimiserit (Above all, since no exception can be taken to anything else in her life except that she left our church without a head). Also see Lois L. Huneycutt, *Matilda of Scotland: A Study in Medieval Queenship* (Woodbridge, 2003), 65, note 42.

36 Pope Honorius's confirmation can be found in *Papsturkunden in England*, ed. Walther Holtzmann (3 vols, Berlin, 1930–52), ii, 141–2. King Henry's charter can be seen in *Charters and Documents Illustrating the History of the Cathedral, City, and Diocese of Salisbury, in the Twelfth and Thirteenth Centuries*, ed. William H. Rich Jones and William Dunn Macray (London, 1891), doc. 6, 6–7; *Regesta*, ii, 1715, 253. Roger probably deposed Eadwulf and left the abbacy vacant for a while, then he took over the abbey after Eadwulf's death. See Nigel Berry, 'The Estates and Privileges of Malmesbury Abbey in the Thirteenth Century' (PhD dissertation, University of Reading, 1989), 465–6; Nigel

William had already shown special concern over the liberty of his monastery before 1125. As Nigel Berry has argued, his translation of the privilege granted by Pope Sergius to Aldhelm from the Old English in the original text of the *GP* was a part of the attempt by the abbey to defend the right of free election of its abbot and remove Salisbury's episcopal control.[37] The privilege's Old English version was probably prepared in the middle of the eleventh century as a counter-argument against Bishop Hereman of Ramsbury's attempt to establish his see at Malmesbury.[38] In his *GP*, William criticized Hereman's worldly ambition and described in detail his failed attempt to make the monastery the seat of his bishopric during the reign of Edward the Confessor: he may have had Roger's threat in mind when he was writing about this event.[39]

His concern obviously continued after 1125. William inserted the charter regarding Leuthere, bishop of the West Saxons, renouncing episcopal rights over Malmesbury Abbey (S 1245) and the document in which Aldhelm confirmed the right of free election of their own abbots at Malmesbury, Frome, and Bradford on Avon after his death (S 1251a), into a blank space in the main text of the Magdalen manuscript, meaning that these two documents may only have reached their current forms at some point after 1125.[40] This is the most obvious evidence of William's concern, and we can assume that he continued such efforts in the redactions of his works until his monastery finally had a new abbot with King Stephen's approval in 1140 or even as late as May 1142, when at last Pope Innocent II confirmed its freedom from the control of the bishops of Salisbury.[41]

Berry, 'St Aldhelm, William of Malmesbury, and the Liberty of Malmesbury Abbey', *Reading Medieval Studies* 16 (1990), 15–38 at 15–17.

[37] Berry, 'St Aldhelm', 15–38.

[38] Berry, 'St Aldhelm', 15–38; *Charters of Malmesbury Abbey*, ed. Kelly, 27–8 and 31.

[39] See William of Malmesbury, *GP*, i, 286–9.

[40] The charters can be found in Oxford, Magdalen College, MS lat. 172, fols 82r and 89r; William of Malmesbury, *GP*, i, 524–7, 566–9. Kelly believed that these two documents were inserted by William between *c.* 1125 and *c.* 1135. See *Charters of Malmesbury Abbey*, ed. Kelly, 28, 31, 127–31, 161–2. In my opinion, although the decade after finishing the main text of the Magdalen manuscript was most likely, the *terminus ante quem* need not be before 1135, for its revision continued to the 1140s.

[41] Bishop Roger died on 11 December 1139, and the monk John was elected as the new abbot in January 1140. See William of Malmesbury, *HN*, 64–5, 70–1. According to the *HN*, the papal legate, Henry of Blois, disapproved of John's election of the abbacy, suspecting simony (a suspicion refuted by William), and this became the reason for his trip to Rome to seek confirmation. His journey was supposed to be narrated in William's *Itinerarium*, which is now lost. The privilege of Innocent II can be seen in *Registrum Malmesburiense: The Register of Malmesbury Abbey Preserved in the Public Record Office*, ed. J.S. Brewer (2 vols, London, 1879–80), i, 346–8. The monks must have launched another petition to the apostolic see at some point between 1141 and 1142, and this time their claim was supported by both King Stephen and Henry of Blois. This confirmation was based on the alleged privilege of Pope Sergius, and Berry argued that it was the text 'improved' by William, rather than other earlier versions. See Berry, 'St Aldhelm', 28.

The most important event in the mid-1130s is King Henry I's death in Normandy on 1 December 1135.⁴² It is likely that William began his journey to the south quickly once the news of the king's death had reached his abbey. The monks might have decided to petition for the liberation of the abbey again, but this time to the new king, Stephen. They needed all the support they could get, and William as the librarian and cantor, was in charge of getting as many oral and written materials as possible to back their claim.⁴³ King Henry's confirmation of Bishop Roger's control over Malmesbury Abbey on 8 September 1131 must have brought great disappointment to the monks and an end of the dispute during his reign; the succession of a new king would have offered the possibility of changing the monastery's fortunes for the better.⁴⁴ Therefore, his travels during this period belong to a larger project: William sought to find more information about St Aldhelm and his own monastery and to reveal the past glory of the monastery from documents elsewhere so that Malmesbury might recover the right of electing a new abbot freely, rid itself of episcopal control, and regain its liberty. If this is true, then William's journey through the south of England might have happened in early 1136, which means that the **B** version of the *GR*

---

⁴² For the death of King Henry I, see C. Warren Hollister, *Henry I* (New Haven, CT, 2001), 473–4; Judith A. Green, *Henry I: King of England and Duke of Normandy* (Cambridge, 2006), 219–23.

⁴³ William clearly said that he was the librarian of his convent in the prologue of his *HN*; see William of Malmesbury, *HN*, 2: 'Willelmus bibliothecarius Malmesberiae' (William the librarian of Malmesbury). He might have been the librarian before 1125, for he once depicted his own labours, following Abbot Godfrey's example, to enlarge the collections of the monastery library in the *GP*. See William of Malmesbury, *GP*, i, 644–5: Quod studium si predico, uideor id quodam meo proprio iure facere, qui nullis maioribus in hoc presertim loco cesserim, immo, nisi quod dico iactantia sit, cunctos facile supergressus sim. Sit qui modo parta conseruet: ego ad legendum multa congessi, probitatem predicandi uiri in hoc dumtaxat emulatus. Ipsius ergo laudabili cepto pro uirili portione non defui. Vtinam sit qui labores nostros foueat! (If I single out this activity, I think I have every right to do so, for in this area especially I have been inferior to none of those who went before; indeed (if I can say this without boasting) I have easily surpassed them all. May there be someone to look after the present stock! I have collected much material for reading, approaching the prowess of my excellent predecessor at least in this respect; I have followed up his laudable start as best I could.) Unlike Thomson's statement that this passage shows that William had worked under Godfrey's supervision for the library, it rather indicates that he was the one continuing Godfrey's work as the librarian of the monastery. Thomson's suggestion can be found in R.M. Thomson, *William of Malmesbury* (Woodbridge, 2003 [1987]), 200. William became the cantor no later than 1137, for Robert of Cricklade referred to him as 'William monk and cantor of the church of Malmesbury' in his *De connubio patriarche Iacob*, which is believed to be written soon after March 1137. See Robert of Cricklade, *De connubio patriarche Iacob*, ii. 22, in Oxford, Bodleian Library, MS Laud Misc. 725, fols 90v–184v at 129v, quoted from R.W. Hunt, 'English Learning in the Late Twelfth Century', *Transactions of the Royal Historical Society* 19 (1936), 19–42 at 31–2: Guillelmi Meldunensis ecclesie monachi et cantoris. William never mentioned his occupation as cantor in his own narratives. For related modern research, see Hayward, 'William of Malmesbury', 222–39.

⁴⁴ For King Henry's charter, see above note 36.

and many corrections in the fifth book of the *GP* in the Magdalen manuscript were probably made in late 1136 or shortly thereafter.

Last, but not least, was the **B** version of the *GR* directly involved in this new petition by Malmesbury Abbey? We know that one copy of the earliest version of the *GR*, which is the **T** version, was presented by the monks to Empress Matilda after their appeal to King David of Scotland later in 1126/27.[45] In letters to both Empress Matilda and King David, William mentioned that Queen Matilda of Scotland had left their church without a head, and his words suggested that the monks were also trying to convey some kind of petition orally through their bearer, which were not suitable to be included in a written communication, probably because they referred to the problem of Roger's seizure of the monastery.[46] Was the **B** version likewise sent to the dedicatee for a similar reason, namely in order to ask for help with the monks' petition for freedom from Bishop Roger's control? The dedicatee is supposed to be Robert, earl of Gloucester, the bastard son of King Henry I, and one presentation copy

---

45 William of Malmesbury, *GR*, ii, xvii–xxii. The manuscript that was close to Empress Matilda's copy is Troyes, Bibliothèque Municipale, MS 0294 bis, fols 1–119v, which includes two letters respectively to King David of Scotland and Empress Matilda. These two letters were first published and analysed in Ewald Könsgen, 'Zwei unbekannte Briefe zu den Gesta Regum Anglorum des Wilhelm von Malmesbury', *Deutsches Archiv für Erforschung des Mittelalters* 31 (1975), 204–14. In the commentary on the *GR*, Thomson provided three possible dates for the writing of these two letters: (1) before the death of Empress Matilda's husband Henry V on 23 May 1125; (2) between the death of Henry V and Empress Matilda's arrival in England in September 1126; (3) when Empress Matilda and King David were both in England later in 1126/7. Of the three possibilities, Thomson thinks the third is the most probable; for his discussion, see William of Malmesbury, *GR*, ii, 6–7. This is also the opinion of Könsgen and Marjorie Chibnall, see Könsgen, 'Zwei unbekannte Briefe', 207; Marjorie Chibnall, *The Empress Matilda: Queen Consort, Queen Mother and Lady of the English* (Oxford, 1999 [1991]), 46–7. Similarly, Tahkokallio has dated this presentation to the second half of 1126. See Tahkokallio, *Anglo-Norman Historical Canon*, 19–21.

46 William of Malmesbury, *GR*, i, 4–5: Hoc solum in habundantia totius bonitatis superfuit, quod absque pastore gregem aecclesiae nostrae liquerit…non indignanter obaudiatis et muneris nostri latorem apud imperatricem regali cura commendetis (One thing alone was wanting in this abundant goodness: she left our church a flock without a shepherd… with kingly forethought to recommend to the empress the bearer of our gift); William of Malmesbury, *GR*, i, 6–7: Maxime uero, cum de uita eius nil aliud reprehendi possit nisi quod ipsam aecclesiam sine rectore dimiserit, iustissimum est tam potentis filiae sapientia corrigi quo beatissimae matris ignorantia hactenus potuit reprehendi (Above all, since no exception can be taken to anything else in her life except that she left our church without a head, it is the height of justice that the wisdom of so powerful a daughter should set right the one point in which a truly blessed mother has so far by her ignorance laid herself open to criticism); William of Malmesbury, *GR*, i, 8–9: Preterea quae uobis per libri latorem mandamus, pro anima matris uestrae et antecessorum uestrorum omnium, imperialiter audite, et nobis misericordiam impendere curate. (Lend your imperial ear, furthermore, for the sake of the souls of your mother and all your predecessors, to the requests which we make by the bearer of the book, and do not forget to show us compassion.)

of **B** was supposed to have been sent to him.⁴⁷ Nevertheless, if Earl Robert did receive one copy, why was it not used as the exemplar for the *GR* text in the manuscript London, BL, Royal MS 13 D II, fols 4–110, which had strong connections with Robert's family and seems to have used both the copies of **A** and **C** versions in Robert's preservation?⁴⁸

A plausible explanation is that Robert was not able to preserve the presentation copy of **B** that he had received but acted as the intermediary and gave it to someone else, probably even at William's own suggestion. We have noted that the monks at Malmesbury were planning a new petition to King Stephen about the liberty of their own monastery in around 1136 and William's journey through the south of England was part of the preparation process, with the finishing of the **B** version in late 1136 or shortly later as one result. Interestingly, Earl Robert was back in England sometime after the Easter of 1136 and reached a reconciliation with King Stephen, marking the beginning of their good relationship and temporary cooperation.⁴⁹ They both went to Normandy separately in March and April in 1137, where Robert fought loyally at the side of Stephen against Count Geoffrey's invasion.⁵⁰ Only after King Stephen's return to England at the end of 1137 did their alliance start to weaken, and finally in May 1138 Robert formally denied his fealty to the king and sided with the Angevins.⁵¹ It may not be a coincidence that the petition of the monks at Malmesbury and the making of the **B** version of the *GR* occurred around the time when Robert and Stephen enjoyed an alliance between 1136 and 1137. It is possible that the monks asked Earl Robert to deliver the copy to King Stephen, or more likely his queen,

---

⁴⁷ Before the **B** version, early versions of the *GR* seemed to have already been dedicated to Earl Robert. The dedication letter to the earl appears for the first time in most copies of the **C** version, but it is located between Book Three and Four. Only in the **B** version is it found in its logical place preceding the first book, so it is suggested that this final version must have been 'formally and explicitly' dedicated to Earl Robert. See William of Malmesbury, *GR*, ii, 6. The **A** version around 1126 may have already been dedicated to Robert as well, because he was greatly praised almost with same words at the end of **A**, **C** and **B** versions. The sentence in c. 446 – Hoc autem opus postquam absolui, circumspectis plurimis, uobis potissimum delegandum credidi. (When I had finished my work, I considered many names, and chose you above all others as its recipient.) – also seemed to imply the dedication. See William of Malmesbury, *GR*, i, 798–9; ii, xxxiii, note 26. This sentence can be found in the manuscripts of the **A** version, such as Paris, Bibliothèque Nationale, MS lat. 6047, fols 1r–139r at 138v, and Cambridge, Trinity College, MS R. 7. 10 (748), fols 2–150r at 150r. This may imply that William had already turned to Robert's patronage as early as 1126.

⁴⁸ The *GR* in the manuscript is based on the **C** version but cautiously corrected against the **A** version. Tahkokallio suggested that the maker of the manuscript may have used all those books (*GR*, *HN*, and Geoffrey of Monmouth's *De gestis Britonum*) that belonged to Robert. See Tahkokallio, *Anglo-Norman Historical Canon*, 25–6.

⁴⁹ Edmund King, *King Stephen* (London, 2010), 61–4; Robert B. Patterson, *The Earl, the Kings, and the Chronicler: Robert Earl of Gloucester and the Reigns of Henry I and Stephen* (Oxford, 2019), 132.

⁵⁰ King, *King Stephen*, 73–4; Patterson, *The Earl*, 135.

⁵¹ King, *King Stephen*, 86–7; Patterson, *The Earl*, 136–7.

Matilda of Boulogne, who was an integral member of Stephen's inner circle, in order to get help with their petition.[52] The emphasis on the blood relationship between St Aldhelm and King Æthelstan may have been intended to touch the emotions of the queen, who also inherited the exalted Anglo-Saxon lineage, a strategy that William had used in his letters to King David and Empress Matilda a decade before.[53] If this is the case, then the presentation copy of the **B** version was probably sent to Robert at the end of 1136 or in early 1137, before he and Stephen left for Normandy, and that he immediately delivered it to the queen without making a copy. Queen Matilda of Boulogne's less active interest in literary patronage than Matilda of Scotland and Earl Robert, and the later break between her husband and Earl Robert, might be the reasons for the limitation of the contemporary distribution of this last version of the *GR*.[54]

In conclusion, the changes in William's narratives and the shifts in tone between various versions of his *GR* and *GP* suggest that William took a trip across

[52] From the investigation of the queen's household staff, Patricia Dark argued that she 'entered into the life of her husband's court to the fullest' and enjoyed great political influence. See Patricia A. Dark, 'The Career of Matilda of Boulogne as Countess and Queen in England, 1135–1152' (PhD dissertation, University of Oxford, 2005), 98–124.

[53] To King David, William claimed his abbey as 'the monastery of St Aldhelm your kinsman', see William of Malmesbury, *GR*, i, 4–5: 'monasterii sancti Aldelmi cognati uestri'. To Empress Matilda, he took Aldhelm's blood relationship with the kings of the West Saxons and her mother, Queen Matilda of Scotland, as the reason for the very start of the launch of the *GR* project. See William of Malmesbury, *GR*, i, 8–9: Semel igitur nobiscum inito sermone de beatissimo Aldelmo, cuius se consanguineam non immerito gloriabatur, seriem eius prosapiae sciscitata est. Acceptoque responso quod eadem esset quae regum Westsaxonum fuisset, rogauit ut totam eius progeniem breui sibi libello disponeremus, se indignam asserens more antiquo uolumine gestorum regum Anglorum honorari. (Thus on one occasion we were engaged in conversation with her on the subject of St Aldhelm, whose kinswoman she claimed with proper pride to be, and she asked for information about his family. When told in reply that his lineage was the same as that of the kings of the West Saxons, she asked us to set out his whole family history in a short work (*libellus*) for her benefit, claiming that she was unworthy to receive the tribute of a volume on traditional lines on the history of the English kings.)

[54] For Queen Matilda of Scotland's literary and artistic patronage and its influence, see Reto R. Bezzola, *Les origines et la formation de la littérature courtoise en Occident (500–1200)* (3 vols, Paris, 1958–63), ii, 422–6; Lois L. Huneycutt, '"Proclaiming Her Dignity Abroad": The Literary and Artistic Network of Matilda of Scotland, Queen of England 1100–1118', in *The Cultural Patronage of Medieval Women*, ed. June Hall McCash (Athens, GA, 1996), 155–74; Huneycutt, *Matilda of Scotland*, 125–43; E.M. Tyler, *England in Europe: English Royal Women and Literary Patronage, c. 1000–c. 1150* (Toronto, 2017), 302–53. For Earl Robert's patronage of literature, see Patterson, *The Earl*, 178–206. Dark compared the two Matildas' involvement in literature and arts and argued that Matilda of Boulogne 'had neither the motive nor the opportunity for such patronage'. See Dark, 'The Career of Matilda of Boulogne', 224. She may have only commissioned the *Beatae Idea Vita*, see *The Warenne (Hyde) Chronicle*, ed. and trans. Elisabeth M.C. van Houts and Rosalind C. Love (Oxford, 2013), xliii, note 131. The limited circulation of the **B** version at an early stage is noted by Tahkokallio, who ascribed it to the availability of previous versions and no addition in its chronological coverage. See Tahkokallio, *Anglo-Norman Historical Canon*, 31.

southern England probably in early 1136, visiting places including Doulting, Muchelney, Sherborne, Milton, Wareham, Corfe, and Winchester, presumably in this order. King Henry I's death in December 1135 and the succession of King Stephen provided an opportunity to organize a new petition to change the fortunes of the monastery, leading William to travel to find more information about St Aldhelm and his own monastery that would support his community's efforts to escape the control of Bishop Roger of Salisbury and regain its liberty. The **B** version of the *GR* and the numerous corrections in the fifth book of the *GP* in the Magdalen manuscript bear silent witness to William's research endeavor in the service of Malmesbury's liberty.

3

Kings in the Cloister: Contemporary Reception of Aelred of Rievaulx's Royal Biographies

W. Tanner Smoot

As the first Cistercian to write ostensive historical works in England, Aelred of Rievaulx (d. 1167) has received increasing attention from scholars interested in both twelfth-century historiography and political theology.[1] Aelred's histories indeed betray a keen interest in contemporary events, making them valuable sources of political commentary for a particularly potent moment of British history. For the mid-twelfth century represented a period of political transition for many across the British Isles. The majority of Aelred's historical works date to the years 1153–5, the conclusion to the so-called 'Anarchy' of King Stephen of Blois (d. 1154).[2] For nearly two decades, a violent succession dispute between Stephen and Empress Matilda (d. 1167), the daughter of Stephen's predecessor, Henry I (d. 1135), had mired many across England and Scotland in civil conflict. Although Stephen's acknowledgement of Matilda's son, Henry of Anjou (d. 1189) as his heir in 1153 brought hostilities to an end, religious leaders like Aelred had reason for concern over a truly peaceful transition of power. In Scotland, the concurrent death of King David I (d. 1153), a great friend and patron of Aelred's Rievaulx, saw the Scottish throne pass to the twelve-year-old Malcolm

---

[1] For Aelred's life and career, see Aelred Squire, *Aelred of Rievaulx: A Study* (Kalamazoo, MI, 1981). For Aelred's role as a historian, in particular, see Elizabeth Freeman, *Narratives of a New Order: Cistercian Historical Writing in England, 1150–1220* (Turnhout, 2002), especially 31–90; Elizabeth Freeman, 'Aelred as a Historian among Historians', in *A Companion to Aelred of Rievaulx (1110–1167)*, ed. Marsha L. Dutton (Leiden, 2017), 113–46; and Jay Paul Gates, '*Quidam Proditor Partis Danicae*: Aelred's Re-Imagining of the Anglo-Saxon Past', in *Remembering the Medieval Present: Generative Uses of England's Pre-Conquest Past, 10th to 15th Centuries*, ed. Jay Paul Gates and Brian O'Camb (Leiden, 2019), 87–116. Other studies have likewise focused on the political theology and accompanying ideals of lay spirituality implicit in Aelred's historical works; see Marsha L. Dutton, 'That Peace Should Guide and Society Unite: Ælred of Rievaulx's Political Philosophy', *Cistercian Studies Quarterly* 47 (2012), 279–95; and Katherine TePas Yohe, 'Working Out One's Salvation in the World: Aelred and Lay Spirituality', in *A Companion to Aelred*, 268–94.

[2] For a general overview of Aelred's historical writings, see *Aelredi Rievallensis: Opera Historica et Hagiographica*, ed. Domenico Pezzini, *CCCM* 3 (Turnhout, 2017), 7–28.

IV (d. 1165), whose minority threatened the stability of northern Britain. Much, therefore, remained uncertain in 1154, as two new kings gripped the reins of power in Britain. This essay examines two of Aelred's works on royal history, namely the *Liber de vita religiosi David regis Scotie* and the *Genealogia regum Anglorum*, as responses to the major political and religious anxieties gripping northern Britain throughout the 1150s.

Understanding the historical contexts in which Aelred wrote remains pivotal for analyzing his various intentions in composing these biographical responses. As the third abbot of the Yorkshire abbey of Rievaulx, Aelred governed during a dynamic period of northern England's political history. Anglo-Norman royal power had collapsed in Northumbria following the death of Henry I in 1135, at which time David I of Scotland imposed his lordship over much of northern England in support of his niece, Matilda.[3] Despite his defeat by the Yorkshire barons at the Battle of the Standard in 1138, David received Stephen's recognition of his northern hegemony, and even secured the earldom of Northumbria for his son Henry (d. 1152).[4] This expanding Scottish lordship, together with an emerging frontier aristocracy, perpetuated a fluid border between the two realms.[5]

Aelred himself exemplified the dynamism of northern England, pursuing an education at Durham Cathedral before serving at the court of David prior to joining Rievaulx in 1134.[6] For all its disorder, Stephen's reign witnessed a proliferation of new monastic communities, with thirty-four founded in the diocese of York alone.[7] Rievaulx's own founder, Walter Espec (d. 1153), had in fact opposed David at the Standard in 1138, an event that seems to have tragically divided Aelred's personal loyalties.[8] Rievaulx, nevertheless, maintained good relations

---

3 Paul Dalton, 'The Governmental Integration of the Far North, 1066–1199', in *Government, Religion, and Society in Northern England, 1000–1700*, ed. John C. Appleby and Paul Dalton (Stroud, 1998), 14–26 at 17; *Gesta Stephani*, ed. and trans. K.R. Potter and R.H.C. Davis (Oxford, 1976), 52–3.
4 Geoffrey W.S. Barrow, 'The Scots and the North of England', in *The Anarchy of King Stephen's Reign*, ed. Edmund King (Oxford, 1994), 231–53 at 247; Richard Oram, *David I: The King Who Made Scotland* (Stroud, 2008), 143.
5 William M. Aird, 'Northern England or Southern Scotland?: The Anglo-Scottish Border in the Eleventh and Twelfth Centuries and the Problem of Perspective', in *Government, Religion, and Society in Northern England*, 27–39 at 32.
6 Emilia Jamroziak, *Rievaulx Abbey and its Social Context, 1132–1300: Memory, Locality, and Networks* (Turnhout, 2005), 2; Jean Traux, *Aelred the Peacemaker: The Public Life of a Cistercian Abbot* (Collegeville, MN, 2017), 35–6, 39; Squire, *Aelred of Rievaulx*, 19.
7 Christopher Holdsworth, 'The Church', in *The Anarchy of King Stephen's Reign*, 207–29 at 218.
8 Pezzini, *Opera Historica et Hagiographica*, 154; see *Relatio de Standardo*, in *Opera Historica et Hagiographica*, ed. Pezzini, 57–75; Marsha L. Dutton, 'Galwegians and Gauls: Aelred of Rievaulx's Dramatisation of Xenophobia in *Relatio de Standardo*', in *Monastic Life in the Medieval British Isles: Essays in Honour of Janet Burton*, ed. Karen Stöber, Julie Kerr and Emilia Jamroziak (Cardiff, 2018), 115–26 at 118. Beyond his personal ties to the main belligerents, Aelred emphasized the bonds of friendship that intersected the battlelines at the Standard.

with both David and Walter Espec, both of whom continued to patronize the abbey's *familia*.[9] Yet, many religious communities in Yorkshire suffered at the hands of feuding barons, who devastated, plundered, and depopulated monastic lands in their pursuit of political dominance.[10] Although David appears to have stabilized his domains north of the Tyne, war still managed to disrupt religious life in Yorkshire throughout the 1140s.

Aelred's interest in historical writing culminated in this context of disruption and growing anxiety.[11] Cistercians had long involved themselves in lay politics, building networks of lay benefactors and proffering advice to secular rulers so as to maintain the welfare of Christian society.[12] From Aelred's perspective, David's death in 1153 jeopardized the relative stability of northern Britain. The crown of Scotland, as well as the earldom of Northumbria, had passed to David's two adolescent grandchildren, Malcolm IV and William I (d. 1214) respectively.[13] Thus, in the wake of David's death Aelred composed his *Liber de vita religiosi David*, itself as much a lament as a general call for peace and fidelity to the king's young heirs.[14]

Whatever Aelred's anxieties over the situation in Scotland, the subsequent death of King Stephen in 1154 exacerbated contemporary concerns in England. For although Stephen had accepted Henry of Anjou as his heir in 1153, their accord merely initiated a peace process between their respective factions, and few at the time could have known if this process would ultimately bear fruit.[15] Such uncertainties elicited a second work from Aelred, the *Genealogia*

---

[9] *The Charters of King David I: The Written Acts of David I King of Scots, 1142–53 and His Son Henry Earl of Northumberland, 1139–52*, ed. Geoffrey W.S. Barrow (Woodbridge, 1999), no. 120; Jamroziak, *Rievaulx Abbey*, 36.
[10] Paul Dalton, 'Ecclesiastical Responses to War in King Stephen's Reign: The Communities of Selby Abbey, Pontefract Priory and York Cathedral', in *Cathedrals, Communities and Conflict in the Anglo-Norman World*, ed. Paul Dalton, Charles Insley, and Louise J. Wilkinson (Woodbridge, 2011), 131–49 at 133–7.
[11] Aelred wrote during a period of great historiographical activity in twelfth-century England. Although English Cistercians engaged in history writing to a lesser degree than their Benedictine (and clerical) co-religious, they nevertheless produced various historiographical works between the twelfth and thirteenth centuries. See Elizabeth Freeman, 'The Many Functions of Cistercian Histories. Using Aelred of Rievaulx's *Relatio de Standardo* as a Case Study', in *The Medieval Chronicle: Proceedings of the 1st International Conference on the Medieval Chronicle, Driebergen/Utrecht 13–16 July 1996*, ed. Erik Kooper (Amsterdam, 1999), 124–32; and Freeman, 'Aelred as a Historian among Historians', 136–8. For more on Angevin historical writing in general, see Michael Staunton, *The Historians of Angevin England* (Oxford, 2017).
[12] Martha G. Newman, *The Boundaries of Charity: Cistercian Culture and Ecclesiastical Reform, 1098–1180* (Stanford, CA, 1996), 170–90, especially 176–83; Traux, *Aelred the Peacemaker*, 14–32.
[13] Barrow, 'The Scots and the North of England', 252.
[14] Aelred of Rievaulx, *Liber de vita religiosi David regis Scotie*, in *Opera Historica et Hagiographica*, ed. Pezzini, 5–21 (hereafter Aelred, *LVD*).
[15] Edmund King, 'The Accession of Henry II', in *Henry II: New Interpretations*, ed. Christopher Harper-Bill and Nicholas Vincent (Woodbridge, 2007), 24–46 at 37.

regum Anglorum, which he addressed personally to Henry of Anjou.[16] In the *Genealogia*, Aelred summarized the virtues of Henry's royal ancestors so as to provide the incoming king with imitable models of kingship. In this way, the *Genealogia* appears a classic example of a 'mirror for princes', a work of political pedagogy designed to assist a young king in ruling well. These two treatises began as separate works, yet quickly became linked in the manuscript tradition; indeed, Aelred himself combined them for Henry in 1154.[17] Medieval audiences therefore encountered these works together, a fact that warrants their collective analysis here.[18]

Although long neglected, more recent scholars have turned to these works for what they suggest about Cistercian political philosophies, lay spirituality, and emerging 'national' identities in England.[19] This attention has largely focused on Aelred's intentions for his supposed lay audiences, especially the moral and political guidance that the abbot addressed to Henry of Anjou.[20] These remain important lines of inquiry, and the scholarship of the last two decades has done much to fill this gap in our understanding of Cistercian historiography. Such studies nevertheless tend to overlook questions concerning the works' reception among contemporary religious communities. The *Genealogia* and *Liber de vita religiosi David* circulated soon after their composition, and complete paired copies survive in thirteen different manuscripts produced in the *scriptoria* of various Benedictine, Augustinian, and Cistercian communities.[21] Amounting to more than just 'mirrors' for princes, Aelred's royal histories appealed to several contemporary audiences and remained popular in English religious communities well after the twelfth century. Yet, while scholars such as Elizabeth Freeman and

---

[16] Aelred of Rievaulx, *Genealogia Regum Anglorum*, in *Opera Historica et Hagiographica*, ed. Pezzini, 2–57 (hereafter Aelred, *GRA*).

[17] Pezzini, *Opera Historica et Hagiographica*, 30–57; Walter Daniel, *The Life of Ailred of Rievaulx*, ed. and trans. Maurice Powicke (Oxford, 1978), 41.

[18] For a contrary approach, see Freeman, *Narratives of a New Order*, 58–9.

[19] See note 1 above. Renewed interest in the *LVD* and *GRA* has likewise occasioned an English translation of these works. See *Aelred of Rievaulx: The Historical Works*, ed. and trans. Jane Patricia Freeland and Marsha L. Dutton (Kalamazoo, MI, 2005).

[20] See Newman, *The Boundaries of Charity*, 181; Marie Anne Mayeski, '*Secundum naturam*: The Inheritance of Virtue in Ælred's *Genealogy of the English Kings*', *Cistercian Studies Quarterly* 37 (2002), 221–8; Marsha L. Dutton, '*Sancto Dunstano Cooperante*: Collaboration between King and Ecclesiastical Advisor in Aelred of Rievaulx's *Genealogy of the Kings of the English*', in *Religious and Laity in Western Europe, 1000–1400: Interaction, Negotiation, and Power*, ed. Emilia Jamroziak and Janet E. Burton (Turnhout, 2006), 183–95 at 183–6; Dutton, 'Ælred of Rievaulx's Political Philosophy', 280–5; Freeman, 'Aelred as a Historian among Historians', 128; and Traux, *Aelred the Peacemaker*, 130–48 and 172–93.

[21] Pezzini, *Opera Historica et Hagiographica*, 37, 121; Freeman, *Narratives of a New Order*, 70. See also Anselm Hoste, *Bibliotheca Aelrediana: A Survey of the Manuscripts, Old Catalogues, Editions and Studies Concerning St. Aelred of Rievaulx* (The Hague, 1962), 111–14. Several communities appear to have possessed a copy of Aelred's *Genealogia* by the thirteenth century, including Kirkham priory, Rievaulx, La Merci-Dieu (Poitou), Peterborough, St Albans, and St Augustine's, Canterbury.

Domenico Pezzini have noted these works' multiple registers of appeal, their didactic allure for religious audiences remains understudied.[22]

In many ways, religious interest in Aelred's histories is unsurprising: monastic communities in particular had long maintained an interest in history. Monastic libraries often included historical works, which monks appear to have read in the refectory, during the liturgy, and individually throughout the year.[23] The *Liber de vita religiosi David* and *Genealogia*, however, often survive in hagiographical manuscripts, appearing alongside collections of *vitae*, sermons, and hymns.[24] Indeed, when composing these works, Aelred adopted a methodology more germane to hagiography than to the types of narrative history flourishing in twelfth-century England. Thus, instead of composing strict chronological narratives, Aelred explained the past using allegorical paradigms intended to elucidate spiritual truths and encourage proper moral conduct.[25] Moreover, despite dedicating these treatises to Henry of Anjou, he incorporated exegetical lessons most readily recognized and understood by religious audiences.[26] Aelred manipulated historical anecdotes to demonstrate religious paradigms rooted in the strictures of the *Rule of Benedict* and conventional tropes of hagiography. Aelred's biographies, then, have less to tell us about his conception of kingship as an office than his belief in the universal applicability of monastic virtues – especially humility, obedience, and patience – to society at large.

Through an examination of Aelred's narrative methodology in the *Liber de vita religiosi David* and *Genealogia*, specifically regarding kings David I, Alfred the Great (d. 899), and Edgar the Peaceful (d. 975), this study will show how the Cistercian abbot used England's royal history to demonstrate the broad spiritual and social benefits of cultivating monastic virtue in both the kingdom and cloister. Specifically, it will explore these texts' didactic value for religious audiences, explicating the ways in which Aelred proffered certain kings as exemplary models of monastic behavior. In so doing, this study will evaluate

---

[22] Freeman, *Narratives of a New Order*, 57–8; Pezzini, *Opera Historica et Hagiographica*, 8–13, and 74–5.
[23] See *Liber Tramitis Aevi Odilonis Abbatis*, ed. Petrus Dinter, *Corpus Consuetudinum Monasticarum* 10 (Siegburg, 1980), 261–4; Hoste, *Bibliotheca Aelrediana*, 147–76; Teresa Webber, 'Reading in the Refectory at Reading Abbey', *Reading Medieval Studies* 42 (2016), 63–87; and Teresa Webber, 'Bede's *Historia Ecclesiastica* as a Source of Lections in Pre- and Post-Conquest England', in *The Long Twelfth-Century View of the Anglo-Saxon Past*, ed. Martin Brett and David A. Woodman (Farnham, 2015), 47–76.
[24] See especially Oxford, Bodl., MS Laud. Misc. 668; London, BL, Cotton MS Vitellius F III; London, BL, Add. MS 35110; London, BL, Add. MS 57533; London, BL, Harley MS 3846; Dublin, Trinity College 172; and Poitiers, Médiathèque, MS 75 (208).
[25] For more on the paradigmatic structure of hagiography, see Thomas J. Heffernan, *Sacred Biography: Saints and Their Biographers in the Middle Ages* (Oxford, 1992); and David Defries, *From Sithiu to Saint-Bertin: Hagiographic Exegesis and Collective Memory in the Early Medieval Cults of Omer and Bertin* (Toronto, 2019), 19–57.
[26] Pezzini, *Opera Historica et Hagiographica*, 32–3; Jamroziak, *Rievaulx Abbey*, 31. It appears as though Kirkham priory, founded alongside Rievaulx by Walter Espec, had already acquired a copy of both the *Liber de vita religiosi David* and *Genealogia* by the late twelfth century.

these works' multiple registers of appeal, which will grant insight into their popularity among contemporary religious communities.

Pious and Religious King: David I of Scotland

Composed shortly after the death of David I in 1153, Aelred's *Liber de vita religiosi David* both commemorates the Scottish king's virtues and laments his passing. The poignancy of Aelred's lament no doubt stemmed from his personal relationship with David, with whom he had associated both as a courtier and later as abbot of Rievaulx.[27] Yet, David's death caused Aelred more than just personal grief, for his demise threatened to upend the stability of northern Britain. With the reins of lordship left in the hands of the youthful Malcolm IV, the potential for a resurgence in political violence loomed.[28] Aelred himself expressed concern over the loyalty of Malcolm's aristocracy, admonishing them to maintain fidelity and concord.[29] He used the *Liber de vita religiosi David* to highlight those Christian virtues necessary for maintaining peace in society, exemplified in the behavior of David himself. Indeed, Aelred explained the king's virtues through frequent appeal to hagiographic paradigms, liturgical allusions, and, especially, the *Rule of Benedict*.[30] In so doing, Aelred demonstrated the universality of monastic virtue, whereby the peace that Benedict's rule established in the monastery might come to shape society at large.[31] In this way, a Scottish king could become a model for all, religious and lay, embodying virtues that both brought worldly success and led to eternal life.

From the outset of his *Liber de vita religiosi David*, Aelred cast the Scottish monarch as a model of Christian virtue, especially in his humility (*humilitas*), justice (*iustitia*), and chastity (*castitas*).[32] David's royal status in fact amplified his virtues, as his power (*potestas*) gave him license to do what he pleased.[33] Despite the opportunity born of his station, David chose not to stray from Christian virtue, becoming modest before his people, equal to his soldiers, and

---

[27] Two of Rievaulx's daughter houses (Melrose and Dundrennan) resided securely within Scottish territory and benefited from the patronage of David's family. See Traux, *Aelred the Peacemaker*, 2, 39–41; *The Charters of King David I*, no. 120; and *The Life of Ailred*, ed. Powicke, 2–9.
[28] Traux, *Aelred the Peacemaker*, 136.
[29] Aelred, *LVD*, 14–15.
[30] Aelred Squire has noted the importance of Aelred's biblical allusions in describing the character of David I, especially in his typological comparison of the king to biblical figures. See Squire, *Aelred of Rievaulx*, 83–4.
[31] For a Carolingian precedent of preaching 'Benedictine' virtues to lay audiences, see Scott G. Bruce, 'Textual Triage and Pastoral Care in the Carolingian Age: The Example of the *Rule of Benedict*', *Traditio* 75 (2020), 127–41.
[32] Aelred, *LVD*, 5. Aelred reiterates these key virtues of David in his dedicatory letter to Henry. See Aelred, *Epistola Ælredi Abbatis Rievallis ad Henricum Ducem Normannie*, in *Opera Historica et Hagiographica*, ed. Pezzini, 3–4 (hereafter Aelred, *Epistola*).
[33] Aelred, *LVD*, 5.

lower than his priests.[34] Aelred's praise resonates with Benedict's description of the good abbot, who accommodates himself to the character of each monk under his charge.[35] Aelred amplified these allusions through a reference to 1 Corinthians 9:22, wherein Paul claimed to have become 'all things to all people' for the sake of winning their salvation.[36] Thus David, like Paul, became 'all things to all people' (*omnibus omnia factus*) so that he might exhort everyone (*omnes*) to virtue.[37] Monastic writers had long regarded these words of Paul as characterizing abbatial authority. In his influential commentary on the *Rule*, for example, Smaragdus of Saint-Mihiel (d. *c*. 840) alluded to this verse when explicating Benedict's description of proper abbatial behavior.[38] In Aelred's own time, hagiographers frequently cited this verse when describing the humility of more conventional saints, making the concept of becoming 'all to all' a common hagiographic trope.[39] From the beginning of the *vita*, therefore, Aelred presented David's royal character as reasonably analogous to that of a saintly abbot, aligning concepts of royal and abbatial virtue.[40]

Aelred went on to detail the way David's 'Benedictine' humility enabled his worldly success, further validating the king's status as a moral exemplar. He asserted that God rewarded David's exceptional moral conduct (*optimi mores*),

---

[34] Aelred, *LVD*, 6. Compare Sir. 31: 9–10. 'qui te modestum plebi, equalem militibus, inferiorem sacerdotibus ostendas'.
[35] *The Rule of St. Benedict: In Latin and English with Notes,* ed. and trans. Timothy Fry et. al. (Collegeville, 1981), 177 (hereafter *RB*). See also *RB*, 279–81 where Benedict describes the rank of monastic brethren, noting that each should strive to give precedence to the other.
[36] 1 Cor. 9:22.
[37] Aelred, *LVD*, 6.
[38] *Smaragdi Abbatis Expositio in Regulam S. Benedicti*, ed. Alfredus Spannagel and Pius Engelbert, *Corpus Consuetudinum Monasticarum* 8 (Siegburg, 1974), 75.
[39] See, for instance, contemporary examples: Eadmer of Canterbury, *Vita S. Oswaldi*, in *Eadmer of Canterbury: Lives and Miracles of Saints Oda, Dunstan, and Oswald*, ed. and trans. Andrew J. Turner and Bernard J. Muir (Oxford, 2006), 242–3; Eadmer of Canterbury, *The Life of St. Anselm*, ed. and trans. R.W. Southern (London, 1962), 20; Baldric of Bourgueil, *Historia Magistri Roberti*, in *Baldricus Burgulianus: Opera Prosaica III*, ed. and trans. Armelle le Huërou (Paris, 2013), 84–5; and Gilbert Crispin, *Vita Domni Herluini Abbatis Beccensis*, in *Gilbert Crispin, Abbot of Westminster: A Study of the Abbey under Norman Rule*, ed. J. Armitage Robinson (Cambridge, 1911), 104.
[40] Aelred's sustained emphasis on royal humility is quite distinctive. While several twelfth-century historians note the humility of secular rulers, they often discuss the virtue in a passing, sometimes tempered way. John of Worcester referred to Edgar the Peaceful as 'humble' (*humilis*) when enumerating his virtues, while Henry of Huntingdon and William of Malmesbury each noted William I's humble attitude to the clergy specifically. When detailing the monkish humility of Richard II of Normandy, however, Malmesbury recounted the ways his presence at Matins could disrupt life at Fécamp. See John of Worcester, *Chronicle*, ii, 413; Henry of Huntingdon, *Historia*, 405; and William of Malmesbury, *GR*, 307. Overall, twelfth-century English historians placed far less emphasis on their kings' humble rulership than their Carolingian forbearers. See Emily A. Winkler, *Royal Responsibility in Anglo-Norman Historical Writing* (Oxford, 2017), 37–41.

fulfilling the promise of Psalm 98:8 whereby the meek inherit the earth and abide in unbridled peace.[41] David had ruled without pride (*nichil superbum in moribus*) and pacified Scotland, whose people submitted to the laws of his royal gentleness (*regia mansuetudo*).[42] Aelred's description of David's worldly success accords well with a monastic tradition that had long distinguished pride as the corresponding vice to humility. The *Rule of Benedict* specifically associates the humble life with the vision of Jacob's Ladder, whereby one ascended toward heavenly exaltation through humility in the world.[43] Pride had the opposite effect, casting down those who exalt themselves away from eternal life. In the 1120s, the Cistercian abbot Bernard of Clairvaux (d. 1153) further explicated the degrees of humility detailed in the *Rule*. In his *On the Steps of Humility and Pride* (*De gradibus humilitatis et superbiae*), Bernard thoroughly described the steps of pride as the inverse of humble behavior.[44] Aelred's description of David's virtues in fact corresponds remarkably well with the steps of humility detailed by Benedict and Bernard. David did not privilege his own will over the laws of God (second degree of humility; eleventh degree of pride), nor exalt himself over his people (seventh degree of humility; eighth degree of pride).[45] Aelred also alluded to the grades of humility elsewhere in the *vita*, clearly construing the success of David's reign as a consequence of his increasingly humble heart.

Aelred's description of David's hegemonic lordship, moreover, frequently accords with monastic ideals of abbatial governance.[46] Aelred argued that David reigned peacefully over so many people because of his equal commitment to stern rule (*seueritas*) and merciful leniency (*lenitas*), leading his people to obey him out of love rather than fear.[47] Such language again resonates with that of the *Rule of Benedict*, specifically in its instructions for abbots teaching their flock and reprimanding errant monks.[48]

Aelred's emphasis upon humility may also have had a particular resonance in the political context of 1154. Matilda, niece of David and mother of the future Henry II, often appears in contemporary sources as perilously haughty. Henry of Huntingdon (d. c. 1157), whose *Historia Anglorum* Aelred knew well, even attributed Matilda's failure during the Anarchy to her overwhelming pride.[49] Where prideful Matilda failed to secure England, David in his humility united

---

[41] Aelred, *LVD*, 6.
[42] Aelred, *LVD*, 6–7.
[43] *RB*, 193.
[44] *De gradibus humilitatis et superbiae*, in *Sancti Bernardi opera*, ed. Jean Leclercq et al. (9 vols, Rome, 1957–99), iii, 13–59.
[45] *RB*, 197, 199–201; *De gradibus*, ed. Leclercq, iii, 53–4, 51.
[46] See Katherine M. Yohe, 'Aelred of Rievaulx on Holy Royalty: A Twelfth-Century View of Lay Spirituality', *Studies in Spirituality* 13 (2003), 169–98 at 194–7; Dutton, 'Ælred of Rievaulx's Political Philosophy', 288; and Freeman, *Narratives of a New Order*, 67–9.
[47] Aelred, *LVD*, 7.
[48] *RB*, 175–7; 223–7; 283.
[49] Henry of Huntingdon, *Historia*, 739. See also *Gesta Stephani*, 212. For Aelred's knowledge of the *Historia Anglorum*, see Gates, '*Quidam Proditor Partis Danicae*', 89.

the diverse peoples of Scotland under one rule.[50] To someone like Henry of Anjou, as lord of an increasingly vast continental empire, Aelred thus offered a particularly apt moral lesson. Even so, he consistently proffered David as a moral exemplar to all, not merely to princes or the secular aristocracy. Finding Scottish churches at risk morally (*mores*) and materially (*res*), David established new bishoprics and monasteries throughout his realm.[51] The king subsequently lived like a monk (*quasi unus ex ipsis*), praising the good while giving deference and attention to all.[52] More than a role model for princes (whether Malcolm or Henry), Aelred's David exemplified the universal applicability of a 'Benedictine' sensibility in the world, made all the more inspiring by his high worldly station.

Aelred further compounded the association between the virtues of David and the *Rule of Benedict* through a detailed description of the king's participation in liturgical ritual. Religious audiences would have easily recognized such allusions, which began with a reference to David's participation in mass, prayers, and the psalmody.[53] Aelred described David's religious life in essentially monastic terms, going so far as to characterize the king's palace as a monastery in the final year of his life.[54] While visiting David during Lent, Aelred himself claimed to have found in the king a monk (*in rege monachum*), in the court a cloister (*claustrum in curia*).[55] David prayed seven times a day, keeping the divine offices and setting aside time for manual labor before retiring to his chaste bed (*castum cubile*) in silence.[56] Aelred later reflected upon David's meditation on the psalms, wherein he alluded to traditional biblical exegesis to elucidate the king's character further.[57] On the Saturday before his death, David repeatedly intoned the petition of Psalm 118:121: 'I have done judgement and justice; do not deliver me to my oppressors!'[58] According to Aelred, David had – like the psalmist – thus escaped divine judgement (*iudicium*) through his self-reproach, an act of penance that would mitigate his punishment in the afterlife. Such an interpretation of this psalm had circulated since at least the time of Cassiodorus

[50] Aelred, *LVD*, 7.
[51] Aelred, *LVD*, 7–8.
[52] Aelred, *LVD*, 8.
[53] Aelred, *LVD*, 11.
[54] Aelred, *LVD*, 14.
[55] Aelred, *LVD*, 14.
[56] Aelred, *LVD*, 14. Compare *RB*, 191, 211, 249–53.
[57] Biblical commentaries, particularly those of the Church Fathers, made up a substantial portion of Cistercian libraries in the twelfth and thirteenth centuries, and Aelred appears to have relied on some of the most popular patristic exegetes when describing David's prayer life. For Cistercian interest in the Latin Fathers, see C.R. Cheney, 'English Cistercian Libraries: The First Century', in *Medieval Texts and Studies*, ed. C.R. Cheney (Oxford, 1973), 328–45; Teresa Webber, 'The Patristic Content of English Book Collections in the Eleventh Century: Towards a Continental Perspective', in *Of the Making of Books: Medieval Manuscripts, Their Scribes and Readers, Essays Presented to M.B. Parkes*, ed. P.R. Robinson and Rivkah Zim (Aldershot, 1997), 191–205; and Constance B. Bouchard, 'The Cistercians and the *Glossa Ordinaria*', *The Catholic Historical Review* 86.2 (2000), 183–92, especially 188.
[58] Aelred, *LVD*, 17: 'Feci iudicium et iustitiam, non tradas me calumniantibus me.'

(d. c. 583), who asserted that whoever judged themselves and punished their own sins had indeed done judgement (*iudicium*) and justice (*iustitia*).[59] For Aelred, David also manifested the justice (*iustitia*) of the psalmist by showing mercy to others.[60] This public understanding of the psalmist's justice accords well with that expounded by Ambrose (d. 397) in his *Expositio* on Psalm 118. For Ambrose, justice (*iustitia*) by definition tends to the goods of others; where justice exists, mercy necessarily follows.[61] Aelred thus appears to have identified a typical royal virtue (*iustitia*), which he then reinterpreted by means of biblical exegesis in order to demonstrate David's Christian character.[62]

Aelred continued to gloss the devotional practices in David's biography as the old king came to reflect upon Psalm 119. David's impending death provided the immediate context for Aelred, who used the verse to allude to the king's humble approach to eternal life. After repeating the verse seven times, David placed his hope in heaven, spurned the earthly, and contemplated celestial things.[63] Psalm 119 marks the beginning of the gradual psalms, the song of ascents long interpreted by patristic exegetes like Augustine (d. 430) and Cassiodorus as denoting the soul's progress towards spiritual understanding.[64] As with the steps of humility in the *Rule of Benedict*, the gradual psalms became exegetically linked with the imagery of Jacob's Ladder in the Middle Ages.[65] Cassiodorus moreover explicitly equated the steps of the psalms with humility.[66] Such allusions by Aelred accord well with the general revival of interest in patristic texts across western Europe during the eleventh and twelfth centuries.[67] They constituted the fundamental guides to the study of Scripture, and monks, more

---

[59] *Magni Aurelii Cassiodori Senatoris Opera, Pars II, 2: Expositio Psalmorum LXXI–CL*, ed. M. Adriaen, *CCSL* 98.2 (Turnhout, 1958), 1112.

[60] Aelred, *LVD*, 18.

[61] *S. Ambrosii Opera, Pars V: Expositio Psalmi CXVIII*, ed. M. Petschenig, *CSEL* 62 (Vienna, 1913), 358–60. Rievaulx appears to have possessed a copy of Ambrose's *Expositio* by at least the thirteenth century. See Hoste, *Bibliotheca Aelrediana*, 155.

[62] For more on contemporary presumptions of royal justice, see Gerald of Wales, *De Principis Instructione*, ed. and trans. Robert Bartlett (Oxford, 2018).

[63] Aelred, *LVD*, 19.

[64] *Aurelii Augustini Opera, Pars X, 3: Enarrationes in Psalmos, CI–CL*, ed. E. Dekkers and J. Fraipont, *CCSL* 40 (Turnhout, 1961), 1776–86; *Cassiodori Senatoris Opera: Expositio Psalmorum*, ed. Adriaen, 1139–44. Augustine's *Enarrationes* features among the titles included in Rievaulx's thirteenth-century catalogue. See Hoste, *Bibliotheca Aelrediana*, 149, 164.

[65] *Cassiodori Senatoris Opera: Expositio Psalmorum*, ed. Adriaen, 1139–40; *Aurelii Augustini Opera: Enarrationes in Psalmos*, ed. Dekkers and Fraipont, 1777–8; *S. Hieronymi Presbyteri Opera, Pars II: Opera Homiletica*, ed. D. Germanus Morin *CCSL* 78 (Turnhout, 1958), 248.

[66] *Cassiodori Senatoris Opera: Expositio Psalmorum*, ed. Adriaen, 1140. See also *RB*, 193; and *De gradibus*, ed. Leclercq, 18.

[67] Webber, 'The Patristic Content of English Book Collections', 197; Teresa Webber, 'Monastic and Cathedral Book Collections in the Late Eleventh and Twelfth Centuries', in *The Cambridge History of Libraries in Britain and Ireland. Vol. I: To 1650*, ed. Elisabeth Leedham-Green and Teresa Webber (Cambridge, 2006), 109–25 at 113.

than most, would have recognized Aelred's exegetical allusions, all of which tend to emphasize the virtues established at the beginning of David's *vita* – especially the king's humility and justice.[68] In detailing the final year of David's life in his cloistered court through the lens of patristic exegesis, Aelred proffered the king as an enduring example for regular religious, not just young princes.

Soldier of Christ: Alfred the Great

Aelred composed the *Genealogia regum Anglorum* shortly after his *Liber de vita religiosi David*, sometime between the Treaty of Winchester (1153) and the coronation of Henry of Anjou (1154). The work catalogues the virtues and family history of England's royal dynasty, ultimately advancing Henry's impending reign as reconciling the kingdom's English and Norman legacies.[69] Aelred in fact dedicated the *Genealogia* to Henry in the hopes that the young duke might imitate the virtues of his ancestors – especially the recently deceased David.[70] The work nevertheless circulated among a wider audience early on, appearing in monastic manuscripts throughout the twelfth and thirteenth centuries. Aelred adapted his narrative from several sources, most notably Bede's *Historia ecclesiastica* (c. 731), Asser's *De rebus gestis Ælfredi* (c. 893), Symeon of Durham's *Historia regum* (c. 1129), Henry of Huntingdon's *Historia Anglorum* (c. 1130), and probably William of Malmesbury's *Gesta regum Anglorum* (c. 1134).[71] Yet, Aelred modified his narrative sources in significant ways, often providing his own exegetical gloss to events by altering descriptive biblical analogies and language. Understanding the ways Aelred deviated from his sources offers insight into the overall purpose and message of the *Genealogia* as it applied to a wider (religious) audience. His particularly rich treatment of kings Alfred and Edgar corresponds to their popularity among twelfth-century historians. As in the *Liber de vita religiosi David*, Aelred promoted a model of virtuous kingship in line with the ethics of the *Rule of Benedict*, with a specific

---

[68] Cistercians, for instance, often read Augustine's *Enarrationes* on the gradual psalms in Matins during Lent. See Webber, 'Reading in the Refectory', 70; and Chrysogonus Waddell, 'More about Saint Augustine and the Gradual Psalms at Early Cîteaux: A Supplementary Note', *Liturgy* 22 (1988), 61–94.

[69] Freeman, *Narratives of a New Order*, 60; Freeman, 'Aelred as a Historian among Historians', 128; Squire, *Aelred of Rievaulx*, 98.

[70] Aelred, *Epistola*, 4.

[71] Aelred also made considerable use of other historical materials produced at Durham cathedral, principally the *Historia de Sancto Cuthberto* and the *Capitula de Miraculis et Translationibus* (see below). Aelred had family ties to Durham, as his great-grandfather Alfred had lived there as a sacristan and custodian of St Cuthbert's shrine. Aelred's grandfather Eilaf had likewise belonged to the chapter of Durham before William of Saint-Calais expelled the clerks from the cathedral. Aelred himself may have received an education at Durham and retained a good relationship with the cathedral throughout his life. For more on Aelred's upbringing, see Traux, *Aelred the Peacemaker*, 35–9. For an overview of Aelred's potential sources, see Gates, '*Quidam Proditor Partis Danicae*', 89 n. 7.

interest in the way the saints reward moral behavior. Yet, by downplaying his sources' emphasis on dynastic legitimacy, Aelred advanced a broader message about the importance of patience in crisis especially relevant to contemporary religious audiences.

In characterizing the reign of Alfred of Wessex, Aelred reveals a special interest in the king's ostensible humility (*humilitas*) and patience (*patientia*). Such virtues naturally correspond, as patience in times of difficulty represents the fourth step of humility in the *Rule of Benedict*.[72] In this way, Aelred construed the political trials of Alfred's life as opportunities for the king's progress towards perfect humility. The account of Alfred's flight from the Vikings in 878 perhaps best exemplifies this method. While hiding in the swamps of Somerset, Alfred shared a portion of his food with a stranger – actually St Cuthbert in disguise. In return for Alfred's generosity, St Cuthbert promised to intercede on the king's behalf, always protecting him and his dynasty if they continued to venerate him.[73] The most immediate sources for Aelred's account come from Durham Cathedral, principally the *Miracula sancti Cuthberti*, though he may have likewise consulted the *Historia de Sancto Cuthberto* and the *Historia regum* of Symeon.[74] The focus of each of these narratives falls squarely on the patronage of Cuthbert, especially the saint's power to intercede for the king and guarantee his rule over Britain.[75] Alfred's almsgiving, discharged on account of the 'condescension of his humanity' (*humanitatis condescensu*) to the disguised Cuthbert, defines the king's moral character in the Durham texts.[76] Due to Alfred's devotion, Cuthbert – servant (*servus*) of God and soldier (*miles*) of Christ – freed the king from his persecution.[77] The entire episode serves to demonstrate Cuthbert's power as an intercessor, someone capable of granting Alfred and his progeny possession of the British *imperium*.[78]

Aelred, however, shifted emphasis in his account of Alfred's encounter with Cuthbert, reimagining the episode so as to highlight Alfred's virtuous character. From the outset, Aelred described the king typologically as Job, an innocent man

---

[72] *RB*, 197.
[73] This story appears in multiple sources, though not in any of the earliest depictions of Alfred's reign. The earliest account appears to come from the eleventh-century *Historia de Sancto Cuthberto*, from which later authors incorporated it into Alfred's legacy. See *Historia de Sancto Cuthberto*, ed. and trans. T. Johnson South (Cambridge, 2002), 90–4.
[74] John R.E. Bliese, 'St. Cuthbert's and Neot's Help in War: Visions and Exhortations', *HSJ* 5 (1995), 39–62 at 54. For history writing at Durham in this period, see now Charles C. Rozier, *Writing History in the Community of St Cuthbert, c.700-1130. From Bede to Symeon of Durham* (York, 2020).
[75] *Capitula de Miraculis et Translationibus Sancti Cuthberti*, in Symeon, *Opera*, i, 229–61, at 232–3.
[76] *Capitula de Miraculis*, 232; *Historia de Sancto Cuthberto*, ed. Johnson South, 55.
[77] *Capitula de Miraculis*, 232; *Historia de Sancto Cuthberto*, ed. Johnson South, 55. The *Capitula* refers to Cuthbert as a 'servant of God' (*servus Dei*), while the *Historia* calls the saint a 'soldier of Christ' (*miles Christi*). Thus, each of these accounts, in their own way, keeps the narrative emphasis squarely on St Cuthbert.
[78] *Capitula de Miraculis*, 234.

who demonstrated exceptional patience during a period of tribulation. As with Job, God allowed the Devil to test Alfred's faith by depriving the king of his realm and forcing him into exile.[79] Alfred endured these trials without complaint, once again eagerly granting the disguised Cuthbert a ration of food and wine.[80] Yet, Aelred altered the rationale for Cuthbert's appearance and intercession, which he characterized as a test of Alfred's purpose of mind and devotion.[81] According to Cuthbert, Christ acknowledged Alfred's patience and consequently ordered an end to his suffering.[82] Among contemporary historians, Aelred alone construed Alfred's political exile in such a way.[83] His evaluation of Alfred's patience reflects the virtue's importance in the *Rule of Benedict*, where the patient endurance of difficulties represents the fourth step towards perfect humility.[84] When addressing his troops on the eve of battle at Assandun, Alfred employed the words of the psalmist to reinforce this association. English fortunes would improve because God considers the prayers of the humble (Ps. 101:18), especially those who struggle in humility against the proud (Ps. 33:19).[85] Here Aelred carefully interpolated psalms that alluded to Alfred's penitential humility, a marked change from his sources' scriptural references. When, for example, the author of the *Historia de Sancto Cuthberto* described the consequences of Cuthbert's patronage of Alfred, he almost exclusively emphasized God's conditional support for and legitimization of the West Saxon ruling dynasty (Ps. 131:11–12).[86]

The interplay between humility and pride as a rationale for Alfred's experience speaks to Aelred's broader treatment of sin in the *Genealogia*. Anglo-Norman historians frequently explained the ninth-century Viking raids as punishment for the sins of the English.[87] Henry of Huntingdon even described the Danes as God's avengers against the immoral English.[88] By framing Alfred as a type of innocent Job, however, Aelred downplayed any of the king's personal failings. God wounded Alfred as he had wounded Job, striking and healing the king in turn, humbling him in order to raise him to new heights.[89] Aelred's typological exegesis accords well with that of Gregory the Great (d. 604), who likewise construed Job's suffering as expiatory.[90] Aelred indeed clarified that the pagan

---

[79] Aelred, *GA*, 27. With reference to Job 1:10–12.
[80] Aelred, *GA*, 27–8.
[81] Aelred, *GA*, 29.
[82] Aelred, *GA*, 28: 'Patientiam tuam, o mi Alurede, Christus ex alto prospiciens, laboribus tuis et erumnis finem imponit.'
[83] Other historians, insofar as they address Alfred's *patientia*, do so in the context of the king's personal illness. See John of Worcester, *Chronicle*, 229, 353.
[84] *RB*, 197.
[85] Aelred, *GA*, 29–30.
[86] *Historia de Sancto Cuthberto*, ed. Johnson South, 57.
[87] Henry of Huntingdon, *Historia*, 275; William of Malmesbury, *GR*, 183.
[88] Henry of Huntingdon, *Historia*, 275.
[89] Aelred, *GA*, 29; Job 5:18; 1 Sm. 2:6–7.
[90] *S. Gregorii Magni Opera: Moralia in Iob, Libri I–X*, ed. M. Adriaen, CCSL 143 (Turnhout, 1979), 314–15; in reference to Job 5:18. The works of Gregory the Great became extremely popular throughout the Middle Ages, especially in monastic circles.

Danes did not so much rage against the English *gens* as against their sins; they were divine tools for their purification (*purgatio*).[91] In this way, Aelred construed Alfred's struggle as a spiritual battle between humility and pride (Ps. 33:19), whereby the English, once tested (*probati*), examined (*examinati*), and purified (*purgati*), stood ready to face the Danes, the representation of England's sins.[92]

Alfred's patience in exile thus set the English on the road towards humble virtue and redemption. Since at least the time of John Cassian (d. c. 435), monastic authorities had understood patience as a mark of humility, itself a condition for securing virtue and purifying vice.[93] Bernard of Clairvaux similarly posited humility as the labor which leads to truth and eternal life.[94] Aelred essentially characterized Alfred as engaged in a similar progress towards virtuous perfection, describing him alternatively as a servant of God (*servus Dei*) and soldier of Christ (*miles Christi*).[95] The Durham texts, upon which Aelred based his account of the swamp miracle, exclusively refer to Cuthbert in this way.[96]

These terms, especially that of *miles Christi*, had a special resonance within a monastic context. Since late antiquity, ecclesiastical writers had understood the monastic life as a type of spiritual military service.[97] Commentaries on the *Rule of Benedict*, particularly that of Smaragdus of Saint-Mihiel, made this association more explicit, detailing how Christ's soldiers fight against the vices in the hopes of winning eternal life.[98] Although the term expanded in the later eleventh century to include certain secular knights – particularly crusaders – serving the church, Aelred seems to have envisioned Alfred's service in spiritual terms.[99] Smaragdus' *Expositio* nevertheless remained popular among the Cistercians, who believed that he explained the simple essence of the *Rule*.[100] Smaragdus even alluded to the experiences of Job when describing cenobites 'soldiering' under a rule.[101] For his part, Aelred explicitly described Alfred as a *miles Christi*

Rievaulx had several copies of the *Moralia* in its thirteenth-century library. See Hoste, *Bibliotheca Aelrediana*, 172.

[91] Aelred, *GA*, 30.
[92] Aelred, *GA*, 30.
[93] *Iohannis Cassiani: De Institutis Coenobiorum*, ed. Michael Petschenig, *CSEL* 17 (Vienna, 1888), 75–6. For Rievaulx's volumes of Cassian, see Hoste, *Bibliotheca Aelrediana*, 164–5.
[94] *De gradibus*, ed. Leclercq, 16–17.
[95] Aelred, *GA*, 28.
[96] *Capitula de Miraculis*, 232; *Historia de Sancto Cuthberto*, ed. Johnson South, 55.
[97] *RB*, 157; Katherine Allen Smith, *War and the Making of Medieval Monastic Culture* (Woodbridge, 2011), 89.
[98] *Smaragdi Abbatis Expositio in Regulam*, ed. Spannagel and Engelbert, 13–14.
[99] Smith, *War and the Making of Medieval Monastic Culture*, 96, 106, who has noted that the concepts of the secular and monastic *miles Christi* shared a common tradition and did not necessarily contradict one another. See also Martha G. Newman, *The Boundaries of Charity*, 29–37.
[100] For the influence of Smaragdus on the Cistercians, see Daniel Marcel La Corte, 'Smaragdus of Saint-Mihiel: Ninth-Century Sources for Twelfth-Century Reformers', *Cistercian Studies Quarterly* 41 (2006), 273–90.
[101] *Smaragdi Abbatis Expositio in Regulam*, ed. Spannagel and Engelbert, 56; Job 7:1.

and *servus Dei* when referring to the king's patience in exile and gift of alms to Cuthbert.[102] Alfred proved himself a *miles Christi* by rejoicing over the loss of his kingdom, as it left the king with more time to focus on God.[103] Alfred remained God's *servus* from his political exile onwards, allowing the Lord to guide him in life until his final journey to the heavenly kingdom.[104] In the main, Aelred appears to have adapted his historical sources in order to shift the focus away from concepts of saintly patronage, dynastic politics, and the general sin of the English, and towards Alfred's humble journey on the road to eternal life. Monastic audiences would have not only understood Aelred's symbolism but also identified with his message.

Royal Preacher: Edgar the Peaceful

As noted above, Aelred's treatment of kings Alfred and Edgar in the *Genealogia* appears especially rich. Edgar's memory had inspired panegyrics almost from the moment of his death, full of praise for the king's strength, justice, and generosity.[105] The great-grandson of Alfred, Edgar won praise for his involvement in the so-called English 'Benedictine Reform' of the tenth century.[106] The king's reign indeed impressed twelfth-century writers, who frequently eulogized Edgar's monastic patronage and hegemonic power in Britain.[107] For his part, Aelred appears to have relied heavily on twelfth-century depictions of Edgar, borrowing numerous metaphors and anecdotes from the works of Henry of Huntingdon, Symeon of Durham, and William of Malmesbury. Aelred nevertheless syncopated their narratives of Edgar's reign, devoting most of his attention to the king's ecclesiastical policies. Aelred's narrative centers around an idealized speech, wherein Edgar admonishes the English clergy to reform their

---

[102] Aelred, *GA*, 28.
[103] Aelred, *GA*, 28.
[104] Aelred, *GA*, 31.
[105] See *ASC*, A 973; Byrhtferth of Ramsey, *Vita S. Oswaldi*, in *Byrhtferth of Ramsey: The Lives of St. Oswald and St. Ecgwine*, ed. and trans. Michael Lapidge (Oxford, 2009), 75; and Wulfstan of Winchester, *Vita S. Æthelwoldi*, in *Wulfstan of Winchester: The Life of St. Æthelwold*, ed. and trans. Michael Lapidge and Michael Winterbottom (Oxford, 1991), 25. For an overview of Edgar's reign and legacy, see *Edgar, King of the English, 959–975*, ed. Donald Scragg (Woodbridge, 2008).
[106] The concept of monastic 'reform', especially in pre-Conquest England, remains a debated topic among scholars. For an overview of the issues involved, see Julia Barrow, 'Ideas and Applications of Reform', in *The Cambridge History of Christianity, 3: Early Medieval Christianities, c. 600–1100*, ed. Thomas F.X. Noble and Julia H.M. Smith (Cambridge, 2008), 345–62; Julia Barrow, 'The Ideology of the Tenth-Century English Benedictine "Reform",' in *Challenging the Boundaries of Medieval History: The Legacy of Timothy Reuter*, ed. Patricia Skinner (Turnhout, 2009), 141–54; and Steven Vanderputten, *Monastic Reform as Process: Realities and Representations in Medieval Flanders, 900–1100* (Ithaca, NY, 2013).
[107] Henry of Huntingdon, *Historia*, 319–23; William of Malmesbury, *GR*, 239–62; Symeon of Durham, *Historia Regum*, in Symeon, *Opera*, ii, 3–283 at 128–32; John of Worcester, *Chronicle*, 397–427.

way of living and adopt the regular life. In this speech, Aelred deviates from his sources significantly, hinting at contemporary anxieties about the current state of monasticism best interpreted in the context of the recent 'Anarchy'.

Aelred's account of Edgar begins with a general overview of the king's reign, noting how none surpassed him in holiness (*sanctitas*) nor sweetness (*suauitas*).[108] Weaving together the imagery of Henry of Huntingdon and Symeon of Durham, Aelred presented Edgar as a type of Solomon (that is to say, peaceful), as beneficial to England as Cyrus to Persia or Romulus to Rome.[109] Yet, Edgar's reform of the English Church occupied most of Aelred's energy. In a manner similar to William of Malmesbury, Aelred envisaged Edgar addressing the English clergy directly in a speech that takes up most of the *Genealogia*'s narrative about the king.[110] This sermon (*sermo*), as Aelred called it, addressed not only the secular priests, as did most other accounts of Edgar's reform, but also the kingdom's bishops, clerics, and monks.[111] Manuscripts of the *Genealogia* typically demarcate the sermon from the rest of the Edgar narrative, usually by an initial or rubricated title.[112] Edgar's speech appears under various titles, though at least one fourteenth-century manuscript entitled the text a 'sermon of King Edgar to the clergy' (*sermo regis Edgari ad clerum*).[113] In expanding the addressees of Edgar's speech, all while framing the 'sermon' in a pastoral style, Aelred could circulate, especially among his religious audiences, his own values and concerns regarding ecclesiastical affairs in twelfth-century Yorkshire.

Directed to the presbyters (*presbyteri*) of the English Church, Edgar's speech begins with a critique of ecclesiastical oversight.[114] Edgar specifically questioned whether England's ministers, monks, and nuns lived chastely, behaved honorably, conducted services appropriately, taught the laity, ate with moderation, dressed with restraint, and judged with discretion.[115] For Edgar, the fact that he knew of these offenses suggested that church leaders had failed to care properly for their clergy.[116]

The critiques that Aelred voiced through Edgar appear much more extensive than those originally expressed by tenth-century reform leaders. Composed around the turn of the first millennium, the earliest hagiographies of the reform bishops Æthelwold of Winchester (d. 984) and Oswald of Worcester (d. 992)

---

[108] Aelred, *GA*, 38. William of Malmesbury, even more than Aelred, depicted Edgar as a 'holy' king. See William of Malmesbury, *GR*, 255, 262.

[109] Aelred, *GA*, 38–9; Henry of Huntingdon, *Historia*, 323; Symeon of Durham, *Historia Regum*, 131.

[110] Aelred, *GA*, 40–3; William of Malmesbury, *GR*, 249–51. William noticeably recorded Edgar's words in the form of a charter presented to the abbey of Malmesbury. John of Worcester similarly noted that Edgar himself exhorted the pastors of England. See John of Worcester, *Chronicle*, 413.

[111] Aelred, *GA*, 40.

[112] For more information on the manuscripts of Aelred's works, see Pezzini, *Opera Historica et Hagiographica*, 29–57.

[113] Dublin, Trinity College 172, p. 74.

[114] Aelred, *GA*, 40.

[115] Aelred, *GA*, 40–1.

[116] Aelred, *GA*, 41.

focused almost exclusively on the issues of liturgical performance and clerical celibacy when defaming the secular clergy.[117] By contrast, twelfth-century writers tended to frame the reform as a response to English clerics' refusal either to live chastely or in accordance with a rule.[118] Aelred nevertheless broadened Edgar's criticisms, chastising the indecent clothing, improper tonsure, base speech, and insolent gestures of the clergy. Religious houses had become little more than brothels, full of drunkenness, dancing, singing, and gambling.[119] For Aelred, such irregular behavior spoke to the madness (*insania*) of the clergy's inner selves.[120] Aelred's hyperbole bears a striking resemblance to that of Cistercian apologists, eager to promote the discipline of the white monks. Bernard of Clairvaux criticized the Cluniacs on similar grounds in his *Apologia*, written around 1125 for William of Saint-Thierry (d. 1148). Like Aelred, Bernard berated the excessive consumption, fashionable attire, and extravagant foods prevalent (or so he believed) in Cluniac houses.[121] Such concern for bodily satisfaction necessarily starved the soul. In various ways, Aelred appears to have shifted the emphasis of Edgar's complaint (as presented in his sources), focusing instead on the particulars of cloistered, Cistercian discipline.

Aelred's particular interest in monastic discipline, coupled with the pastoral tone of Edgar's *sermo*, likely reflects the context in which he wrote the *Genealogia*. Even as the 'Anarchy' of King Stephen disrupted ecclesiastical life in Yorkshire, some thirty-two new religious houses emerged in the diocese of York after 1140.[122] Prior to his abbacy at Rievaulx, Aelred had governed its daughter house of Revesby from *c*. 1141 to 1147, a role that had accustomed him to the difficulties of organizing a new religious institution.[123] As an abbot, Aelred managed his community's spiritual and material wellbeing, and new foundations like Revesby – and even Rievaulx itself – relied on a pious laity for support.[124] Monastic communities of all stripes depended on the acquisition and maintenance of land rights for their economic wellbeing, and Cistercians frequently sought to consolidate their properties by requesting, exchanging, and purchasing land from their lay neighbors.[125] Since its own foundation in 1132, Rievaulx maintained close relationships with its most important local

---

[117] Byrhtferth of Ramsey, *Vita S. Oswaldi*, ed. Lapidge, 35; Wulfstan of Winchester, *Vita S. Æthelwoldi*, ed. Lapidge and Winterbottom, 31. Wulfstan does mention the Winchester canons' excessive eating and drinking, though his main complaint centers around proper liturgical celebration and the clerics' illicit sexual relationships.
[118] William of Malmesbury, *GR*, 251; Henry of Huntingdon, *Historia*, 321; Symeon of Durham, *Historia Regum*, 129; John of Worcester, *Chronicle*, 413; Eadmer of Canterbury, *Vita S. Dunstani*, in *Eadmer of Canterbury*, ed. Turner and Muir, 139.
[119] Aelred, *GA*, 41.
[120] Aelred, *GA*, 41.
[121] *Apologia ad Guillelmum abbatem*, in *Sancti Bernardi opera*, iii, 62–108 at 97–102.
[122] Holdsworth, 'The Church', 220.
[123] Walter Daniel, *The Life of Ailred of Rievaulx*, ed. Powicke, 28; Dalton, 'Ecclesiastical Responses', 144–5.
[124] Traux, *Aelred the Peacemaker*, 65–8; Walter Daniel, *The Life of Ailred of Rievaulx*, ed. Powicke, 28.
[125] Newman, *The Boundaries of Charity*, 71.

patrons.[126] Aelred alluded to the importance of such lay patronage, as well as the concomitant duties of monks, in the *sermo Edgari*. After detailing the clergy's impropriety, Edgar complained that they had squandered royal patrimonies (*patrimonia regum*), the treasure (*thesaurus*) his ancestors had donated to the Church.[127] The clergy had exploited royal generosity in order to satisfy their material wants, neglecting their liturgical duties and the dictates of God's law.[128]

Religious communities relied, at least in part, on their public image to attract lay patrons. Indeed, Aelred's biographer, Walter Daniel, attributed the gifts of lay and ecclesiastical patrons alike to their reverence (*reuerencia*) and affection (*amor*) for both Revesby and Aelred himself.[129] The misuse of such patronage thus threatened a community's material security during an admittedly disturbed (*turbata*) and chaotic (*confusa*) time.[130] Aelred further underscored the importance of maintaining moral probity in the face of material wellbeing, when he observed how the entire kingdom of England abounded in devotion, discipline, and justice once the clergy had either renounced their luxuries or were expelled and replaced by more worthy individuals.[131] Writing in a context of new foundations, uncertain patronage, and intermittent war, Aelred's expanded version of Edgar's sermon on ecclesiastical behavior provided an apt commentary for contemporary times.

In sum, Aelred of Rievaulx suffused his *Liber de vita religiosi David* and *Genealogia regum Anglorum* with vocabulary, allusions, and tropes especially perceptible to religious audiences. His appeal to monastic virtues, especially those expressed in the *Rule of Benedict*, ensured that monastic readers could absorb moral lessons from Britain's virtuous kings; indeed, the degree to which Aelred's concepts of lay piety and monastic devotion converge is striking. Like his contemporaries, Aelred accepted the concept of a royal *ministerium*, the representation of kingship as a divine vocation.[132] Yet, Aelred saturated his royal narratives with exegetical allusions that espouse the universal applicability of monastic virtues. As a result, Aelred could construe Britain's historical kings as moral exemplars, not only for young Henry of Anjou and Malcolm of

---

[126] The Ros family, as heirs of Rievaulx's founder Walter Espec, appear to have somewhat neglected their role as benefactors of the abbey. Consequently, Rievaulx relied on a support network that included powerful local patrons such as Eustace Fitz John (d. 1157), William de Vesci (d. 1184), Roger de Mowbray (d. 1188) and bishops William of St. Barbara (d. 1152) and Hugh de Puiset (d. 1195) of Durham. See Jamroziak, *Rievaulx Abbey*, 38–9, and 87–8; and Emilia Jamroziak, 'How Rievaulx Abbey Remembered its Benefactors', in *Religious and Laity in Western Europe, 1000–1400*, 63–76 at 64 and 66–7.

[127] Aelred, *GA*, 41.

[128] Aelred, *GA*, 41–2.

[129] Walter Daniel, *The Life of Ailred of Rievaulx*, ed. Powicke, 28.

[130] Walter Daniel, *The Life of Ailred of Rievaulx*, ed. Powicke, 28.

[131] Aelred, *GA*, 41–3.

[132] Aelred, *GA*, 42. During his *sermo*, Edgar appeals to the so-called doctrine of the two swords when describing his authority. See also Newman, *The Boundaries of Charity*, 176–7; Yohe, 'Aelred of Rievaulx on Holy Royalty', 183.

Scotland, but also for those religious audiences most likely to encounter these works. Indeed, the manuscripts of these works themselves illustrate the varied and enduring interests of their audiences, as several bear marginal annotations drawing readers' attention to notable examples of royal piety.[133] Thus, the *Liber de vita religiosi David* and the *Genealogia* perhaps speak less to Aelred's ideas of kingship as a political role than to his esteem for the practice of humility, patience, and discipline in the cloister and beyond. This itself remains a significant point; even Bede had once critiqued the temperament of a king as better suited for the episcopacy than the throne.[134] Aelred, in contrast, made less of a distinction between the sorts of behaviors appropriate to kings and the clergy, merging royal and monastic virtues whenever the opportunity arose. For someone committed to a community united by charity, the virtues of the cloister seemed a balm for an otherwise fragmented and fractious world.[135]

[133] See London, BL, Royal MS 13 D V, fols 142r–51v. Produced at St Albans during the thirteenth century, this manuscript features a heavily annotated copy of the *Liber de vita religiosi David* and *Genealogia*. Although written in a humanist script, perhaps from the later fifteenth century, the annotations nevertheless demonstrate both a continued interest in the kings' Christian virtues and the enduring relevancy of Aelred's royal biographies. See also Dublin, Trinity College 172, pp. 75–6, which features several manicules pointing out sections of Edgar's speech where he chastises the clergy for misusing royal donations.
[134] Bede, *EH* 4.11, 365. According to Bede, King Sebbi of the East Angles yearned for the monastic life most of his reign, finally converting to the habit after thirty years of rule.
[135] Walter Daniel, *The Life of Ailred of Rievaulx*, ed. Powicke, 11: 'caritate iungitur'.

Bethell Prize Essay 2021

Heretics, Miracles, and Cistercian Preachers: The Influence of Henry of Marcy on Herbert of Clairvaux's *Liber visionum et miraculorum Clarevallensium*[1]

Emmie Rose Price-Goodfellow

In 1178, Herbert, a monk at the Cistercian abbey of Clairvaux, created a collection of exemplary miracle stories, now known to us as the *Liber visionum et miraculorum Clarevallensium* (hereafter *Liber miraculorum*).[2] Information on its author and dating comes to us via the *Chronicon Clarevallense*, written at Clairvaux in the early thirteenth century:

And in this year [1178], Dom Herbert, who was then monk at Clairvaux and had been abbot of Mores, wrote a book of miracles [*librum miraculorum*] at Clairvaux… From the testimony of Dom Gossuinus, who was once a monk at Clairvaux… '… And Dom Herbert, who was once the chaplain of Abbot Henry, produced quite a large volume of various visions and miracles, and later became archbishop in Sardinia thanks to God's providence.'[3]

---

[1] I would like to thank the judge of the Denis Bethell prize, as well as the *HSJ* editors, for their constructive comments on this essay, which have improved it immeasurably. Thanks also to my doctoral supervisor, Dr Sethina Watson, for our many conversations about this topic, and to Dr Tess Wingard, for reading and commenting on an earlier draft.

[2] A new edition of Herbert's collection has recently been published, *Herberti Turritani Archiepiscopi. Liber Visionum et Miraculorum Clarevallensium*, ed. Giancarlo Zichi, Graziono Fois, and Stefano Mula (Turnhout, 2017). All quotations from the *Liber miraculorum* in this essay are from this edition.

[3] *PL* 185, cols 1247–8: Et hoc anno [1178] domnus Herbertus monachus Claraevallis, qui fuerat abbas de Moris, librum miraculorum apud Claramvallem conscripsit… Testimonium domni Gossuini monachi quondam Claraevallis…Praeterea et domnus Herbertus, qui aliquando capellanus domni Henrici exstitit abbatis, magnum satis diversarum visionum et miraculorum edidit volumen: qui postea Dei providentia Sardiniae fuit archiepiscopus.'". All translations are my own, unless otherwise indicated. Stefano Mula has identified the author of the *Chronicon Clarevallense* as the Cistercian

Scholars have long thought of Herbert's *Liber miraculorum* as an unstructured series of anecdotes from his fellow monks at Clairvaux, in contrast to later collections such as Conrad of Eberbach's *Exordium magnum* and Caesarius of Heisterbach's *Dialogus miraculorum*, in which the exempla are organized into thematic divisions.[4] As Brian Patrick McGuire has said of Herbert's work, 'His job is to impress the reader by the number of his wonders, not to interpret them or to integrate them into some system.'[5] This characterization is thanks in large part to an edition, produced by the Jesuit Father Chifflet in the seventeenth century, and reproduced in the *Patrologia Latina*, which was based on two unrepresentative manuscript copies.[6] One of these manuscripts uniquely divides the collection into three parts, and unbeknownst to the editor, both were abridged. The recent publication of a new critical edition, based on a survey of the complete and incomplete manuscripts, and which largely reproduces the earliest twelfth-century witness (Munich, Bayerische Staatsbibliothek, Clm 2607, henceforth Clm 2607), has provided a clearer picture of Herbert's collection and the manuscript history.[7] Far from being a random collection of stories about life in a Cistercian monastery, the material is split evenly between stories of Clairvaux and other monasteries, and stories that feature lay people and take place in the secular world. Though Herbert's text is not explicitly organized in the manner of Caesarius's or Conrad's collections, a number of themes recur in the latter half: unbelief and heresy, eucharistic miracles, crusade and the conversion of pagans in Eastern Europe, and the divine punishments incurred by the sinful behavior of the laity. It is a more varied and complex text, with a more secular focus, than has hitherto been recognized.

Alberic of Trois Fontaines. See now Stefano Mula, 'Looking for an Author: Alberic of Trois Fontaines and the *Chronicon Clarevallense*', *Cîteaux: Commentarii Cistercienses* 60 (2009), 5–25. Mula has also produced a new edition of the chronicle, Stefano Mula, 'Il considetto *Chronicon Clarevallense*. Edizione sal ms. Firenze, Bibl. Laurenziana, Ashburnham 1906', *Herbertus* 5.4 (2005), 5–48.

[4] Brian Patrick McGuire, 'A Lost Clairvaux Exemplum Collection Found: The *Liber Visionum et Miraculorum* Compiled under Prior John of Clairvaux (1171–79)', *Analecta Cisterciensia* 39 (1983), 26–62 at 26; Brian Patrick McGuire, *The Difficult Saint: Bernard of Clairvaux and His Tradition*, (Kalamazoo, MI, 1991), 164; Michael Casey, 'Herbert of Clairvaux's "Book of Wonderful Happenings"', *Cistercian Studies Quarterly* 25 (1990), 37–64 at 41.

[5] Brian Patrick McGuire, 'The Cistercians and the Rise of the Exemplum in Early Thirteenth Century France: A Reevaluation of Paris *BN MS lat. 15912*', *Classica et Mediaevalia: Revue Danoise de Philologie et d'Histoire* 34 (1983), 211–67 at 213.

[6] *PL* 185, cols 1271–1384, with additional fragments in *PL* 185, cols 453–66. For Chifflet's edition, see *Sancti Bernardi Clarevallensis abbatis genus illustre assertum. Accedunt Odonis de Diogilo, Iohannis Eremitae, Herberti Turrium Sardiniae archiepiscopi, aliorumque aliquot scriptorum opuscola, duodecimi post Christum seculi historiam spectantia: quorum seriem proxima post epistolam nuncupatoriam pagina dabit*, ed. Petrus Franciscus Chiffletius (Paris, 1660).

[7] For further information on the manuscript and edition history, see the introduction to the new edition, *Liber miraculorum*, VII–CXI.

In 1178, the year in which it is reported that Herbert wrote this collection, he was acting as chaplain to Henry of Marcy, the abbot of Clairvaux. That year, Henry spent several months in the south of France, as part of a mission against heretics supported by Pope Alexander III. Yet Herbert's relationship with Henry has not been used as a lens through which to explore the *Liber miraculorum*, even though, as Henry's chaplain, Herbert likely accompanied him to Toulouse. Herbert's collection, with its stories of knights, heretics, usurers, devil-worshippers, crusaders, and pagan peoples, was supposed to edify his fellow monks, and the exempla about holy men at Clairvaux did provide his audience with models of virtuous Cistercian life to emulate. The educative role of the stories about the laity, however, has not been explored. As abbot, Henry left the monastery to contend with heretics and preach to the laity on behalf of the papacy, and was later involved in the crusades to the Middle East; his activities covered many of the themes seen in Herbert's exempla. The question explored here is, what influence did Henry of Marcy and the events of 1178 have on the exempla Herbert chose to include in his *Liber miraculorum*?

Despite the positions he held, as abbot and archbishop, little is known of Herbert's life. He may have been born in Spain, but there is insufficient evidence to make this claim with certainty.[8] He appears to have entered Clairvaux as a novice after the death of St Bernard in 1153, since the stories about Bernard in the *Liber miraculorum* came second-hand from older monks. He described being a novice under Achard, who held the position from sometime around 1140 and died after 1170.[9] He also wrote about serving at the table of Fastrad, abbot 1157–61: 'By what sober living and, what's more, by what rigid fasting he kept his body under control once he became a monk, I refrain from saying... Indeed, I became familiar with and noted enough about this during the many years I served at his table.'[10] Herbert seems therefore to have made his profession by 1157, and likely entered the novitiate in 1154 or 1155. Sometime between 1168 and 1177 he left Clairvaux to become the third abbot of Mores, a Cistercian abbey in the diocese of Langres, not far from Clairvaux, which had been founded by Bernard between 1151 and 1152.[11] The fourth abbot, Ugo, was recorded on

---

[8] *Liber miraculorum*, LV–LXVII; Bruno Griesser, 'Herbert von Clairvaux und sein Liber Miraculorum', *Cistercienser Chronik* 54 (1947), 21–39.
[9] *Exordium Magnum Cisterciense oder Bericht von Anfang des Zisterzienserordens*, trans. Heinz Piesik (2 vols, Langwaden, 2000–02), i, 509 note 442.
[10] *Liber miraculorum*, c. 46: Iam uero monachus factus, quam sobrie uiuendo, immo quam rigide abstinendo corpus in seruitutem redegerit supersedeo dicere quia, ut uerum fatear, uehementior extitit in hac parte. Satis etenim illum super huiusmodi noui atque notaui, quippe qui pluribus annis eidem in mensa sua ministraui. For the rules concerning the abbot's kitchen helpers, see *Les Ecclesiastica Officia Cisterciens Du XIIème Siècle: Texte Latin Selon Les Manuscrits Édités de Trente 1711, Ljubljana 31 et Dijon 114, Version Française, Annexe Liturgique, Notes, Index et Table*, ed. Danièle Choisselet and Placide Vernet (Reiningue, 1989), c. 109, and *RB 1980: The Rule of Benedict in Latin and English with Notes*, ed. and trans. Timothy Fry OSB (Collegeville, MN, 1981), c. 53.
[11] *Liber miraculorum*, LVII–LVIII.

documents from 1178; Herbert likely stepped down as abbot and returned to Clairvaux in 1177 or early 1178 at the latest.

Upon his return he became chaplain to Abbot Henry of Marcy, otherwise known as Henry of Clairvaux or Henry of Albano. Henry, the son of a noble family, had entered Clairvaux as a novice at a similar time to Herbert, and made his profession in 1156.[12] Given their later relationship, it is likely that he and Herbert were in the novitiate together. Henry left Clairvaux in 1160 while still a very young man to become abbot of Hautecombe, another French Clairvaux daughter founded in 1135, near to the modern border with Switzerland. As French abbots, Herbert and Henry would have attended the General Chapter every year, and we can imagine a friendship that began as novices continuing through these annual reunions. As abbot of Hautecombe, Henry would have travelled to visit its daughter-houses, including Fossanova to the south of Rome, whose abbot from 1170 was Geoffrey of Auxerre, St Bernard's erstwhile secretary and hagiographer. Geoffrey had also been abbot of Clairvaux (1162–5), albeit briefly; after Henry's election as abbot of Clairvaux in 1177, Geoffrey succeeded him as abbot of Hautecombe. Henry's predecessor at Clairvaux, Gerard, was murdered by a rebellious monk at Igny, an incident recounted in a later exempla collection, Conrad of Eberbach's *Exordium magnum*.[13] Stories about Henry are also told in Conrad's collection, but he is mostly absent from Herbert's, despite their relationship.

As Herbert also returned to Clairvaux in 1177 and became Henry's chaplain, he likely left his position as abbot at Henry's request. Henry was returning to Clairvaux after an absence of nearly two decades. Asking Herbert, who had likewise been away for many years, to serve as his chaplain perhaps avoided disturbing the internal politics of the house, and gave Henry a friend and confidante he could trust. The editors of the new edition of the *Liber miraculorum* note that it was not uncommon for monks to return to Clairvaux, especially to spend their final years.[14] But after only a short time at the abbey, on 14 March 1179, Henry was made Cardinal-Bishop of Albano by Alexander III at the Third Lateran Council, and left the abbey, and Herbert followed him shortly thereafter.[15] Herbert's second tenure at Clairvaux therefore seems to have been tied to Henry's.

Evidence of the esteem in which Herbert was held by his French Cistercian contemporaries comes from his time as Henry's chaplain. A letter to Henry from Abbot William of Auberive, another Clairvaux daughter in the diocese of Langres, requested Herbert's opinion as well as his own regarding a difficult

---

[12] Yves Congar, 'Henri de Marcy, abbé de Clairvaux, cardinal-évêque d'Albano et légat pontifical', *Analecta Monastica*, Studia Anselmiana 43, Series 5 (1958), 1–91 at 1–2.
[13] Conrad of Eberbach, *Exordium Magnum Cisterciense, Sive Narratio de Initio Cisterciensis Ordinis*, ed. Bruno Griesser (Rome, 1961; reprinted with additional notes Turnhout, 1994), II.28. Stories of Henry can also be found in Conrad's collection; see *Exordium magnum*, II.30–31.
[14] *Liber miraculorum*, LIX.
[15] Congar, 'Henri de Marcy', 26–30.

theological question that William and another abbot were discussing.[16] The role of a Cistercian abbot's chaplain in the twelfth century is not clear; it is not mentioned in either the *Rule of St Benedict* or the *Ecclesiastica Officia*, the Cistercian customary.[17] The editors of the *Liber miraculorum* refer to Herbert only as a chaplain, since the evidence we have, the *Chronicon Clarevallense*, calls him Henry's *capellanus*. However, given Herbert's literary work, and the reference to him in William's letter, other scholars have described him as both chaplain and secretary.[18] An appropriate model for Herbert's role may be Geoffrey of Auxerre, who acted as Bernard's secretary and accompanied him on the missions that took him away from Clairvaux – though Geoffrey was described as Bernard's *notarius*, not *capellanus*. There are other monastic examples of chaplain-secretaries and their close relationships with their abbots or bishops: Eadmer (d. 1126), for example, was chaplain, secretary, and friend to Anselm of Canterbury (d. 1109) and wrote his *vita* after his death.[19]

Herbert remained at Clairvaux until 1181 when he was elected archbishop of Torres in Sardinia. No records survive from his time as archbishop, but one document suggests that he died sometime in or before 1196: on 14 August 1196 one *magister* Bandino, from Pisa, was referred to as the newly elected Archbishop of Torres.[20] Herbert appears to have left a copy of the *Liber miraculorum* at Clairvaux before he departed for Sardinia, and from it, his collection was copied and disseminated throughout Europe over the course of the twelfth and thirteenth centuries. The editors of the new edition have argued that the earliest surviving manuscript witness, Clm 2607, comes from this now lost Clairvaux manuscript.[21]

In the new critical edition, the *Liber miraculorum* comprises 165 chapters. In Clm 2607, the collection only has 152 chapters (fols 16r–130r); however, this is due to different practices of chapter numbering, and not any difference in content.[22] There is little explicit internal textual organization in the *Liber miraculorum*: no thematic or temporal divisions of the exempla, and no prologue

---

[16] *Liber miraculorum*, LXI.
[17] For the chapters concerning abbots, see *Ecclesiastica Officia*, c. 110 and *Rule of Benedict*, cc. 2 and 64. What the *Rule* has to say concerning ordained priests in the monastery can be found in cc. 60 and 62.
[18] Griesser, 'Herbert von Clairvaux', 26.
[19] *The Life of St Anselm, Archbishop of Canterbury*, ed. and trans. R.W. Southern (Oxford, 1972); R.W. Southern, *Saint Anselm and his Biographer: A Study of Monastic Life and Thought, 1059–c.1130* (Cambridge, 1963).
[20] *Liber miraculorum*, LXV.
[21] *Liber miraculorum*, XCVIII–XCIX.
[22] Clm 2607 has been digitised, 'Liber de miraculis S. Brandani abbatis. De visionibus, quae variis monachis Cisterciensibus, inprimis Clarevallenisbus apparuerunt – BSB Clm 2601', *Münchener Digitalisierungs Zentrum, Digitale Bibliothek*, accessed 12 December 2021, www.digitale-sammlungen.de/en/details/bsb00048177. Herbert's collection begins on fol. 16v. For a discussion of the chapter numbering in the edition and manuscripts, see *Liber miraculorum*, LXXXI–LXXXV. Throughout, I will refer to the chapter numbers in the edition, for ease and consistency of reference.

or final summary. However, there is a discernible shift in focus across the text, from Cistercian stories in the first half of the collection to stories featuring laypeople in the latter half. The majority of the exempla in the first half – up to chapter 85 – are about Cistercians, and mostly monks or lay brothers from Clairvaux. There are very few stories about monks from other orders; for the most part, the monastic life is represented by Cistercians. As other scholars have noted, the majority of these exempla about the Cistercian Order concern visions experienced by monks within the monastery, and in particular deathbed visions: a monk sees angels, Christ, the Virgin Mary or a saint as he lies dying, or has a vision which foretells the death of someone else.[23] In one typical exemplum, Abbot Robert of Clairvaux (1153–7) sees a vision in which angels are preparing for the arrival of a new saint, and shortly afterwards a holy brother dies (c. 8); in another, a lay brother sees angels approaching his bed as he lies dying, and so tells those around him to sound the board for his death (c. 14). Others feature visions of holy persons that were experienced when a monk was in the chapel or at prayer, such as the monk who had a vision of the crucified Christ on Good Friday (c. 23). Visions often revealed misbehavior by members of the monastic community: in one, a monk considering leaving the monastery has a vision of Saints Bernard and Malachy, and is beaten by Bernard for wanting to leave (c. 27); in another, a monk sees demons offering roast chicken or glasses of red wine to the lazy and negligent during Vigils (c. 5).

In reading these stories about Cistercian monks, Michael Casey and Stefano Mula have identified recurring themes and plot points.[24] The daily life of the monastery, its rules and its challenges come up repeatedly: the hard work, the liturgical calendar, the challenges of abbatial responsibilities, the procedures to be followed when a monk is dying, and the different lives lived by monks and lay brothers. Mula has argued that this repetition of themes was central to Herbert's strategy of edification, affirming and improving his audience's understanding of the core principles of Cistercian life.[25] This is an important insight regarding the exempla about other Cistercians, yet it still leaves nearly half of the 165 chapters unexamined, rendering an understanding of Herbert's work incomplete.

For the *Liber miraculorum* was not just an exempla collection that showed Cistercian monks how to behave well through stories of their virtuous forebears and contemporaries. Just as Mula and Casey have identified repeated lessons in the Cistercian stories, specific themes recur in the second half: the sacrament of the altar, heresy and unbelief, lay sinfulness, conversion, and the peripheries of Christendom (Scandinavia, Eastern Europe, and Iberia). This was not a Cistercian collection comprising solely stories that showed monks examples

---

[23] Casey, 'Book of Wonderful Happenings', 56–9; Stefano Mula, 'Herbert de Torrès et l'autoreprésentation de l'ordre Cistercien dans les recueils d'exempla', in *Le Tonnerre des exemples: Exempla et médiation culturelle dans l'Occident médiéval*, ed. Marie Anne Polo de Beaulieu, Pascal Collomb, and Jacques Berlioz (Rennes, 2010), 187–200 at 190–7.
[24] Casey, 'Book of Wonderful Happenings', 37–64; Mula, 'Herbert de Torrès', 187–97.
[25] Mula, 'Herbert de Torrès', 198–9.

of holy lives, lived according to the rules of Cistercian life within the walls of the monastery. It contained by design a significant number of exempla that dealt with the world outside. From chapter 85, eucharistic miracles, involving the miraculous transformation or preservation of a host wafer, are especially common (cc. 85–96). Several stories about paganism, devil-worship and the Christianization of Eastern Europe also feature (cc. 100–104). There are a number of exempla about the church and laity in Denmark, probably told at Clairvaux by the Danish Archbishop Eskil, who retired there in the 1170s (cc. 99, 105–106).[26] These Danish stories are followed by one of a Jewish man who converts to Christianity (c. 107). There are then nine miracle stories (cc. 110–118) taken from William of Malmesbury's *Gesta regum Anglorum* (hereafter *GR*).[27] This work, which William finished around February 1126, related England's secular history from Bede's time until his own.[28] The majority of Herbert's exempla came from oral sources: in sixty-seven he explicitly named his source, and in another eighty the word-of-mouth transmission is implicit.[29] The *GR*, from which sixteen exempla were drawn, was the textual source used most frequently in the *Liber miraculorum*.[30] These are for the most part not stories of English kings, but fantastic miracle stories William included as digressions, such as the story of several villagers who danced in the churchyard for a whole year in Saxony (c. 110) and the tale of a young Roman man who accidentally married a statue of Venus (c. 112).

After the stories from the *GR*, many of the remaining exempla deal with examples of lay sinfulness and its punishments. Several are about heretics: men who disparage the sacrament of the altar and die horribly (cc. 143–144) and a woman who gives birth to a demon (c. 125). Herbert also included a number of stories concerning lay misbehavior: men who swear on Christ's body and limbs and suffer horrible punishments, like the soldier whose beard and chin skin fall off (cc. 134–136); criminals who abuse pilgrims and are driven mad or killed as a result (cc. 137–138); men who attempt to rape virtuous women and nuns (cc. 63–64, 97, 138); and a multitude of lay people, both good and evil, who give their soul to the devil or are otherwise tormented by demons (cc. 111, 139, 141, 149, 159, 162, 164–165). Amongst these are only a few stories of wrongdoing committed by clerics, nuns, monks, and prelates. The final story in the collection

---

[26] On Archbishop Eskil and the Cistercians in Denmark, see Brian Patrick McGuire, *The Cistercians in Denmark* (Kalamazoo, MI, 1982), especially 39–73, and James France, 'St Bernard, Archbishop Eskil and the Danish Cistercians', *Cîteaux: Commentarii Cistercienses* 39 (1988), 232–48.
[27] Herbert's sources are laid out in the *Index Fontium* in the new edition, *Liber miraculorum*, 432–38. In order, chapters 110–18 in the *Liber miraculorum* are drawn from *GR* II, 174; II, 204; II, 205; II, 205; II, 207; II, 207; II, 225; III, 268; III, 293 (references are to book and chapter number).
[28] William of Malmesbury, *Gesta regum Anglorum*, ed. and trans. R.A.B. Mynors, R.M. Thomson and M. Winterbottom (2 vols, Oxford, 1998–9).
[29] *Liber miraculorum*, LXXIX.
[30] Paul Lehmann, 'Ein Mirakelbuch des Zisterziensersordens', *Studien und Mitteilungen zur Geschichte des Benediktinerordens* 45 (1927), 72–93; *Liber miraculorum*, LXXV.

(c. 165) tells the story of a woman plagued by demons. Both a cleric and a Clairvaux monk come to her aid, and Herbert ends by saying that he has heard that the woman has recently overcome the persecution.

The change in the content of the exempla at chapter 85, when the eucharistic miracles are introduced, is abrupt. The few chapters immediately preceding this point concern monks from Clairvaux, and visions they experienced of either Christ or the Virgin Mary. They show the special care Jesus and his mother have for the Order: in one, a monk sees the Virgin feeding sweet medicine to his brothers (c. 82), while another is about a monk who sees a vision of Christ telling him how greatly he loves the tears of penitents (c. 84). There is then a sudden shift to eucharistic miracles featuring lay people. Whilst there are a few stories about non-Cistercians in the first half of the collection, before chapter 85 Herbert always returned to Cistercian stories after these brief forays into the secular world. After the eucharistic miracles (c. 85–96), the collection does not come back inside the walls of the monastery, but strays far from Clairvaux: chapter 108 does take place inside a Cistercian monastery, but the rest are stories of the outside world. Thus, chapter 85 marks a definitive shift in the content of the exempla.

Other Cistercian authors noted the differences in the two parts of the collection as well. Conrad of Eberbach made extensive use of the Cistercian material in the first half of the *Liber miraculorum* but did not reuse Herbert's stories of the outside world in his *Exordium magnum*.[31] For Conrad, only the corpus of exempla concerning the Cistercian Order was of use to him; Herbert's text was received by his contemporaries as having two parts, each with its own distinct character.

The miracles of the eucharist represent the largest group of miracles on a single theme: fifteen chapters in total, nearly a fifth of the material in the latter half of the collection. The repetitive nature of these miracles, and their identity as a gathered cohort on the theme, is highlighted by the fact that in Clm 2607 many are grouped together under a single chapter heading. The first – chapter 85 in the edition – is titled 'A recent miracle of the sacrament of the altar', with the four following stories merely given the heading 'Another' and no new chapter number. Though two of the miracles in this section (cc. 91–92) occurred within Cistercian monasteries (though to lay brothers, not choir monks), the majority took place in the world outside the monastery. Exempla demonstrating the miraculous power and transformation of the eucharist were common throughout the late twelfth and early thirteenth century, used by preachers to strengthen the belief of the faithful and confound heretics.[32] Similarly, Herbert used the

---

[31] For an analysis of Conrad's use of the *Liber miraculorum*, see Brian Patrick McGuire, 'Structure and Consciousness in the "Exordium Magnum Cisterciense": The Clairvaux Cistercians after Bernard', *Cahiers de l'Institut du Moyen-Âge Grec et Latin* 30 (1979), 33–90 at 45–9.

[32] This is the common argument. See Jessalynn Bird, 'The Construction of Orthodoxy and the (De)Construction of Heretical Attacks on the Eucharist in Pastoralia from Peter the Chanter's Circle in Paris', in *Texts and the Repression of Medieval Heresy*, ed.

eucharistic exempla in his collection to explain the miraculous sacrality of the host wafer (c. 85), to demonstrate the true nature of the eucharist as the actual flesh and blood of Christ (cc. 85–87), to warn against superstitious or talismanic use of the host by lay persons (cc. 93–95), and to rebuke those who do not believe in the sacrament (cc. 143–144).

So while the *Liber miraculorum* may not have any explicit textual organization, there are repeated themes in the exempla Herbert included. The author also worked to link these themes; chapters 143 and 144 are about laymen who disparage the sacrament of the eucharist. By including these stories among others that concerned misbehaving lay people, and not with the other eucharist exempla, he connected the eucharistic miracles thematically with the stories of lay sinfulness that appear in the latter half of the collection. Likewise, by following the exempla concerning the eucharist with several tales of paganism on the fringes of Europe, he connected these themes as well. In Herbert's thinking, the sins committed by the laity, the sacrament of the eucharist and associated miracles, and the Christianization of Europe were thematically linked. The miracles of the sacrament of the altar are pivotal to this collection; Herbert used them to move his audience away from thinking about life in the Cistercian monastery, to thinking about lay unbelief, heresy, sin, and conversion.

The eucharist thus literally and figuratively lies at the center of Herbert's collection. It sits between the stories of monks in the first half and those of the laity in the second half, and links the themes outlined above. This is not a coincidence. The sacrament of the eucharist was central to the rituals of monastic life. Cistercian monks took communion every Sunday, at Christmas, on Holy Thursday, Easter Day, and Pentecost. If they could not take communion on Sunday, they would do so on another weekday.[33] Though yearly communion did not become mandatory for the laity until 1215, it has been argued that from the twelfth century onwards the eucharist was the foremost sacrament of the church.[34] In the transformation of the bread into Christ's body, it allowed for direct human interaction with the divine and cemented the power of the priest as mediator between believer and God. It was also a unifying symbol, thanks to the universality of the ritual of mass and communion. As Miri Rubin has argued, 'The eucharist emerged [in the eleventh and twelfth centuries] as a unifying symbol for a complex world.'[35] Communion, as a ritual in which they all partook, was a point of connection between the very different lives lived by monks, priests, and laypeople. As the foremost symbol of Christian belief and unity, the eucharist

---

Caterina Bruschi and Peter Biller (York, 2003), 45–61 at 53–9; Miri Rubin, *Corpus Christi: The Eucharist in Late Medieval Culture* (Cambridge, 1991), 109–20. For a skeptical view, see Steven Justice, 'Eucharistic Miracle and Eucharistic Doubt', *Journal of Medieval and Early Modern Studies* 42 (2012), 307–32.
33 *Ecclesiastica Officia*, c. 66.
34 Gary Macy, 'The Dogma of Transubstantiation in the Middle Ages', *Journal of Ecclesiastical History* 45 (1994), 11–41; Rubin, *Corpus Christi*, 12–14 and 35–82.
35 Rubin, *Corpus Christi*, 348.

could lie at the center of the matrix of themes and associations that Herbert built: heresy and belief, conversion, sin, divine power, and divine punishment.

The sacrament of the eucharist also lay at the heart of disputes between churchmen and heretics in these years. In 1178, when it is recorded that Herbert wrote the *Liber miraculorum*, Henry of Marcy spent the summer and autumn in the south of France on an anti-heresy mission. Reports of heretical activity in France, especially in the south, had proliferated in the years before, as Beverly Mayne Kienzle has outlined in her account of the events of 1178.[36] In September 1177, Count Raymond V of Toulouse appealed to the Cistercian General Chapter for help against the increasingly powerful heretics in his domain, as part of a mission supported by the kings of both France and England.[37] Henry was central to the planning of this mission, as his surviving letters show. In one, written to Alexander III, he transposed the logic of crusade in the Holy Land to heretics within Europe's borders, laying the intellectual and spiritual groundwork for armed campaigns against heresy, as Yves Congar and Kienzle have argued.[38] In this same letter, from May 1178, he also begged the pope to extend Peter of St Chrysogonous's (d. 1182) authority as papal legate to include the fight against heresy. He believed that only the intervention of the papacy would be effective against heretics.

Henry's entreaties were successful. The 1178 mission, which lasted from August to October 1178, was headed by the papal legate and included, alongside Henry, the archbishop of Narbonne; the bishop of Poitiers; Raymond V; and Reginald Fitz Jocelin, bishop of Bath. Henry recorded the events in a letter he wrote after his return, known from its opening words as *Audite coeli*. Here he described the mission and its participants:

Recently, at the command of the lord pope, and at the request of the pious princes, Louis, king of the French, and Henry, king of the English, I accompanied the venerable Peter, legate of the Apostolic See, and those wise men the bishop of Poitiers and the bishop of Bath, to Toulouse, which is an extremely populous city, said to be the mother of heresy and fountainhead of error.[39]

According to the papal legate's account, the delegation included almost 300 people.[40] While we have no direct evidence that Herbert was one of them,

---

[36] Beverly Mayne Kienzle, *Cistercians, Heresy and Crusade in Occitania, 1145–1229: Preaching in the Lord's Vineyards* (York, 2001), chapter 4.
[37] Congar, 'Henri de Marcy', 10–12.
[38] Congar, 'Henri de Marcy', 18; Kienzle, *Cistercians, Heresy and Crusade*, 113–21.
[39] Henry's *Epistola* 29 is in *PL* 204, cols 235–40 at 235D–236A: Contigit enim nuper ad imperium domini papae, et hortatu piissimorum principum Ludovici Francorum, et Henrici Anglorum, regum, venerabilem Petrum apostolicae sedis legatum, virosque discretos Pictavensem et Bathoniensem episcopos, nosque in comitatu eorum urbem adire Tolosam, quae sicut erat civitas maximae multitudinis, ita etiam dicebatur mater haeresis et caput erroris. An English translation can be found in R.I. Moore, *The Birth of Popular Heresy* (London, 1975), 116–22. For an analysis of the letter see Kienzle, *Cistercians, Heresy and Crusade*, 121–7.
[40] Congar, 'Henri de Marcy', 19.

as Henry's chaplain (and possibly secretary) it is likely that he was there. The example of Geoffrey of Auxerre, who accompanied Bernard on his own preaching mission to the south of France in 1145, suggests that Herbert would have travelled with Henry.⁴¹ We know that Herbert accompanied Henry's successor, Abbot Peter Monoculus, on a visitation to a Clairvaux daughter house in the province of Reims in early 1181; it is improbable that he would have stayed behind at Clairvaux while Henry was in Toulouse for several months.⁴²

Our evidence for the mission comes from the letters written afterwards by the papal legate and by Henry, and entries in the *Gesta Henrici* and Roger of Howden's chronicle that reproduce the letters.⁴³ Henry's letter begins by arguing that heretical beliefs were widespread and heretics gaining in power, especially in the south of France. This was exemplified by the conditions in Toulouse, where heretics openly preached their dangerous ideology:

We found the city so diseased that from the soles of its feet to the top of its head there was not a healthy piece in it... Heretics ruled the people and lorded it over the clergy... When heretics spoke, everyone applauded... The plague was so strong in the land that they had not only their bishops and priests, but their own evangelists as well... who seduced the people and preached to them new doctrines drawn from their own evil hearts.⁴⁴

Both his letter and that written by the legate make clear that not believing in the sacraments of the church, including baptism, and especially denying the sacrament of the eucharist was a key tenet of this heretical doctrine with which they had to contend. In his account of the interrogation of Peter Maurand, a notorious heretic from Toulouse, Henry wrote:

Peter was required, according to this oath, simply to tell us, without deceit, what he believed about the eucharist... he said that he held, by a new doctrine, that the holy bread of eternal life consecrated by a priest in the word of the Lord does not become the body of the Lord... Peter was adjudged a criminal and a heretic.⁴⁵

---

⁴¹ On Bernard's preaching mission, see Kienzle, *Cistercians, Heresy and Crusade*, chapter 3.
⁴² *Liber miraculorum*, LXI–LXIII.
⁴³ For the legate's letter, *PL* 199, cols 1119–24, and translated in Moore, *Birth of Popular Heresy*, 113–16. The relevant entry from Roger of Howden's chronicle is translated in Walter L. Wakefield and Austin P. Evans, *Heresies of the High Middle Ages* (New York and London, 1969), 194–200.
⁴⁴ *PL* 204, cols 236A–236B: Et ecce inventa est plaga eius magnanimis, ita ut a planta pedis usque ad verticem non esset in ea sanitas... Ibi haeretici principabantur in populo, dominabantur in clero... Loquebantur haeretici, et omnes admirabantur... Interim praevaluerat pestis in terra, quod illi sibi non solum sacerdotes et pontifices fecerant, sed etiam evangelistas habebant, qui... de corde suo nequam recentia dogmata seducto populo praedicarent.
⁴⁵ *PL* 204, col. 236D: At nobis instantibus, ut de sacramento altaris suam nobis finem sine fraude aliqua fateretur... sed contra id quod de omnibus mentiri decreverat, falsitatis suae prodidit veritatem, et panem sanctum vitae aeternae sacerdotis ministerio in verbo Domini consecratum, non esse corpus Christi novo dogmate contendebat.

Henry and the rest of the delegation attempted to preach the true faith, to counter these heretical preachers: 'one of our number was appointed to preach the word, and to discuss the rule of the true faith before the crowd of infidels. When orthodoxy had been preached to the people, the sinners were humiliated in Zion.'[46] Henry wrote of the divine support they had in this work. When he and the bishop of Bath had gone to Béziers, to secure the release of the bishop of Albi from Roger, the heretical lord of that region, they had found a castle full of unbelievers. Nevertheless, God was on their side:

Almost all the inhabitants of the castle were either heretics or their sympathizers, and the power of the Lord above prevented them from presuming to murmur against the faith which we preached. Although we were there in their lands, in their power since we were surrounded by heretics on every side, the word of the Lord which we showered on them in continual rebuke and exhortation was not obstructed.[47]

Thanks to the intervention of God, Henry was able to continue preaching. In *Audite coeli*, preaching is both the method through which heretical doctrine is spread and a crucial weapon in the fight against it, one exercised with divine sanction and support.

The impact of other signs of divine power on believers and heretics alike is also described in Henry's letter. At one point, during the interrogation and confession of Peter Maurand, relics were brought in so that he could swear an oath: 'The relics of the saints were soon respectfully brought in and received with such solemn reverence and devotion that the faithful were moved to tears, while the heretics who were at the meeting found their hiding places preferable to such a sight.'[48] Peter was also later frightened into confessing by a miracle, and the gathered believers took great pleasure in this divine intervention: 'The mouths of the faithful were opened, Oh Christ, and Catholic lips unsealed in your praise.'[49] A combination of preaching, relics, and miraculous occurrences were used to confound the heretics and compel them to confess, and through them the faithful were also confirmed in their beliefs. Though at the end of the

---

[46] *PL* 204, col. 238B : ...nuntiatum est uni de nobis verbum exhortationis assumere... Habito autem sermone orthodoxae praedicationis ad plebem, conterriti sunt in Sion peccatores.

[47] *PL* 204, col. 240B: Omnes fere habitatores illius castri, vel haeretici, vel haereticorum complices erant, licet sola Domini virtute repressi, nihil contra fidem quam praedicabamus praesumerat vel mutire. Quamvis enim essemus et nos in manibus ipsorum positi, et velut intra quosdam potentiae complices haeretica undique multitudine corcumventi, verbum tamen Domini non erat alligatum, quin eos continuis invectionibus et increpationibus feriremus.

[48] *PL* 204, cols 237D–238A: Mox igitur sanctorum reliquiae honorabiliter efferuntur, cum tam solemni reverentia et devotione susceptae, ut et de fidelis populus compungeretur lacrymas; haereticos vero, qui convenerant, latebrae potius quam talia spectacula delectarent.

[49] *PL* 204, col. 238C: ...aperiuntur ora fidelium, et catholicae plebis labia in tua, Christe, praeconia resolvuntur.

letter Henry advocated for future (possibly armed) missions against heretical strongholds, he also praised the success of their non-violent preaching tour:

> It is clear from this that a fine door is open to Christian princes to avenge the wounds of Christ, and bring to the desert the garden of the Lord, and to the wilderness the sweetness of paradise. In case anyone thinks that nothing can be done against them, everyone should know that it was the general opinion in the city of Toulouse that if our visit had been three years later, we would hardly have found anyone there who would call upon the name of Christ.[50]

According to Henry, their sermons and the public interrogation of heretics, and the divine signs that accompanied this, were responsible for turning the tide against heresy in Toulouse. Later, in 1181, Henry returned to the Languedoc at the head of an armed mission against Roger of Béziers.[51] Even in the midst of this armed mission, preaching was still important. Geoffrey of Auxerre reported Henry's success in converting two heretics: the Holy Spirit moved him to such eloquence that his preaching caused the two heretics to emotionally confess their errors.[52] Henry's skill as a preacher, coupled with divine assistance, remained a key weapon in his arsenal, even as his army wielded actual steel against the heretics.

Though the fight against heresy took him away from his duties as abbot, and would eventually lead him to leave Clairvaux altogether, Martha Newman has argued that Henry viewed his missions on behalf of the papacy as a Cistercian duty.[53] His crusade treatise, *De peregrinante civitate Dei*, written sometime before his death in January 1189, was a distillation of his thinking on the state of Christianity and the duty of all believers – including Cistercian monks. The treatise itself was dedicated to the brothers of Clairvaux, and directed their attention to the condition of the Church on earth first and then, ultimately, towards the heavenly Jerusalem. It was here that he believed he and his monks would be reunited, but only if they worked to ensure its existence: 'So, what else now remains but that we should eagerly sow fields, plant vineyards, and make a fruitful yield so that, after the many and various disturbances described above, the city with dwelling places is finally found?'[54] This was a broad understanding

---

[50] *PL* 204, col. 240C: Ecce amodo satis apparet quam grande et evidens ostium patet principibus Christianis, et Christi ulciscantur injurias, ponantque desertum illud quasi hortum Domini, et solitudinem eius in delicias paradisi. Ne autem vel parum, vel nihil contra illos posse causentur, sciant omnes generalem fuisse in urbe Tolosana sententiam, quod si visitatio ista fuisset adhuc triennio retardata, vix inveniretur in ea qui nomen Christi amplius invocaret.
[51] Congar, 'Henri de Marcy', 31–41; Kienzle, *Cistercians, Heresy and Crusade*, 132–4.
[52] Kienzle, *Cistercians, Heresy and Crusade*, 133.
[53] Martha G. Newman, *The Boundaries of Charity: Cistercian Culture and Ecclesiastical Reform, 1090–1180* (Stanford, CA, 1996), 229–43.
[54] *De peregrinante civitati Dei* can be found in *PL* 204, cols 251–402, here 253B: Quid igitur restare aliud iam videtur, nisi ut post multos et varios fluctus superius descriptos, civitate tandem habitationis inventa, seminare agros, plantare vineas et fructum navitatis

of the Cistercian value of *caritas*, which argued for Cistercian involvement in healing the wounds of the church, such as those caused by heresy.[55] This ideology had been elaborated by earlier Cistercian writers, starting with Bernard himself, as Newman has explored.[56] In several sermons from the 1160s, Geoffrey of Auxerre, speaking in defense of Cistercian activities against heresy on behalf of Alexander III, argued that the monastic life could not please God if it existed without a unified Church. For Henry, heresy was a particular threat to a united Church and thus to salvation.[57] His promotion of Cistercian activity against heresy on behalf of the papacy, and his belief that faith must be coupled with action in an imperfect world, had deep roots in Cistercian thinking.

In 1178, while acting as chaplain and friend to an abbot who argued for Cistercian participation in papally mandated anti-heresy efforts, Herbert wrote the *Liber miraculorum*. Midway through the collection, at the point where Herbert moves his audience from Cistercian to non-Cistercian stories, he referenced the very French heretics that Henry was contending with, and used them to explain why he had included eucharistic miracles in his collection:

Whence we are given to understand, because of the most foul heresies in the kingdom of France... [which are] sending forth poisonous shoots and greatly disparaging the sacrament of the altar, the Lord Jesus Christ has deigned to reveal abundant miracles concerning the sacrament of His body and His blood, in this time and in these regions, in order to reinforce the faith of believers.[58]

Heresy was spreading in France, but God was sending miracles to counter it and comfort believers; through his collection, Herbert disseminated these miracles. Though in the edition this transition from Cistercian to lay stories is in chapter 86, and chapter 85 is the first miracle of the eucharist, in Clm 2607 they are all part of one chapter. This passage informed a Cistercian audience of the dangers of heretics and the spread of their influence, told them something about the content of their beliefs, and then argued for the importance of miracles in such a moment. As Herbert told his audience, at a time of heretical attacks on the eucharist, divine signs were sent to confirm the beliefs of the faithful, just as the believers described in Henry's letter were comforted by relics and the miracles they witnessed during Peter Maurand's confession. There is a further link between Henry's work and Herbert's inclusion of these stories: Herbert says

---

facere studeamus? For the translation and interpretation, I have referred to Newman, *Boundaries of Charity*, 241–2.
[55] Newman, *Boundaries of Charity*, in particular chapter 9.
[56] Newman, *Boundaries of Charity*, 235–43.
[57] Newman, *Boundaries of Charity*, 233.
[58] *Liber miraculorum*, c. 86: Unde datur intelligi quia propter spurcissimas hereses in regno Gallie... uirulento germine pullulantes et sacramento altaris maxime detrahentes, Dominus Ihesus Christus de ipso sacramento corporis et sanguinis sui temporibus et regionibus istis ad roborandam credentium fidem crebriora solito miracula demonstrare dignatur.

that several of the miracles of the eucharist were told to him by King Louis, one of the supporters of the 1178 mission.

Proofs of such miraculous events were provided not only by miracle stories like the ones Herbert offered, but also by relics, as shown in Henry's letter, and the preservation of miraculous hosts is also a key component in Herbert's eucharistic miracles. In one, a priest who saw the host wafer turn to flesh and the wine into blood was later reprimanded by his bishop for not preserving the miraculous host, and instead continuing to take communion (c. 87). The next week, with the bishop watching, the same thing happened again: the miracle repeated so that the host, now transformed into flesh, could be preserved and seen by a greater number of people. In a similar exemplum, in which the host wafer transformed into flesh everywhere except where the priest's fingers touched, Herbert noted that this relic was later kept in a crystal reliquary where it could be seen and revered by all (c. 86).

Alongside these miracles of the eucharist, Herbert's *Liber miraculorum* contains further stories that demonstrate the power of divine signs to convert, or confirm the faith of the newly converted, especially when interpreted by a priest or monk learned enough to understand them. Following the eucharistic miracles in his collection, Herbert included two stories about pious women on the peripheries of Christendom: one was newly converted from Islam in Spain (c. 97), the other was a Danish woman whose husband and his family did not share her piety (c. 99). Both women are cruelly killed, but later venerated for their faith, with the Danish woman's grave becoming a shrine where miracles occur. After these come stories of pagan peoples, crusade, and conversion in Eastern Europe. In one of these (c. 102), a town of pagans, recently converted to Christianity, is terrified one night by the sound of an army in retreat. The next day, when Cistercian monks arrive to baptize them, they are able to explain to the townspeople that what they heard was the demons who had once plagued them retreating:

Then truly it manifestly became known to all the faithful that the nocturnal commotion was nothing other than legions of demons, who had rebuked God, who fled from the humans they had besieged, not able to withstand the presence of holy angels and the arrival of the Holy Spirit. Thanks to this event all were consoled by God, especially the newly converted, who were liberated from the wicked dominion [of the devils].[59]

Thanks to the explanation of this supernatural event, the newly converted were 'consoled by God'. But Herbert made clear that there was a need for explication that the monks provided: only after their arrival and the baptism

---

[59] *Liber miraculorum*, c. 102: Tunc uero fidelibus cunctis manifeste innotuit quia tumultus ille nocturnus nichil aliud extitit nisi demonum legiones ab obsessis hominibus, increpante Domino, fugientes, qui beatorum angelorum presenciam et Sancti Spiritus aduentum sustinere non poterant. De qua uidelicet re multum in Domino consolati sunt uniuersi, precipue uero nephiti illi, qui ab immunda dominacione fuerant liberati.

(another sacrament denied by contemporary heretics) is an explanation of what the townspeople heard the night before offered in the narrative. Like the new converts, Herbert's audience was not given an explanation for the supernatural events until the arrival of the Cistercian monks into the story; their experience mirrored that of the converted townspeople, and so the explanation to the converts within the narrative served also to illuminate the message of the exemplum to Herbert's audience. By the end of the narrative they, like the townspeople, understood that it demonstrated that demons assault non-believers, but Christians are protected from them. The next chapter likewise testifies to the power of conversion and baptism: a pagan woman, accidentally splashed by a monk with holy water, feels a burning sensation in her body whenever she invokes the name of the demon she worships. But when she realizes her error, converts, and invokes the name of Christ, the pain stops, and she understands that she will be saved in both body and soul.

Herbert emphasized this need for interpretation in the following chapter (c. 104), the final exemplum concerning Cistercian activities in Slavic lands. In the aftermath of a mighty battle between Christians and pagans, the bones of all lie unburied in a field. Later, Cistercian monks come to the spot and find crosses on the skulls of the Christians. The Cistercian monks immediately understand that the crosses signify which bones are Christian; the recently converted locals, in their ignorance, had ignored this manifestation of divine power.[60] Without an explanation by Cistercian monks, the converts were not strengthened in their faith by this sign; they were not 'consoled'. Herbert again emphasized the need for monks to interpret miracles and other signs of divine power to laypeople with this exemplum. This explication, done within the narrative to the converts, also explained the sign of divine approval for the crusaders to his audience. This explanation was likely not intended for the Cistercian reader who would already have understood what the crosses signified; it suggests a second imagined audience for the exempla in the collection.

With the eucharistic miracles, alongside the stories of crusade and conversion that follow, Herbert demonstrated three points: first, the role of miracles and wonders in strengthening faith, and the need for this at a moment of heretical attack; second, the need for learned Cistercian monks to explain the significance of such signs, in order for them to have the desired effect; and, finally, that Cistercian monks, in carrying out missionary activities, and by explaining divine signs and miracles, could convert non-Christian peoples and console the faithful. These exempla in the *Liber miraculorum* were proofs of the power of miracles to persuade and convert, so long as they were properly explained and expounded.

A clear overview can therefore be sketched of the content and didactic purpose of each part of this so-called unstructured and unwieldy text. The first half of the *Liber miraculorum* primarily tells stories about Cistercian monks, often from

---

[60] *Liber miraculorum*, c. 104: Porro homines loci, cum antea ydolatre existerent, miraculum illud minime aduertebant, quia de signo crucis aut nichil sciebant aut nichil omnino curabant

Clairvaux, that take place mostly within the walls of the monastery. They show the rules of Cistercian life in narrative form, and by repeating the same themes taught a monastic audience to live a virtuous cenobitic life. Midway through the collection, as noted above, the content and setting of the exempla abruptly change to the world outside the monastery. At this point, Herbert included a number of eucharistic miracles, whose presence he explained through the need to confront heretics and strengthen the faithful, given the spread of heresy in France. There are then a number of stories about crusade and conversion, which further his argument about the power of miracle stories to convert non-Christians and console believers, so long as they are explicated by Cistercian monks. The remainder of the collection then catalogues various kinds of bad behavior on the part of the laity. These exemplary narratives in the second half of Herbert's text are of a type that could be used in the kinds of preaching events that he and Henry were involved with in 1178 – laypeople listening to a sermon were Herbert's second imagined audience.

A monk reading Herbert's collection would thus have learnt, in order: how to lead a good Cistercian life within the walls of the monastery; the dangers of heretics who disparage the sacraments, and the appearance of miracles to counter them; the power of miracles to persuade and convert; and the various kinds of wrongdoing, heresy, and sin that existed in the world. He would then have ended the collection on a story which showed a monk from Clairvaux successfully intervening alongside a secular cleric to help a lay woman escape from demons and sin. The two corpuses of material within the *Liber miraculorum* argued for the life of a Cistercian monk to be both contemplative and bounded by the walls of the monastery, and active in the service of papal anti-heresy and crusade efforts.

Was Henry involved in its production? The *Liber miraculorum*'s combination of exempla about virtuous Cistercian living and focus on the problems of the world mirrors Henry's own thoughts in *De peregrinante* on the need for Cistercians to work actively in the world as part of their journey towards virtue. His involvement would explain his otherwise puzzling absence in the text, since although Herbert included stories valorizing the other abbots of Clairvaux he had known and the senior monks who had inspired him, there are no similar stories about Henry.

Furthermore, the initial composition of the collection during the 1178 preaching campaign would provide an explanation for Herbert's use of William of Malmesbury's *GR*. William's works were available at Clairvaux, but, in the bountiful library there, why was it to the *GR* alone that Herbert turned for miracle stories? It is almost the only written source Herbert seems to have consulted, and he copied William's words verbatim; indeed, he must have had the text in front of him. One of the members of the 1178 legation was Reginald Fitz Jocelin, Bishop of Bath. After preaching in Toulouse, Henry was keen to return to Cîteaux for the General Chapter, but the papal legate first tasked him and Reginald with going to Béziers to secure the release of the bishop of Albi.[61] Henry and Herbert thus spent longer on the road with Reginald and his retinue. Reginald was the son of Jocelin de Bohun, bishop of Salisbury from 1142 until he retired to a Cistercian monastery shortly before his death in 1184.[62] Malmesbury Abbey was in the diocese of Salisbury, and Reginald's diocese, Bath, neighbored his father's. If Herbert wrote the *Liber miraculorum* not at Clairvaux, but on the preaching tour, he would have had access to a more limited library. Factoring in the presence of Reginald and his retinue, and the books they may have brought with them, it is possible that a copy of the *GR* was one of the only books available to him. It explains why most of the stories in the collection were acquired by word of mouth – Herbert had been told these previously and remembered them – and why he relied so infrequently on written miracle collections.

With the *Liber miraculorum*, Herbert created a collection that suggested that a key component of Cistercian life was activity in the world in the service of the papacy, and provided numerous exempla that both taught his audience of the problems of the world and were themselves illustrative narratives that could be used as part of a sermon. It also argued that reform of the self, the monastic preacher, had to precede that engagement with the laity. Following the logic of the collection, the eager Cistercian had to model himself on the example of the virtuous monks portrayed in the first half of the text; only then, upon learning of the dangers of the world, could he go forth and attempt to ameliorate them.

The preaching Herbert envisaged, modelled no doubt on Henry's, was thus truly evangelical, in the sense that the preacher had to be a virtuous man and an example himself when he went forth to preach. This idea, that historians have more readily associated with the mendicant preachers and their role as the shock troops of the papacy in the thirteenth century, is found here in the *Liber miraculorum*, the result of the close relationship between Herbert of Clairvaux and his friend, Henry of Marcy.

---

[61] Congar, 'Henri de Marcy', 22.
[62] B.R. Kemp, 'Jocelin de Bohunn', in *Oxford Dictionary of National Biography* (Oxford, 2004), doi: 10.1093/ref:odnb/50340; Charles Duggan, 'Reginald *fitz* Jocelin', in *Oxford Dictionary of National Biography* (Oxford, 2004), doi: 10.1093/ref:odnb/9613.

5

Some Problems of the Peace: Angels in America (and Angevin England)[1]

Simon Yarrow

> More than to the Black race within her borders, America owes to the world the solution of her race problem, from this very year.
>
> W.E.B. Du Bois, *Letter to President Woodrow Wilson* (1918)[2]

This essay – speculative and historical – is an enquiry into the nature of immanent and transcendent forms of power and the ways in which, in several specific different settings, modern and medieval, contemporary scholars have sought to understand the nature of power in their world by invoking some transcendent force or referent as well as the more earthly ones of violence and administration. Furthermore, as will be shown, the medieval and modern worlds have come to be refracted through each other, at once producing distortions and the opportunity for new insights.

Haskins, the State, and the Problem of Peace

When Charles Homer Haskins attended the Paris Peace Conference in 1919 in the immediate aftermath of the Great War, he represented 'history in the making' in both senses of the phrase. First, he was the founder of American medieval historiography and had already distinguished himself in the provincial archives of France, preparing his *Norman Institutions* for publication in 1917.[3] Second, he was a co-architect of America's rebuilding of a new world order from the moral

---

[1] My thanks to Marcus Bull for inviting me to speak at the 38th Annual Haskins Society Conference, Chapel Hill, North Carolina, in 2019; to Laura Gathagan and William North for their editorial guidance; and to the Haskins Society. The publication of this essay was much delayed by the pandemic conditions.
[2] *W.E.B. Du Bois: International Thought*, ed. A. Getachow and J. Pitts (Cambridge, 2022), 52–4.
[3] M. Chibnall, *The Debate on the Norman Conquest* (Manchester, 1999), 70–1, for his more professional and rewarding approach to the sources than that of his English contemporary, J.H. Round.

and economic ruins of old Europe.[4] Haskins' contribution to a co-authored account of the Paris conference, *Some Problems of the Peace Conference*, made no simple association of medieval precedent with the immediate task of redrawing Europe's boundaries.[5] Peace would instead be forged through a commission of inquiry involving the judicious gathering, interpretation, and application of thousands of report findings prepared by US historians, political scientists, and geographers on the social, economic, and demographic conditions on the ground.[6] But this example of Wilsonian progressivism, that took 'seeing like a state' to new levels,[7] was at odds with the more famous Wilsonian principle of the peace, 'self-determination', and the opportunity it gave different peoples to pursue sovereign identities free of imperial powers or to resist consolidation into blocks defined by others' geopolitical economic strategy. Haskins' dual role exposed him in two ways to these conflicting priorities. First, as a diplomat, he found himself between realist *Weltpolitik* and democratic consent of the governed; and second, as a historian, he stood between the painstaking rebuilding of the past from its archives and the historian's temptation to be a narrator of providence. In both situations, of course, all actors operated along one or both of these continua between realism and liberalism, positivism and idealism. Matthew Specter has usefully portrayed the first as a mode of conversation among governing elites – the Atlantic realists – over the role of the state in the projection of power or the pursuit of utopian values. He refers to a 'disavowed shadow-side of liberalism' to explain how Wilson took a 'realist position on race relations at home and abroad' whilst simultaneously espousing liberal internationalism.[8]

The shadow-side of liberalism affected the problems of Haskins' peace chiefly in the drawing of Europe's frontiers and in the relative weight given to their historically complex emergence from the various and often incommensurate building blocks of self-determination: geography, natural resource distribution, trade and communication as well as language, race, politics and ethnicity. Though he recognized race as a valid category of identity, Haskins set no great store by it nor by ethno-nationalism, as criteria for self-determination in Europe.[9] Others

---

[4] See H. Blurton, 'An American in Paris: Charles Homer Haskins at the Paris Peace Conference', in *Medievalisms in the Postcolonial World*, ed. K. Davis and N. Altschul (Baltimore, MD, 2009), 265–85.
[5] C.H. Haskins, *Some Problems of the Peace Conference* (London, 2018) (hereafter *SPOPC*).
[6] 'Never before in history, perhaps, have the universities played so dominant a part in world statesmanship', P. Slossen, 'The Constitution of the Peace Conference', *Political Science Quarterly* 35 (1920), 360–71 at 369.
[7] See James Scott, *Seeing Like a State* (New Haven, CT, 1998), 4–5, for the beginnings of developmental theory in 1918, characterized by administrative ordering and measuring of nature and society, and a high modernist, 'scientific' ideology prepared to employ 'ends–means' state power upon a prostrate civil society.
[8] M. Specter, *The Atlantic Realists: Empire and International Political Thought between Germany and the United States* (Stanford, CA, 2022), 5–6.
[9] Haskins mentioned race as an obsolete category of identity for a Europe whose Mediterranean, Teutonic and Alpine 'races' had long since intermingled; *SPOPC*, 14.

did, however, and his economic argument for combining into one national entity the resources of Belgium and Luxembourg to bolster France's eastern frontier with Germany, lost out to nationalist appeals.

In one special case, Haskins accepted his co-author Robert Howard Lord's evocation of 'a ghost roaming the Sarmatian plain, revived but with no knowledge of its home, nor what this disembodied spirit would look like if clothed again in flesh and blood', in support of modern Polish nation-making.[10] The success of Sarmatianism – the origin myth according to which the eighteenth-century Polish ruling elite were said to be descendants of Iranian ethno-cultural stock – was the 'righting of an historical wrong'[11] and was swiftly vindicated by the 'miracle of the Vistula', when newly independent Poland repelled the Red Army in the summer of 1920. The event was also seen as an 'Aryan' victory over a Slavic people.

It may have embarrassed Wilson, leader of the first Southern Democrat administration since the Secession – a symbol, Adam Tooze notes, 'of the reconciliation of 'White America', and a license to step forward from the Civil War'[12] – to be skewered by German diplomats applying the principle of self-determination to their maps of 'Hawaii, St Thomas, Florida, and Texas'.[13] But then again, perhaps he was not, given his open racial segregation of White House staff, his screening there of the lost-cause epic film *The Birth of a Nation*, and his fondness for the Confederate uniform.[14] Haskins did not share such nostalgia, but he could be adamant that the 'aim of the conference was not to do abstract justice in every corner of the earth'. Indeed, there was consensus over arrangements in Africa: though it might be an 'imperative of action', self-determination could only be granted to those with the 'maturity, and self-control' with 'experience in self-governance, or some means of political self-expression'. For this reason, it was not applicable to 'the downtrodden natives of the German colonies'.[15]

---

[10] *SPOPC*, 279.
[11] P.J. Geary, *The Myth of Nations: The Medieval Origins of Europe* (Princeton, NJ, 2002), 21.
[12] A. Tooze, *The Deluge: The Great War and the Remaking of Global Order, 1916–1931* (London, 2014), 14.
[13] *SPOPC*, 14.
[14] 'Permit me to refer at this point to a pleasing incident in which that distinguished son of the South, Woodrow Wilson, President of the United States, had the leading part. A year or two ago diplomas were given by our university to all the students who had interrupted their studies to enter the military service of the Confederacy. Mr. Wilson, then President of Princeton University delivered these diplomas. One man only of the Class [handwritten – that Matriculated in 1862] wearing the Confederate uniform, came forward to receive that highly prized token. It was the humble individual who now addresses you. At the dinner, later in the day, Professor Wilson greeted me with the remark that in many years nothing had so much touched and warmed his heart as the sight of that Confederate uniform.' Excerpt from Chapel Hill alumnus, Julian Carr's Silent Sam Inauguration Speech, transcribed by Hilary N. Green, https://hgreen.people.ua.edu/transcription-carr-speech.html.
[15] *SPOPC*, 14.

With these words American pragmatism struck the discreet balance between self-determination and old-world imperialism.

The second tension Haskins faced, as a historian, between positivism and presentism, has received attention from two illustrious historians born during the Second World War. In her 2017 chapter on 'Why Reinventing Medieval History is a Good Idea', Janet Nelson, recalling the 'prospective retro-medievalism' of Norman Cantor's *Inventing the Middle Ages, The Lives, Works and Ideas of the Great Medievalists of the 20th Century*,[16] proposed the 'time-required, positive, medieval-style invention' of a new medieval history.[17] In her recent three-part meditation, *On the Judgment of History*, Joan Scott reflected on the politics of an eighteenth-century idea of history that – in taking 'the nation state to be the "tip of the arrow" of the direction of history' – insulated itself from the moral reproach of those whose experience of the secular, liberal state entailed a more complex and conflicted understanding of its history.[18] Both Nelson and Scott affirm that history writing is always implicated in an emergent present.[19] Integral to Nelson's moment of medieval reinvention is the need for improved language training to address the corrosive effect – through its populist, 'end of history' antipathy to the humanities – of neoliberal governance in the UK's Higher Education sector.

Scott surveys our dark political times more broadly and reflects on the continued messianic allure – 'even for sceptical secularists like myself' – of history as the ultimate court of moral appeal.[20] In the wake of the events in Charlottesville, Virgina; the ongoing rallies of neo-Nazis, Klansmen, and groups like the 'Proud Boys'; and the attack on the Capitol,[21] much rides on the answer to Scott's question: are such fantasies about history's and historians' jurisdiction a spur to action or a symptom of (and consolation for) political impotence? If historical time is (as it was for Haskins) out of joint, how is our reinvention of medieval history to help set the problems of the peace aright?

How much of the Parisian atmosphere of 1919 did the historian-diplomat absorb as diplomat-historian? He sketches a somber scene in *Some Problems of the Peace*: 'an influenza epidemic, displaced people, the sorrowful trips by foreign nationals to hastily buried loved ones, many bodies still lying unburied

---

[16] (New York, NY, 1991).

[17] J. Nelson, 'Why Reinventing Medieval History is a Good Idea', in *The Making of Medieval History*, ed. G.A. Loud and M. Staub (York, 2017), 17–36.

[18] J.W. Scott, *On the Judgment of History* (New York, NY, 2020), 80.

[19] For recent debates on presentism, see M. Rubin, 'Presentism's Useful Anachronisms', *PP* 234 (2017), 236–44, P. Coss, 'Presentism and the "Myth" of Magna Carta', *PP* 234 (2017), 227–35, and F. Hartog, *Regimes of Historicity: Presentism and Experiences of Time*, trans. S. Brown (New York, NY, 2015).

[20] Scott, *On the Judgment of History*, xii.

[21] The events referenced here are the 'Unite the Right' rally on 11–12 August 2017 in Charlottesville, VA; the demonstrations of a range of far-right-wing political groups such as the 'Proud Boys'; and the storming of the US Capitol building on 6 January 2020 by demonstrators supporting presidential candidate Donald Trump and denying the results of the 2020 election in favor of Joseph Biden.

at the front... no dancing or gaiety, like at Vienna'.²² But it would be a mistake to infer it left him with abidingly gloomy expectations. The full panorama, of course, emerges in his 1927 *The Renaissance of the Twelfth Century*, his optimistic account of a Europe of regions and dynamic peoples, chief among them the Norman diaspora, and of universities and courts fostering fresh intellectual endeavors.²³ Taken all together, there emerges the consistency of a man engaged in nothing less than the translation as well as the moral rehabilitation of western civilization.

This much is well known, thanks, among others, to Paul Freedman, Bruce Holsinger, Gabrielle Spiegel, and Robin Fleming.²⁴ But what else might Haskins have noticed had he had the time to take in more of the Parisian air? As Erez Manela has shown us, the Wilsonian moment in Paris was a transcultural and global conjuncture. Side experiments in the settling of peace germinated out in the cold 'cosmopolitan caravanserai' beyond the top table at Paris, and grew in its wake.²⁵ John Maynard Keynes left Paris early to write his damning audit of the *Economic Consequences of the Peace*, and W.E.B. Du Bois returned from Paris to write *The Gift of Black Folk* (1924)²⁶ to American nationhood, after, I would like to think, exchanging thoughts with Marcel Mauss, who at the time was running a co-operative society in Paris and publicly writing in favor of the deferral of German reparation payments, and a book on social contracting called *The Gift* (1925).²⁷ Soon after (in January 1922), André Breton moved into the Rue de Fontaine, wrote his first *Surrealist Manifesto*, and began collecting indigenous African art and 'ethnographic objects'.²⁸ Bolshevism –

---

²² *SPOPC*, 4, 8.
²³ (Cambridge, MA, 1927). On the background to Haskins' work and its use of the term 'renaissance', see A. Novikoff, 'The Renaissance of the Twelfth Century Before Haskins', *HSJ* 16 (2005), 104–16.
²⁴ P. Freedman, and G.M. Spiegel, 'Medievalisms Old and New: The Rediscovery of Alterity in North American Medieval Studies', *AHR* 103 (1998), 677–704; Bruce W. Holsinger, 'Medieval Studies, Postcolonial Studies, and the Genealogies of Critique', *Speculum* 77 (2002), 1195–227; R. Fleming, 'Picturesque History and the Medieval in Nineteenth-Century America', *AHR* 100 (1995), 1061–94.
²⁵ E. Manela, *The Wilsonian Moment: Self-Determination and the International Origins of Anticolonial Nationalism* (Oxford, 2007). For the cosmopolitan dimension of the Paris Conference, see *Transcultural History*, ed. M. Herren et al. (Heidelberg, 2012), 1–10, citing E.J. Dillon, *The Inside Story of the Peace Conference* (New York and London, 1920), 4.
²⁶ 'The Negro folk song – the singular spiritual heritage of the nation and the greatest gift of the Negro people', W.E.B. Du Bois, *The Souls of Black Folk* (New York, NY, 1989), 178.
²⁷ See C.L. Stewart, 'Civil Religion, Civil Society, and the Performative Life and Work of W. E. B. Du Bois', *The Journal of Religion* 88 (2008), 307–30, esp. 310, for the comment, 'Had one not known otherwise, one might have thought that Mauss's study, *The Gift*, was actually based upon the life and work of Du Bois. Mauss's work affirms in such a definite manner Du Bois's understanding of the nature and meaning of the gift in the life of society.'
²⁸ G. Mallard, *Gift Exchange: The Transnational History of a Political Idea* (Cambridge, 2019), 14, notes that Mauss's 'social capital' as an anthropologist was due to 'external

Lenin's vision of self-determination and progressive modernity – caught the eye of many anticolonial internationalists in Paris as an alternative to the Wilsonian mirage of self-determination, and if embraced by some (Ho Chi Minh, Mao Zedong) as a plan for action, it could be seen as leverage by others (Lajpat Rai) in their efforts to hold the new League of Nations to its word.[29] Though they were differently measured and configured, common to these many economic imaginaries of Paris, were questions of peace and justice, and the relationship between state and people, and the relationship of both of these with sovereignty in a world of national, transnational, and colonial governance.

Haskins' reinvention of a medieval Europe for American consumption achieved a *translatio studii* of European heritage, to match the United States' ascent to world power status.[30] But with its elevation from the nation of the freeborn Anglo-Saxon stock of its founding fathers to the inheritor of Europe's heritage, something in America's own historical experience of race within that shadow-side of liberalism passed inchoate into the new variant of prospective retro-medievalism.[31]

Towards a Theology of Politics

One Continental European reaction against the peace enacted at Versailles that also invoked medieval precedent in its justification of state sovereignty, was elaborated by Carl Schmitt in his *Political Theology* (1922). A work of authoritarian mysticism, Schmitt's *Political Theology* fashioned a legal rubric for political authority designed to protect the Weimar Republic's territorial integrity and sovereignty against foreign liberal interference. In circumstances

---

political factors – the expansion of the French Empire as a result of the 1919 peace of Versailles – and more local factors – the infatuation of Parisian art collectors for "primitive" fetishes'. For the anticolonial, antiracist nature of the surrealist movement, see *Black, Brown, & Beige: Surrealist Writings from Africa and the Diaspora*, ed. F. Rosemont and R.D.G. Kelly (Austin, TX, 2010).

[29] E. Manela, *The Wilsonian Moment: Self-Determination and the International Origins of Anticolonial Nationalism* (Oxford, 2007), 3–4, 173–4, 194–5. Ho Chi Minh (1890–1969) was central to Vietnam's emergence as nation independent of French colonial rule and led the evolving polity, 1945–69; Mao Zedong (1893–1976) led the Communist revolution in China after the Second World War and established the People's Republic of China; Lajpat Rai (1865–1928) was a major figure in the Indian National Congress and an outspoken critic of British colonial rule.

[30] For the arrival of US as a world power between 1898 and 1917, see M. Specter, *The Atlantic Realists Empire and International thought between Germany and the United States* (Stanford, CA, 2022), 31–9.

[31] At the same time African American writers were already putting the medieval literary canon to a progressive use. In 1928, W.E.B. du Bois published the historical romance, *Dark Princess*. His colleague, and literary editor of *The Crisis*, Jessie Redmon Fauset, 'midwife' of the Harlem Renaissance, used medieval themes to articulate modern African American female experience in her writing. See C.J. Whitaker, 'The Middle Ages in the Harlem Renaissance', in *Whose Middle Ages Teachable Moments for an Ill-Used Past*, ed. Mary C. Erler, Nicholas Paul et al. (New York, NY, 2019), 80–93.

of hyperinflation and a French army occupying and extracting reparations from the Ruhr region, center of Germany's heavy industry, Schmitt's failsafe politico-juridical mechanism entailed an emergent leader invoking a state of exception to break with the law to save the law and assert the political will of the law's subjects against its enemies. Schmitt justified this sovereign decisionism through the recuperation of medieval theological concepts from their secular interment, he claimed, within all modern liberal theories of the state.[32] The antisemitic vein running through this particular defense of Weimar sovereignty against American liberal economic hegemony grew ever more visible after 1933 with Schmitt's open support for National Socialism.[33]

The word 'state' appears only once in the index to Haskins' *Renaissance*. He uses it obliquely to illustrate the twelfth-century's philosophical occupation with universals and nominals, and incidentally, to point out a political incertitude he felt liberal modernity had inherited from the Middle Ages: 'Apply it [the universal] to the state, and where does political authority reside, in a sovereign whole, or in the individual citizens? In this form, at least, the problem is still with us.'[34] With this aside, Haskins intuitively brought modern political thought into alignment with twelfth-century eucharistic thought, inviting consideration of such problems as what is real about the state, whether language allows us entirely to understand what about the state is real, or if it merely names and assigns a relational, indexed value to the state, and if so, then how do we account for, and where do we locate, those aspects of the state that exceed language? Upon the answers to these conundrums depended an understanding of the associations between the state as the scene of legitimate governance, and its agents and peoples, beneficiaries and enemy-victims.[35] Haskins' unresolved problem – like Schmitt's – is one of political theology. It links modern constitutional understandings of the state with trace theological discussions of the relationship between earthly institutions and the divine. It poses questions for liberal constitutionalists about the legitimate operations of executive power at moments of perceived emergency, for example, in the case of counter-majoritarian supreme court rulings, stop and frisk policing, the use of advanced interrogation techniques, activation of the nuclear codes, attempted coups.[36] Solutions to such questions are clearly not in the gift of historians, but they lie

---

[32] C. Schmitt, *Political Theology. Four Chapters on the Concept of Sovereignty*, trans. G. Schwab (Chicago, IL, 2005), 36.
[33] J. Israel, 'Narratives of Disenchantment, Narratives of Secularization', in *Narratives of Disenchantment and Secularization: Critiquing Max Weber's Idea of Modernity*, ed. R.A. Yelle and L. Trein (London, 2021), 111–28 at 123.
[34] C.H. Haskins, *The Renaissance of the Twelfth Century* (Cambridge, MA, 1927, rev. ed., 1971), 352.
[35] For Schmitt, this is resolved in the sovereign who decides the exception, i.e. occupies the positions of both nominal and real simultaneously.
[36] P.H. Kahn, *Political Theology: Four New Chapters on the Concept of Sovereignty* (New York, NY, 2012), a timely study of the relationship of liberal political theories of American exceptionalism to the sacred.

in the background of historical judgment, they weighed heavily on the minds of some of Haskins' more immediate successors, and they inform the problems of our decolonizing present, upon which Joan Scott reflects.[37]

Among Haskins' successors, two stand out as curators of this modern myth of the state: Ernst Kantorowicz and Joseph Strayer. Robert Lerner's biography of the former has clearly demonstrated their mutual intellectual indebtedness, not least in terms of their interest – independently of Schmitt – in *liturgical* myths of the state and political theology.[38] Moreover, the conditions in which they encountered Haskins' version of the state as unfinished theological business were different to those of Schmitt.

Integral to Strayer's story was the laicization of ecclesiastical precepts and practices by medieval French kings and their development, ultimately, into the practices and principles of liberal administration and statecraft. Churchmen surrounded Christian kings with glorious reflections of royal authority, a power domesticated by being made visible. Strayer's examples of this gradual provisioning of political authority with divine sources of legitimacy were realized in great undertakings like the organization of resources to support crusading or the use of a 'defence of the realm' rationale by thirteenth-century French kings to 'excuse actions which carried royal power far beyond its old limits', among them the increased regulation of trade and baronial coinage, the commandeering of rights in property, and taxation in the furtherance of war.[39]

All this was elegantly crystallized in his *Medieval Origins of the Modern State*, a textbook published in 1970 for political scientists, national security administrators, and other constituents of the US governing establishment, as well as for historians.[40] The book's secular theologizing is essentially Weberian, with the difference that Strayer takes his cue for the routinization of charisma from twelfth-century bishops and kings rather than sixteenth-century puritans. Its ethos is rehearsed in this unexpectedly soteriological vein:

A man can lead a reasonably full life without a family, a fixed local residence, or a religious affiliation but if he is stateless, he is nothing. He has no rights, no security, and little opportunity for a useful career. There is no salvation outside the framework of an organized state... [it is] a framework for organization... we cannot escape from the state.

---

[37] See above note 18.

[38] Lerner found no trace of reference to Schmitt in Kantorowicz's published papers or letters and refers the reader to his annotations to a methods seminar of 1949 that associate 'political theology' with J. Strayer's article of the same year, 'Defence of the Realm'; see R. E. Lerner, *Ernst Kantorowicz a Life* (Princeton, NJ, 2017), 347.

[39] J.R. Strayer, 'Defence of the Realm and Royal Power in France', in *Medieval Statecraft and the Perspectives of History* (Princeton, NJ, 1971), 297.

[40] J.R. Strayer, *On the Medieval Origins of the Modern State* (Princeton, NJ, 1970). For the intended audience, see the remarks of William Chester Jordan, in J.R. Strayer, *The Medieval Origins of the Modern State* with forewords by Charles Tilly and William Chester Jordan (new ed., Princeton, NJ, 2016), xix–xxi.

And yet, he continues,

> A state exists chiefly in the hearts and minds of its people, if they do not believe it is there, no logical exercise will bring it to life… [and finally, exists]… the most important, also most nebulous sign of the state… moral authority.[41]

Strayer's use of theological language in his rooting of the modern state in late twelfth- and thirteenth-century Latin Christendom was rooted in his confidence in the power of the administrative state to accomplish great projects. Yet it may also have derived from a more fragile wish that his own involvement and that of others in the morally ambiguous operations of the CIA and other aspects of what Dwight Eisenhower dubbed the military-industrial complex might find justification in the valorization of secular administrative service with a providential sense of righteous necessity.[42] In such terms, the work of political administration, including its shadier arts, became the sacred business of *Heilsgeschichte*.

Kantorowicz's *The King's Two Bodies A Study in Mediaeval Political Theology* surveys the underlying conceptual and ritual strata for the landscape that Strayer sought to map. His thesis, so far as one can be discerned from such an exhaustively erudite yet ill-organized study, was both something less than and something more than a claim for the invention by medieval theology of the concept of the king's two bodies. According to this, the physical person of the secular ruler was enveloped in another transcendent 'body', one rooted not in any earthly polity but in the mystical body of Christ with its many associations.[43] *The King's Two Bodies* has been read as a work of constitutional semantics, a deep history of renaissance political theory, a legal anthropology, and as 'an anthology of disquisitions concerning transmutations of Christian theological formulations into political ones'.[44] One reviewer, Beryl Smalley, who knew a thing or two about schoolmen through the ages, praised it as 'a golden treasury of political metaphors', before voicing – in the comic mode – her ultimate frustration: 'By the end of the book, I felt as queasy as one would after a diet of jam without bread.'[45] Political metaphors might be important, but the historian 'has to measure their distance from the *facts of life… actual* problems

---

[41] Strayer, *The Medieval Origins* (1st ed.), 19–23.
[42] Dwight Eisenhower coined this phrase in his Farewell Address in 1961: www.archives.gov/milestone-documents/president-dwight-d-eisenhowers-farewell-address.
[43] Important precursors to Strayer's stage in this process was the eighth and ninth century use of *laudes regia* rites in the coronation of Carolingian kings, and the liturgical kingship represented in Ottonian visual culture. See E. Kantorowicz, *The King's Two Bodies A Study in Medieval Political Theology* (Princeton, NJ, 2016), 61–78, and G. Agamben, *The Kingdom and the Glory: For a Theological Genealogy of Economy and Government*, trans. L. Chiesa (Stanford, CA, 2011), 189–90, on the liturgical practice of acclamation that he notes was revived with the rise of fascist dictatorships in the 1920s.
[44] R.E. Lerner, *Ernst Kantorowicz. A Life* (Princeton, NJ, 2017), 348.
[45] B. Smalley, 'Review: The King's Two Bodies. A Study in Mediaeval Political Theology', *PP* 20 (1961), 3–35 at 30 and 32. For a rather indiscreet depiction of the schoolmen of Smalley's generation, see P. Brown, 'What's in a Name?, a Talk Given

and conflicts... *actual* function and powers'.[46] Smalley had in mind here the behavior of the Angevin kings, and especially Henry II, whom she regarded, agreeing with J.E.A. Jolliffe, as 'on a sustained course of intrigue and violence which can by no stretch of the argument be justified within any conventional limits of legitimate power'.[47]

In fact, Kantorowicz's interest in culture-power, gender and the body as well as his focus on discourse anticipated the themes of a new medieval history that emerged in the 1970s and flourishes today.[48] The 'grotesque', as Freedman and Spiegel name it, embraces the strangeness of the Middle Ages, replacing a view of alterity as origin with one of alterity as difference explored through 'post-structural' techniques of discourse analysis, the linguistic turn, and gender – more jam, in Smalley's terms. The 'facts of life... the actual problems and conflicts... actual functions and power' of church, state, and 'administrative kingship', were dealt a particular blow by Peggy Brown and Susan Reynolds, two of the shrewder observers of the schoolmen.[49] By exposing feudalism as an abiding legal myth of male political bonding that prepared the way for the state proper, they felled a hoary old oak and cleared space for new scholarship, including women's and gender history, the history of identities, postcolonial, and, ultimately, 'postmedieval' medievalism. Kathleen Davis has taken these insights furthest – in conversation with, among others, Dipesh Chakrabarty and Gil Anidjar – arguing that the epochal transformations implicated in the European medieval–modern periodization have little value for historians working outside that tradition, not only because the binary was never designed for such histories, but because this periodization came to serve civilizing, liberal colonial projects in its deployment of the rhetoric of race, religion, education, and culture to justify the violent intervention in and re-ordering of non-European societies. Davis thus drew attention back to the entanglement of the notions of the liturgical state with its salvific mission with the peculiarly racially inflected myth of American exceptionalism.[50]

---

at the Opening of the Oxford Centre for Late Antiquity on Friday 28 September, 2007', www.ocla.ox.ac.uk/sites/default/files/ocla_opening_talk.pdf?time=1577640804436, 6–7.
[46] Smalley, 'Review: The King's Two Bodies', 32.
[47] Smalley, 'Review: The King's Two Bodies', 33, referencing J.E.A. Jolliffe, *Angevin Kingship* (Oxford, 1955), 13.
[48] As noted by C. Leyser in his introduction to Ernst Kantorowicz, *The King's Two Bodies. A Study in Medieval Theology* (3rd ed., Princeton, NJ, 2016), xv–xix.
[49] For this classic challenge, see Elizabeth A.R. Brown, "The Tyranny of a Construct: Feudalism and Historians of Medieval Europe', *AHR* 79 (1974), 1063–88; and more recently Susan Reynolds, *Fiefs and Vassals. The Medieval Evidence Reinterpreted* (Oxford, 1994), and 'Still Fussing about Feudalism', in *Italy and Early Medieval Europe. Papers for Chris Wickham*, ed. R. Balzaretti, J. Barrow, and P. Skinner (Oxford, 2018), 87–94.
[50] See K. Davis, *Periodization and Sovereignty: How Ideas of Feudalism and Secularization Govern the Politics of Time* (Philadelphia, PA, 2008); D. Chakrabarty, *Provincializing Europe: Postcolonial Thought and Historical Difference* (Princeton, NJ, 2000); G. Anidjar, 'Secularism', *Critical Enquiry* 33 (2006), 52–77; and for the particular

Thomas Bisson's *The Crisis of the Twelfth Century. Power, Lordship, and the Origins of European Government* is an underappreciated book.[51] Bisson shares with Strayer the bureaucratic state as his destination but he gets there later and by other means. He presents a twelfth century largely without 'government', '*res publica*' or 'politics', a world without centralized political agency, where political ideas and practices found no traction. Instead, there was the power of affective lordship whether in the person of the lord-king or that of the lord.

Bisson treats the experience of that power as a continuous passive reckoning with arbitrary, unpolitical violence.[52] He sees not 'state-building', but violence, rapine and arbitrary exaction by lords and ruler-lords, only gradually reined in by cultures of expertise including 'the songs of the troubadours, courtly discourses, and academic moralities'.[53] In penitential theology for example, the school masters taught lords a path to salvation through attention to the status of their peasants; status in this context meaning not publicly guaranteed civil rights, forms of consent, representation, or protection from distraint of person or property by a rule of law, but the voluntary norms of moral treatment or statecraft lords might, through their own spiritual inclinations, grant people. He narrates the state into being through a regional survey of events that proceed from lordship brought to account through new techniques of resource management, witnessed first in late twelfth-century Angevin England. Bisson unfashionably laid insights from social science and poststructuralism aside in his enquiry into the 'twelfth-century relationship of human suffering to power'.[54] Consequently, his description of the evolution of power relations retains a sense of Weberian destiny, thus remaining – somewhat like feudalism – a male-dominated enterprise of castle-based, affective violence, absent the more diffuse kinds and currents of power found in the more recent 'grotesque' historiographies.

So where does that leave us with the problems of the American peace among nations inherited from Haskins's medievalism? Interestingly, Haskins framed the problem of peace as analogous to that of the eucharist, when he asked what does an object retain of its own being and becoming that is independent of its nominative being. For Kantorowicz, the medieval state constituted itself in the Christ-like body of the king. For Carl Schmitt, the modern state manifested itself in the sovereign exception embodied by the Messiah-like figure of the *Führer*.[55] For Strayer, the modern, secular state was a vehicle for divine administration, bestowing upon the citizen an identity and a vocation, and guiding (invariably) him toward salvation through great feats of collective organization and civil

---

flourishing in the US of histories of medieval race, see, among others, G. Heng for *The Invention of Race in the European Middle Ages* (Cambridge, 2018).
[51] (Princeton, NJ, 2009).
[52] See also T.N. Bisson, *Tormented Voices: Power, Crisis, and Humanity in Rural Catalonia, 1140–1200* (Cambridge, MA, 1998).
[53] Bisson, *The Crisis of the Twelfth Century*, 454.
[54] Bisson, *The Crisis of the Twelfth Century*, 20.
[55] See above, p. 75.

service.[56] All these scholars bridged Smalley's gap between metaphor and reality with theological constructions of one sort or another. The peace of the state, in other words, was not ensured by unassailable principles of authority or by immanent institutions but by a revelatory momentum, superior to any institutional apparatus, that was choreographed by white men in governing positions of moral trust. Or, to use the language of Giorgio Agamben, the state is a theological-economic phenomenon comprising and commingling the kingdom and the glory, and service of the state a liturgical undertaking conducted by men capable of operating ethically, if necessary, with indifference to judicial regimes.[57] By encompassing Bisson's thesis and the 'grotesque' history of power as gender and discourse within the purview of economic theology, we might thereby differentiate among various emergent reifications of power in the workings of the peace.[58] Moreover, in such circumstances, we might reasonably ask whether this is a habit associated solely with Western figurations of power and governance,[59] and if so, whether we might take Davis's advice to unpick the threads of sovereign decisionism behind ideas of feudalism and secularization, better to compare it with alternative configurations of divine governance.

In the remainder of this essay, I explore the tensions within the theological-economic paradigm of the Cistercian imaginary by means of their treatment of angelic governance. Yet my subject is not the Cistercians, or twelfth-century angelology, nor is it the eremitic life. Not all Cistercian spirituality was about angelic governance, and not all angelic governance was Cistercian. It explores instead that point of convergence between all three and the place of 'angelic poetics' in economic theology, and in which Bisson's 'ruler-lord' was also implicated. I shall investigate a small selection of hagiography, spiritual texts, and letters representative of a certain kind of Cistercian 'economizing' in Angevin England.[60]

---

[56] See above, p. 77.
[57] For this phrase, see Agamben, *The Kingdom and the Glory*, 47, 66, 167; and for the life of service to state as a kind of liturgical and ethical observance, see Agamben, *The Highest Poverty, Monastic Rules and Form of Life*, trans. A. Kotsko (Stanford, CA, 2011), 79–85.
[58] See C. West, *Reframing the Feudal Revolution: Political and Social Transformation Between Marne and Moselle, c. 800–c.1100* (Cambridge, 2013).
[59] For a medieval example of which see J. Dale, *Inauguration and Liturgical Kingship in the Long Twelfth Century* (York, 2019), 14–15.
[60] John of Forde, *Vita Wulfrici*, in *Wulfric of Hazelbury by John, Abbot of Ford*, ed. M. Bell, Somerset Record Society 47 (1933), and *John of Forde, The Life of Wulfric of Haselbury, Anchorite*, trans., P. Matarasso (Collegeville, MN, 2011); T. Licence, 'The Life and Miracles of Godric of Throckenholt', *Analecta Bollandiana* 124 (2006), 15–43; Walter Daniel, *Life of Ailred of Rievaulx*, ed. and trans. M. Powicke (Oxford, 1978); Bernard of Clairvaux, *Five Books on Consideration*, in *Sancti Bernardi*, ed. J. Leclercq, H.M. Rochais et al. (8 vols, Rome, 1957–77), iii, 381–493; Bernard of Clairvaux, *Five Books on Consideration Advice to a Pope*, trans. J.D. Anderson and E.T. Kennan (Athens, OH, 1976; repr. Collegeville, MN, 2004).

Cistercian Angelic Poetics

The most successful trans-European spiritual diaspora of the twelfth century, Cistercian monasticism spread by means of local arrangements brokered between lords and religious across borders and kingdoms. Many Cistercian monasteries developed from eremitical experimentation into communities that sent out further spores resulting in the foundation of new daughter houses. Following William I's harrying of the north of England, an ensuing ascetic invasion revived monasticism at Durham, St Mary's York, Jarrow, Monkwearmouth and Whitby.[61] A Cistercian colonization, especially in the north, accelerated during the disturbed peace of Stephen's reign. Between 1135 and 1147, the number of foundations increased from five to twenty-seven, many of them filial spurs of Clairvaux.[62] Clairvaux's close institutional links with English Cistercian monasteries ensured communication and collaboration across the Channel. Bernard commissioned Ailred to write his *Mirror of Charity*, an apologia for the Cistercian spiritual practice, and Bernard's own work, the *Five Books on Consideration* survives, among others, in a group of English manuscript copies.[63]

One feature of the twelfth-century renaissance, remarked Ernst Kantorowicz, was that scholarly minds 'began to discover the intellectual joy and stimulus emanating from angelological investigations'.[64] For example, John Sarazin of St Denis wrote a commentary on Pseudo-Dionysius dedicated to John of Salisbury.[65] Pseudo-Dionysius was studied by the canons regular, particularly Hugh and Richard of St Victor. Hugh of St Victor was interested in *speculatio* as a hermeneutic aid to scriptural exegesis and knowledge of the created world, which could be gained through contemplation and reflection.[66] The idea of *hierarchy*, a word coined by Pseudo-Dionysius, stimulated thought about relations, behaviors, and boundaries and on 'proper measure (*mensura*) in desire, thought and act', in one's habits of posture, eating and contemplation.[67] To be sure, Jean Leclercq saw the Cistercians as less interested than the

---

[61] J. Burton, 'The Eremitical Tradition and the Development of Post-Conquest Life in Northern England', *Trivium* 26 (1991), 18–39.
[62] See E.T. Kennan, 'Introduction', in Bernard of Clairvaux, *Five Books on Consideration Advice to a Pope*, trans. J.D. Anderson and E.T. Kennan (Athens, OH, 1976, 2004), 10; and J. Burton, 'Citadels of God: Monasteries, Violence, and the Struggle for Power in Northern England, 1135–1154', *ANS* 31 (2008), 17–30.
[63] Ailred of Rievaulx, *The Mirror of Charity*, trans. Elizabeth Connor (Collegeville, MN, 1990); and Bernard of Clairvaux, *Five Books on Consideration*.
[64] Kantorowicz, *The King's Two Bodies*, 280.
[65] J. Leclercq, 'Influence and noninfluence of Dionysius in the Western Middle Ages', in *Pseudo-Dionysius, The Complete Works*, trans. C. Luibheid (New York, NY, 1987), 27.
[66] D.M. Coulter, 'Contemplation as "Speculation": A Comparison of Boethius, Hugh of St Victor, and Richard of St Victor', in *From Knowledge to Beatitude, St Victor. Twelfth-Century Scholars and Beyond Essays in Honor of Grover A Zinn, Jr.*, ed. E. Ann Matter and L. Smith (Notre Dame, IN, 2013), 204–28 at 212–14.
[67] See B.T. Coolman, '"Trangressing [its] measure… trespassing the mode and law of

Victorines in Pseudo-Dionysius. He notes, however, that his work was copied at Citeaux, that Bernard and Ailred knew it, that Isaac of Stella used him, and that Garnier, late twelfth-century abbot of Clairvaux, preached to the General Chapter on his work.[68] The degree to which it informed Cistercian intellectual thought, certainly in the Greek, needs further attention, but in terms of 'applied Cistercian spirituality' the *vita angelica* was a point of reference for Cistercian self-identity. An instructive example of Cistercian thinking with angels is the *De Consideratione* (or '*Five Books On Consideration*', 1148–53), the mirror for a papal prince, Eugenius III (1145–53), written by his spiritual mentor and fellow Cistercian, Bernard of Clairvaux.[69]

In this work, Bernard uses the angelic hierarchy to expand upon Paul's comments to the Corinthians on the relationship between apostolic ministry and earthly power.[70] 'Just as', he notes, 'in heaven the Seraphim and Cherubim and each of the other ranks down to the angels and archangels are arranged under one hand, God; likewise, here on earth the primates or patriarchs, archbishops, bishops, priests or abbots, and all the rest are arranged under one supreme pontiff.'[71] Even though the Church is arranged under the supreme apostolic power of the pontiff, Bernard cautions Eugenius not to confuse that supremacy with monopoly. There are others to whom apostolic powers are available, '[dispensors] who are required to be found faithful'.[72]

Bernard's Pauline allusions are those Agamben regards as evidence of the absorption of the Hellenistic language of domestic administration (*oikonomia*) into early Christian theology to denote, in Paul's case, the duty of Christians in the faithful service of the unfolding of salvation.[73] Bernard shows that though each level of the hierarchy ministers or 'weighs out' to that below it (*dispensatio*), the actions of all would-be dispensors (*oikonomoi*) degrade to those of ruinous scattering (*dissipatio*) unless conditions of utility and necessity – to be revealed

---

its beauty." Sin and the Beauty of the Soul in Hugh of St Victor', in *From Knowledge to Beatitude*, ed. Matter and Smith, 186–203 at 187, for Hugh of St Victor's Christological framing of *hierarchy* in the aesthetic terms of measure, mode and order in the observation of justice and virtue.

[68] Leclercq, 'Influence and Noninfluence of Dionysius in the Western Middle Ages', 28–9.

[69] C. Egger, 'Curial Politics and Papal Power: Eugenius III, the Curia, and contemporary theological controversy', in *Pope Eugenius III (1145–1153): The First Cistercian Pope*, ed. I. Fonnesburg-Schmidt and A. Jotischky (Amsterdam, 2018), 69–100 at 96–100, for Bernard's intentions for *De Consideratione*.

[70] Corinthians 10:8 and 1 Corinthians 4:2.

[71] *Sancti Bernardi Opera*, iii, 445: quod sicut illic Seraphim et Cherubim, ac ceteri quique usque ad angelus et archangelos, ordinantur sub sub uno capite Deo, ita hic quoque sub uno summo Pontifice primates vel patriarchae, archiepiscopi, episcopi, presbyteri vel abbates, et reliqui in hunc modum; trans. Bernard of Clairvaux, *Five Books on Consideration*, 102–03.

[72] *Sancti Bernardi Opera*, iii, 445, citing 1 Cor. 4.2: Queritur inter dispensatores, ut fidelis quis inveniatur.

[73] For this discussion, see Agamben, *The Power and the Glory*, 17–49, esp. 21–5 for Pauline usage.

ultimately through divine not earthly judgement – are met.[74] All this reminds Eugenius of what Bernard had stated at the outset of the work, that 'your power is over sin and not property... to exclude sinners, not possessors... tell me, which is the greater honour and greater power: to forgive sins or to divide estates?'[75]

The consideration Bernard attempted to foster in Eugenius was rational but also spiritually comforting for a simple monk. It prized an ethos of service over the legal and administrative technicalities with which advisers besieged him in the Roman curia.[76] In book five, Bernard turns from discussion of Eugenius' active responsibilities toward the faithful, to consideration of things 'above you' (*supra te*). Consideration is 'practical (*dispensativam*), scientific (*aestimativam*), and speculative (*speculativam*)',[77] but for the pope, 'Your portion is spirit... God is the spirit, and his Holy Angels; these are above you, the former superior by nature, the latter by grace... you and the angels have one excellence: reason.'[78] The angels are 'citizens of the heavenly Jerusalem, powerful spirits, ethereal, pure, kind, pious, chaste, secure in peace, dedicated to divine praise and service' and known by nine names reflecting office, rank, and function.[79] Among them, Seraphim burn with fire, Cherubim shine with knowledge, Powers exhibit strength in countering darkness, and Virtues 'arouse the sluggish hearts of men by a show of signs'.[80]

In its description of angels, *The Celestial Hierarchy* modelled a division and ranking of labour relative to the divine that was underwritten by grace. For those aspiring to be good Christian dispensors without proof of grace, hierarchy was an uncertain experience of becoming – that is, striving toward the divine, and in the aesthetic sense of embodying and truly making present the virtues one practiced – dependent upon the use of 'opinion, faith, and understanding' in the exercise of free will. Bernard even goes on to say, in his 'Letter to Sophia', that whereas the angels have all the virtues, and are happy, yet they still envy the

---

[74] The translators of Bernard use the words, 'to dispense, dispensors', and a 'dispensation', to render Bernard's own Latin rendering, *dispensor*, in accordance with the Vulgate, of Paul's original Greek, *oikonomos, oikonomoi*, or treasurer(s).
[75] *Sancti Bernardi Opera*, iii, 402: Ergo in criminibus, non in possessionibus potestas vestra... praevaricatores utique, non possessores... Quaenam tibi maior videtur et dignitas et potestas, dimittendo peccata an praedia dividendi?'; Trans. *Five Books on Consideration*, 36.
[76] C. Egger, 'Curial Politics and Papal Power', 98–9.
[77] That is, empirical, abstract and reflective, *Sancti Bernardi Opera, III*, 469; trans. Bernard of Clairvaux, *Five Books on Consideration*, 142.
[78] *Sancti Bernardi Opera*, iii, 470: Tui portio spiritus est... Porro spiritus est Deus, sunt et angelis sancti, et hi supra te. Sed Deus natura, angeli gratia superiores sunt. Unum siquidem tui et angeli optimum, ratio est; trans. Bernard of Clairvaux, *Five Books on Consideration*, 144.
[79] *Sancti Bernardi Opera*, iii, 471: Cives spiritus... potentes... divinis laudibus et obsequiis deditos. (Seraphim, Cherubim, Thrones, Dominions, Principalities, Powers, Virtues, Archangels, Angels), 147.
[80] *Sancti Bernardi Opera*, iii, 476: Virtutes pro suo ministerio satagunt excitare corda torpentia hominum exhibitione signorum; trans Bernard of Clairvaux, *Five Books on Consideration*, 152–3.

body of Sophia, formed in the disciplined life of the heroic person. For Bernard, governance was a profoundly ethical, embodied, economic undertaking realized through Cistercian monasticism; in Weberian terms, he placed the charismatic economy of the monastery over the intellect and office of the Roman curia and used a Pseudo-Dionysian hierarchy to portray its internal dynamics.[81]

Encounters with Angels

In weighing the lives of monks and hermits in terms of the active and contemplative expertise modelled by angels, Cistercian writers, through an ethos of angelic economizing (*dispensatio*), fashioned a technology for brokering peace through appeals to moral order. Walter Daniel described Ailred of Rievaulx as an angel and observed that in his letters Ailred 'left a living image of himself, for what he there commended in writing, he himself practiced in life and lived much better than he could say'.[82] He called the Cistercians at Rievaulx 'wonderful men... as the angels might be, they were clothed in undyed wool spun and woven from the pure fleece of the sheep... they shine as they walk, with the whiteness of snow',[83] and 'on feast days you might see the church crowded with the brethren like bees in a hive... compacted into one angelic body'.[84] The use of angelic associations as a language of esteem among Cistercian networks is evidenced in the story related by Ailred of Rievaulx to the monks of Durham, of the hermit Godric of Finchale, who prophesied the death of Robert, Rievaulx alumnus and founding abbot of Newminster Abbey, his soul being joined with the heavenly angels.[85] In his later years, Ailred took to a small, grave-like space in the oratory where 'the light of angelic visitation shone there upon his head'.[86]

Walter Daniel also calls him an *echonomus*, a synonym for *dapifer*, a steward or manager of resources. During Stephen's reign, Ailred won benefactions for Revesby Abbey by speaking with bishops, earls and barons, and 'preaching to clergy in the local synods'. His appeals for land from benefactors targeted these powerful men's calculations of self-interest: 'he realized that in this unsettled time such gifts profited knights and monks alike... so disturbed and chaotic was the land, reduced almost to desert by the malice, slaughters and harrying

---

[81] C.S. Jaeger, *The Envy of Angels Cathedral Schools and Social Ideas in Medieval Europe, 950–1200* (Philadelphia, PA, 1994), 8 and 270–3.

[82] Walter Daniel, *Life of Ailred of Rievaulx*, ed. and trans. M. Powicke (Oxford, 1978), 42: in quibus viventem sibi reliquit imaginem, quia quod ibi literis commendavit hoc in vita ipse complevit et multo melius vixit quam ibi dicere potuit.

[83] Walter Daniel, *Life of Ailred of Rievaulx*, ed. and trans. Powicke, 10–11: mirabiles quidem... quod ovis vellere puro in filum producto et in telam deducto sine fuco cuiuslibet coloris angelice satis tegeruntur... velut candore nivis dum incedunt albescunt.

[84] Walter Daniel, *Life of Ailred of Rievaulx*, ed. and trans. Powicke, 38: Videres festis diebus in oratorio, tamquam in alveolo apes... et collegiatas unum quoddam exprimere corpus angelicum.

[85] Reginald of Durham, *The Life and Miracles of Saint Godric, Hermit of Finchale*, ed. M. Coombe (Oxford, 2022), 298.

[86] Walter Daniel, *Life of Ailred of Rievaulx* ed. and trans. Powicke, 50: lux angelice visitacionis resplenduit super caput eius.

of evil men... for which almost all men were fighting to the death'.[87] If in these circumstances monastic lordship replaced the immediate dangers of aristocratic competition over land, this did not always secure the status of those who made a living on it. Ros Faith has shown how the reorganization of the Revesby estate into a grange imposed new labour services on some and forced others off the land. Faith notes, too, that villeinage took on a more servile and legally extensive meaning over this period.[88]

Of course, not all Cistercians were as skilled as Ailred in combining the active and contemplative elements of their shared religious vocation. Great discretion was needed to avoid attracting accusations of hypocrisy from critics of the order. 'They wear white to make a show of righteousness', said Orderic Vitalis, 'voluntary poverty, contempt for the world and true religion inspire many of them, but 'many hypocrites and plausible counterfeiters are mixed with them'.[89] Others under Cistercian pastoral care were so active in their worldly charity as to attract similar suspicions of their religious vocations. In his advice to recluses, Ailred's image of entrepreneurial anchoresses 'finding pasture for their flocks and shepherds to tend them; demanding a statement of the numbers, weight and value of the flock's yearly produce; following the fluctuations of the market', can be compared with John of Forde's defense of Wulfric of Hazelbury against accusations that inappropriate amounts of money accumulated in his hands. Drogo de Munci, a noble of King Henry's household, and Robert of Cirencester, at the time a minor clerk, were struck with ill health after slandering Wulfric over his unseemly liquidity.[90] Indeed, wealthy visitors seeking advice at his hermitage frequently gave Wulfric money and material benefits when they sought advice at his hermitage. But John is at pains to show Wulfric as a conduit not only of worldly things (*carnalia*), which he dispensed to 'Christ's poor men of Forde [the Cistercians]', to put to the service of piety (*serviens pietati*), but he 'poured out on them the wealth of his simplicity, for he held them especially close in God's love, and reverenced them as angels'.[91]

The responsible handling by religious of worldly resources required extreme care, a predicament nicely summed up by Ailred in his pastoral advice to Yvo, a monk and spiritual friend of Warden Abbey, 'not to neglect wholly the

---

[87] Walter Daniel, *Life of Ailred of Rievaulx* ed. and trans. Powicke, 28: In synodis iubet illum antistes sermonem facere ad clericos... quia noverat hoc illo in tempore militibus prodesse et monachis... quia omnis terra malorum malicia cede ac vastatione turbata et confusa prope modum redacta fuerat in desertum.

[88] R. Faith, *The English Peasantry and the Growth of Lordship* (Leicester, 1997), 189, 251–2; and P. Hyams, *Kings, Lords and Peasants* (Oxford, 1980).

[89] Orderic Vitalis, *The Ecclesiastical History of Orderic Vitalis*, ed. and trans., M. Chibnall (6 vols, Oxford, 1969–80), iv, 312–13: sed plures eius hypocritae seductoriique simulatores permiscentur.

[90] *John of Forde, The Life of Wulfric of Haselbury, Anchorite*, trans. P. Matarasso Collegeville, MN, 2011). For Drogo de Munci, see 150–1 [ed. Bell, 65], and for Robert of Cirencester, 197–8 [ed. Bell, 88].

[91] John of Forde, *The Life of Wulfric*, trans. Matarasso, 151 [ed. Bell, 65]: In pauperes etiam Christi de Forda in divitiis simplicitatis suae liberaliter abundavit eo quod in caritate Dei specialiter eos amplexaretur et sicut angelos Deo veneraretur.

contemplation of god for the sake of our neighbor's welfare, nor again to neglect our neighbor's welfare for the delights of contemplation... Above all, never rely on your own unaided judgment to discern the time of these spiritual alterations, that is to say, when you are to go down to Nazareth, or go up to Jerusalem, but always ask the advice of your elders.'[92]

Cistercians had friends in high places, and in even higher places; but they kept their feet on the ground. The angelic economy they practiced and envisioned for the hermits about whom they wrote promoted peace as a kind of communism of the elite. At the same time, through this reservoir of angelic labour filled by the actions of hermits like Wulfric, they also intruded new patterns of work, scales of production, divisions of labour, and distributive opportunities upon the livelihoods of local communities.

These developments in resource management stimulated a keen interest in measurement of values, material and spiritual. Cistercian hagiography is littered with the language of measuring of lands, the exchange of gifts, tokens, and money, and the payment of debt. We have already heard from Ailred about recluses dispensing charity in the community. Walter Daniel cites Wisdom 11:21 in saying that 'For them [the Cistercians] everything is fixed by weight, measure and number.'[93] During the day Wulfric would pay what was owed to nature in the matter of sleep 'as with dues meted out by weight and measure'.[94] Emmeline of Chinnock sent Wulfric loaves of bread 'the gracious kindness (*munus*) having become like a rent (*pensio*) to be paid at due times'.[95] Another woman sent silk to cover a psalter and faithfully paid Wulfric, even after his death, an annual due at the right season by visiting him on pilgrimage from Kent.[96] John notes of Wulfric of Hazelbury that although 'he lauded the order to the heavens', he still criticized them for the fact that they 'exploit gifts, that is, properties, in their jurisdiction over-freely' and 'in the case of those committed to their patronage, seemed insufficiently mindful of what was due to kindness'.[97] Interestingly, however, these deficiencies did not stop him from regarding them as '*similis eos Angelis Dei*' in their self-denial when it came to food, bodily discipline, clothing, and charity.[98] Before Wulfric became a hermit, he met a beggar who predicted he would find in his purse coins newly minted by Henry I's moneyers. 'There is good reason to believe that this man was an angel of

---

[92] Ailred of Rievaulx, *On Jesus at the Age of Twelve*, in, *Treatises and Pastoral Prayer*, ed. M.B. Pennington (Kalamazoo, MI, 1971), 37–9.
[93] Wisdom 11.21, Walter Daniel, *Life of Ailred of Rievaulx*, ed. and trans. Powicke, 11.
[94] John of Forde, *The Life of Wulfric*, trans. Matarasso, 103 [ed. Bell, 18]: in pensionibus fieri consuevit in pondere atque mensura.
[95] John of Forde, *The Life of Wulfric*, trans. Matarasso, 145 [ed. Bell, 62]: cumque voluntarium munus quasi necessarium pensionem solveret temporibus suis.
[96] John of Forde, *The Life of Wulfric*, trans. Matarasso, 214.
[97] John of Forde, *The Life of Wulfric*, trans. Matarasso, 152 [ed. Bell, 66]: professionem hanc summis laudibus attollens... quod in datis videlicet possessionibus liberius suo jure uterentur, et magis attendentes quod licet quam quod expedit, in causa hominum qui eorum patrocinio commendato sunt non quod satis est pietatis recordari viderentur.
[98] John of Forde, *The Life of Wulfric*, trans. Matarasso, 152.

the lord pointing toward the new man he was asking for in terms of a new currency.'[99] Wulfric's 'reverencing of the poor of Forde as angels', his criticisms of Cistercian harshness, and his redistributions of money are intriguing. Does John of Forde provide enough clues for us to imagine Wulfric as a kind of local credit provider?[100]

He does seem to operate a kind of token or 'truck system' in the community.[101] John of Forde describes, a little hesitantly, Wulfric's miraculous ability to unhitch the ringlets from the penitential hauberk of chainmail gifted to him by Alan fitz Walter, and his habit of distributing them to visitors: 'and still to this day', says John, 'these rings can be found throughout the district in the keeping of the pious who treasure them as a gift – a testimony to holiness or a guarantee of health – either way a sacred and sure deposit'.[102] Thus Wulfric illustrated the biblical image of the turning of the 'arms of the world into weapons of righteousness'.[103] This kind of practice, evidence for which exists for other hermits, marks a point of conversion between Bisson's theme of the 'experience of power', and that of West's 'reifications of power'.[104] It shows how the presence of angelic men like Wulfric made moral and material hierarchies symbolically visible in their communities. Wulfric's tokens or pledges (*pignora*) were media of exchange that helped to create patron–client relations. These, in turn, enabled resource transfers in increasingly unequal and socially mobile societies, where livelihoods were under threat, many were vulnerable to arbitrary violence, and others were one step from disaster.

The activities of the Exchequer, so systematically detailed in the *Dialogus de Scaccario*, were analogously understood, perhaps with Wulfric's chainmail rings in mind, as pious work as well as statecraft. Its author, Richard fitz Nigel – whose father, Nigel, bishop of Ely, was, like Walter Espec (the founder of Rievaulx), one of Henry I's new men, who helped to restore the fiscal system in the early reign of Henry II, and who at least once visited a hermit called Godric of Throckmorton – seemed to think so: 'In the whole account of the exchequer, holy mysteries hide themselves.'[105] Henry's second wife, Adelizia of Louvain, begged her king to visit Wulfric, 'who by his prayers and merits could confer

---

99 John of Forde, *The Life of Wulfric*, trans. Matarasso, 98–9 [ed. Bell, 14]: Non immerito is angelus domino fuisse credendus est, novum hominem significans et expetens simul in nummo novo.
100 To reprise a question first posed by Henry Mayr-Harting in his 'Functions of a Twelfth-Century Recluse', *History* 60 (1975), 337–52 at 343.
101 A 'truck system' was a kind of closed economic system in which workers would be paid in goods or in tokens redeemable for goods.
102 John of Forde, *The Life of Wulfric*, trans. Matarasso 110 [ed. Bell, 24]: Useque nunc annuli hi in minibus piorum passim per regionem istam, magni scilicet instar muneris atque ad testimonium et memoriam sanctitatis, seu etiam ad sanitatum compendia, sacrum et fidele depositum.
103 Romans 6:13.
104 Bisson, *The Crisis of the Twelfth Century*, 84–181, and West, *Reframing the Feudal Revolution*, 184–98.
105 *Dialogus de* Scaccario. *The Dialogue of the Exchequer; Constitutio Domus Regis:*

great benefit both on himself and on his kingdom'.[106] Management of the royal fisc, like that of pious gifts to monks and hermits, was a dispensation intrinsically linked to the king's ethical projection of 'prudence, fortitude, temperance and justice'; his duty was 'not hoarding treasure but spending it as it should be spent, in due place and time and on fit persons'.[107] Richard fitz Nigel praises the king for consulting with his father, Nigel, hoping that 'with your generous hand, obeying your noble mind, you may spend to the best advantage'.[108]

Hermits and anchorites were among those fit persons on the king's payroll, as Thomas Licence has argued, because 'In a sin-troubled age, *anchoresis* was set to become a new gold standard for holiness.'[109] The economic metaphor here is suggestive in its deliberate anachronism, especially when we add Adeliza's advice to her husband to the evidence of the Pipe Rolls.[110] Of course, hermits did not literally act as a 'gold standard' fixing the value of media of commercial exchange. Nor, I suspect, is it useful to think of twelfth-century society's increased sensitivity to sin and experimentation with new forms of penance, as if it were an issue of demand or supply.[111] However, the metaphor makes more sense if we see economy as the governance of resources rather than exchange activity in the market. In these broader terms, economy becomes the working through of functional differences in governance through discrete value forms rendered poetically continuous, convertible, and translatable through the work of metaphorical association carried out by the authors of our texts, themselves seeking new providential idioms to describe new social relations in an increasingly hierarchical, urbanized, and commercialized world.

In these terms, sin, devotion, the earmarking of land, money, gifts or other kindnesses for particular sacred outlets, were opportunities to initiate terms of dependence or association with a lord, a monastery, a local cult, a priest, or hermit, to solicit their patronage, moral warrant, care, and potential material benefit. For example, the niece of a hermit called Godric, Wulfgifu Greve, was famous for her meads and ales. At her request, Godric prayed for her and was told by a dove that she was free of her sins. He told her the news and instructed her to increase

---

Disposition of the King's Household, ed. E. Amt and S.D. Church (Oxford, 2007), 39–40: in tota scaccarii descriptione sacramentorum quedam latibula sunt.

[106] John of Forde, *The Life of Wulfric*, trans. Matarasso, 150 [ed. Bell, 64]: qui orationibus et meritis suis ipsi multum conferre posset et regno eius.

[107] *Dialogus de Scaccario*, ed. Amt and Church, 2–3: prudentia, fortitudine, temperantia sive iustitia... non parcentem quidem pecuniae thesauris, set pro loco, pro tempore, pro personis legittimis sumptibus insistentem.

[108] *Dialogus de Scaccario*, ed. Amt and Church, 4: que possit oportune nobilissime mentis tue ministra manus effundere.

[109] T. Licence, *Hermits and Recluses in English Society, 950–1200* (Oxford, 2011), 114.

[110] Licence, *Hermits and Recluses*, 86, and A.K. Warren, *Anchorites and their Patrons in Medieval England* (Berkeley, CA, 1985), 130–46.

[111] That is, whether the religious were meeting rising lay demand for forgiveness or were themselves increasingly intolerant of lay behavior seems difficult to reduce to historical explanation.

the measure of brew she was accustomed to serve.[112] This was a gendered as well as hierarchical economy within which circulated tokens, pledges, money, and bodily gesture and affliction, linking family, lord, monastery, and king, where diffuse social relationships encountered the problems of the peace, where sin was instrumentalized, and informal dispensations diffusely conferred. It was a world in which angels could be administrators and administrators angels.

Conclusions

In this essay I have explored an aporia at the heart of Wilsonian progressivism, impressions of which are left in the legacy of Charles Homer Haskins, both in his invention of modern American medievalism, and in his reflections on the problems of the peace in the wake of the First World War. In short, it is the predicament described above by Matthew Specter as the disavowed shadow-side of liberalism that, according to Jonathon Kahn, bases American liberal constitutionalism upon 'racialized and anti-black' sacred foundations.[113] Those troubled by this idea might be asked: how much 'peace' can old, invented truths bear before they break, and what is the price, and what is the value of a new peace to those seeking justice and moral order?

In the face of such questions, I am inspired by Janet Nelson's call for an *aggiornamento* in the field of medieval history, and Joan Scott's subjection of the nation-state to radical historiographical reckoning, to propose Agamben's notion of economic theology as a means to interrogate that aporia and address racial injustice, nostalgia, xenophobia, boosterism, and rapture as national destiny, to which it is vulnerable. Here 'economic theology' designates an area of historical enquiry spanning the state in its broadest civic sense, as a complex of judicial, legislative, and fiscal systems in the modern western tradition, *and* those religious orders, beliefs, and practices, normally treated separately within that tradition. I have used examples of Angevin 'angels' as a case study of the state as a complex entanglement of Weberian routine and sacred, providential idioms and the potential of this 'synoptic' approach to yield insights.

When we return to Haskins and Strayer's work and to the political theology of Kantorowicz in the light of this example, soteriological continuities submerged within modern American medievalism become visible. Inasmuch as they envisioned a medieval civilization of Normans and Franks, Haskins and Strayer, although White Ango-Saxon Protestants, were not Angles. But angels? In answering this question, I might consult my *Celestial Hierarchy* and suggest that they were Powers, that is, they felt it their duty to go into the darkness and dwell in its profound moral ambiguity, in a sincere and undoubtedly fallible,

---

[112] T. Licence, 'The Life and Miracles of Godric of Throckenholt', *Analecta Bollandiana* 124 (2006), 15–43 at 37.
[113] Jonathon Kahn, 'At the End of Liberal Theory', Political Theology Network, 30 July 2019, https://politicaltheology.com/at-the-end-of-liberal-theory/; and P.W. Kahn, *Political Theology Four New Chapters on the Concept of Sovereignty* (Ithaca, NY, 2012).

attempt to mitigate its worst effects. To those Powers might be added the glory of the Virtues, those angels who 'arouse the sluggish hearts of men with signs', and who might teach us how to mourn as well as love the state.[114] Among them, members of that great American lineage culminating in the Black Lives Matter movement, including W.E.B. Du Bois, with his pageants and spirituals, Gil Scott-Heron, pioneer of rap and hip hop, Toni Morrison, poet of moral dignity and fortitude in struggle, and Supreme Court Justice Sonia Sottomeyer, reviser of Princeton University's motto,[115] offer an economic theology to reckon with liberal white supremacy, and that all medieval historians might use to contemplate 'the problems of the peace' in our own moment.

---

[114] See note 89.
[115] In 2016, Princeton University added the phrase 'And the service of humanity' to its original motto, 'In the Nation's Service', upon her suggestion at the Woodrow Wilson Award Day, 2014. I want to thank Prof. Lester Little for drawing this to my attention, and for his generous, moving, and invaluable advice and comments on this essay, and to apologize for my shameful failure promptly to thank him for it at the time.

6

Purgatory Revisited

Carl Watkins

It is forty years since Jacques Le Goff traced the emergence of 'the middle place' to the twelfth and thirteenth centuries in his seminal book *The Birth of Purgatory*.[1] The book's provocative analysis famously pinpointed the coinage of the noun *purgatorium* and a process of 'spatialization' as central to the construction of a new geography of the afterlife by the Church of the High Middle Ages. At this time the otherworld ceased to comprise many 'tiny receptacles', and in their place there loomed up 'vast territories'.[2] The dissemination of knowledge of this new geography through preaching and teaching was, in Le Goff's analysis, culturally transformatory, helping to usher in a late medieval order in which the living, bound by obligations of memory and prayer, were in service of the dead.

Le Goff's thesis was almost immediately the object of a good deal of criticism.[3] Graham Edwards and Claude Carozzi argued for a much earlier gestation of the idea of purgatory, and Aron Gurevich suggested Le Goff had given too much weight to theology in explaining the idea's development.[4] Medievalists have since elaborated such critiques. Isabel Moreira has fleshed out arguments for the development of purgatory during the early Middle Ages, attaching particular significance in its development to the writings of Bede.[5] Peter Brown has developed a broader argument that a new style of Christianity began to take hold in the later sixth and seventh centuries in which 'a more sharply focused emphasis

---

[1] J. Le Goff, *La Naissance du purgatoire* (Paris, 1981); *The Birth of Purgatory*, trans. A. Goldhammer (London, 1984); see also for my own earlier contributions to aspects of the debate Carl Watkins, 'Doctrine, Politics and Purgation', *JMH* 22 (1996), 225–36; and Carl Watkins, 'Sin, Penance and Purgatory in the Anglo-Norman Realm: the evidence of visions and ghost stories', *PP* 175 (2002), 3–33.
[2] Le Goff, *Purgatory*, esp. 154–76, 362–6.
[3] R. W. Southern, 'Between Heaven and Hell', *Times Literary Supplement* (1982), 651–2.
[4] C. Carozzi, 'La géographie de l'au delà et sa signification pendant le haut moyen âge', in *Popoli e paesi nella cultura altomedievale*, Settimane di studio del Centro italiano di studi sull'alto medioevo 29 (1983), 423–81; G.R. Edwards, 'Purgatory: Birth or Evolution', *JEH* 36 (1985), 634–46; Aron J. Gurevich, 'Popular and Scholarly Medieval Cultural Traditions: Notes in the Margins of Jacques Le Goff's Book', *JMH* 9 (1983), 71–90.
[5] Isabel Moreira, *Heaven's Purge: Purgatory in Late Antiquity* (Oxford, 2010).

on the world beyond the grave' is a prominent feature.⁶ Brown's identification of this cultural watershed helps to turn the period from the late sixth century through to the end of the Middle Ages into a continuum after the great fracture of those early centuries sundered late antique Christianity decisively from its medieval successor. Where Le Goff had placed the moment of decisive change in the High Middle Ages, recent work has located it in Late Antiquity and the early Middle Ages. What remained for the twelfth and thirteenth centuries was therefore not so much invention as the theological rationalization of ideas about otherworld space that had already been developed.

This revisionist backdating makes a great deal of sense, but one element of Le Goff's argument that has remained relatively resistant to criticism is his suggestion that a clarified geography – even a cartography – of the afterlife was at the heart of purgatory's tightening hold on high and late medieval imaginations. The notion of the 'geography of the afterlife', and that this geography acquired sharper definition during the Middle Ages, has remained potent in historiographical terms. Indeed, it is striking that a number of early medievalists have measured the rudimentary post-mortem geographies in their own period against what they assume to be the clarity of 'mature' conceptualizations of the later Middle Ages. Isabel Moreira notes that no normative position on the place of the dead had taken hold in the early medieval period, implying that this was a characteristic that differentiated it from what came later.⁷ Sarah Foot, in contesting the notion that an idea of purgatory was to be found in Anglo-Saxon England, set the undeveloped (and sometimes contradictory) early accounts of the geography of the afterlife against the putative clarity of its late medieval successor.⁸ Richard Sowerby has also noted that 'late antique and early medieval Christians possessed no single, uniform picture that looked like the tripartite otherworld ... adhered to by late medieval Christians'.⁹

Some historians writing about the later period, however, have observed that too much attention may have been concentrated on the idea of purgatory as a defined 'space'. R.N. Swanson has noted the importance of purgatory as *state of being*, and Robert Mills has suggested that it mattered more as *time* rather than place.¹⁰ In this essay, I explore purgatory in the imagination of the twelfth and

---

⁶ Peter Brown, 'Gloriosus Obitus: The End of the Ancient Other World', in *The Limits of Ancient Christianity: Essays on Late Antique Thought and Culture in Honor of R.A. Markus*, ed. W. Klingshirn and M. Vessey (Ann Arbor, MI, 1999), 289–314; Peter Brown, *The Ransom of the Soul: Afterlife and Wealth in Early Western Christianity* (Cambridge, MA, 2015), 201–11.
⁷ Isabel Moreira, 'Purgatory's Intercessors: Bishops, Ghosts and Angry Wives', in *Imagining the Medieval Afterlife*, ed. Richard M. Pollard (Cambridge, 2020), 133–52 at 134.
⁸ Sarah Foot, 'Anglo-Saxon "Purgatory"', in *The Church, the Afterlife and the Fate of the Soul*, ed. Peter Clarke and Tony Claydon (Woodbridge, 2009), 87–96 at 96.
⁹ Richard Sowerby, *Angels in Early Medieval England* (Oxford, 2016), 113.
¹⁰ Robert N. Swanson, *Indulgences in Late Medieval England: Passports to Paradise?* (Cambridge, 2007); Robert Mills, 'God's Time? Purgatory and Temporality in Late Medieval Art', in *Time and Eternity: The Medieval Discourse*, ed. G. Jaritz and G. Moreno-Riano (Turnhout, 2003), 477–98.

thirteenth centuries and suggest that purgatory mattered to the Church primarily as a state or condition, about which there was growing clarity and coherence, whereas visual and spatial conceptualizations of place continued to be various.

If purgatory was, in fact, 'designed' as a distinctive space by theologians of the twelfth and thirteenth centuries and then preached by the Church, as Le Goff suggested, then we run into a number of difficulties. Here, it is worth dwelling on evidence for an ongoing *lack* of agreement about post-mortem geography even among theologians at work in the thirteenth century – men such as William of Auvergne, Alexander of Hales, Bonaventure, and Thomas Aquinas, all of whom were considered by Le Goff.[11] For if there was a measure of clarity in the writings of some individual authors, there was certainly no agreement between them. It is also striking that the question of the place, or places, of purgation was never central to their analyses. They had other emphases such as: Who was in the purgatorial state? What was the nature of the fire? How do suffrages help souls?[12] Le Goff's own summary is notable in this respect: theologians of this period, he says, were 'doubtful about [Purgatory's] location and discreet as to its more concrete manifestations, affording it a relatively minor place in their theological systems'.[13] This is a rather surprising synopsis of the thought of leading theologians in the very century during which ideas about 'purgatory-the-place' were supposedly systematized. If we turn our gaze to the famous papal pronouncements on the topic of purgatory, these, too, are, in fact, rather ambiguous. For example, while Innocent IV sent a letter to his legate to the Greeks in 1254 identifying the place of purgation as purgatory, the Church's conciliar statement of 1274 was worded more vaguely, without explicit reference to 'purgatory-the-place' or even to the idea of purgatorial fire.[14]

If there was ambiguity in theology and conciliar statements then one should probably not expect greater clarity in the Church's instructional materials. And lack of clarity is indeed what we find. The great homiletic collection *Legenda Aurea* illustrates the point. Offering morally improving readings on the lives of the saints, it was composed in the second half of the thirteenth century by Jacobus de Voragine and circulated very widely in the later Middle Ages in both Latin and vernacular translations. Its material for the commemoration of All Souls was, unsurprisingly, taken as an opportunity to expound in some detail the fate of the dead. Yet, although we do find in these portions of *Legenda Aurea* precision about the theology of purgation, they contain precious little certainty about place.[15] Where purgatory was, where purgation might happen: these were still open questions.

The same is true of *exempla*. There is little instruction about 'purgatory-the-place' in *exempla*-collections of the thirteenth century, such as those produced

---

[11] Le Goff, *Purgatory*, 241–56, 266–78.
[12] Le Goff, *Purgatory*, 263.
[13] Le Goff, *Purgatory*, 266.
[14] Le Goff, *Purgatory*, 283–6.
[15] *The Golden Legend: Readings on the Saints*, chapter 163, trans. W. Granger Ryan (2 vols, Princeton, NJ, 2012), ii, 280–90.

by Caesarius of Heisterbach, Jacques de Vitry,[16] and Stephen of Bourbon.[17] Le Goff had suggested that friars were in the vanguard of disseminating news of purgatory's birth, but it is far from clear that they were nearly as deeply engaged in this enterprise as he supposed.[18] For example, the anonymous authors of two early mendicant collections of *exempla* from the British Isles – the *Liber Exemplorum*, which was the work of a Franciscan writing probably between 1275 and 1279,[19] and the so-called Cambridge Dominican collection, likely completed between 1270 and 1292[20] – make little attempt to expound post-mortem geography. This pattern of inattention repeats in *exempla* of the fourteenth and fifteenth centuries, too, and so one cannot argue that one needs to look at later evidence because the work of evangelization began at a later date.[21] Evidence from other genres corroborates this impression. 'Purgatory-the-place' is rarely a subject tackled in late medieval sermons,[22] and, as Paul Binski and others have observed, it does not figure very prominently in later medieval art.[23]

An inspection of high and late medieval evidence suggests that late medieval teachers thought their audiences did not need to be told about a place called purgatory. It may be that they were confident that they already knew about it thanks to its long gestation in the early Middle Ages. Or it may be because they anticipated that their audiences were equipped with a concept of purgatorial suffering and so preaching about a unitary place in which it happened was superfluous rather than, as Le Goff suggested, an important tool that facilitated instruction about a new idea. That the geography of the hereafter remained inchoate even at the very end of the Middle Ages might point us towards the latter conclusion rather than the former.[24] For although late medieval authors depended on a shared repertoire of images – pits of fire, boiling rivers – their sense of how these elements fitted together to form otherworldly space was not necessarily any clearer than that of their early medieval counterparts. It might, then, be a mistake to see the High and Late Middle Ages as periods of consolidation, in which a clarified geography of the afterlife came into being. Indeed, our readiness to think and write about the afterlife using the language of geography

---

[16] *The Exempla or Illustrative stories from the Sermones Vulgares of Jacques de Vitry*, ed. Thomas F. Crane (London, 1890).
[17] *Anecdotes historiques, légendes et apologues tirés du recueil inédit d'Étienne de Bourbon, Dominicain du XIIIe siècle*, ed. A. Lecoy de La Marche (Paris, 1877).
[18] Le Goff, *Purgatory*, 300.
[19] *Liber Exemplorum ad usum praedicantium saeculo xiii compositus a quodam Fratre Minore anglico de provincia Hiberniae*, ed. A.G. Little (Aberdeen, 1908).
[20] S.D. Forte, 'A Cambridge Dominican Collector of Exempla in the Thirteenth Century', *Archivum Fratrum Praedicatorum* 28 (1958), 115–48.
[21] Carl Watkins, 'Landscapes of the Dead in the Late Medieval Imagination', *JMH* 48 (2022), 250–64.
[22] Watkins, 'Landscapes', 252–3.
[23] Paul Binski, *Medieval Death: Ritual and Representation* (London, 1996), 70. For a qualification and the risk of under-counting artistic representations, see Mills, 'God's Time'.
[24] For this point, see Watkins, 'Landscapes', 254–8.

and cartography might risk making it more difficult to recover how medieval men and women actually conceptualized the soul's fate.

One place where clarity about the space of purgation might be expected is in those most obviously 'geographical' of writings about the afterlife, vision-narratives. Indeed, these accounts, which proliferated during the High Middle Ages, might plausibly be expected to communicate messages about the tripartite division of the afterlife into heaven, hell and purgatory. It is worth dwelling for a moment, however, on the evidence, or rather the absence of evidence, of visions discharging such a function. The Vision of Owein at St Patrick's Purgatory, recorded in the *Tractatus de Purgatorio Sancti Patricii*, is an important case. Written by a Cistercian monk of Sawtry in the 1180s it relates how the knight, Owein, passed through a cave into the subterranean realm in which St Patrick, centuries before, had been shown the fate of the dead.[25] Its extraordinary popularity in the later Middle Ages, in Latin and many vernaculars, makes it appear, on first inspection, a plausible vector for spreading new ideas.[26] But while its prologue declared that 'there is after death a punishment that is called purgatorial', the 'Purgatory' of the *Tractatus* seems to add up to little more than the Pit itself.[27] The author explained that 'material punishments are prepared by God' for the re-embodied souls of the dead, and that 'material places have been arranged where these punishments can take place'.[28] This line of thinking also leads the monk of Sawtry to argue that his vision bears out Augustine's claim that the dead were detained in various receptacles of pain and rest before the general judgement. The monk's recurrence to authorities is, as Robert Easting has pointed out, seemingly born of a discomfort about one especially unusual characteristic of his story, namely that Owein had entered the afterlife in the flesh rather than, as was customary among visionaries, in a dream or trance.[29] But the author's readiness to concede at the very outset that there were many places of pain and rest – not a single purgatory – as the price of Augustine's endorsement suggests the minimal importance of the theme of 'purgatory-the-place' in his message.

Many of the other popular vision-narratives of the High and Late Middle Ages also do not have a clearly delineated purgatorial space; in fact, most of them do not. The early thirteenth-century Vision of Thurkill is the major

[25] *St Patrick's Purgatory: Two Versions of* Owayne Miles *and the* Vision of William Stranton *Together with the Long Text of the* Tractatus de Purgatorio Sancti Patricii, ed. Robert Easting (Oxford, 1991), 121–54.
[26] Le Goff, *Purgatory*, 193–201. Note also that it is 'one of the most widely disseminated texts in the Middle Ages, with 170 Latin MSS and translations into some thirty languages'; Aisling Byrne, *Otherworlds: Fantasy and History in Medieval Literature* (Oxford, 2016), 74.
[27] *St Patrick's Purgatory*, ed. Easting, 122: 'pena tamen post mortem esse dicitur, que purgatoria nominatur'.
[28] *St Patrick's Purgatory*, ed. Easting, 122: '… a Deo corporales pene dicuntur preparate, ita ipsis penis loca corporalia, in quibus sunt, dicuntur esse distincta'.
[29] Robert Easting, *Visions of the Otherworld in Middle English* (Cambridge, 1997), 44; see also Byrne, *Otherworlds*, 75–7.

exception.³⁰ Peter of Cornwall uses the verb *purgare* in the Vision of Ailsi, and purgation is very clearly present in his visualization of souls whose sins are progressively boiled away in a superheated river, but the noun *purgatorium* does not appear.³¹ Although the word *does* appear in the Vision of the Monk of Eynsham it is used only seldom, and there is little sense that one is being instructed in this vision about a new space.³² In the Vision of Tundal, which was composed in the middle of the twelfth century and vies with that of Owein in terms of numbers of extant manuscript copies, the hereafter was split into five principal and additional subsidiary spaces within each of which was placed a distinct group.³³ There were sinners (with tailored punishments) and the meritorious (martyrs or faithful spouses), and there was also room in this scheme for custom-made compartments, where, for example, punishments were visited on named Irish kings in order to make a political point.³⁴ Tundal's vision comprised loose-linked theological and didactic vignettes, forming not so much a route-map as a moral compass. What is perhaps more interesting is that even in later copies, translations and reworkings of these visions there is only very limited interest in clarifying all this spatial complexity.³⁵

We do sometimes find authors reaching for the word purgatory as a portmanteau term in what appears to be a kind of linguistic tidying. The author of the *South English Legendary* (1275x85) offers the best example of this. He epitomized the Vision of Owein and, in so doing, rebranded the 'places of torment' as 'pultatorie'.³⁶ But even here, when the same author got to a more detailed exposition in his 'Sermon for All Souls Day', he portrayed an afterlife that was more spatially complicated but less firmly defined, allowing for some five purgatorial places where souls (*gostes*) suffer: 'in the firmament'; in the air; in water; 'under the earth deep, beside hell'; and 'on earth, among us'.³⁷ Even in vision-narratives and even regarding the big building blocks of post-mortem space, therefore, we are not on a trajectory of 'growing clarity' about otherworldly geography.

At the level of more granular topographical detail, too, we find not convergence but rich plurality in the portrayal of the soul's fate. Visions of the twelfth and thirteenth centuries continued very frequently to suggest the soul's motion

---

30 On the exceptionality of Thurkill, see Alison Morgan, *Dante and the Medieval Other World* (Cambridge, 1990), 155–6.
31 *Peter of Cornwall's Book of Revelations*, ed. and trans. R. Sharpe and R. Easting (Toronto, 2013), 206–08. Peter uses the verb *purgare* only once, more generally using *punio* or formulations in which he describes *poena* or *tormentum*.
32 A point made in B.P. McGuire, 'Purgatory, the Communion of Saints and Medieval Change', *Viator* 20 (1989), 61–84 at 81.
33 *Visio Tnugdali: lateinisch und altdeutsch*, ed. Albrecht Wagner (Erlangen, 1882).
34 *Visio Tnugdali*, ed. Wagner, 42–5.
35 Watkins, 'Landscapes', 254–8; Takami Matsuda, *Death and Purgatory in Middle English Didactic Poetry* (Cambridge, 1997), 39–45, 52.
36 *South English Legendary*, ed. Charlotte D'Evelyn and Anna J. Mill (3 vols, Oxford, 1956), iii, 85–110.
37 For this point, see Matsuda, *Death and Purgatory*, 80–2.

happened in space that possessed only weak and shifting definition. Of course, space *was* still implicated in projecting the soul's fate. The 'otherworld journeys' recounted by vision-narrators reveal death conceptualized as longitudinal extension and onward motion; a forward momentum of a re-embodied soul. Yet we find that, in the vision-narratives, while the authors conceptualized the fate of the soul *in* space, they did not attempt the conceptualization *of* space. In the Vision of Charles the Fat as recorded by William of Malmesbury the afterlife is maze-like. The visionary entered labyrinthine space armed with a clue so that he might find his way back out again.[38] As they go deeper, visionaries often have only the haziest notion of where they are or of directions of travel. The course of the knight Owein's journey was, for example, plotted vaguely, at one point heading towards the 'midsummer sunset' and then, later, towards the midwinter one.[39] Indeed, few visionaries seem to have known where they were going. None is shown to have had a map in their heads. Richard Sowerby notes of early medieval visions how souls were lost as they left the body, depending on angelic guides to orientate them in uncertain space.[40] Some of that same uncertainty prevails in later visions, too. Practically all visionaries relied on a guide, whether saint or angel, to show them the way, a dependency dramatized in many examples by the guide's sudden, but temporary, disappearance that leaves the soul-traveler unmoored in an immensity of indeterminate space and unsure where to turn.

What then is the relationship between the varied accounts of post-mortem space presented in vision-narratives and contemporary perceptions of the authenticity of the visionaries' claims? In raising this question, I am mindful that at the beginning of the Reformation Protestant polemicists also exposed differences in portrayals of the afterlife as contradictions in order to call into question the Catholic Church's teachings about the fate of the soul.[41] But these differences, though they became grist to the mill of Protestant polemic, somehow remained latent and un-activated during the Middle Ages. This was so even though medieval vision-writers were eager to authenticate new visions by referencing established ones, whether by way of simple mention or through collecting examples together in a single manuscript, the texts constituting a network of mutual support. This practice suggests that vision-writers were comfortable with the fact that the visions that they recorded and referenced often revealed very different things. For example, Simeon of Durham (d. after 1129) recorded in his *Libellus* a vision ascribed to a man called Eadwulf.[42] He noted

---

[38] William of Malmesbury, *Gesta regum Anglorum*, ed. and trans. R.A.B. Mynors, R.M. Thomson and M. Winterbottom (2 vols, Oxford, 1998–9), i, 162–71.
[39] *St Patrick's Purgatory*, ed. Easting, 130.
[40] Sowerby, *Angels*, 110–16.
[41] Marshall, 'Map of God's Word', 113–16; Peter Marshall, *Beliefs and the Dead in Reformation England* (Oxford, 2002), 53–64.
[42] Simeon of Durham, *Libellus de exordio atque procursu istius, hoc est Dunhelmensis, ecclesie: Tract on the Origins and Progress of this the Church of Durham*, ed. and trans. David Rollason (Oxford, 2000), 211–18.

that 'almost the same miracle happened in the province of the Northumbrians', associating Eadwulf's vision with Bede's account of Dryhthelm's, but it seems not to have bothered Simeon that the topography of his new vision had only the weakest resemblance to that recorded by Bede.

This *sang-froid* amidst difference is the more striking because vision-narratives were sometimes mobilized, at least ostensibly, as a means to rebut skepticism. Writing at the start of the thirteenth century, the Augustinian canon Peter of Cornwall revived a version of Gregory the Great's argument that stories of visions and ghosts would win people over who otherwise believed only what could see and touch.[43] He put that claim at the head of his compendious *Book of Revelations*,[44] but then copied stories that seemed to reveal different pictures of the place of the dead. We cannot simply write Peter's book off as the work of a magpie-like collector of stories, unthinkingly gathering whatever materials caught his eye, because he showed himself, in other ways, alert to the danger of false reports and skeptical reactions. For example, he first wrote up the (relatively newly composed) Vision of the Monk of Eynsham but crossed it out.[45] He then changed his mind again and reinstated it. We cannot discern what prompted Peter's reticence (although perennial watchfulness about fakery and delusion likely would surely have played a part) but whatever worried him, it seems unlikely that it was any contradiction between the description of afterlife in the Eynsham account and that offered by others he had recorded. For such contradictions honeycombed the stories that formed his sprawling book. The works of writers such as Symeon of Durham and Peter of Cornwall thus suggest that, *pace* Le Goff, contemporaries 'invested' little intellectual energy in the unification of the 'middle spaces'. Diverse conceptualizations continued to co-exist, and those who read and heard these varied accounts either did not see or successfully accommodated what might seem to be contradictions to a modern reader or Protestant critic.

What, then, were the conditions that permitted different visualizations of the afterlife to co-exist not only freely but seemingly fruitfully? One answer might lie in the manner of reception: visions were not necessarily 'consumed' on the terms set by the churchmen who originally composed them and narratives designed originally to reinforce belief might turn into mere entertainments. Contradictions might disappear when stories were taken up more lightly than we imagine. Indeed, some historians have noted the affinities of visions and romance as evidence that otherworld journeys might have been construed as 'fictions'.[46] It is striking in this connection that the two most widely reproduced vision-narratives

---

[43] Gregory the Great, *Dialogues* III.38 and IV.3, trans. O. Zimmerman (Washington, DC, 1959), 186 and 192.
[44] *Peter of Cornwall*, ed. Sharpe and Easting, 78–87.
[45] *Peter of Cornwall*, ed. Sharpe and Easting, 57–8.
[46] Stephen Greenblatt, *Hamlet in Purgatory* (Princeton, NJ, 2001), 47–9. Byrne observes that later versions of Owein are turned explicitly into romance, a trend evident in Marie de France's version where the work is labelled as *romanz* and *aventure*. See Byrne, *Otherworlds*, 82.

of the later Middle Ages, those of Tundal and Owein, had warrior-heroic figures as their protagonists. Owein, in particular, was a questing knight in spiritualized guise. Not only the content but also context might suggest that visions were read through the prism of romance. At the same time, to see in the dissemination and reception of vision-narratives a process of fictionalization is surely a mistake. Although visions might, in narrative terms, *work* in ways akin to romances, they were *not* like romances in terms of genre. The special imaginative power of the most popular visions, measured in crude terms by extant manuscript copies, must have lain precisely in the marriage of narrative tricks of romance to the claim that this extraordinary story was true. Romance shared with visions the important technique of combining and adapting established elements, recurring elements identified by some literary scholars as medieval antecedents of the modern meme, such that a new story was simultaneously familiar and fresh.[47] Of course, the authors of vision-narratives substituted for enchanted castles and dream-inducing summer glades a grimmer repertory of tormented souls, boiling rivers, passages over test-bridges and scenes in which sin was weighed in the balance, but they were engaging in a similar authorial practice as their romance-writing peers, generating texts in which meaning and power derived not from originality but the novel combination of often familiar elements.[48]

It would be an error, however, to collapse the distance between vision-narrative and romance completely. While shared elements in visions themselves helped to generate a measure of verisimilitude, the hard evidence of authenticity further reinforced the vision-narrator's truth-claim, separating romance from vision. Where the action of romance might be located in indeterminate time, the vision-narrative was much more firmly anchored. Where chains of testimony linking past to present were often broken in romance by remoteness of time or place, in otherworld journeys the line of transmission was detailed and shown to be strong and reliable (and the credentials and the credibility of the visionary were exhaustively rehearsed). Authors noted that even visionaries' bodies sometimes testified to their claims. Those who had entered the afterlife in the flesh sometimes bore the scars to prove it. And some who entered only in spirit nonetheless found that the pains they had experienced were inscribed on the sleeping bodies that they had left behind. So it was perfectly possible for visions to share the storytelling strategies of romance, and even to keep the company of romance between the boards of a single manuscript book, without the 'fictional' connotations of romance bleeding into perceptions of the vision.[49]

---

[47] Cooper, *Romance*, 3–7.

[48] Elizabeth Boyle also notes of Irish vision-narratives that 'unique purpose, sophistication and meaning' are not the product of 'originality' but of the author's selection and combination from a range 'universal archetypes' and 'culturally specific elements' belonging to a 'pre-existing repertoire'. See Elizabeth Boyle, 'The Afterlife in the Medieval Celtic-Speaking World', in *Imagining the Medieval Afterlife*, ed. Pollard, 62–78 at 68.

[49] Byrne also makes the point that many of the tropes shared between romance and

Discrepant visualizations of the soul's fate could also co-exist because what visionaries saw was the shadow and not the truth, a proposition axiomatic to learned discourse but one also likely to have had more general imaginative power. Though visions augmented details about death that were unrevealed in the Bible, these elements were necessarily apprehended by way of limited human senses and cognition. In his prologue to the Vision of Owein, for example, the monk of Sawtry stressed that in revelations everything appeared as if it were concrete.[50] He was, as we have seen, keen to explain how Owein had entered the afterlife in his very body, but he did so by explaining that all visionaries – whether travelling in the spirit or the flesh – necessarily saw material signs of spiritual things so that they could perceive them 'while living in the body and knowing only material things'.[51] Another example is found in the curious Vision of Bricius related by Peter of Cornwall. Here the visionary was led through 'diverse places and torments' but we also learn that things 'as they say, do not happen to him bodily but spiritually in the imagination'.[52] This idea of the limits of perception and cognition was captured in vision-narratives not only abstractly but in experiential ways, too. When visionaries entered the afterlife the authors often emphasized what the visionaries could not see: darkness shrouded them; light dazzled them; vast, indeterminate space unfolded around them, such that its bounds were not visible. A theological argument in vernacular dress, learned and unlearned alike could understand it and share a strong sense that they were exploring insights about the world beyond the grave that they could never fully grasp.

The specific terms in which writers and readers of visions conceptualized the soul's fate further reinforced that awareness of the limitations of what could be known. Travel in this world was, preponderantly, pedestrian. It was also informed by itineraries, sometimes textual but more often mental, rather than the map form. The power of such experience of movement to structure narratives of travel has also been observed in romance where the 'space of romance' was conceived not cartographically but in terms of points plotted along the linear extension of the protagonist's travels.[53] Visions obeyed similar logic. They were *ambulant* experiences. Sarah Foot has observed of early medieval visions that visionaries often walked rather as they might in the countryside.[54] This remains true of later narratives, too. The vision of Tundal, for example, is all about

---

vision are derived from the common stock of the bible. See Byrne, *Otherworlds*, 89.
[50] *St Patrick's Purgatory*, ed. Easting, 122.
[51] *St Patrick's Purgatory*, ed. Easting, 123: 'in corpore uiuentibus et corporalia tantum scientibus'. On the question of the spiritual apprehended in material form and the limits of human cognition see a very valuable discussion in Michael D. Barbezat, '"He Doubted these Things Actually Happened": Knowing the otherworld in the *Tractatus de Purgatorio Sancti Patricii*', *History of Religions* 57 (2018), 321–47.
[52] *Peter of Cornwall*, ed. Sharpe and Easting, 133: 'per diuersa loca et tormenta'; '... non in rei ueritate corporaliter set ymaginarie spiritualiter...'
[53] Cooper, *Romance*, 70.
[54] Foot, 'Anglo-Saxon "Purgatory"', 90.

walking. The visionary moves down paths, traverses narrow ways and crosses test-bridges, one of which, spiked with nails, lacerates his feet, leaving him for a time unable to walk and so unable to go on.[55] This method of portrayal was an invitation for readers to put themselves in the visionaries' shoes. But, of course, if the mechanism of locomotion was familiar, the terrain was radically alien. Not only did impressions of it overwhelm the senses, transcending the powers of language and comprehension as visionaries tried to articulate what they were seeing, but pedestrian exploration, guided through uncertain space, also opened up the possibility of unique routes as well, adding another layer of subjectivity. Final destinations in the otherworld were surely fixed – both the pit of hell and the shining city tended to be described in terms similarly anchored in scriptural language and imagery – but in the nearer reaches of the places of the dead scripture was no certain guide because it had so little to say. It was possible for visionaries to tread different paths and to see different things, maintaining in the gaps between hell and heaven a plurality of possibilities.

The circumstances of purgatory's development might help to explain why the Church accommodated the plurality of ways in which purgation was visualized and emplaced and did not work towards unification. Here it is helpful to see purgatory as not simply an idea emerging over a long span of time, one rooted in early medieval changes of the kinds traced by Peter Brown and Isabel Moreira, but also, as Aron Gurevich observed in his early response to Jacques Le Goff's work, an idea that had long existed in 'popular consciousness' before being 'forced on the attention' of theologians writing in the twelfth and thirteenth centuries.[56] Such an interpretation of purgatorial thinking as something emerging 'from below' still retains at least some of its force, and it makes particular sense if one considers how problems of late repentance and the failure of sinners to make proper amendment during their lives must have been confronted during the early Middle Ages. Exposure to the penitential system became general enough to seed very widely anxieties about how and when – and indeed whether – penance undischarged in life might be completed.[57] Purgatorial punishment resolved the question by locating it after death.[58] It possessed both an emotional and intellectual justification, for how else might the demands of penance be squared with idea of a God who was just, and so required a penalty, but also loving and merciful such that he did not demand damnation as the price of unresolved sin? Bede, in his Vision of Dryhthelm, made the resolution plain at an early date.[59]

---

[55] *Visio Tnugdali*, ed. Wagner, 19 and 22.
[56] Gurevich, 'Cultural Traditions', 71–90.
[57] See Victoria Thompson, 'The Pastoral Contract in Late Anglo-Saxon England: priest and parishioner in Oxford Bodleian Library, MS Laud. Miscellaneous 482', in *Pastoral Care in Late Anglo-Saxon England*, ed. F. Tinti (Woodbridge, 2005), 106–20.
[58] Sarah Foot notes that, amidst the diversity of Anglo-Saxon visions of the otherworld there was convergence on the point that penance left incomplete in life could be completed after death. See Foot, 'Anglo-Saxon "Purgatory"', 89–90 and 94–5.
[59] *Bede's Ecclesiastical History* v.12, ed. and trans. Bertram Colgrave and Roger A.B. Mynors (Oxford, 1969), 488–99; Moreira, *Heaven's Purge*, 147–76.

Dryhthelm witnessed souls suffering pains until Judgment Day in a place that he took to be hell but which his angelic guide explained was not. In this space-that-was-not-hell even grave offences (*scelera*) might be redeemed in fire and ice so long as they had been confessed. Evidence of this genealogy of purgatory is also visible later in the ways in which post-mortem satisfaction was still sometimes conceptualized in penitential terms. The theologian-bishop William of Auvergne, to take just one example, continued in the thirteenth century to construe purgatorial suffering as a sublimation of penance.[60]

This view of purgatory as something more organic, emerging 'from below', helps to make sense of the very different understandings of the place where penance incomplete at death might be fulfilled. Furthermore, the dead continued to be imagined in varied purgatorial conditions not only beyond the world but also within the world.[61] Gervase of Tilbury, writing in the early thirteenth century, told a number of stories about purgatory in *Otia Imperialia*. In one a ghost from Beaucaire described purgatory as a unitary space located in the air, but Gervase suggested the location of the dead was less clear-cut.[62] They lurked 'in the places of punishment' that 'verge and border' on this world, whence they were able to appear to family and friends by divine permission, 'sometimes in dreams, sometimes openly in the semblance of their former bodies', ceasing to appear only when their time in 'purgatory' was done.[63] Such souls might also be trapped in the world, purged of their sins within it rather than around its edges. For Gervase, it seems, there were many purgatorial places but there was a single purgatorial state.

A similar opinion emerges in the roughly contemporary *exempla* of Caesarius of Heisterbach (d. 1240). Caesarius, in addition to the two eternal destinations for the dead, heaven and hell, knew of 'a third place, after this life appointed for some and deputed for their purgation and for that reason called purgatory', one which would exist only for a season, until the Day of Judgment, but, once again, this 'place' had multiple identities and varied locations.[64] When the

---

[60] In *De Uniuerso*. On this point, see Le Goff, *Purgatory*, 242–4.
[61] Victoria Thompson, 'Constructing Salvation: A Homiletic and Penitential Context for Late Anglo-Saxon Burial Practice', in *Burial in Early Medieval England and Wales*, ed. Sam Lucy and Andrew Reynolds (London, 2002), 229–40; Sarah Semple, 'Illustrations of Damnation in Late Anglo-Saxon Manuscripts', *ASE* 32 (2003), 231–45.
[62] See for a different interpretation: Paolo Cherchi, 'Gervase of Tilbury and the Birth of Purgatory', *Medioevo Romanzo* 14 (1989), 97–110.
[63] Gervase of Tilbury, *Otia Imperialia: Recreation for an Emperor*, ed. S.E. Banks and J.W. Binns (Oxford, 2002), 588–91: Asserunt enim animas, quamdiu in locis penalibus quasi nobis vicinis et coniunctis sunt, per visiones nunc sompniorum, nunc manifeste in corporum pristinorum similitudine, ex divina dispensatione cumfinibus et amicis frequenter ut licenter apparere, statusque sui miseriam et necessitate pandere; verum cum ad altiora gaudia purgatorio exacto evecte fuerint, iam ad nostram non se offerunt visionem.
[64] Caesarius of Heisterbach, *Dialogus Miraculorum*, 12.1, ed. J. Strange (2 vols in 1, Köln, 1851), ii, 317–18: Adhuc est tertius locus post hanc vitam quibusdam electis ad purgandum deputans, at a rei purgatorium vocitatus.

monk-narrator of *Dialogus Miraculorum* was asked directly by his interlocutor, a novice, where exactly purgatory was, the monk replied that 'as much as is gathered from various visions, it is in several places of this world'.[65] One of them, he said, was surely St Patrick's Purgatory in Ireland. The monk suggested that any who had 'doubts about purgatory' should go there to have them allayed, leading the excited novice to exclaim 'I would like to know for certain about *that* purgatory...'[66] There were also, as this exchange suggests, other purgatories. Caesarius added stories, for example, about fiery mountains, telling of Stromboli where the soul of a certain deceased steward of Kolmere had been discovered in torment; he encouraged his wife to go on pilgrimage to shrines of the saints and offer up alms and prayers to bring about his release.[67] In other stories Caesarius was alert to the possibility that the dead were purged at the site of their sins. One story had the rubric 'Of the purgatory of a certain Mary in Friesland' suggesting the possibility of customized purgatorial conditions. Caesarius related that when a churchman visited a community of nuns, he encountered one of the dead sisters 'in a place enclosed by walls, in which he heard very great sighing and groaning'.[68] Such stories of purgatories – whether the Pit of St Patrick in Ireland, the volcanic mountains of the Mediterranean, or the fiery lava flows of Iceland, or the personal place of purgation in the interstices of the everyday – persisted in the later Middle Ages, but they represent, not confusion or odd hold outs in the face of an otherwise unified and accepted notion of purgatorial space but an accepted and expected spatial plurality.[69]

Convictions about purgatorial suffering in the world enjoyed at least a measure of theological approbation, having been authorized by no less a figure than Gregory the Great who had allowed in the fourth book of his *Dialogues* that the dead might suffer temporal punishment in the midst of the living, telling, for example, a story of a soul constrained to labour as a ghostly bath-attendant in lieu of penance incomplete at death.[70] The pattern suggested by Gregory persisted, and his stories continued to be widely recapitulated. Caesarius turned to them in his discussion of the fates of the dead as did Jacobus de Voragine in the *Legenda Aurea*, which proliferated in vernacular manuscript, and later

---

[65] Caesarius of Heisterbach, *Dialogus Miraculorum*, 12.38, ed. Strange, ii, 347: Ubi est purgatorium? ... Quantum ex variis colligitur uisionibus, in diuersis locis huius mundi.
[66] Caesarius of Heisterbach, *Dialogus Miraculorum*, 12.38, ed. Strange, ii, 347: Qui uero de purgatorio dubitat... Vellem aliquid certe nosse de eodem purgatorio...
[67] Caesarius of Heisterbach, *Dialogus Miraculorum*, 12.7, ed. Strange, ii, 322. Caesarius also suggests elsewhere that volcanic mountains are infernal rather than purgatorial, characterizing them as the 'jaws of hell'. See Caesarius of Heisterbach, *Dialogus Miraculorum*, 12.13, ed. Strange, ii, 325–6.
[68] Caesarius of Heisterbach, *Dialogus Miraculorum*, 12.26, ed. Strange, II, pp. 337–8: 'De purgatorio cuiusdam Mariae in Frisia', 'Videbatur sibi esse in quodam loco parietibus clause, in quo quidem grauissima suspiria et gemitus audiuit'. See other examples: 12.30, 12.31.
[69] For example, 'Twelve Medieval Ghost Stories', ed. Montague Rhodes James, *EHR* 37 (1922), 413–22.
[70] Gregory the Great, *Dialogues* iv.42, 249–50.

print, versions down to the end of the Middle Ages.⁷¹ In the *Supplementum* ascribed to Thomas Aquinas (but completed by others after his death), too, although the author rejected the notion that souls might suffer post-mortem punishment at the site of the sin, there was still allowance for both 'common' and 'special' purgatories, the latter located variously in the world, a distinction which usefully accommodated claims that at least some of the dead were more durably 'present' among the living than accounts of simple visits by the dead to deliver messages would permit.⁷² But this accommodation should not necessarily be understood in terms of an oppositional dynamic, pitting learned against unlearned, in which theologians were 'forced' to accept diverse ideas about the fate of souls in quite the manner suggested by Gurevich. The interaction was likely more subtle than that.

William of Auvergne, for example, already confident that purgation after death must happen, was not at all sure about where it might occur. He appealed, then, to the testimony of visions and apparitions that would give the process of purgation shape and form; visualizations of the purgatorial condition 'in the world' were thus able to flow back into theological rationalizations. Something similar is visible in the *Dialogus* of Caesarius of Heisterbach, too, as he appealed to 'various visions' in suggesting purgatory happened in multiple places in the world.⁷³ Finally, Aquinas himself observed that neither scripture nor reason but rather visionary revelation was the basis for what was known of purgatory.⁷⁴

If the concept of purgatorial suffering had already developed in the early Middle Ages as a means to address the problem of satisfaction for sin left incomplete at death, it was not necessary to create a 'new' and spatially coherent idea of purgatory in later centuries as a tool of instruction for its dissemination. More importantly, if these 'ideas of purgatory' had already emerged from below in an organic but idiosyncratic fashion, then the fate of those suffering temporal punishment might continue to be worked out with a similar pluralism: in various ways and in varied spaces of this world and the next.⁷⁵ Churchmen did not need to define a geography of the afterlife in order to teach a *concept* (of a purgatorial suffering) that was already widely diffused. Instead, the Church's teaching about

---

⁷¹ Caesarius of Heisterbach, 12.38, ed. Strange, ii, 347; *Golden Legend*, c. 163, trans. Ryan, ii, 284; on Gregory, see Jesse Keskiaho, 'Visions and the Afterlife in Gregory's Dialogues', in *Imagining the Medieval Afterlife*, ed. Pollard, 225–46.

⁷² See H. Kelly, 'Common and Special Purgatories, Authorized Revenge and Hamlet's Ghost', *Studies in Medieval and Renaissance History*, n.s., 9 (2012), 255–305, esp. 257–61.

⁷³ Caesarius of Heisterbach, *Dialogus Miraculorum*, 12.38, ed. Strange, II, 347. See Le Goff, *Purgatory*, 242–4. And see also on the importance of visions as a supplementary route to knowledge about the fates of the dead Hugh of St Victor, *De Sacramentis*, 2.16.2, *Patrologia Latina*, cols 173–618 at cols 580–4.

⁷⁴ Kelly, 'Common and Special Purgatories', 257–61.

⁷⁵ Note also other contexts in which bespoke purgatories proved attractive, including a Cistercian exemplum portraying the special purgatory of that order, where monks were punished in fire but also eased by a draught of wind generated by prayers of living monks. For this example, see McGuire, 'Purgatory', 77.

purgatory sought to provide a framework within which these varied visualizations and localizations of post-mortem suffering might be accommodated along with moral and doctrinal messages. For this reason, what was needed were not claims about place but rather narratives about the soul's trajectory and how it was to be helped after death.

In her study of Anglo-Saxon burials, Victoria Thompson has observed the absence of clearly defined 'scripts' in Anglo-Saxon England explaining what happened to the soul.[76] Likewise, as Richard Sowerby has noted, there was no early medieval analogue of the *ars moriendi*, curating events of the deathbed and explaining what was required of the dying person, priest and bystanders.[77] With the growing emphasis on confession and repentance in these centuries, identifying pathways to salvation that any 'ordinarily obedient and repentant Christian' might follow, was becoming an ever more important concern and encouraged the sharper formulation of ideas about penitence and the purgatorial process.[78]

In this regard, the *exempla*-collections emerging in this period articulated with particular force two messages, or more accurately two loose clusters of messages: the saving power of contrition and confession, and the beneficial effects of suffrages on the state of the dead. Attention to contrition and confession was hardly novel, and had a long intellectual lineage and was visible, for example, in the reflections of scholars such as Hrabanus Maurus and Alcuin in the ninth century.[79] But in the twelfth and thirteenth centuries it was coming to have a new significance. In Bede's Vision of Dryhthelm, sorrow had been enough to save those who felt it only on the deathbed, but it is telling that Dryhthelm himself thought the place in which he found these souls was hell and, by implication, that these were the souls of the damned.[80] For Bede and his contemporaries, therefore, an argument in favor of the saving power of last-minute repentance was present, but, as Augustine had cautioned, one could never be sure that this inner sorrow at the last would be sufficient and thus about the fate of the late penitent. In the thirteenth century, however, though Caesarius of Heisterbach reprised Augustine's very words on this subject, his *exempla* collectively told a different story, or at least contained a different emphasis.[81] For through them Caesarius stressed not uncertainty but rather redemptive possibility, revealing how even the most sin-stained of souls – the usurer, the heretic and the apostate – were delivered through genuine sorrow. Such beliefs about

---

[76] Thompson, 'Constructing Salvation', 229–40.
[77] A point made in Sowerby, *Angels*, 115–16; note also Marcus Bull, *Knightly Piety and the Lay Response to the First Crusade* (Oxford, 1993), 191–203, for ongoing uncertainty among arms-bearing families in the eleventh and early twelfth centuries about the location of the dead.
[78] Southern, 'Between Heaven and Hell', 652.
[79] See Helen Foxhall Forbes, 'The Theology of the Afterlife in the Early Middle Ages, 400–1100', in *Imagining the Medieval Afterlife*, ed. Pollard, 153–75 at 165.
[80] *Bede's Ecclesiastical History* v.12, ed. and trans. Colgrave and Mynors, 490–1; and on Bede's Dryhthelm, see Sowerby, *Angels*, 117–23.
[81] Caesarius, II.13, ed. Strange, I, 82.

the salvific power of contrition and confession reinforced the conviction that penance undischarged in life might be commuted into corporeal pain after death. The hard realities of this circumstance and the trauma of those pains were also signatures of the *exempla*.

Through these *exempla*, however, the Church also sought to send clear messages about the power of suffrages to ameliorate the suffering of the dead. From an early date there was considerable agreement that prayers, alms and masses aided souls, but there was less agreement about how such ministrations worked to bring relief.[82] Many vision-narratives, such as those of the Monk of Wenlock, Fursey and Boniface, skated lightly over the issue, perhaps because they had an essentially monitory agenda, warning against sin and revealing its consequences rather than elaborating on how the dead were to be helped.[83] These early visions, while allowing for post-mortem satisfaction, wished even more to encourage their readers and hearers to a penitent life in the world and so did not dwell on suffrages as means to expurgate pains after death.

This pattern, in which suffrages were accepted but not strongly emphasized, continued to hold in at least some of the new vision-narratives of the twelfth century, including some of the most prominent ones. Neither the monk Marcus, who composed the Vision of Tundal, nor Peter of Cornwall in his own Vision of Ailsi treated the subject. In the case of Ailsi the vision simply revealed to him 'the punishment of the wicked' and the 'rewards of the good'.[84] Both visions stressed the transformation of the visionary through the prospect of their own future punishment. A similar monitory emphasis recurs in the visions of Boso and Eadwulf recounted by Simeon of Durham.[85] In another early twelfth-century vision, that of a boy named Orm, prayers for the dead do appear but they are connected to a girl who is among the saved and seem to function more as thank-offering than means of assistance.[86] In the vision of the Norman priest Walchelin, ascribed by Orderic Vitalis to the year 1091 but recorded in the second quarter of the twelfth century, souls are imprisoned in an itinerant host and, although some can be freed through the intercession of the living, the dead

---

[82] Earlier important works include: Giles Constable, 'The Commemoration of the Dead in the Early Middle Ages', in *Early Medieval Rome and the Christian West: Essays in Honour of Donald Bullough*, ed. Julia M.H. Smith (Leiden, 2000), 169–95; Arnold Angenendt, 'Missa Specialis: Zugleich ein Beitrag zur Entstehung der Privatmessen', *Frühmittelalterliche Studien* 17 (1983), 153–221; Arnold Angenendt, 'Theologie und Liturgie der mittelalterlichen Totenmemoria', in *Memoria: der geschichtliche Zeugniswert*, ed. K. Schmid and J. Wollasch (Munich, 1984), 79–199; Megan McLaughlin, *Consorting with Saints: Prayer for the Dead in Early Medieval France* (Ithaca, NY, 1994). And for more recent discussion: R.S. Choy, *Intercessory Prayer and the Monastic Ideal in the Time of the Carolingian Reforms* (Oxford, 2017).
[83] Sarah Foot observes amidst the variety there is convergence in Anglo-Saxon England on the idea that suffrages were efficacious. See Foot, 'Anglo-Saxon "Purgatory"', 94–5.
[84] *Peter of Cornwall*, 202–03: ...de penis malorum et premiis bonorum.
[85] Simeon of Durham, *Libellus*, 212–17; 246–51.
[86] Hugh Farmer, 'The Vision of Orm', *Analecta Bollandiana* 75 (1957), 72–82.

have to argue the point to a skeptical visionary.[87] Even the Vision of Owein has nothing to say about suffrages until the very end of the protagonist's tour of the afterlife, whereupon a brief account of the value of prayer for the dead is added, a piece of theological boilerplate summing up all that a faithful Christian needed to know and to do. This emphasis contrasts sharply with that of visions at the end of the Middle Ages. For although late medieval visions continued to warn against sin by revealing its gory consequences for souls imprisoned after death in fire, ice, and darkness, a commanding message concerns the obligation of the living to offer help to the souls of the dead, to expedite their progress through purgatorial pains, and not to slide into negligence.[88]

That same preoccupation with the need for the living to help the dead, along with an explanation of how that help worked, is powerfully present in *exempla*-collections of the thirteenth century and beyond, works that also concentrate attention on related issues, such as the implications of excommunication or failure to make restitution as barriers to the efficacy of prayer for the dead. Here, then, is another shift of emphasis. Clarification and standardization of how suffrages worked – often making use of numbers to take account of days in purgatory and days remitted thanks to prayers, masses and alms offered up by the living – when linked to 'mass' communication of the message to the laity through preaching, ensured that the effects of this shift of emphasis were widely felt.

The Church's more tightly formulated and standardized claims about penitence, confession, satisfaction and suffrages could be, and were, inserted into manifold visualizations of the fate of souls. It is striking, however, that *exempla*-authors had recourse much more commonly to ghost stories than visions of the otherworld itself when they sought to illustrate these teachings. The ghosts of *exempla* took stereotyped forms but also revealed their own distinctive biographies – why they were in pain, how intense those pains were, how they were tailored to their sins, and how the living might help them. Many stories turned on a series of visitations, in which a soul, initially charred black or burning became pallid and emaciated on its second appearance, and then, on a third, joyful and dazzling white, illustrating the purgatorial process and the power of suffrages to accelerate progress towards heaven.[89] Ghost stories revealed souls *in* space, in the sense that they were firmly in three dimensions, re-embodied, simulacra of their former selves, suffering in aerial flesh. It might – or it might not – be spelled out that the soul was 'in purgatory', but what or where that place might be was more often elided than explicated. The concentration was on the story of a soul and its relationship with a percipient constrained to provide help. Thus, there was in the *exempla* only a weak commitment to the

---

[87] *The Ecclesiastical History of Orderic Vitalis*, ed. and trans. Marjorie Chibnall (6 vols, Oxford, 1969–80), iv, 238–49.
[88] McGuire, 'Purgatory', 61–84.
[89] J.-C. Schmitt, *Ghosts in the Middle Ages*, trans. Theresa Lavender Fagan (London, 1998), 133–40.

definition of otherworldly space. There might well be value in assigning souls to 'purgatory', but there was also merit in not confronting difficult and pedagogically peripheral questions about what or where purgatory was, since answers, as we have seen, risked cutting across a variety of pre-existing commitments and assumptions about where the newly dead might be. It was better to let this plurality endure, folding the diversity of ideas about *place* into a unified conception of *state*, with a focus on what was needed to enter it at death and how the living might help the dead trapped in this condition to move out of it.

Varied conceptions of where purgation happened arose because of the diverse circumstances in which the idea of 'purgatory' emerged. They persisted because the stories that bore the idea in all its variety were inherited and reused by those continuing to reflect on the fate of the dead during the twelfth and thirteenth centuries (and beyond). It is, indeed, the case that some of those writing in the period tried to define purgatory in spatial terms, but, when we find such attempts, they were usually subordinate to a more fundamental interest in defining the purgatorial condition. The development of a new post-mortem geography thus was not the cause of the transformation that made provision for departed souls such a powerful concern in the later Middle Ages. Rather this seems to have arisen more straightforwardly from the way in which the Church responded to deep human impulses – inspired by loss and grief – to provide help for the dead. It sought to define these theologically and to lay on the living an obligation to the dead that was to be discharged through measures that took practical form, especially the performance of suffrages, and which could be shown to have practical effect. An explanation – increasingly standard in form – of what the living owed to those who were already dead (as well as of what the living needed to do before they died) could be, and was, readily inserted into very various stories about visions and ghosts (which were often old, or suffused with motifs and tropes that were old). And preaching, as it became more widespread from the thirteenth century onwards, made possible the mass communication of messages about what was to be done for the deceased, fixing and magnifying the needs of the dead – family, neighbors, friends; the future self – in late medieval imaginations.

7

Bethell Prize Essay 2022

The Exemplary Knighting of Geoffrey Plantagenet: A Historiographical and Documentary Reappraisal

Arnaud Montreuil[1]

> There is only one historical source of the twelfth century that describes in considerable detail the procedure of a princely knighting ritual: Jean de Marmoutier's account – written around 1180 – of the knighting of Geoffrey Plantagenet of Anjou (d. 1151), celebrated in Rouen in 1127 on the occasion of his betrothal to the daughter of King Henry I of England.
>
> Joachim Bumke[2]

The tale of Geoffrey Plantagenet's knighting written down by John of Marmoutier in the *Historia Gaufredi Ducis* is regularly featured in modern scholarship as one of the best, if not the best, example of dubbing ceremonies in twelfth-century north-western Europe. However, the historiographical tradition which propelled this text to the forefront of chivalric studies and the documentary basis on which it is built has seldom been explored. The purpose of this essay is to reappraise the status of exemplarity usually associated with this distinctive text that may be much better known and appreciated now than it was during the twelfth and thirteen centuries.

The delivery of arms to Geoffrey Plantagenet (1113–51), heir to the county of Anjou, by the hand of Henry I, King of England, Duke of Normandy, on

---

[1] I would like to offer my warmest thanks to Frances Andrews and William North for their careful evaluation, patient review, enlightening comments, and wise suggestions. My gratitude also goes to T.J.H. McCarthy, Laura Morreale, Nicholas L. Paul, Robert Berkhofer, Heather J. Tanner, and Leland Grigoli for their critical and favorable reception of this research. I am more broadly indebted to the warm welcome of all members of the Haskins Society, to the organizers of the Richmond conference (Laura Gathagan, Steven Isaac, Joanna Drell), to Jennifer Paxton, and to the support of the Thomas Keefe Memorial Fund.
[2] Joachim Bumke, *Courtly Culture: Literature and Society in the High Middle Ages*, trans. Thomas Dunlap (Berkeley, CA, 1991), 235.

the feast of Whitsun held at Rouen in 1128, was a major event in Anglo-French history of the first half of the twelfth century.[3] Prelude to the matrimonial alliance which tied the future count of Anjou to the heiress of the Anglo-Norman realm, it marked an important shift in the balance of power in north-western France. For decades, Angevins and Normans had been rivals, fighting border skirmishes,[4] negotiating the status of the county of Maine through homage,[5] and meddling in each other's internal affairs. Souring relations between the two neighboring powers led to open conflict in 1117, when count Fulk V of Anjou, supporting rebellions in Normandy and laying siege to Henry's castles, joined Louis VI and Baldwin VII in an attempt to challenge Anglo-Norman dominance in north-western France. After two years of setbacks, King Henry scored a diplomatic victory by convincing Fulk to join his side, in return for a large sum of money and the promise of an alliance between the Normans and the Angevins. Peace was to prevail thanks to the wedding of Matilda, daughter of the count of Anjou, to William Adelin, heir apparent to the English throne.[6] Celebrated in Lisieux's cathedral in 1119, this union proved to be short-lived. During the night of 25 November 1120, William Adelin and many other young aristocrats embarked on the White Ship, a beautiful vessel which was to take them from Normandy to England. This simple crossing of the Channel turned into a tragic shipwreck as the inebriated guests and crew crashed against coastal rocks near Barfleur. The peace between Henry and Fulk perished alongside William Adelin and his unfortunate companions. Matilda, who was still alive (she took another ship to England), was sent home in 1121 at Fulk's request, and Henry's refusal to return the young widow's dowry in 1122 led the count of Anjou not only to renounce the alliance with the king of England, but also to support his maternal uncle Amaury de Montfort in his 1123–4 rebellion against King Henry.[7]

In 1126–7, King Henry, without a male heir, designated his daughter Maud as his successor. In the wake of his nephew William Clito's rise to power as the

---

[3] Scholars such as Jean Flori and David Crouch have shown that knighting rituals, considered as social practices which explicitly created knights as defined through a shared chivalric representation system, were invented and formalized at the end of the twelfth century. This is why in this article I refer to the historical event of 1128 as a delivery of arms (*remise d'armes* in French) and to John of Marmoutier's description c. 1180 as a knighting (*adoubement chevaleresque* in French). See Jean Flori, *L'essor de la chevalerie* (Geneva, 1986), and David Crouch, *The Chivalric Turn: Conduct and Hegemony in Europe before 1300* (Oxford, 2019). I therefore disagree, on this very specific point, with Max Liberman's suggestion to refrain from using this terminology. Max Lieberman, 'A New Approach to the Knighting Ritual', *Speculum* 90 (2015), 391–423 at 421.
[4] C. Warren Hollister and Amanda Clark Frost, *Henry I* (New Haven, CT, 2008), 239–40.
[5] Hollister and Frost, *Henry I*, 249.
[6] This alliance had been designed already in 1113, but never accomplished. Hollister and Frost, *Henry I*, 261.
[7] Amaury de Montfort even designed an alliance between the second daughter of Fulk, Sybil, and William Clito, who was at the time Henry I's main contender for the English throne. Hollister and Frost, *Henry I*, 292.

count of Flanders and as the most serious contender to the English throne, the king sought to renew his alliance with Anjou to secure Maud's queenship. He convinced Fulk to agree to a betrothal, this time between Geoffrey, the count's young son (aged fourteen at the time of the events), and Maud, who was to be queen of England and duchess of Normandy. The following year, Geoffrey Plantagenet, who was now aged fifteen but who did not yet bear arms, was invited by Henry I in Rouen solemnly to receive knightly weapons in prospect of the upcoming marriage (Henry's gift of arms to Geoffrey took place just eight days before the wedding). That Pentecost, by offering a sword and equestrian arms to his soon to be son-in-law in front of his court at Rouen, King Henry publicly recognized that the future count of Anjou was old enough to exert lordship over men and lands, that he was ready to wage war, and that he could legitimately wed and have children; that is to say, he was now to be considered a full-fledged aristocrat of the twelfth century.

The historical importance of this chain of events – betrothal, delivery of arms, wedding – lies in the fact that Geoffrey effectively acted as a link between Anjou and Anglo-Norman England, paving the way for Anglo-Angevin kingship. Mark Blincoe has shown that this union allowed Geoffrey to claim the right to govern Normandy and the Anglo-Norman realm alongside his wife, as was usually the case with twelfth-century weddings.[8] Moreover, Maud and Geoffrey produced a son, later King Henry II, who successfully claimed both inheritances. Yet, there is another reason, albeit more historiographical than historical, why the events of 1128 and more precisely the delivery of arms to Geoffrey is important: because it has acquired a venerable status of exemplarity, thanks to the masterful retelling of this event by the monk John of Marmoutier in a famous work entitled the *Historia Gaufredi Ducis*. The details of Geoffrey's knighting are found at the beginning of John's tale, right after the prologue. It is an unusually long scene of more than 600 words, which opens briefly on Geoffrey's betrothal to Maud, and then describes at length the dubbing of the future knight. The *Historia Gaufredi* relates that when he arrived at Rouen for the feast of Whitsun in 1128, Geoffrey was duly received by the king, whom he impressed with his wisdom and prudence, and that he was instructed to prepare himself for his knighting which, according to the text, proceeded as follows:

On the great day, as required by the custom for making knights, baths were prepared for use. After having cleansed his body, and come from the purification of bathing, the noble offspring of the count of Anjou dressed himself in a linen undershirt, putting on a robe woven with gold and a surcoat of a rich purple hue. His stockings were of silk, and on his feet he wore shoes with little golden lions on them. His companions, who were to be knighted with him, were all clothed in linen and purple. He left his privy chamber and paraded in public, accompanied by his noble retinue. The horses were led, arms carried to be distributed to each in turn… He wore a matching hauberk made of double mail To his ankles were fastened golden spurs. A shield hung from his neck on which were golden images of lioncels he

---

[8] Mark Blincoe, 'Geoffrey le Bel of Anjou and Political Inheritance in the Anglo-Norman Realm', *The Haskins Society Journal* 27 (2015), 79–100.

carried a sword from the royal treasure, bearing an ancient inscription which attributed it to the mystical smith Wayland.[9]

Finally, Geoffrey showed everyone his remarkable physical strength by jumping into the saddle without using the stirrups, and his dubbing was enhanced by a whole week of feasts and warlike exercises.

For centuries, this magnificent knighting has been showcased as a model example of the *adoubement* in French historiography. In 1683, the antiquarian Claude-François Menestrier published his book *De la chevalerie ancienne et moderne avec les moyens d'en faire les preuves*.[10] This work, which is a serious contender for the honor of being considered the first empirical and critical study of the history of chivalry, already treated Geoffrey's knighting told by John of Marmoutier as a historically accurate and complete description of the social practice through which a young man received equestrian arms and joined the social group of knights. A few decades later, Menestrier was followed by Honoré de Sainte-Marie, who in 1718 presented Geoffrey's knighting as 'the way Chivalry was given during the twelfth century'.[11] From the beginning of the nineteenth century until the First World War, the exemplarity of Geoffrey's *adoubement* became well entrenched. Librarians and archivists trained at the École des chartes,[12] professional historians teaching at la Sorbonne,[13] and polymaths such as Émile de la Bedollière[14] all contributed to the scholarly fate of this textual excerpt. Léon Gautier, author of the influential book *La Chevalerie*, relied heavily on John of Marmoutier's depiction of Geoffrey's knighting to develop his theory of the progressive christianization of knighting practices. He considered this particular dubbing as the epitome of secular, militaristic dubbing before the Church took control over this performance.[15]

After a decline in interest in chivalric studies in the early decades of the twentieth century,[16] historical works for a short time tended not to feature the

---

[9] This translation comes from Nigel Saul, *Chivalry in Medieval England* (Cambridge, 2011), 21. The Latin version of the text is discussed later in this essay.
[10] Claude-François Ménestrier, *De la Chevalerie ancienne et moderne, avec la manière d'en faire les preuves* (Paris, 1683), 129–30.
[11] Honoré de Sainte-Marie, *Dissertations historiques et critiques sur la chevalerie ancienne et moderne* (Paris, 1718), 346–7.
[12] Henri Bordier et Édouard Charton, *Histoire de France* (2 vols, Paris, 1859), i, 264–7.
[13] Charles-Victor Langlois, *Lectures historiques* (Paris, 1890), 174; Charles Bémont, *Histoire de l'Europe et en particulier de la France de 395 à 1270* (Paris, 1896), 262–3; The *Historia Gaufredi Ducis* serves as documentary evidence in Paul Guilhiermoz, *Essai sur l'origine de la noblesse en France au Moyen Âge* (Paris, 1902), 346–7, 397, 412, 414, 418, 472.
[14] Émile de la Bedollière, *Histoire des mœurs et de la vie privée des Français* (3 vols, Paris, 1849), iii, 137–58.
[15] Léon Gautier, *La Chevalerie* (Paris, 1884), 274–8.
[16] On this decline in interest, see Pierre Toubert et al., 'Conclusion', in *Chevalerie et christianisme aux XIIe et XIIIe siècles*, ed. Martin Aurell and Catalina Gîrbea (Rennes, 2013), 315–21.

Plantagenet's famous *adoubement*.[17] But the importance of the *adoubement* re-emerged in the 1970s, when Georges Duby placed the mentalities and representations governing lay aristocratic society between the tenth and the twelfth century at the forefront of medieval historiography. In his masterwork *Les trois ordres ou l'imaginaire du féodalisme*, Georges Duby discussed the *Historia Gaufredi Ducis* as a text promoting an ideal representation of a lay sovereign, both lord and knight. He also underlined that Geoffrey's knighting is to be understood as one of the rituals (along with the betrothals and wedding) which legitimized the future count's dominion over Anjou and the Anglo-Norman world.[18]

Since the publication of Georges Duby's seminal work, most French historians interested in the study of chivalry have integrated Geoffrey's knighting into their works. This goes without saying for major writers on the history of knighthood such as Jean Flori and Dominique Barthélemy, for specialists of Anglo-Angevin kingship like Martin Aurell and Amaury Chauou, or for scholars focusing on lay aristocracy, but it is also true for literary historians as well as for the authors of more synthetic histories.[19]

In Anglophone historiography, in contrast, John of Marmoutier's account of Geoffrey's knighting was not enshrined as exemplary either as early or as strongly. According to the earliest evidence I have yet discovered, it seems to have entered mid-nineteenth-century literature through the romantic celebration of chivalry[20] and historical biographies of the English monarchs.[21] For a large part of the twentieth century, chivalry (and hence John of Marmoutier's lavish depiction of a knighting performance) did not attract the attention of historians of the English empirical tradition, who, as David Crouch argues, 'tended to play down the influence of chivalry as no more than a hypocritical veneer concealing the brutal and unscrupulous nature of the medieval aristocracy'.[22]

---

[17] A notable exception is found in Augustin Fliche, *La chrétienté médiévale (395–1254)* (Paris, 1929), 456–8.
[18] Georges Duby, *Les trois ordres ou l'imaginaire du féodalisme* (Paris, 1978), 361–2.
[19] Flori, *L'Essor de la Chevalerie*, 304–08; Dominique Barthélemy, *La chevalerie. De la Germanie antique au XIIe siècle* (Paris, 2012), 399–402; Dominique Barthélemy, 'Chivalry in Feudal Society According to French Evidence', in *Knighthood and Society in the High Middle Ages*, ed. David Crouch and Jeroen Deploige (Leuven, 2020), 29–50 at 49–50; Martin Aurell, *Le chevalier lettré* (Paris, 2011), 396–7; Amaury Chauou, *L'Idéologie Plantagenêt. Royauté arthurienne et monarchie politique dans l'espace Plantagenêt (XIIe–XIIIe siècles)* (Rennes, 2001), 51–60; Régine Le Jan, *Famille et pouvoir dans le monde franc (VIIe–Xe siècles): essai d'anthropologie sociale* (Paris, 2003), 79; Joseph Morsel, *L'aristocratie médiévale (V^e–XVe siècle)* (Paris, 2004), 119; Philippe Walter, *La mémoire du temps* (Paris, 1989), 353; Dominique Boutet, *Charlemagne et Arthur, ou le roi imaginaire* (Paris, 1992), 38; Denise Péricard-Méa, *Le Moyen Âge* (Quintin, 2006), 36–7; Florian Mazel, *Féodalités 888–1180* (Paris, 2011), 605–06.
[20] Menella Bute Smedley, *Lays and Ballads from English History* (London, 1850), 12–15; Charles Lethbridge Kingsford, *The Song of Lewes* (Oxford, 1990), 63–5.
[21] Agnes Strickland, *Lives of the Queens of England from the Norman Conquest* (12 vols, London, 1840), i, 229–31; Kate Norgate, *England under the Angevin Kings* (2 vols, London, 1887), i, 258–9; M.F. Johnston, *Coronation of a King* (London, 1902), 191–3.
[22] David Crouch, *The Birth of Nobility: Constructing Aristocracy in England and*

In a fashion which echoes Georges Duby's influence on French historiography, this particular historiographical situation was completely reversed thanks to Maurice Keen's *Chivalry* (1984), a true milestone in the contemporary study of knighthood. Without doubt, Maurice Keen contributed tremendously to the visibility of John of Marmoutier's narration. He opened his chapter on knighting practices by presenting Geoffrey's *adoubement* as the exemplar of a lay, secular dubbing ceremony,[23] which stemmed from royal coronation and would never be controlled by the Church. Since then this scene has made its way into studies on Angevin lordship as well as major books on knighthood and chivalry[24] such as those written by David Crouch, Peter Coss, and Nigel Saul.[25] Geoffrey's dubbing has appeared in a recent *Companion to Chivalry*[26] as well as in historical books intended for popular audiences.[27] Since John of Marmoutier describes the heraldic trappings on the chivalric equipment offered to the newly made knight, both French[28] and English[29] scholars also deem this part of the *Historia Gaufredi Ducis* to be one of the earliest examples of heraldic description.

In addition to the status conferred upon it through its presence in French and English scholarly traditions, three complementary reasons, elaborated gradually over time, explain the importance acquired by the knighting scene narrated by John of Marmoutier. First, the *Historia Gaufredi Ducis* in general is seen to be an important historical witness to the emergence of chivalry in the later twelfth century,[30] and that the excerpt of the dubbing scene in particular is, to quote Dominique Barthélemy, 'a bit of an anthology, with the lustral bath

---

France 900–1300 (London and New York, 2005), 14.
[23] Maurice Keen, *Chivalry* (New Haven, CT, 1984), 65.
[24] A notable exception to this rule is Maurice Keen, *Medieval Chivalry* (New Haven, CT, 2016).
[25] Jim Bradbury, 'Geoffroy V of Anjou, Count and Knight', in *The Ideals and Practice of Medieval Knighthood III*, ed. Christopher Harper-Bill and Ruth Harvey (Woodbridge, 1990), 21–38; Jeffrey Anderson, *Angevin Dynasties of Europe 900–1500* (London, 2019); David Crouch, *The Image of Aristocracy in Britain, 1000–1300* (London and New York, 1992), 104–105, and Crouch, *The Chivalric Turn*, 270; Peter Coss, *The Knight in Medieval England: 1000–1400* (Conshohocken, PA, 1996), 52; Saul, *Chivalry in Medieval England*, 21. Interestingly, in his *Medieval Chivalry* (Cambridge, 2016), Richard Kaeuper makes no mention of Geoffrey's knighting; it is the exception that proves the rule.
[26] Peter Coss, 'The Origins and Diffusion of Chivalry', in *A Companion to Chivalry*, ed. Robert W. Jones and Peter Coss (Woodbridge, 2019), 7–38 at 26–7.
[27] Dan Jones, *The Plantagenets: The Kings Who Made England* (London, 2012).
[28] Michel Pastoureau, *Traité d'héraldique* (Paris, 1979), 30, 200; Dominique Boutet, *Charlemagne et Arthur*, 727; Jean-François Nieus, 'L'invention des armoiries en contexte. Haute aristocratie, identités familiales et culture chevaleresque entre France et Angleterre, 1100–1160', *Journal des savants* 1 (2017), 93–155 at 135.
[29] Richard Marks and Ann Payne, *British Heraldry from its Origins to C. 1800* (London, 1978), 11; Michael J. Huxtable, 'Aspects of Armorial Colour and its Perception in Medieval Writing', in *New Directions in Colour Studies*, ed. Carole Biggam, Carole Hough, and Christine Kay (Amsterdam and Philadelphia, PA, 2011), 194–5; Gabriel Esposito, *Armies of Plantagenet England, 1135–1337* (Barnsley, 2022).
[30] Flori, *L'essor de la chevalerie*, 305–06.

and the conferral of wondrously beautiful arms'.[31] The second reason is that it is widely considered the first 'historical' depiction of the performance of knighting,[32] that is, an account derived from the documentary genre of annals, chronicles and histories rather than vernacular French literature. As Jean Flori has shown,[33] the *chansons de geste* and the romances of Chrétien de Troyes are the only documents composed during the twelfth century in which *adoubement* is described (or rather represented, staged, and discussed) in detail, with its gestures, objects, and oral formulas.[34] In this regard, the *Historia Gaufredi Ducis* is indeed exceptional, since it is the sole Latin text that comes close, in terms of style, precision and length, to what can be quite frequently observed in vernacular literature. Finally, it is by far the most detailed account of a knighting ceremony in the whole corpus of historical writings of the twelfth and thirteenth centuries from north-western Europe, and possibly in that of the entire Middle Ages.

Although these three reasons may explain why the tale of King Henry's *adoubement* of Geoffrey has become the standard example of knighting rituals, it is nevertheless important to recognize several limitations. The most evident one is that this account of Geoffrey's knighting should not be considered an accurate depiction of what happened in 1128. John of Marmoutier, who was not at Rouen for the feast, wrote his *Historia Gaufredi ducis* between 1170 and 1180, more than forty years after the event. In the light of this timelapse of four decades, I wholeheartedly agree with Peter Coss, who has warned that 'as always, we need to be extremely cautious when it comes to backward projection by medieval writers. [The *Historia Gaufredi Ducis*] is most assuredly evidence of the world of 1180 not that of the 1120s.'[35] This point about anachronism, however, is not always made clear, even in recent literature and especially in books targeting readerships outside academia.[36]

A second caution: although Geoffrey's knighting is well known to modern scholars, this was most likely not the case during the Middle Ages. The *Historia Gaufredi Ducis* was not widely copied and the original manuscript remains unknown. The *Historia Gaufredi Ducis* has come down to us in two later versions, now preserved in the Bibliothèque nationale de France. The earliest

---

[31] Barthélemy, *La chevalerie*, 400: '"un morceau d'anthologie, avec le bain lustral et la remise d'armes fabuleusement belles'.
[32] Peter Coss, for instance, stated that 'the first description of [a knighting ceremony] comes from John of Marmoutier who was writing in about 1180 of the knighting of Geoffrey V, count of Anjou, at Whitsun 1128.' Coss, 'The Origins and Diffusion of Chivalry', 26.
[33] Jean Flori, 'Pour une histoire de la chevalerie. L'adoubement dans les romans de chrétien de Troyes', *Romania* 100 (1979), 21–53, and 'Sémantique et société médiévale. Le verbe adouber et son évolution au XIIe siècle', *Annales. Économies, sociétés, civilisations* 31 (1976), 915–40.
[34] Barthélemy, *La chevalerie*, 399.
[35] Coss, 'The Origins and Diffusion of Chivalry', 26.
[36] Jones, *The Plantagenets*; Thomas Asbridge, *The Greatest Knight: The Remarkable Life of William Marshal, the Power behind Five English Thrones* (London, 2015).

surviving witness is found in the BnF Latin MS 15067, which was produced in the fourteenth century; it is incomplete. This miscellaneous codex opens with the *Gesta consulum Andegavorum* (*Chronicle of the counts of Anjou*), followed by an incomplete version of the *Historia Gaufredi Ducis*.[37] The missing section consists precisely in the prologue and Geoffrey's magnificent dubbing: folio 39v ends in the middle of a sentence and a catchword at the bottom of the page indicates that the next folio should begin by the verb 'ama', but folio 40r, on which the incomplete version of John of Marmoutier's work commences, starts with the words 'Rex vero genero suo et filie' which belong to the part of the *Historia* directly following Geoffrey's knighting and wedding to Maud.

Fortunately, a full version of the *Historia Gaufredi Ducis* can be found in the sixteenth-century BnF Latin MS 6005, again at the end of the *Chronicle of the counts of Anjou* and preceding what seems to be a compilation (*compendiosum*) of a chronicle attributed to Ivo of Chartres. The versions in both manuscripts 15067 and 6005 pertain to the same textual tradition, but it is not the only one. A third manuscript must have served as the model for the first printed edition of the *Historia Gaufredi Ducis*, made in 1610 by the Parisian lawyer and humanist Laurent Bouchel (1559–1629), although this can only be hypothetically reconstructed through observation of the differences between Laurent Bouchel's edition and the two surviving manuscripts.[38]

If we assume that the number of manuscript witnesses that have come down to us, in spite of losses and destructions (voluntary or not), offer some sign of the success and importance of a text for medieval society, we are forced to admit that the *Historia Gaufredi Ducis* was not a major document. While this text must have been important to some contemporary writers, readers, and listeners, it is nonetheless impossible, given the available evidence, to assert that it had a wider reception than Touraine and quite probably Maine.[39] In this regard, the local or regional reception of the *Historia Gaufredi Ducis* could have been similar to the reception of the *Liber de compositione castri Ambaziae et ipsius dominorum gesta*, the *Chronica de gestis consulum Andegavorum*, and the *Gesta Ambaziensium dominorum* that are contained in BnF MSS Latin 6218 and 6006. Indeed, Nicholas Paul has shown that these three historical narratives

---

[37] The other works are a fragmentary copy of the *Liber Aristotelis de Secretis secretorum*, the *Vita virginis Marie*, and a short piece titled *Contre l'espidemie*. This manuscript has been fully digitalized in color and can be accessed on the website of the Bibliothèque nationale de France.

[38] The *Historia Gaufredi Ducis* was twice included in learned editions of the *Gesta consulum Andegavorum*: *Chroniques des comtes d'Anjou*, ed. Paul-Alexandre Marchegay and André Salmon (2 vols, Paris, 1856–71), i, 229–310; and John of Marmoutier, *Historia Gaufredi Ducis*, in *Chroniques des comtes d'Anjou et des seigneurs d'Amboise*, ed. Louis Halphen and René Poupardin (Paris, 1913), 172–231.This edition is mainly based on BnF Latin MS 15067, and on BnF Latin MS. 6005 for the missing parts (prologue, betrothal, knighting, wedding).557

[39] Touraine, because the document was produced by a monk of Marmoutier, and Maine, since the dedicatee (see below note 41), Guillaume of Passavant, was bishop of Le Mans, and because Marmoutier held lands in Maine.

produced in the Loire Valley during the twelfth century were most likely produced around Amboise with aim of inscribing this county in the broader spatial and historical context of the Anglo-Angevin domain.[40] In short, in the case of the *Historia Gaufredi Ducis*, scholars and historians have taken as paradigmatic a narrative, or rather a single excerpt from a narrative (Geoffrey's *adoubement*) that is absolutely remarkable in its content, but probably minor in its contemporary reach.

Caution is all the more necessary since nothing is known about the circulation of this work within the literary networks of the late twelfth century. In *Les trois ordres*, Georges Duby led one to believe that Henry II (1133–89) was the addressee of the work:

Henry II expected to hear a long description of the initiation ceremony in John of Marmoutier's life of his father Geoffrey. For him, this rite of passage, embedded between the betrothal and the wedding feast, at the heart of the dual ceremonial which, when it had united the heir to the county of Anjou with the heir to Normandy and the kingdom of England, was essential, as it prepared the elevation of the Plantagenet above all the powers of the earth. Henry was undoubtedly very pleased that the docile writer showed only the profane part of this ceremony, speaking of the ritual bath as a simple preparation of the body, and alluding to the sacred only through a reminder of the chosen day: Whitsun, the moment when the holy spirit is sent to mankind. [author's translation][41]

As convincing as Georges Duby sounds, one can only hypothesize that the *Historia Gaufredi Ducis* was intended for King Henry II's royal court, family, or entourage.[42] It is true that the *Gesta Consulum Andegavorum*, which John of Marmoutier finalized between 1164 and 1173 and is presented as the result of successive literary efforts by Thomas of Loches, a certain monk named Robin, Brito of Amboise, and himself, was explicitly dedicated to Henry.[43] But this is not the case with his narration of Geoffrey's life, whose addressee was Guillaume of Passavant,[44] bishop of Le Mans between 1145 and 1187, and commissioner of a magnificent tomb, embellished with a splendid enamel, for Geoffrey Plantagenet in the Le Mans cathedral.[45] The *Historia Gaufredi Ducis*

---

[40] Nicholas L. Paul, 'An Angevin Imperial Context for the Amboise–Anjou Narrative Programme', *ANS* 41 (2018), 103–18.
[41] Georges Duby, *Les trois ordres*, 361–2.
[42] C. Stephen Jaeger also understood that Henry II and his entourage were the intended public of the work; see C. Stephen Jaeger, *The Origins of Courtliness. Civilizing Trends and the Formation of Courtly Ideals, 939–1210* (Philadelphia, PA, 1985), 204–12.
[43] *Chroniques des comtes d'Anjou et des seigneurs d'Amboise*, 162: Domino Henrico, regi Anglorum, duci Normannorum, comiti Andegavorum, Turonorum et Cenomannorum, principi Aquitanorum, duci Guasconum et Arvernorum, duci etiam Britonum.
[44] John of Marmoutier, *Historia Gaufredi Ducis*, 172: Domino Guillelmo, reverendo episcopo Cenomannensi, specimini clericorum et speculo, frater Johannes, Majoris Monasterii humillimus monachorum et per ipsum clericorum, modicum id quod est.
[45] Robert Favreau, 'L'épitaphe d'Henri II Plantagenêt à Fontevraud', *Cahiers de civilisation médiévale* 50 (2007), 3–10 at 3–4.

might have been, as Jean Flori tentatively suggests, a discourse intended to help Henry win the hearts of his knights,[46] in essence a work of propaganda. Yet, given the fact that it is impossible to affirm that John's *opus* even reached Guillaume of Passavant, let alone Henry II, it seems overbold to assert that it was intended as a work of propaganda for Henry II's court rather than (and this would be my hypothesis, alas unprovable) a local attempt to bolster the position of Le Mans and its cathedral as the conservatory of the *memoria* of one of the founders of the Plantagenet dynasty.[47] In other words, readily available scientific editions and a robust scholarly tradition have disguised the fact that the most celebrated depiction of a knighting, considered exemplary for the development and evolution of this chivalric practice and supposedly linked to King Henry II himself, is known only through one sixteenth-century copy of a lost original of what might have been a very localized history.

The *Historia Gaufredi Ducis* is not only a rare work with regard to its manuscript tradition. It is also, as stated above, a singular text, the only known Latin text in the twelfth- and thirteenth-century historiographical corpus which describes a knighting practice in the detailed way in which Geoffrey's dubbing is depicted. To some degree, this absence is not surprising. As heirs to a double tradition of ancient Greco-Latin and Judeo-Christian history, medieval historical writings claim to narrate 'what has been done'. They can also offer a performative narrative retelling of the events of the divine story (*geste divine*), or more precisely, a narrative of the actions of men and women in the face of God's will. In medieval historical writing, audiences can reflect on the use women and men make of their free will as well as on the beneficial (in the case of saints, courtly knights, and arguably Geoffrey according to John of Marmoutier) or terrible (in the case of traitors and other felons) consequences of conformity or non-conformity to Christian principles.

As a consequence, the structure of these writings does not, generally speaking, lead to or allow for elaborate descriptions of knighting rituals. In the vast majority of chronicles, histories, and annals, references to dubbing mention only the date and place on which the performance took place, and sometimes, if the reader is lucky, an associated event, such as a homage, a military campaign, a banquet, a tournament or, in Geoffrey's case, a wedding that took place after the *adoubement*. Thus, in any given text, knighting may very much resemble the following sentence taken from the *Annales de Dunstaplia*, which relates David I of Scotland's delivery of arms to Henry II: 'Henry II is made a knight by David, king of the Scots. He did homage to Louis, king of the Franks, for the duchy of

---

[46] Flori, *L'essor de la Chevalerie*, 305–08.
[47] For a general study of this phenomenon, see Michel Lauwers, *La mémoire des ancêtres, le souci des morts. Fonctions et usages du culte des morts dans l'occident médiéval* (Paris, 1997). For a recent case study, see Nicholas L. Paul, 'Writing the Knight, Staging the Crusader: Manasses of Hierges and the Monks of Brogne', in *Knighthood and society in the High Middle Ages*, ed. David Crouch and Jeroen Deploige (Leuven, 2020), 167–91.

Normandy and the county of Anjou.'[48] Even the *Gesta Consulum Andegavorum*, completed by the same John of Marmoutier, simply indicates: 'Fulco bore from the daughter of Count Helia, his wife, Geoffrey who, as an adult knight, became mighty in arms and took as wife Matilda, daughter of King Henry of England who had been the wife of the emperor of Germany.'[49] References to dubbing like these two, amounting to just a few words, are representative of how little knighting practices appear in chronicles. In comparison, Geoffrey's knighting in the *Historia Gaufredi Ducis*, with all of its elaborate details, is over 600 words and is in a class of its own. In my research on knighting rituals in twelfth- and thirteenth-century France and England, I compiled 320 mentions of the *adoubement* found in more than ninety chronicles, histories, and annals, and not a single one of these selections come close to the detail, length, or narrative structure of Geoffrey's dubbing.[50] In other words, the monk of Marmoutier's description of Geoffrey's knighting is a *hapax* not at all representative or typical of what is found in medieval writing of this type.

This observation on the excerpt of Geoffrey's knighting echoes the wider conclusions drawn by Jim Bradbury in his essay 'Geoffroy V of Anjou, Count and Knight', in which he underlined the fact the *Historia Gaufredi Ducis* was not really a history:

The *History of Duke Geoffrey* is rather an exceptional work. Although it is in a sense a continuation of the *Gesta*, it is in a very different form to that work. It is not an ordinary medieval chronicle. It is broadly chronological, but does not attempt to give a detailed narrative of Geoffrey's career. It is a kind of biography, with some classical and medieval models, but nor entirely like any of those models. Its basic intention is to show Geoffrey as an ideal ruler. It is structured around certain admirable traits in his character, each illustrated by anecdotes.[51]

What Jim Bradbury describes here is, in fact, the literary model of a *vita*, the life of a saint, applied here to the life of a great secular lord.[52] Under John

---

[48] *Annales de Dunstaplia*, in *Annales Monastici*, ed. Henry Richard Luard (4 vols, London, 1866), iii, 16: Anno MCXLVIII. Henricus secundus fit miles a David, rege Scottorum. Qui fecit homagium Lodoico, regi Francorum, de ducatu Normanniae, et comitatu Andegaviae.

[49] *Chroniques des comtes d'Anjou*, 69: Fulco ex filia comitis Helie uxora sua genuit Gosfridum, qui adultus miles, armis prepotens effectus, Meltidem filiam Henrici regis Anglie, que uxor fuerat inperatoris Alemannie, uxorem duxit.

[50] Arnaud Montreuil, 'Écrire, décrire, saisir l'adoubement chevaleresque: une histoire de l'hippogenèse dans l'Europe du Nord-Ouest, le Midi de la France et l'Italie centro-septentrionale (v.1175–v.1300)' (PhD dissertation, Paris 1 Panthéon-Sorbonne and University of Ottawa, 2022), 73–4. As of February 2024, it has not been published, but I will be happy to communicate these findings on request.

[51] Bradbury, 'Geoffroy V of Anjou, Count and Knight', 23.

[52] There was a broader cultural context favorable to the production of this type of document (e.g., the *Vita Ludovici grossi regis* by Suger). C. Stephen Jaeger notes that the years 1120–70 'marked the flowering of the episcopal *vita*, with a high-point being reached between 1145–1160'; Jaeger, *The Origins of Courtliness*, 205–06.

of Marmoutier's pen, the historical Geoffrey disappears behind his figure's role as a catalog of virtues,[53] governed by the maxim 'spare subjects and vanquish the proud' (*parcere subjectis et debellare superbos*). According to Bernard Guenée, this is a core characteristic of historical works composed in monastic circles. These texts shared with hagiographical texts a strong concern for moral edification. After all, as texts often designed to be read during *lectiones* in the refectory, they were meant to have an edifying function, they were intended for the same public, and they were written by authors who were often hagiographers before they were historians, and who therefore often owed their training as historians to hagiography.[54] The structure of the *Historia Gaufredi Ducis* itself is reminiscent of hagiography (which was, given the prestige of this genre, the matrix for the composition of *vitae* of powerful laymen), since it closely follows the classical tripartite model of: 1) lineage, childhood, and coming of age; 2) personal qualities and noteworthy deeds; 3) circumstances that lead to death.[55] Thus, in form and style, the *Historia Gaufredi Ducis* is closer to hagiography than it is to chronicle writing.

While the *Historia Gaufredi Ducis* stylistically and structurally is an example of lay hagiography, this is not the case from a thematic point of view. Hagiographies seldom feature knighting performances,[56] let alone one like Geoffrey's dubbing narrated by John. To find inspiration, the monk of Marmoutier turned to the vernacular genre of the *chansons de geste*, which were of major importance in shaping of a chivalric system of representations in late twelfth-century aristocratic society. Indeed, Léon Gautier wrote that Geoffrey's dubbing seems either to borrow from a *chanson de geste* or to have been written to resemble a vernacular poetic text.[57] Jean Flori judged that John's depiction of a knighting was in nearly all respects consonant with chivalric epics;[58] and Dominique Barthélemy underlined the fact that the mystical smith Wayland who forged the sword presented to Geoffrey appears in *chansons de geste*.[59]

I agree with all these scholars, but I argue that this hypothesis needs to be taken further. Geoffrey's knighting is indeed a scene pertaining to the genre of

---

[53] Geoffrey's *Historia* is not unique, as it was generally the case. Jacques Le Goff showed that it is the case of every *vita* of Louis IX excepted the one written by Jean de Joinville. Jacques Le Goff, *Saint Louis* (Paris, 1996), reprinted in *Héros du Moyen Âge, le Saint et le Roi* (Paris, 2004), 571–5.
[54] Bernard Guenée argues that historical texts written by monks in cloisters, and most notably those of Orderic Vitalis, were composed primarily for their immediate brethren, in a way that was appropriate for *lectiones* in the refectory. Bernard Guenée, *Histoire et culture historique dans l'Occident médiéval* (Paris, 1980), 51–4 and esp. 53.
[55] Amaury Chauou, *L'idéologie Plantagenêt*, 51–60. It is important, however, not to insist too much on this as a hagiographic schema. It is, after all, the pattern of secular biographies as well.
[56] Although a thorough study of this subject in a corpus of warrior saints' lives (e.g. Martin of Tours, Georges, Maurice) has yet to be done.
[57] Gautier, *La Chevalerie*, 275.
[58] Flori, *L'essor de la chevalerie*, 306.
[59] Barthélemy, *La chevalerie*, 402.

chanson de geste and directly woven into Geoffrey's *vita*. This process is quite frequent between the various genres of chivalric literature. For instance, the motif of knighting as it appears in *chansons de geste* has frequently been transferred to other genres such as verse and prose romances. Patrick Moran coined the concept of a *patron générique exportable*,[60] or exportable genre template, to designate a section of a literary text that is borrowed in an aesthetic sense from another literary genre. According to Moran, those extra-generic patterns were fully recognizable as such by medieval readers, without making a whole work unrecognizable from the point of view of genre. In other words, the audience of the *Historia Gaufredi Ducis* would have immediately been able to recognize Geoffrey's knighting as an exportable generic template, and to understand its close association with *chansons de geste*, without considering the work as a whole a *chanson de geste*. John of Marmoutier was furthermore a specialist of this specific form of literary borrowing. Neil Wright has studied the intertextuality displayed by John of Marmoutier in his works, and showed that a battle scene included in the *Historia Gaufredi Ducis* was composed from verses of Statius's *Thebaid*.[61] In the introduction to their critical edition, André Salmon and Paul Marcheguay described John's literary process less favorably as consisting in sewing together anecdotes borrowed from many hands and from the most diverse sources.[62] This negative opinion stems from the fact that the second half of Geoffrey's *vita* is mostly based on Henry of Huntington's *Historia*.

John of Marmoutier manifested a strong taste for intertextuality, including the use of an exportable genre template, that can be identified clearly in Geoffrey's knighting scene. In *chansons de geste*, knighting performances are, as a rule, structured and described in as many as thirteen steps, from the preparation of the ceremony to the presentation and equipping of each weapon and piece of armor to girding of the sword and the demonstration of knightly abilities. The order in which the various steps are accomplished will differ from one *chanson de geste* to another, but these core steps remain the same.[63] As an ideal, a complete knighting performance would include the following thirteen steps: 1) the ceremony is prepared (mass, bath, etc.); 2) the weapons are presented; 3) the boots are laced; 4) the spurs are tied to the feet; 5) a shirt is put on; 6) the hauberk is donned; 7) the helmet is set; 8) the sword is girded; 9) the accolade is given; 10) the shield is hung at the neck; 11) the spear is seized; 12) the horse is brought forward; 13) the new knight shows his ability.

To take a medieval example, here is Rainier's knighting in *Girart de Vienne*, a *chanson de geste* from the late twelfth or early thirteenth century. Most of the

---

[60] Patrick Moran, 'La guerre comme marqueur générique dans la littérature narrative des XIIe et XIIIe siècles', *Le Moyen Âge* 125 (2019), 21–35.
[61] Neil Wright, 'Epic and Romance in the Chronicles of Anjou', *ANS 26* (2003), 177–89.
[62] *Chroniques des comtes d'Anjou*, ed. Paul-Alexandre Marchegay and André Salmon, i, p. xxxviii.
[63] This description of an ideal knighting is inspired by documentary observations and by Jean-Pierre Martin, *Les motifs dans la chanson de geste. Définition et utilisation* (Paris, 2017).

formal gestures and knightly objects showcased in the ideal knighting mentioned above are found in Rainier's dubbing, with the exception of the spurs (4) and the shirt (5).

> (1) *Après la messe en ont mené Rainier*
> *Por adouber ou grant palais plainier*
> (2) *Ses garnemans ont fait aparilier,*
> (3) *Chausses de fer li font aparilier.*
> (6) *El dos li vestent .i. frès haubert doublier.*
> (7) *El chief li lacent .i. vert elme d'or mier.*
> (8) *Li rois li çaint .i. riche branc d'acier,*
> (9) *El col li fiert l'emperere a vis fier;*
> (12) *On li amoine .i. auferrant destrier;*
> *Il i monta par le senestre estrier.*
> (10) *A col li pendent .i. escu de quartier,*
> (11) *Et en son poing .i. roit espie d'acier.*
> (13) *Fist .i. eslès sor l'auferrant corsier.*[64]

> 1) After the mass, they led Rainier/to the great palace to knight him.
> 2) They prepared his knightly gear.
> 3) They made him put his mail leggings on.
> 6) They dress him with a newly-made doubly-woven hauberk.
> 7) They lace to his head a new helmet made of pure gold.
> 8) The king girded him with a precious steel sword.
> 9) The proud-faced emperor strikes him on the neck.
> 12) A warhorse is brought to him; /he mounted it using the left stirrup.
> 10) They hang a quartered shield around his neck,
> 11) and in his fist a stiff steel spear.
> 13) He left on the fast warhorse.

Those thirteen steps can also be identified in Geoffrey's knighting in the *Historia Gaufredi Ducis*:

> (1) *Illucescente die altera, balneorum usus, uti tyrocinii suscipiendi consuetudo expostulat, paratus est.*
> (5) [...] *Gaufredus byssi retorta ad carnem induitur, cyclade auro texta supervestitur, clamide conchilii et muricis sanguine tincta tegitur, caligis olosericis calciatur, pedes ejus sotularibus in superficie leunculos aureos habentibus muniuntur.*
> (1) *Talibus itaque, ut pretaxatum est, ornamentis decoratur regius gener, quasi flos lilii candens roseoque superfusus rubore, cum illo suo nobili collectaneo comitatu, de secreto thalami processit in publicum.*
> (2) *Adducti sunt equi, allata sunt arma, distribuuntur singulis prout opus erat.*

---

[64] Bertrand de Bar-sur-Aube, *Girart de Vienne*, ed. Frederic G. Yeandle (New York, NY 1930), 34–5.

The Exemplary Knighting of Geoffrey Plantagenet 123

(12) *Andegavensi vero adductus est miri decoris equus Hispaniensis, qui tante, ut aiunt, velocitatis erat ut multe aves in volando eo tardiores essent.*
(6) *Induitur lorica incomparabili, que, maculis duplicibus intexta, nullius lancee vel jaculi cujuslibet ictibus transforabilis haberetur ;*
(3) *calciatus est caligis ferreis ex maculis itidem duplicibus compactis ;*
(4) *calcaribus aureis pedes ejus astricti sunt ;*
(10) *clipeus, leunculos auros ymaginarios habens, collo ejus suspenditur ;*
(7) *imposita est capiti ejus cassis multo lapide pretioso relucens, que talis temperature erat ut nullius ensis acumine incidi vel falsificari valeret ;*
(11) *allate est ei hasta fraxinea, ferrum Pictavense pretendens ;*
(8) *ad ultimum allatus est ei ensis de thesauro regio, ab antiquo ibidem signatus, in quo fabricando fabrorum superlativus Galannus multa opera et studio desudavit.*
(13) *Taliter ergo armatus tyro noster, novus militie postmodum flos futurus, mira agilitate absque stapia, gratia invelocitatis, equum prosilit. Quid plura ? dies illa, tyrocinii honori et gaudio dicata, tota in ludi bellici exercitio et procurandis splendide corporibus elapsa est. Septem ex integro dies apud regem tyrocinii celebre gaudium continuavit.*[65]

[1) On this illustrious day, baths were prepared at dawn, as the custom demands for someone about to be knighted. 5) Geoffrey is dressed in a coat of fine linen, adorned with gold embroidery, covered with a mantle dyed with the blood of shellfish and murex, shod in silken stockings, his feet protected with golden shoes shaped like little lions. 1) Thus adorned, the royal son-in-law, shining like a bright lily with a purple hue, proceeds with his noble companions from the privacy of his chamber into the public space. 2) Horses are brought forth, arms and armors are supplied, and each one is equipped as needed. 12) A horse of incredible beauty from Spain, reputed to be so swift that many birds would be slower in flight, is brought for the young man from Anjou. 6) He is clothed in an incomparable hauberk made of doubly-woven mail, impervious to any blows from lances or javelin. 3) He wears similarly doubly-woven boots, 4) and golden spurs are fastened to his feet. 10) A shield painted with the image of golden lions is hung around his neck. 7) A shining helmet adorned with precious stones is placed on his head, forged in such a way that no sword blade could cut through it. 11) He is given an ash spear, made of iron from Poitiers. 8) Finally, he is presented with a sword from the royal treasury, bearing an inscription from ancient times, in the making of which the expert Wayland labored with great effort. 13) Thus armed, our young novice, destined to become a flower of chivalry, leaps onto his horse with remarkable agility, without the need for stirrups, exuding grace and swiftness. What more could we say? That day, dedicated to the honor and joy of chivalry, is devoted entirely to playful martial exercises and to the acquisition of splendid bodies. The celebration of this knighting continued at the court of the king for seven whole days.]

Thus, John of Marmoutier carefully included everything in his masterful depiction. Each step is there: the formal preparations, the pieces of armor, the sword, the horse, the spear, the display of bravery. The 'exportable generic

---

[65] John of Marmoutier, *Historia Gaufredi Ducis*, 177–81.

template' used by John undeniably comes from the *chanson de geste*, which was, in his lifetime, the only literary genre featuring such elaborate descriptions of knighting performances.[66] This is of great consequence for the value of Geoffrey's dubbing as a staple example of knighting performances. Not only is it not representative of medieval historical documentary production, but it has the same thematic exemplary qualities as regular knighting scenes in late twelfth-century *chansons de geste* (and, I would argue, late twelfth- and early thirteenth-century versified and proses romances).[67] The centuries-long identification of Geoffrey's knighting described by John of Marmoutier as the first historical depiction of an *adoubement* thus acts like the tree that hides the forest, and the academic divisions between historians and specialists of medieval literature, especially in France, led scholars to lose sight of what was probably evident for a medieval reader or listener to the *Historia Gaufredi Ducis*.

This does not mean, however, that *Historia Gaufredi Ducis* has nothing to tell us about the ritual and culture of *adoubement*. John of Marmoutier did produce an exceptional text with some striking literary qualities. There is a genuine form of invention in the monk's work, which comes from the fact that he undertook a twofold transposition. He translated into Latin words and sentences on a subject (knighting) that was mostly expressed and thought about in Old French. At the same time, he also partially broke free from the metrical cadence of these words and sentences, moving away from the stereotyped assonance of *laisses* characteristic of *chansons de geste*. John finely mingles clauses of different length, using long sentences (see above 1, 5, and 13) to frame and encompass shorter ones (see above 2, 3, 4, 6, 7, 8, 10, 11, 12), some of which are quite reminiscent of the length of a *laisse* (see above 2, 3, 4, 10, 11). The stylistic freedom offered by prose thus allowed John to circumvent the formulaic constraints governing the way dubbing appears in *chansons de geste* in order to create something new: an original, enhanced, and unique literary depiction of a knighting ritual. Through his skillful pen, he succeeded in elevating the level of his description to what should be seen as a kind of *ekphrasis*, that is to say, a splendid word-painting of a building or an object that demonstrates the rhetoric mastery of its author.

But John's *ekphrasis* is not just a piece of writerly bravura. This literary process, based on exhaustive and meticulous description, is designed to bring readers and listeners affectively to believe and imagine they are in the material presence of the object or the monument so vividly depicted.[68] This approach to

---

[66] To be clear, both derive from the contemporary practice which they were narratively retelling and reshaping, but I argue that the generic exportable template of the *chanson de geste* is fundamental within John of Marmoutier's tale of Geoffrey's dubbing.

[67] See, for instance, the satirical knighting of Fergus in Guillaume le Clerc, *Fergus*, ed. Ernst Martin (Halle, 1872), 15–17, lines 519–613, or the magnificent dubbing of Gawain and his peers in *Les premiers faits du roi Arthur*, ed. Philippe Walter, in *Le livre du Graal I*, ed. Daniel Poirion (Paris, 2011), 1161, § 355.

[68] Sophie Coussemaker and Julia Roumier, 'En guise d'introduction: *Ekphrasis* et hypotypose: les écritures de l'enargeia dans la péninsule Ibérique médiévale et moderne', *e-Spania* 37 (2020), https://journals.openedition.org/e-spania/35993.

presenting Geoffrey's knighting may have led readers and listeners to see it as more real because they could picture it with ease. In medieval historiography, the author's ability to show through words, to describe objects, persons, or events so vividly and convincingly that the reader or the listener could represent them in his heart and mind in order to observe them with the eyes of the soul, was indeed one of the keys to establishing the credibility of both the author and his or her story.[69] As Ghislaine Fournès showed in her case study of the *Castigos del rey don Sancho IV*, the effectiveness of an *ekphrasis* lies, on the one hand, in the awakening of emotions that trigger admiration, and, on the other, in the fact that it is more easily inscribed in the memory and performatively associated with other systems of images already existing in the mind of readers and listeners.[70] Finally, since medieval literary descriptions are often crafted to convey either praise or blame,[71] John exalts the memory of this knighting not only through the clearly laudatory tone and words used, but also structurally by the simple fact that he chose to slow down the rhythm of the narration to depict something in detail and in a positive light.

Of course, these observations on the rhetorical effects of Geoffrey's knighting's as an *ekphrasis* assume that there was a readership or an audience to move and sway with this exceptional word-painting. Yet, as noted above, the contemporary reception of this work is unknown, and for a long time it might only have been enjoyed by monks and priests, high-ranking members of Le Mans's Church like the bishop Guillaume of Passavant (who had been the local promoter of the late count of Anjou's *memoria*), and their lay guests.

As the above investigation has shown, the arguments and assumptions which supposedly make Geoffrey's knighting the standard example of a historical knighting have led to a scholarly misunderstanding: the interpretation of a genre template (the *adoubement* as it appears in *chansons de geste*) as a lived ritual reality through its insertion in a Latin lay hagiographical text. Geoffrey's description of knighting is a documentary *hapax* turned mainstream by more than three hundred years of modern use as a remarkable testimony – useful in its meticulous narrative detail – to the emergence of knighting performances. We should think twice before using John of Marmoutier's work of Geoffrey's dubbing as an exemplary historical knighting, both because it is not, in fact, more accurate or truer than dubbing scenes found in late twelfth-century *chanson de geste* for being composed in Latin prose, and because it is not representative of how medieval chronicles, histories and annals generally portray the *adoubement*.

---

[69] Béranger Boulay, 'Effets de présence et effets de vérité dans l'historiographie', *Littérature* 50 (2010), 26–38, addressing reflections by Umberto Eco in his 'Ekphrasis and Quotations', *Tijdschrift voor filosofie* 50 (1988), 3–19.
[70] Ghislaine Fournès, 'L'ekphrasis au service de l'idéologie royale dans les Castigos del rey don Sancho IV (fin XIIIe siècle)', *e-Spania* 37 (2020), § 19–20, http://journals.openedition.org/e-spania/35997.
[71] Huguette Legros, 'L'armement du chevalier : d'une topique à une *senefiance*', in *Lire les objets médiévaux: Quand les choses font signe et sens* (Rennes, 2017), 145–67 at 147.

But refraining from considering Geoffrey's *adoubement* as exemplary does not mean abandoning this text excerpt altogether as evidence. We should celebrate it as an exceptional document, as a testament to the creative possibilities of medieval literature produced in a cloister, and as proof that monastic authors such as John of Marmoutier knew how to write perfect knighting scenes but chose not to insert such scenes in chronicles because it did not fit their purposes nor the rules of this literary genre.

The *Historia Gaufridi ducis'* portrayal of Geoffrey's knighting also offers an example of how, in medieval society, a new social practice could be legitimized by temporal retrojection. By depicting an early twelfth-century delivery of arms using the form of a late twelfth-century knighting performance, John of Marmoutier enhanced the legitimacy of the later knightly ritual by making it seem to continue an earlier tradition. If we assume, with Joseph Morsel,[72] that what underlies the invention and uses of written traditions is the affirmation of a seignorial power against both its seignorial competitors and his own subordinates, then we can postulate that the existence of the scriptural tradition of *adoubement* was one of the conditions of its effectiveness in the construction of the symbolic power of the lay aristocracy in relation with the clerics and the rest of the population. In this regard, through his *Historia Gaufredi Ducis*, the monk of Marmoutier took part in the construction of the symbolic power of chivalry and to the legitimation of the social dominance of the lay aristocrats who could successfully be recognized as *chevaliers*.

For historians, however, the real value of this story of the creation of Geoffrey's knighting in the *Historia Gaufredi Ducis* as an exemplar maybe that it shows how we historians work and think,[73] and it illustrates how ignorance or neglect of the scholarly history of a document coupled with a somewhat rigid understanding of medieval documentary genres can sometimes involuntarily and unconsciously turn very peculiar texts, known to us only through a thin chain of one or two fragmentary manuscripts, into historiographical monuments.

---

[72] Joseph Morsel, 'Ce qu'écrire veut dire au Moyen Âge... Observations préliminaires à une étude de la scripturalité médiévale', *Memini. Travaux et documents* 4 (2000), 3–43.
[73] See Joseph Morsel, 'Quand l'historien masque que la norme fabrique le crime... Le cas du registre de l'officialité de Cerisy en 1314–1315', *Genèses* 110 (2018), 55–78.

8

The Repentance of Geoffroy de Milly: Anger, Penance, and the Limits of Sovereign Authority in Thirteenth-Century France[1]

Anne E. Lester

Thus the Lord, the God of Israel, said to me: 'Take from my hand this cup of the wine of wrath, and make all the nations to whom I send you drink it. They shall drink and stagger and be crazed because of the sword that I am sending among them.

Jeremiah 25:15–16

In 1347, the canons of the Cathedral of Amiens drew up an inventory itemizing all the precious objects in their church treasury.[2] Copied into a modest parchment *libellus,* or booklet – following entries for the relics of John the Baptist and Saint

---

[1] I am grateful for the opportunity to have presented a version of this essay as a featured lecture at the Haskins Society Meeting in October 2022 and to the audience there in attendance. I thank William Chester Jordan for his encouragement and for his close reading. I also thank my colleague Nathan Connolly, whose question to me about changes in the urban landscape of Amiens and the displacement of people has stayed with me. This is, in part, my attempt to answer that question. Conversations with Julie Barrau, Pascale Bermon, Scott Bruce, Bill North, Liêm Tuttle, Liesbeth Van Houts and Nicholas Vincent yielded valuable advice, bibliography, and comments for which I am extremely grateful. I dedicate the essay to the memory of Paul Hyams, a teacher to so many of us.

[2] The original text, an octo volume of vellum, Amiens, A[rchive] D[épartementales de la] Somme, 4 G1 134 (1347) was drawn up by one Hugh de Mosterolio who is identified as the provost and custodian of the treasury of Amiens and one J. Fructerius. Several other local officials were in attendance when the objects were itemized as noted on fol. 1r. The volume has only eight folios and contains only the text of the cathedral treasury inventory. I suspect that it was created to be used in the space of the cathedral as a handlist of all the relevant objects and books used in the church. Together with Laura Morreale, I have completed a new edition of this text accessible with manuscript images on the DALME website: https://dalme.org/collections/records/40b0df7f-bdcc-489f-80e5-3ca72f0fd316/1r/. The inventory was drawn up during the episcopate of Jean de *Cherchermont* (18 February 1326–26 January 1373), who is mentioned in the text. Bishop Jean was generous to the community and donated funds for a chaplainry as well as a series of sumptuous ornaments and textiles. The inventory was probably drawn up in response to pressures during the Hundred Years' War. See Pierre Desportes and Hélène Millet, *Fasti Ecclesiae Gallicanae: Répertoire prosopographique des évêques,*

Firmin, Amiens's powerful patron saints, numerous opulent clerical vestments, crosses and pyxes, crystal vases, gem-encrusted chalices, and dozens of books – is an outlier: a simple record that reads, *Item*, 'likewise, six silver basins hanging in the church'.[3] Strikingly, the same entry continues and offers a more precise description, noting that 'one is hanging before the crucifix, another in the middle of the choir, and three others similarly before the altar, and the sixth before the body of the saints', that is, before the main altar.[4] The basins were hung at the key intervals above the choir, the sacred space reserved for the cathedral canons, in the middle of the church. When Jacques Garnier first edited the inventory in 1850, he added a curious note: 'No doubt these are the five basins, each made of five marks of silver which had been given in 1244 by the *bailli* Geoffroy de Milly (*Gaudridus de Milliaco*), in expiation for the death of the [five] clerics that he had executed.'[5] Garnier drew his note, as all good antiquarian editors would have, from his own reading and local knowledge of the corresponding archival tradition and from the older histories of Amiens he had to hand as he worked.[6] In local memory, the story of Geoffroy de Milly was a well-known, even notorious, incident, one that persisted over time through the very objects the royal *bailli* donated and in the space of the sanctuary itself. And this was precisely the point, for Geoffroy's basins were designed as commemorative objects to which a history and, as we shall see, his own repentance, were affixed.

The story as it comes down to us in the archival record is truncated: only the episcopal sentence survives. It exists in a single parchment text kept as part of the archives of the chapter of the cathedral of Amiens, and as a copy in the cathedral

---

dignitaries et chanoines de France de 1200 à 1500, t. 1: Diocese d'Amiens (Turnhout, 1996), 62–4.

3 'Item sex bachinos argenteos pendentes in ecclesia'. AD Somme, 4 G1 134 (1347), fol. 3r.

4 'Scilicet unum ante crucifixum alium in medio chori. Tres simul vinctos ante altare. Et sextum ante corpora sanctorum', AD Somme, 4 G1 134 (1347), fol. 3r.

5 'Lá, sans doute, sont les cinq bassins d'argent de 5 marcs qu'avait donnés, en 1244, le bailly Geoffroy de Milly, en expiation de la mort des six clercs qu'il avait fait exécuter'. M. Jacques Garnier, 'Inventaires du Trésor de la cathédrale d'Amiens, publiés d'après les manuscrits', *Mémoires de la Société des antiquaries de Picardie* 10 (1850), 229–391 at 261n2. At the time, Jacques Garnier (1808–88) was serving as the Secrétaire-Perpétuel of the Société des Antiquaires de Picardie and the Conservateur de la Bibliothèque communale d'Amiens (as noted on p. 623 of the same volume). He was also the principal editor of the *Dictionnaire topographique du département de la Somme* (2 vols, Amiens, 1867–78). Commemoration of the clerics was inserted into the Necrology of cathedral as well, see M. Roze, 'Nécrologe de l'Eglise d'Amiens, suivi des distributions aux fêtes', *Mémoires de la Société des antiquaires de Picardie* 28 (1838), 265–504, at 367 and 373.

6 Primarily, one presumes, he drew from the charters and cartularies of the bishop and canons of Amiens. These were later edited by Abbot J. Rose and introduced by J. Roux, *Cartulaire du chapiter de la Cathedral d'Amiens* (Amiens, 1905–13), 379–81, no. 327 (December 1244). Garnier also cites two eighteenth-century histories: Louis-François Daire, *Histoire de la ville d'Amiens, depuis son origine jusque'à present* (2 vols, Paris, 1757), i, 210–12; and Adrian de la Morliere, *Le premier livre des antiquitez, histoires, et choses plus remarquables de la ville d'Amiens* (Paris, 1627), 201–3.

cartulary.⁷ By reading backwards and piecing events together, a scene emerges. On the Saturday after the feast of Saint Martin (11 November), therefore on 18 November 1243, the then *bailli* of Amiens, Geoffroy de Milly, had five clerics, who had been in his service, seized and detained in the city prison. He then had them 'most cruelly and violently torn apart and suspended through the city of Amiens (*fecit per civitatem Ambianensem turpissime ac crudelissime distrahi et suspendi)*'.⁸ This may have entailed something like ordering them to be drawn, although their bodies we know remained intact. The point was, he punished them cruelly, publicly, and unto death. Moreover, as the bishop's text makes clear, Geoffroy allowed this to take place without a confession or a conviction, nor was anyone called to speak verbally on this judgement; rather, the *bailli* condemned the clerics himself to a final sentence.⁹ Two weeks later, on the day after the feast of Saint Andrew (2 December), Geoffroy publicly confessed to this rash act and swore before the bishop, before members of his own family and acquaintances standing surety for him (*fidejussoribus*), and before all in attendance, to accept the elaborate punishment (*poena*) and penance that Bishop Arnould de la Pierre imposed upon him, in the bishop's words, 'for the aforesaid malicious deed (*pro dicto maleficio infligenda)*'.¹⁰

The punishment itself reveals other dimensions of the story, for as was often the case with the prescription of aristocratic penance, its precise stipulations

---

7   Both versions of the episcopal sentence have been edited. See *Inventaire sommaire des Archives départementales antérieures à 1790: Somme*, ed. Georges Durand, (6 vols, Amiens, 1883–1910), series G, ii, 5–6, no. 652 (now available online: https://archives.somme.fr/page/series-anciennes-anterieures-a-1790-) [= *Inv. Som.* G]; and Rose and Roux, *Cartulaire du chapiter de la Cathedral d'Amiens,* i, 379–81. Both copies are dated to the day after the feast of St André (1 December 1243 (n.d. 1244)). Although not ideal, I have worked from these editions.

8   *Inv. Som.* G, ii, 6, no. 652. The version in the cartulary is slightly different: 'fecit per civitatem Ambianensis turpissime ac crudelissime distrahi et suspendi', Rose and Roux, *Cartulaire,* i, 379. There are small differences of syntax between the two versions. I follow that in the archive rather than the cartulary in what follows. The story is also described by Daire, *Histoire d'Amiens,* i, *pièces justificatives,* 528; and from the perspective of the town, in Janvier, *Livre d'or de la municipalité amiénoise,* 7, https://gallica.bnf.fr/ark:/12148/bpt6k3794471/f7.vertical.

9   ... et de facto nec confessi nec convicti fuissent, quorum et si alterum affuisset quod coram non suo judice verbaliter, nec, quod insolentius est, fuissent etiam per diffinitivam sententiam condempnati.

10 Both copies of the text begin in effect as a confession: 'Noverit universitas vestra quod cum Gaufridus de Milliaco confessus fuerit coram nobis', *Inv. Som.* G, ii, 6, no. 652; and Rose and Roux, *Cartulaire,* i, 379. On Bishop Arnould, see the entry in the *Gallia Christiana* 10, cols 1184–5, which gives a short biography of Arnould and summarizes these events among others. Arnould took the Franciscan habit while training in Paris, where he participated in a series of disputes as part of university life, and was then present for a number of reforming church councils before rising to the episcopate of Amiens in 1236. In 1243 and 1244 he welcomed the Dominicans and Franciscans to Amiens respectively. He was present at the translation of the body of St Edmund to the abbey of Pontigny and then died before June 1247.

were designed to fit the crime.[11] Bishop Arnould ordered that on the following Saturday (7 December), after Prime but before Vespers, therefore at some point between seven in the morning and six at night, in bare feet and without clothes except a shirt and belt made of sackcloth, 'with a noose hanging around his neck – which was called a *hars* in French *(laqueo suspensorio circa collum qui vulgariter dicitur* hars)' – and with hands clearly or visibly tied behind his back, 'in the way that mercenaries and criminals are accustomed to be tied who were led to the gibbet (*eo modo quo ligari solent latronibus, qui ad patibulum ducebantur*)', Geoffroy was to begin a penitential procession (*quantulacumque statione peracta*), passing through specific locations within the city. From the place which is called *Mala Domus* he should be taken to the place of the forks (*ad locum furcarum*), and from there taken by way of the church of St-Montianus, and then finally returned in the same way.[12] There, with his hands unbound, he was to take up one of the bodies of the clerics – wrapped in silk cloth which Geoffroy himself had to purchase at great expense (*palla serica ipsius Gaufridi emenda sumptibus*) – and carry the same cleric on his back solemnly and devoutly to the mother church (the cathedral), and from there, journey to the public cemetery next to St-Denis, where the cleric was to be buried. In a similar way, for the four days that followed, one after another, Geoffroy was to process, 'carrying the remaining bodies of the other four clerics, following the conditions described above (*reliqua quatuor corpora delaturus, observatis usquequaque conditionibus antedictis*)'. Once this was done, Geoffroy was to

---

[11] The classic study remains Mary C. Mansfield, *The Humiliation of Sinners: Public Penance in Thirteenth-Century France* (Ithaca, NY, 1995). Far more scholarly attention has been given to early medieval penance and the study of penitential handbooks: see, for example, Rob Meens, *Penance in Medieval Europe, 600–1200* (Cambridge, 2014); Sarah Hamilton, *The Practice of Penance, 900–1500* (Woodbridge, 2001); as well as the landmark studies by Mayke de Jong, 'Power and Humility in Carolingian Society: The Public Penance of Louis the Pious', *Early Medieval Europe* 1 (1992), 29–52; and her overview, de Jong, 'Transformations of Penance', in *Rituals of Power: From Late Antiquity to the Early Middle Ages*, ed. Frans Theuws and Janet L. Nelson (Leiden, 2000), 185–224. See also Mayke de Jong, *The Penitential State: Authority and Atonement in the Age of Louis the Pious, 814–840* (Cambridge, 2009). For the later medieval period, penance in England has garnered far more attention than in the French context. See James Masschaele, 'The Public Space of the Marketplace in Medieval England', *Speculum* 77 (2002), 383–421, esp. 406–15; and David Postles, 'Penance and the Market Place: A Reformation Dialogue with the Medieval Church (c. 1250–1600)', *The Journal of Ecclesiastical History* 54 (2003), 441–68; and for the specific role of bishops in administering public penances and the tension that ensued involving rank, a situation not dissimilar to that of Geoffroy de Milly, see Rosalind Hill, 'Public Penance: Some Problems of a Thirteenth-Century Bishop', *History* 36 (1951), 213–26. On the broader context of penance, pleading and public shame and pain, see Sara M. Butler, *Pain, Penance, and Protest: Peine Forte et Dure in Medieval England* (Cambridge, 2021).

[12] '*Ad locum furcarum*,' or in French, '*des fourches partibulaires*', was another term for a gallows or gibbet. Often *fourcari* were places under episcopal jurisdiction, that is, where bishops oversaw justice or had rights to justice. On the terms here and on different jurisdictions regarding capital punishment, see Lucie Ecorchard, *Les lieux de justice parisiens à la fin du Moyen Âge* (Paris, 2022).

follow the same procedures at the church of Reims and in all the episcopal churches in the province of Reims, as well as in the churches of Rouen, Sens, Paris, and Orleans, according to the same prescriptions: similarly attired in only a sackcloth shirt, with a noose (*hars*) around his neck, hands tied behind his back, and he should process solemnly between Sundays and feast days and he should make a gift or donation with each procession. Finally, he was made to swear that he would never serve as an administrative official in any of these lands, and he promised to carry letters patent sealed with his seal back to the chapter attesting to when and where his punishment was carried out. All of this should be completed by Easter.

The bishop's penance went on to stipulate, 'so that the enormity of his deed is not abolished and the punishment is sufficient to ensure that the memory is not lost (*tam enormis facti vestigium, pena non sufficit que post se memoriam non relinquat*)', Geoffroy had to have five basins of silver, each of five marks to the measure of Troyes, sumptuously made (*volumus ut quinque pelves argenteas, singulas quinque marcharum ad pondus Trecense, suis faciat sumptibus fabricari*). And he had to purchase annual rents at the value of 75 *lbs* Paris for five candles made to weigh three pounds each, to be placed in perpetuity before the relics contained (*theca*) in the church of Amiens. And he should assign the same rents as a commemoration in the church, so that from the day of Pentecost when the basins were to be made, the same rents should be paid and assigned to that use. To give some sense of the value of what was imposed, it should be noted that 5 marks of silver is just over 5 pounds, or 240 silver pennies. In 1243, the silver penny, or *denarius* either of Paris or Tours, would have been the money of account. A *bailli* would have made an annual salary of approximately 365 *lbs* a year.[13] Each basin was therefore made from 1200 coins or its equivalent in silver. These were, in short, not small vessels, but of significant size, sumptuous in their weight. With the additional rents of 75 *lbs* for candles for each basin, this was a material donation meant to be keenly felt and to endure over time. And then, Bishop Arnould concluded, after the feast of the Nativity of John the Baptist (24 June) Geoffroy must undertake the journey to Jerusalem and never be allowed to return, unless each and every canon in chapter of Amiens offered their consent (*tandem intra Nativitatem beati Johannis Baptiste iter arripiat ad terram Jherosolomitanam eundi, nunquam inde de cetero reversurus, nisi de nostra et singulorum de Ambianensi capitulo voluntate*).[14]

---

[13] This is an average estimate that comes to about 1 *lb* or between 12 and 15 *sous* a day. The salaries of some *baillis*, like those of Normandy for example, could be higher, closer to 500–600 *lbs* per annum. For salary calculations and comparisons, see Joseph R. Strayer, *The Administration of Normandy under Saint Louis* (Cambridge, MA, 1932), 119–20; Joseph Strayer, *The Reign of Philip the Fair* (Princeton, NJ, 1980), 55–7, 112–13; John W. Baldwin, *The Government of Philip Augustus: Foundations of French Royal Power in the Middle Ages* (Berkeley, CA, 1986), on the *baillis* generally, 125–36, for salaries, 133.

[14] I have summarized the very long and detailed sentence Bishop Arnould imposed. For the full text, see as above, *Inv. Som.* G, ii, 6, no. 652 (December 1243). I have put the Latin in the text above when useful for clarification or revealing for word choice.

The repentance of Geoffroy de Milly has much to tell us about the interstices of royal and ecclesiastical justice at a pivotal moment of transition in the mid-thirteenth century. In the years and months that followed Geoffroy's punishment and penance, the French king, Louis IX, would take a first vow to go on crusade and would initiate one of the most influential reform measures of his own government by sending out teams of *enquêteurs* to investigate the behavior of his *baillis* and other royal officials.[15] Increasingly, Louis understood the working of his government in moral terms: if his representatives were not upstanding men, his realm could not be governed in accord with divine will. The present essay considers, first, Geoffroy's role as a *bailli*, an official of the highest rank representing royal governance in the years before the advent of the *enquêteurs*, thus as part of a group of officials we know relatively little about. The nature of Geoffroy's misdeed, his *maleficium*, and the punishment imposed, suggests the ways in which jurisdiction – royal, episcopal, and local – in the 1240s, and specifically in the bailliage of Amiens, was still intertwined and ripe for dispute and conflict. Geoffroy's decision to have five clerics strung up and killed – a decision made in the middle of the night, quickly, and decisively – was, I will argue, the product of anger. What then was the place of anger in governance or in responding to injustice? This was a question on the minds of many at that time and it was not easily disentangled from practices of governance, as personal wrongs and perceived injustices would continue to come into tension with and chafe against ideals of sovereign authority through much of Louis's reign. Finally, in light of such anger, the article concludes by asking what the surviving archival record consigns to silence and to suggest what this means for us as historians who are left nearly always to navigate a partial source base, left nearly always partly in the dark.

I

Geoffroy first appears in the archival record in 1228 when he is attested collecting revenues for the king in his capacity as *bailli* in the newly created *bailliage* of Amiens. It is in this manner that Léopold Delisle initially lists him in the *Chronologie des Baillis et des Sénéchaux* in volume twenty-four of the *Recueil des Historiens de Gaules et de la France*.[16] As Henri Stein affirmed, Geoffroy hailed from the region of the Beauvaisis, from a small hamlet which

---

[15] The landmark study of Louis's crusade and governmental reforms, remains that of Jordan, *Louis IX and the Challenge of the Crusade: A Study in Rulership* (Princeton, 1979); for the advent of the *enquêteurs*, see 51–64. More recently, concerning the *enquêtes*, see Maire Dejoux, *Les enquêtes de Saint Louis: Couverner et sauver son âme* (Paris, 2014).

[16] Léopold Delisle, 'Chronologie des Baillis et des sénéchaux royaux depuis les origines jusqu'à l'avènement de Philippe de Valois', in M. Bouquet et al., eds, *Recueil des Historiens de Gaules et de la France* (24 vols, Paris, 1738–1904), xxiv.1, 78* [hereafter *RHGF*]. It was Delisle, however, who was the principal editor of the *enquêtes* materials in parts 1 and 2 of volume 24.

is today called Milly-sur-Thérain located fourteen kilometers north of Beauvais, and south of Amiens.[17] He was, as was true of most *baillis* in the first half of the thirteenth century, from a knightly family, although not a member of the upper nobility. His branch of the Milly must be distinguished from that of the Milly(-le-Fôret) in the region of the Gâtinais, in the present-day department of the Essonnes. Although the two families may at some point have been related, by the 1230s they were separate, and Geoffroy's family was far less well connected with the regional aristocracy.[18] As *bailli* of Amiens he oversaw an administrative region that ran through Amiens and Péronne and encompassed Abbeville in the west, Roye to the south, and Bapaume to the north.[19]

It is possible to trace his activities on behalf of the crown over a ten-year period before his penance and exile. On Monday 19 and Tuesday 20 August 1230, he was part of an inquest at the order of the king or perhaps, given the year, the king and his mother, Blanche of Castile, to determine if one Bernard Double, whom the *bailli* had arrested, was a burgher of Péronne or a cleric of Lihons.[20] In April 1232 he was present on behalf of the king, named as the *bailli* of the lord king for Amiens (*baillius domini regis Ambianensis*), when the knight, Eudes de Monchy, sold his house and fortress at Mouchy to the crown. In effect, Eudes sold his fief to the king and became a royal vassal. The transfer was overseen by Peter *Fabri* the prévôt of Péronne and Geoffroy took possession, by his own hands, of the estate, on behalf of Louis IX.[21] In 1234, 1236, and 1237 he appears again, having journeyed to Paris to render accounts for the bailliage.[22] In 1237,

---

[17] Henri Stein, 'Recherches sur quelques fonctionnaires royaux des XIIIe et XIVe siècles originaires du Gâtinais', *Annales de la société historique et archéologique du Gâtinais* 20 (1902), 1–23; 21 (1903), 343–72; 32 (1914), 195–221; 34 (1918–19), 1–103, at 25; and Jordan, *Louis IX*, 225.
[18] Stein, 'Recherches sur quelques fonctionnaires', 25–6. This point is also made clearly by E. Richemond, *Recherches généalogiques sur la famille des seigneurs de Nemours du XIIe au XVe siècle* (2 vols, Fontainebleau, 1907), i, 180–1, 315–16 with remarks about their seals.
[19] Baldwin, *Government of Philip Augustus*, 130 which describes the boundaries of the newly created bailliage of Amiens. On the history of the *bailliage*, see Michel Fleury, 'Le bailliage d'Amiens: son resort et le problème des limites administratives au Moyen Âge', *BEC* 114 (1956), 45–59.
[20] Alexandre Teulet et al., eds, *Layettes du trésor des chartes* (6 vols, Paris, 1863–1909), ii, 184, no. 2071. The editors date this inquest to 1230 seemingly on the basis of his work collecting revenue on the part of the crown in the same year. See also Léon Louis Borrelli de Serres, *Recherches sur divers services publics du XIIIe au XVIIe siècle* (3 vols, Paris, 1895–1909), i, 63, 72–3. Both cite the revenues coming into the crown, edited in *RHGF*, xxi, 252 C–D, however, this entry, noted below, pertains to 1238 not 1230. There was a misreading of the date, perhaps by Tuelet, and this error persisted. The Layette document, Paris, AN J.232, makes it clear that Geoffroy was serving as *bailli* of Amiens by August 1230.
[21] Teulet, *Layettes*, ii, 233–4, no. 2180 (11–30 April, after Easter 1232): 'dictam saisinam rerum venditarum predictarum recepit in manu sua pro domino rege.'
[22] Delisle, 'Chronologie', *RHGF*, xxiv.1, 78*, citing Nicolas Brussel, *Nouvel examen de l'usage général des fiefs en France pendant le XI, le XII, le XIII, et le XIVe siècle, pour servir à l'intelligence des plus anciens titres du domaine de la Couronne* (2 vols,

again acting for the king, he took possession of the rights to the fishponds of Bies, located at Doullens to the north of Amiens, which Pavie the wife of Bernard de Moreuil held as part of her dower and which the couple sold to the king. In this case, the bishop of Amiens, Arnould, oversaw the transfer and invested Geoffroy with the rights through the formal document.[23] Between 1237 and 1243, Geoffroy continued to appear in the account records of the crown, rendering revenues generated in the bailliage of Amiens. For the accounts cast on Ascension (13 May), 1238, he submitted returns from the bailliage to the crown of a relatively meager 322 *lbs* 13 *denarii*. These were specifically tied to revenue from the fishponds of Athies, Doullens, and Péronne, and included 80 *lbs* of revenue from the goods seized from heretics at Miraumont as well as *tailles* and labor services worth 180 *lbs*.[24] Finally, at some point after the king acquired the rights to the fishponds at Doullens, Geoffroy, working with the mayor of Doullens, and Robert Fretel and Gerard de Altrebatus, undertook another inquest at the order of the king to find who was responsible for repairing damages incurred due to flooding.[25] Here, Geoffroy is present in the countryside, interviewing witnesses and townsmen about what they saw and heard, and what was in the king's best interests.

Strikingly, the records also give us a glimpse of Geoffroy after his fall, after his condemnation and banishment from the *bailliage* and from France. For he also appears, in staccato memories, piecemeal in the first *enquête* returns of 1247. We learn of two complaints about his conduct, incidents that by the time they were recorded had taken place five or even eight years earlier. Here Geoffroy

---

Paris, 1727–8), i, 487, which lists Geoffroy rendering accounts in Paris. I thank Cecilia Gaposchkin for facilitating my consultation of Brussel's text when I was visiting Dartmouth College.

[23] Teulet, *Layettes*, ii, 346 (13 June 1237). For an overview of Geoffroy's dealings as *bailli*, see the comments in Léopold Delisle, 'Fragment d'un register des enquêteurs de saint Louis', *Comptes rendus des séance de l'Académe des Inscriptions et Belles-Lettres* 33 (1889), 315–26, where he describes the *enquête* material recovered from nineteenth-century book bindings, part of which include material from Picardy that concerns Geoffroy de Milly (see pp. 318–20).

[24] *RHGF*, xxi, 252 (May 1238): 'de cataulis haereticorum de Miraumont', 'De espletis'. On the heretics seized at Miraumont, see the brief discussion in Charles Homer Haskins, 'Robert Le Bougre and the Beginnings of the Inquisition in Northern France', *AHR* 4 (1902), 631–52, at 632–3, who notes that 'Pieron Malkasin and Matthieu de Lauvin, their wives, and Robert de Lauvin, were burnt. Matthieu's pregnant daughter was also taken, but by the intercession of the French Queen her life was spared on profession of orthodoxy'. The comment in *Chronicle of Hainaut* by Baudoin d'Avesnes, *RHGF*, xxi.1, 166, notes that heretics were seized in 1235, therefore during the time Geoffroy was active as *bailli* in the north. More work is needed on this episode.

[25] Paris, AN J/1034 no. 35 (s.d. before 1270): 'Hec est inquesta de mandato domini regis facta per Gaufridum de Milliaco, ballivum Ambianensem, et per majorem Dullendii'. The inquest was recorded on a role of parchment, an edited extract is found in E. Boutaric, *Actes du Parlement de Paris* (2 vols, Paris, 1863), i, 139, no. 1560C; and Teulet, *Layettes*, v, 318–19 no. 888. I thank Jean-François Moufflet for allowing me to consult the original in the AN.

was accused of extortion or taking money from several people – without right and without judgement. In the first instance, he extorted 100 *sous parisis* from one Peter de Vermans, a knight (*extorserunt ab eo, sine lege et judicio, c solidos parisiensium*) for permission to hunt one hare (*unum leporem*).[26] In the second case, he took 7 *lbs parisis* (*extorserunt ab ea sine lege et judicio VII libras parisiensium*) to clear Agnes de Bievilla's two sons from accusations of wrongdoing (*forefactum*).[27] In the second instance, Geoffroy is cited acting with Peter Faber and William de Milly, who were serving as the *prévôts* of Péronne.[28]

None of this behavior is at all surprising or out of the ordinary. Overall, Geoffroy appears to have been a diligent and forthright official. Present, carrying out the business of the king, hearing civil cases and grievances, and imposing fines and collecting fees for justice, he did what was asked of a competent *bailli*.[29] From time to time, the memory of his actions seemed harsh and arbitrary. That he acted without law and judgement (*sine lege et judicio*) was a serious critique of a *bailli* whose function was precisely to uphold the law and bring cases to justice. Some of Geoffroy's work certainly incurred the frustrations of both local knights and women protective of their own status and rights, and that of their children.

There is, of course, so much about everyday behavior that we simply cannot know. But what remains important in Geoffroy's case is how a *bailli* was meant to act. The *baillis* were first and foremost representatives of the king in the countryside. They 'constituted the fundamental administrative contact between the king and his subjects'.[30] *Baillis* who acted in the capacity that Geoffroy did were a relatively new cadre of officials. Their reach and authority were given formal definition in 1190, as John Baldwin has shown, in the reform ordinance-testament of Philip Augustus.[31] The *baillis* were relied upon 'chiefly

---

[26] *RHGF*, xxiv.2, 735 C, no. 35 (1247–8); here Geoffroy is accused with Matheaus Torel, *prévôt* of Aties.
[27] *RHGF*, xxiv.2, 736 J, no. 53 (1247–8).
[28] Here William de Milly should not be mistaken for Guillaume de Milly, the seigneur of Milly in the Gâtinais who would not have served as a *prévôt* at this time. See the comments in Richemond, *Recherches généalogiques*, 180.
[29] For the day-to-day work of *baillis*, see the descriptions given in Joseph R. Strayer, *The Administration of Normandy under Saint Louis* (Cambridge, MA, 1932), 12–31; although rather dated, it is unsurpassed.
[30] Jordan, *Louis IX*, 47. On the authority and duties of the *baillis*, see also Baldwin, *Government*, 125–36; more generally, Jordan, *Louis IX*, 45–64; Strayer, *The Reign of Philip the Fair*, 111–42; Hiroshi Takayama, 'The Local Administrative System of France Under Philip IV (1285–1314) – *Baillis* and Seneschals', *JMH* 21 (1995), 167–93; and Andrew Jeffrey Collings, 'The King Cannot Be Everywhere: Royal Governance and Local Society in the Reign of Louis IX' (PhD dissertation, Princeton University, 2018).
[31] Baldwin describes this transformation very clearly and links it to the reform Ordinance-Testament. As was the case with Louis IX in 1247–8, Philip's crusade ambitions profoundly reshaped and extended royal authority into the countryside by means of the *baillis*. See Baldwin, *Government*, 125–6. Amiens, as Baldwin shows, was one of the key regions where this transformation occurred. See Baldwin, *Government*, 126–7.

as judicial officers. ... They were instructed to hold monthly assizes in their regions, where they heard pleas and recorded fines.'[32] When pleas to the crown were heard and renders taken, at least 'three times a year in Paris, the *baillis* were required to attend and to give account of the affairs of the realm', as they saw it.[33] Distinct from the *prévôts*, whose primary function was the collection of taxes and dues to the crown, the *baillis* were responsible for collecting and reporting on fees from justice rendered in the king's name as well as occasional or exceptional revenues such as collections from enforcing regalian rights, forest income, *tailles*, and as we saw with Geoffroy, rights and renders from fishponds, fines for illegal hunting and poaching, and the like. In short, the role of the *baillis* was 'to conduct the exercise of royal power on the part of the king... [and enforce] jurisdiction over the king's agents and those who reported directly to him as well as over specifically royal matters'.[34] As Ada Kuskowski notes, after Louis IX's reforms, '[the *baillis*] also had jurisdiction over local appeals to the crown'.[35]

The duties of the *baillis* also ran the other way. They were conduits of information *from* the crown as well, charged with overseeing the protection of churches, the outgoing payments of royal alms, tending to the needs of widows, women, and orphans, and – again, as we saw Geoffroy doing – convening 'inquests to inform the king about his rights and resources' throughout his domains.[36] In their outgoing functions, they must have on occasion overlapped or possibly overstepped the authority or jurisdiction of the bishop and his officials, who also oversaw the distribution of alms, served (in name) as protectors of widows, orphans, and the poor, and held inquisitions into all manner of questions.[37]

By the late 1230s, however, the *baillis* of the north in particular had become a relatively 'entrenched and exclusive group'.[38] Indeed, Geoffroy de Milly was only the fourth *bailli* to serve in what was a relatively new administrative unit, elevated from the provostship of Amiens only in 1196/1197.[39] Pierre de

[32] Baldwin, *Government*, 126.
[33] Baldwin, *Government*, 126. Such official business, and in particular, the auditing of accounts, took place at Ascension (May or June), All Saints (1 November), and Candlemas (2 February).
[34] Ada Marie Kuskowski, *Vernacular Law: Writing and the Reinvention of Customary Law in Medieval France* (Cambridge, 2023), 112.
[35] Kuskowski makes a persuasive argument that much of the learning and expertise codified in the French royal and regional *coutumiers* drew upon the 'observation, experience, and opinion' of baillis, and several of the texts' authors had served as *baillis* for the crown or local princely governments. See Kuskowski, *Vernacular Law*, 112.
[36] Baldwin, *Government*, 126.
[37] Strayer noted this tension when he observed that 'The Church was unable to find any permanent safeguard against the *baillis*. Interdicts, excommunications, appeals to the king might result in confirmation of their rights, but in the long run the Church lost ground.' Strayer, *The Administration of Normandy*, 29. The arrest of clerks, to say nothing of their imprisonment and murder, as we find with the case of Geoffroy de Milly, is a good example of this growing jurisdictional tension.
[38] Jordan, *Louis IX*, 47.
[39] Baldwin, *Government*, 126-36; and Delisle, 'Chronologie', RHGF xxiv.1, *76-8.

Villevoudée, who held a fief in Louvre-en-Parisis (as was true for many of the early *baillis*, located in lands not far from Paris), was formally appointed as the first *bailli* of Amiens in 1196/97.[40] From 1197 onwards, he worked closely with Pierre de Béthisy, who initially served as *prévôt* of Amiens but came to hold the title *bailli de roi*.[41] Pierre is also associated in the documents with Renaud de Béthisy, his brother, who served for a time as *bailli* of Pierrefonds, closer to Soissons, but still squarely in Picardy. All three men collaborated and worked as a team in hearing pleas, issuing commands, attesting charters, holding inquests, and overseeing the king's interests in the region.[42] By 1202/1203, as Baldwin has shown, twelve *baillis* were active in the royal domain, all worked in different directions outward from Paris, 'and each *bailli*'s sphere of operations overlapped and interlaced with those of his neighbors', as the administrative networks of Pierre and Renaud demonstrate.[43] The point is not that the positions were in any way hereditary (they were not), but they did need to function well as a group of men, strictly loyal to Paris and to the king, who – together – carved out a new kind of authority, mutually reinforcing each other even as they worked in separate, if not yet fully distinct, domains that would come to be called '*bailliages*'.

In the years of transition between the reign of Philip Augustus and that of Louis IX, this cadre of officials was crucial for defining and carrying out royal authority. As Louis IX came into his own between 1230 and 1244, his rule – that is, his functional authority in the countryside and provinces of the royal domain—'rested on this small group of regional salaried officials', the *grands baillis* and, to the south, the *sénechaux*, who together constituted 'no more than about twenty men at any one time between 1226 and 1270'.[44] Moreover, as Jordan has noted, 'technically, they owed their appointment[s] to the king'.[45] But as is clear in the case of the Béthisy family and even the Milly, men (brothers, cousins, nephews) must have been recommended and thus probably often preferred for such positions, moving in and around a familiar if not familial geography of

---

[40] Delisle, 'Chronologie', *RHGF* xxiv.1, *76. For the geographical background of many of the newer *baillis* and men at court, see Quentin Griffiths, 'New Men Among the Lay Counselors of Saint Louis', *Medieval Studies* 32 (1970), 234–72.

[41] Pierre de Béthisy served as *prévôt-bailli* of Amiens and was active there and in Péronne and reached as far as Abbeville in the west, Roye to the south, and Bapaume to the North. See the mini-biographies given in Delisle, 'Chronologie', *RHGF* xxiv.1, *76–7. Delisle composed his notes and tracked the whereabouts of these men through references in regional cartularies including the cartularies of Lihons and Chaalis in this case.

[42] Baldwin, *Government*, 127–8; and Joseph Estienne, 'Trois baillis du roi en Vermandois: Pierre de Villevaudé, Pierre de Béthisy, Guillaume Paté (1197–1200)', *BEC* 97 (1936), 82–90. From time to time, they also worked with another relative, Guy to Béthisy, who served to the east with Laon as his central base.

[43] Baldwin, *Government*, 128.

[44] Jordan, *Louis IX*, 48.

[45] Jordan, *Louis IX*, 48 and appendix one; and Griffiths, 'New Men Among the Lay Counselors of Saint Louis'.

appointment and service, not unlike service in the episcopal and ecclesiastical networks of administration. Indeed, one Adam of Milly served as *bailli* of Artois from 1223 to 1228, and he appears to have been, according to Henri Stein, from the same branch of the family as our Geoffroy.[46] Likewise, in the first *enquête* of 1247–8, Geoffroy is listed with a William (*Willelmus*) of Milly, who worked at the time as *prévôt* of Péronne. William was perhaps a nephew or cousin.[47] This close circle of officials is further borne out among those who stand surety, or stand as pledges, on Geoffroy's behalf, upon his condemnation. These men included: his son, Adam; his wife's husband, that is, his brother-in-law (*genero*) Walois; his sister's husband (*sororio suo*); another brother-in-law, Evard; and Robert de Béthisy and Renard de Béthisy – all were men in the circle of the former *bailli* of Amiens and were thus part of his closest social network.[48]

Although the *baillis* were deliberately not drawn from among the upper nobility, nor were they meant to hold lands or fiefs within the territory they administered, they were rapidly becoming a class or cadre of men who possessed great wealth, and therefore, a certain kind of status that could provoke the ire of others, as is abundantly clear from the *enquêtes* returns. Most *baillis* were knights, and in some cases in major cities or towns, bourgeois or urban citizens (*cives*). But the real markers of status came from their moveable wealth. The *baillis* in France, unlike their counterparts in England, were paid officials, and from the start they were compensated well. The crown understood that, in Baldwin's words, 'renumeration was the most effective means of controlling royal officials'.[49] Most *baillis* were paid salaries between 10 and 15 *sous* a day, or on average about one *livre* or one pound a day. Thus, scholars have adopted an average salary of 365 pounds per annum, although by 1248 this amount in some cases was much higher, up to nearly 700 pounds per year. And for the 1260s we have much more precise information that confirms these numbers.[50] In addition, *baillis*, as members of the royal government, if not the royal household, were

---

[46] Stein, 'Recherches' (1919), 25.
[47] *RHGF* xxiv.1, 736, no. 53 with Geoffroy; and 736, no. 49, where William is listed with Pierre Faber, who also worked alongside Geoffroy in earlier inquests.
[48] See *Inv. Som.* G 652, 2: 6 (December 1243). For an excellent study of a single *bailli* and his network and a model for the present study, see Robert-Henri Bautier, 'Guillaume de Mussy, bailli, enquêteur royal, panetier de France sous Philippe le Bel', *BEC* 105 (1944), 64–98.
[49] Baldwin, *Government*, 133.
[50] William Chester Jordan, 'Anti-Corruption Campaigns in Thirteenth-Century Europe', *JMH* 35 (2009), 204–19. For specific salaries paid to the *baillis* of the north during the reign of Philip III, see Louis Carolus-Barré, 'Essai sur les *baillis* de Philippe le Hardi', *Annuaire-Bulletin de la Société de l'histoire de France* (1966–7), 115, 117–45, at 132, which forms part of a longer study by Carolus-Barré, 'Les *baillis* de Philippe III le Hardi. Recherches sur le milieu social et la carrière des agents du pouvoir royal dans la seconde moitié du XIIIe siècle', in the same issue of the *Annuaire-Bulletin de la Société de l'histoire de France* (1966–7), 111–244. This study includes over two dozen mini-biographies much like that completed by Delisle.

also from time to time given gifts of clothing from the royal wardrobe, and gifts of precious stones as recorded in the royal jewel account.[51]

An anecdote embedded in an *enquête* return from 1261 recounts a group of *baillis* standing around in the royal garden, perhaps waiting for an audience or an account session to begin, boasting of the cups and maplewood goblets (*ciphos mazerinos*) that they had and comparing their beauty, manufacture, and materials.[52] The *bailli* who was the subject of the investigation, Mathieu de Beaune, then ordered his clerk to procure for him one yet more beautiful than the others. His clerk, in the company of Étienne de Berron, the *prévôt* of Crépy-en-Valois who Mathieu instructed to accompany him and one Jean Selvestre, a burgher of Crépy-en-Valois, then procured a maple goblet (*ciphum maderinum*) fitted with a silver footing worth 70 *sous*.[53] It came to sit on Mathieu's table, a marker of his status for all to see when they came into his chambers when the *bailli* was at work.[54] The point here is that *baillis*, men who were always on the move so the king need not be, were associated with moveable wealth, and wealth that must at times have seemed to be, or perhaps had been, the property of others. After the crown began to fine misbehaving officials following the first *enquêtes*, this was wealth that could be mobilized to pay such fines.[55] And in part, the donation of six basins was just such a fine of moveable wealth, paid to the cathedral as recompense for Geoffroy's actions.

If we return to the 1240s, when the evidence is not as rich and we cannot yet avail ourselves of the more detailed anecdotes recounted before friar-*enquêteurs* in the decades to follow, there certainly seems to have been a perception that at times the king's officials overstepped their purview and abused their appointed privileges. This was true for lesser officials – foresters, *prévôts*, sergeants, viscounts and the like – but also true of *baillis*. Complaints ranged from accusation

---

[51] Pierre de Béthisy was one such recipient of precious stones. See Baldwin, *Government*, 133, 495n274; Carolus-Barré, 'Essai sur les *baillis* de Philippe le Hardi', 132, which breaks down monies paid for wages and that for clothing and horses.
[52] Jordan is the first I know of to cite this story; see Jordan, *Louis IX*, 58. It was first redacted and edited by Delisle in *RHGF*, xxiv.1, 'Preuves de la Preface', no. 152, p. 326*, deposition 198. I thank him for his help in translating the term here.
[53] Andrew Collings has transcribed the original *enquête* return: Paris, AN J 1028A, no. 4, fol. 49v–50r. The incident is discussed in his masterful dissertation, Collings, 'The King Cannot be Everywhere', 99–100.
[54] The *enquête* then relates that the funds used to purchase the goblet 'had been reimbursed by the town of Crépy-en-Valois from the municipal accounts'. Collings, *The King Cannot be Everywhere*, 100.
[55] Louis IX cracked down on such behavior as well as the taking of bribes and other forms of corruption through the introduction of the *enquêteurs* and by issuing the so-called *Grande Ordonnance* of 1254, which was reissued in 1256. See Louis Carolus-Barré, 'La grande ordonnance de réformation de 1254', *Comptes rendus des séances de l'Académie des Inscriptions et Belles-Lettres* 117 (1973), 181–6, reissued and expanded in Carolus-Barré, 'La grande ordonnance de 1254 sur la reform de l'administration et la police due royaume', in *Septième centenaire de la mort de Saint Louis: actes des colloques de Royaumont et de Paris, 21–27 mai 1970* (Paris, 1976), 88–90; and Jordan, 'Anti-Corruption Campaigns'. More work is needed on the *ordonnance*.

of graft and theft – or coerced takings – of overcoats, sheets, heavy blankets, as well as wine, measures of wheat, corn, and meat; and metal objects like utensils, kitchen pots, and tools. All of these objects could be appropriated and integrated into one's own household with ease. Such abuses had been long-standing. The *baillis*, however, especially given their purview over matters of justice (hearing complaints, overseeing inquests, and informing those in the provinces of new royal ordinances) were more often accused of extorsion or demanding overly large fines and fees for poaching game, for damage to the king's lands and rights, for *tailles* and fines left unpaid, and for matters of jurisdiction. The most common complaints in the 1247–8 *enquêtes* touching the *baillis* of the north, and Geoffroy in particular, had to do with matters of justice that were seemingly arbitrarily determined, that is, 'without right or judgement', which is to say exercising power outside of the law and without a formal hearing. In short, what was most frustrating was when the king's men took justice into their own hands, moving beyond the law.

II

Let us return to Geoffroy and to his punishment. For a close reading of the details of his public penance sheds further light on what was at stake in the crimes *he* committed: that is, in his seemingly arbitrary enforcement of a punishment and the overstepping of his jurisdiction. Indeed, in the eyes of Bishop Arnould, Geoffroy's greatest fault was in hanging five clerics. That action was a two-fold transgression in the bishop's eyes for it both condemned the men to death, a permanent and unappealable sentence, and it reached beyond the boundaries of a *bailli*'s jurisdiction. By virtue of their clerical status, the condemned clerks were outside the jurisdiction of secular law until found guilty of a crime, rendering Geoffroy's actions arbitrary and a breach of the coveted canonical protections that were meant to cover all men of the church.[56] Geoffroy's elaborate punishment – one which the bishop of Amiens and seemingly his own redacting clerk took pains and perhaps pleasure in recounting in full detail – emphasized his position as a layman of status. His station, as a public official of the crown, a man of wealth, and a knight, demanded a public facing penance, not just prison or simple ignominy.[57] Each facet of Geoffroy's punishment had a long-standing

---

[56] The scholarship on jurisdiction and medieval canon law is vast. See the general, but excellent, discussion in and throughout James A. Brundage, *Medieval Canon Law* (2nd ed., London, 2022); and Richard H. Helmholz, *The Canon Law and Ecclesiastical Jurisdiction from 597 to the 1640s* (Oxford, 2004), which deals with England, but with many observations about legal norms on the Continent. See also the beautiful essay that addresses just such exceptions and their longer history in the Anglo-American legal tradition by Emily Steiner, 'Neck Verse', *New Literary History* 53 (2022), 333–63.
[57] On the insistence of public penance for individuals of such stature, see Mansfield, *The Humiliation of Sinners*, 92–129. For other examples of similar rituals of humiliation, see Jean-Marie Moeglin, 'Harmiscara-Harmischar-Hachee: Le dossier des rituels d'humiliation et de soumission au Moyen Âge', *Archivum Latinitatis Medii Aevi* 54 (1996),

ritual element that was legible to those who witnessed his submission and further communicated the infringement of jurisdiction.

To be sure, Geoffroy's attire – barefoot and without vestments except a shirt and belt of sackcloth – was a form of humiliation. But far more striking was what in French was called (*qui vulgariter dicitur*) the *hars*, what is clearly a *harmiscara* or a noose that he was to wear around his neck. Coupled with the fact that Geoffroy's hands were to be tied behind his back 'in the same way in which [hands] are customarily bound for thieves being led to the gibbet (*eo modo quo ligari solent latronibus qui ad patibulum ducebantur*)', the entire scene created a spectacle of deference and, again, enforced humiliation. It rendered him ritually a condemned public criminal.[58] The *harmiscara*, or bearing a noose around the neck, often while carrying a symbolic object – a dog or a piece of cloth – had been prescribed as a form of public penance since the Carolingian period. It signaled the submission of the penitent to their lord by transforming them into a submitted slave or captive, bound and processed publicly.[59] By the thirteenth century, it was a favored ritual penance of bishops when imposed on nobles and officials, emphasizing their submission to the church and deference to clerics.

The term conjoined *hars*, from the Old German, meaning 'suffering, or pain', and from which we derive our modern 'harm', with *scara*, meaning a service imposed or rendered. Thus, together *harmiscara* means a harm or pain, penance, imposed, in the service of suffering humility or humiliation.[60] Although reserved for extraordinary penances, it had also taken on an additional dimension of submission and atonement for sins. In 1258, a group of burghers from Namur came to plead before the *Parlement* in Paris following the murder of a local *bailli*. Pierre of Fontaine, the great jurist and judge, chided them that they should return home, wearing nooses around their necks – that is, as penitents – and ask the countess of Namur for forgiveness.[61] Wearing the noose or *hars* had become a

---

11–65, esp. notes 113–15; and Alain Saint-Denis, 'L'expiation publique des grands et des notables dans les villes due nord de la France aux XIIe et XIIIe siècles', in *Ordre moral et délinquance de l'Antiquité au XXe siècle,* ed. Benoît Garnot (Dijon, 1994), 383–90.

[58] For such rituals of public punishment and humiliation more broadly, see Lucie Ecorchard, *Les lieux de justice parisiens à la fin due Moyen Âge* (Paris, 2022); and Claude Gauvard, *Condamner à mort au Moyen Âge: Practiques de la peine capital en France, XIIIe–XVe siècles* (Paris, 2018).

[59] See Moeglin, 'Harmiscara-Harmischar-Hachee', 11–65.

[60] Moeglin, 'Harmiscara-Harmischar-Hachee', 19.

[61] This incident is reported in the *Récits d'un ménestrel de Reims au treizième siècle,* ed. Natalis de Wailly (Paris, 1876); for the English translation, see *Tales of a Minstrel of Reims in the Thirteenth century,* trans. Samuel N. Rosenberg (Washington, DC, 2022), paragraphs 443–8. For our purposes, tellingly, the incident involves a group of young men who were terrorizing the town of Namur, and who killed a *bailli* of the countess. While this elaborated case is less a question of conflict of jurisdictions, it certainly points to the challenges a new countess faced in imposing her authority over influential burghers (those who appealed the case to Paris), and the uncontrollable young men. For a discussion of this case and the reference to the *harmiscara*, see William Chester Jordan, 'Rustics Petitioning to *Parlement* in the Thirteenth Century: A Case Study', *HSJ* 31 (2019), 205–19, at 214–15.

visible ritualized form of abasement. Indeed, forty years after Geoffroy wore the *hars*, Louis IX's son, Pierre d'Alençon (d. 1283), had a noose placed around his neck as he prepared for his own death, having fallen gravely ill, while fighting for his brother Charles of Anjou in Sicily. Modeling his last moments on those of his father, the noose referenced his own condition as a miserable sinner, in his words, a 'serf' of Christ, someone willingly submitting himself to the mercy of God, just as the repentant thief had done, who was crucified beside Jesus and who had received God's mercy.[62] Indeed, in Geoffroy's penance, the parallel with the thieves hanging next to Jesus was made clear in that he was to be tied 'like a thief... and led to the gibbet'. Unlike the king's son's purely metaphorical submission, however, Geoffroy's was real and formalized. And importantly, it was to be reiterated five times over successive days in Amiens for each of the five clerics' bodies, and then again, throughout the dioceses of northern France. His crime and most importantly his submission to the bishop were to be broadcast publicly across ecclesiastical and secular jurisdictions, throughout the interlaced *bailliages* that supported Geoffroy's former position. Similarly, the stipulation that he commission and then donate five silver basins appears to be referencing precisely the sorts of moveable wealth and status objects associated with *baillis*, the kinds of drinking vessels that set them apart from the clergy and those laymen below them who might admire their wealth displayed in their chambers, visible to those who came to petition for the king's justice. Finally, the imposition of a punishment as close to exile as was permissible for a bishop, that is, a journey to Jerusalem, an endless pilgrimage, again emphasized the difference of jurisdiction and of the bishop's power over Geoffrey's person as well as his soul.[63]

How should we fit this severe and elaborate punishment into the context of Geoffroy's work and operations in Amiens in the 1230 and 1240s? What had he witnessed? What kinds of cases and decisions, inquests and infractions, especially of royal authority, would have been familiar to him? Other than the few surviving inquests, the tri-annual returns of royal revenues paid in Paris,

---

[62] Pierre died 6 April 1283/4. As Xavier Hélary notes, Pierre's wife, Jeanne de Châtillon (d. 1292) also put on the *harmiscara* when she lay dying, however, she fashioned it herself out of her own head-covering. Like her husband, she then died as a penitent. Report of Pierre's death was recorded and circulated back to France and would be recopied among other short devotional texts at the end of a personal breviary codex, possibly belonging to Marguerite of Burgundy (daughter of Eudes of Nevers), queen of Sicily and second wife of Charles of Anjou, now in Paris, Bibliothèque Sainte-Geneviève ms 1273, fols 193v–194. See Xavier Hélary, 'La mort de Pierre, comte d'Alençon (1283), fils de Saint Louis, dans la mémoire capétienne', *Revue d'histoire de l'eglise de France* 94 (2008), 5–22. On the report of the death of Jeanne de Châtillon, see Henri Platelle, 'Les Regrets de la Comtesse d'Alençon (d. 1292): un nouveau manuscript, un nouveau texte, un modèle religieux', *Romania* 110 (1989), 426–65. The point being that over time, wearing a ritualized *harmiscarum* became a sign of a virtuous noble death.

[63] On the growing understanding and theology concerning punishment, intention and jurisdictions, see Virpi Makinen and Heikki Pihlajamaki, 'The Individualization of Crime in Medieval Canon Law', *Journal of the History of Ideas* 65 (2004), 525–42.

and the hints from the memories resuscitated before the *enquêteurs*, we have no precise evidence for what Geoffroy saw or did as an official or resident of Amiens. What is clear, however, is that his time as *bailli* coincided with a tremendous transformation of the city's geography and regulated spaces.

In 1218, the cathedral of Amiens caught fire and burned, destroying most of the building. Rebuilding on a much grander scale, as Stephen Murray has so carefully described, began in 1220 during the episcopate of Évrard de Fouilloy.[64] Between 1220 and 1236 the nave and the west aisle of the transept were built under the supervision of Master Robert de Luzarches. From 1236/41 to 1269 a second phase was initiated that saw the east aisle of the transept and the choir rise to historic heights.[65] As Murray notes, 'the new project demanded substantial adjustments to the urban fabric in the immediate vicinity: the eastern end of the new cathedral would project beyond the old Roman wall. To the north the old Hôtel-Dieu and the collegiate church of Saint-Firmin would both have to be relocated: the bishop would need all his powers of persuasion to make it happen.'[66] It fell mainly to Bishop Geoffroy d'Eu and his successor, our Arnould de la Pierre, to oversee the reestablishment of the Hôtel-Dieu, that is, the hospital which had been adjacent to the old cathedral to the north-west. It was moved further north out of the city center, to the parish of Saint-Leu.[67] Similarly, the collegiate church of Saint-Firmin was demolished to make room for the new north transept, and that community was likewise moved to the site of the Hôtel-Dieu.[68] What did these developments mean when seen not through the lens of the triumph of gothic building but through the eyes of a royal official or the people living in Amiens during this period of intense destruction and reconstruction? Certainly, as Murray notes, it involved frequent 'negotiations with outside agencies: the abbot and community of Saint-Martin-aux-Jumeaux who controlled the parish of Saint-Leu, as well as the king (Amiens was a royal city) and the municipality'.[69] Between 1228 and 1244, negotiations with the king

---

[64] On the contours of medieval Amiens, see C. Chatelain, 'Amiens médiéval, ville du roy, de l'évêque et des bourgeois', in *Histoire d'une ville*, ed. X. Bailly and J.-B. Dupont (Amiens, 2013), 47–65. See also Stephen Murray, *Notre-Dame Cathedral of Amiens: The Power of Change in Gothic* (Cambridge, 1996); and most recently, his synthesis, *Notre-Dame of Amiens: Life of the Gothic Cathedral* (New York, NY, 2021) which is more attentive to the overall dynamics of the city and the cathedral. See also *La grâce d'une cathédrale: Amiens*, ed. Jean-Juc Bouilleret et al. (Strasbourg, 2012).

[65] Stephen Murray, 'Looking for Robert de Luzarches: The Early Work at Amiens Cathedral', *Gesta* 29 (1990), 111–31; and Stephen Murray and James Addiss, 'Plan and Space at Amiens Cathedral: With a New Plan Drawn by James Addiss', *Journal of the Society of Architectural Historians* 49 (1990), 44–66.

[66] Murray, *Notre-Dame of Amiens*, 166.

[67] Murray charts this movement and supplies editions and translations of the documents that record the new placement of the cathedral and consequent displacement of the hospital in Murray, 'Looking for Robert de Luzarches', 112–14, and Appendix 1, 130–1; and Murray, *Notre-Dame Cathedral of Amiens*, Appendix A.

[68] Murray, 'Looking for Robert de Luzarches', 114.

[69] Murray, 'Looking for Robert de Luzarches', 113.

surely would have gone through Geoffroy de Milly. Archival documents reveal a different, ambivalent story, one in which women and families were displaced from their homes, new spaces were cordoned off for the exclusive use of the clergy and clerics of Amiens with a newly entrenched claustral zone running along the north side of the new building, and of course the city's central and oldest hospital was relocated across the Somme and beyond the network of canals that support the city to the south.[70] By 1244, tensions in the city were high, and to many it must have seemed that the bishop and the cathedral clergy had overreached. Had it been exhausting for Geoffroy to continue to maintain the rights and privileges of the king in the face of such episcopal expansion? Perhaps.

III

Perhaps, on that night in November, something in Geoffroy simply snapped. One gets the sense that this was the case. Indeed, I submit that behind Geoffroy's action there was something more, something beyond questions of jurisdiction or clerical privilege, or even the rights of his king. When the archival record goes silent, one must look elsewhere.[71] Here, the local tradition, what some might call a 'Romance' tradition, gives us other clues. I have only been able to trace the story in narrative form to an eighteenth-century source, but there, it is alleged, and, as far as I can tell, all of the antiquarian historians that follow reaffirm, that Geoffroy's reaction – rash, rapid, in the middle of the night – was in response to a painful personal wrong: the seizure, if not also, as is carried in that umbrella term, *capio*, the possession, seizing, and rape of his daughter by five or more clerics.[72]

---

[70] Much of this urban change is charted in general contours by Murray especially in the documents he has gathered in Murray, *Notre-Dame Cathedral of Amiens*, Appendix A, esp. 129–41; see also his comments on 'Cathedral Construction and Social Change', 74–6. Other more precise indications of sales, donations, and changes to the urban fabric can be gleaned more generally from the documents edited or partially edited in the *Inventaire Sommaire des archives départementales antérieures 1790: Département de la Somme*, Séries 4G (2 parts): Fonds du chapiter cathedral d'Amiens.

[71] There is now quite a developed tradition coming out of feminist scholarship and critical race studies of reading sources differently to look through or beyond the archive. The bibliography here is vast, but for some methodological interventions, see, for example: Michel-Rolph Trouillot, *Silencing the Past: Power and the Production of History* (Boston, MA, 1995); David Thomas, Simon Fowler, and Valarie Johnson, *The Silence of the Archive* (London, 2017); and Joseph Pugliese, 'Embodied Archives', *Journal of the Association for the Study of Australian Literature. Special Issue: Archive Madness* 11 (2011), online.

[72] The trail to this accusation is circuitous and may not satisfy all scholars. See B. Winkles, *French Cathedrals: From Drawings by R. Garland* (London, 1837), 24–5, who states: 'In the year 1244, Geoffroy de Milly, chief baillif of Amiens, hung five scholars without any legal process, who had been accused by his daughter of an assault to her person.' Winkles references Daire, *Histoire de la Ville d'Amiens, depuis son origine jusqu'a present* (Paris, 1757), i, 527. The story and Geoffrey's condemnation appears in *Daire*, i, 210–12, with documents at 527–31. The role of the *échevins* and mayor, Mathieu le Maugnier, is elaborated there as well. The *prévôt* of Amiens, the mayor, and

What was one to do upon learning of this? What crime, what personal wrong, would cut so deep as to make a *bailli* arrest – and here the municipal record differs and expands the episcopal archive – seventeen clerics, put them in prison, and charge the *prévôt* of Amiens with keeping them there? According to the municipal record, one of those clerics died in prison, hence the *six* basins, for in fact six clerics died that night. The other five Geoffroy had violently 'suspended and drawn', and then paraded around the city.[73] I submit that even if the details that have come down to us through this other record, one spoken and not recorded by clerical hands; one that hangs in the air, scandalous and bound to make no one look good – neither lustful young clerics nor a vengeful raging representative of the king – even if these details are no longer perfect or verifiable, they do move us closer to the mark.[74] Enraged, in the middle of the night, upon learning of the abduction and possible rape of his daughter, Geoffroy de Milly set aside protocols of comportment and strung up unto death the five men he felt were responsible.

Confronted, as I think we are, by a rash act done in anger, we return then to the question of anger. What are we to do with anger and politics; or even anger and justice? Where is the place for anger in political expression?[75] In the

---

the townsmen were also implicated in the arrest, mistreatment and execution of the six clerics. The bishop also condemned their actions and elaborated a sentence that included founding six benefices to honor the six clerics who died, two in the cemetery of St-Denis and four connected to two altars in the cathedral. The long condemnation document is also reproduced in Daire as well and makes it clear that this was to be a negotiated agreement and it was unlikely the townsmen would supply all the funds needed. This settlement is worthy of its own study. The story is also recounted in George Durand, *Monographie de l'église Notre-Dame cathédrale d'Amiens* ii: 302. Durand cites François-Irénée Darsy, *Bénéfices de l'église d'Amiens, ou État general des biens, revenus et charges du clergé du diocese d'Amiens en 1730, avec des notes* (2 vols, Amiens, 1869–71), i, 52, 'Le 3 juillet 1244 le bailli d'Amiens, Geoffroy de Milly, avait fait emprisonner au beffroi et fustiger 17 clercs ou écoliers, accuses d'avoir déshonoré sa fille'. A version of the same story is repeated in Maurice Leroy, 'Histoire des chapelains de la cathédrale Notre-Dame d'Amiens', *Mémoires de la Société des antiquaries de Picardie* 35 (1838), 249–480, at 611–15; and Maurice Rivoire, *Description de l'église cathédrale de'Amiens* (Amiens, 1806), 87–95, who also reiterates the story of the clerics seizing Geoffroy's daughter and taking her into a nearby wood. See also Jacques Foucart, 'L'église Saint-Firmin-le-Confesseur et la cathédrale d'Amiens', *Cahiers archéologiques de Picardie* 7 (1980), 301–10 at note 33.
73 *Inv. Som.* G, ii, 6, no. 652. The version in the cartulary is slightly different: 'fecit per civitatem Ambianensis turpissime ac crudelissime distrahi et suspendi', Rose and Roux, *Cartulaire*, i, 379. For the municipal record, see Janvier, *Livre d'or de la municipalité amiénoise*, 7, https://gallica.bnf.fr/ark:/12148/bpt6k3794471/f7.vertical.
74 While I cannot verify exactly what happened and what motivated Geoffroy, the fact that the bishop let the bodies of the five clerics sit and presumably suffer from decay over the course of the following days it took to execute Geoffroy's punishment, suggests an acknowledgement of guilt; that they too deserved a delayed burial, implying some malfeasance committed by the clerics that Bishop Arnould recognized. I thank Bill North for this insight.
75 Quite a lot has been written about the effects of and place for anger in political expression, to say nothing of the anger of kings, sovereigns, or those who hold political

legal system of the thirteenth century – a system which, according to some nineteenth-century scholars, brought us to the position we are in today, angrily debating the fates of women and women's bodies[76] – there were virtually no channels for the successful prosecution of clerics for a crime, whether abduction, harassment, taunting, cruelties, or indeed rape, like the one that may have been inflicted on Geoffroy's daughter.[77] There were also few public procedures and legal mechanisms or judgements to assuage the anger either of a father or of his wronged daughter. Indeed, Geoffroy certainly knew that this was, in theory, the case. He would have been familiar with ideas that come to us in written form, for example, in the *Etablissement* of Saint Louis, the collection of legal codes pertaining to the royal domains and other sets of customs still to be written down that *baillis* helped shape and create in the later thirteenth century.[78] The *Customs of Touraine and Anjou*, for example, state quite clearly that:

If the king or the count, or a baron or some vassal who has the administration of justice in his lands arrests a clerk, or a crusader, or some man in religion, even though he were a layman, he should be handed over to Holy Church, whatever crime he had committed. And if a clerk <commits an offense for which he should be hanged or killed, and he> does not have a tonsure, the secular authority should deal with him. <And if he has a tonsure and a clerk's habit and can read, no admission and no answer he makes can be to his detriment; for [the secular judge] is not the

---

power more broadly I have found the work of Martha Nussbaum on this topic – both ancient and contemporary – particularly useful. See Martha C. Nussbaum, *Political Emotions: Why Love Matters for Justice* (Cambridge, MA, 2013); Martha C. Nussbaum, *Anger and Forgiveness: Resentment, Generosity, Justice* (Oxford, 2016); and Martha C. Nussbaum, *The Monarchy of Fear: A Philosopher Looks at Our Political Crisis* (New York, NY, 2018). For the medieval period, see Paul R. Hyams, *Rancor and Reconciliation in Medieval England* (Ithaca, NY, 2003); and *Anger's Past: The Social Uses of an Emotion in the Middle Ages*, ed. Barbara H. Rosenwein (Ithaca, NY, 1998). I would differentiate, however, as Smail does between 'anger' and 'hatred' in that they operate differently and have different social functions. See Daniel Lord Smail, 'Hatred as a Social Institution in Late-Medieval Society', *Speculum* 76 (2001), 90–126.

[76] See Justice Samuel L. Alito's opinion in the Dobbs decision, which displays arguments that historians have made clear are both wrong and misplaced. See 'Dobbs v. Jackson Women's Health Organization (6/24/2022), No. 19–1392', www.supremecourt.gov/opinions/21pdf/19-1392_6j37.pdf; and Sara M. Butler, 'Alito's Leaked Draft Majority Opinion and the Medieval History of Abortion', *Legal History Miscellany,* posted 13 May 2022: https://legalhistorymiscellany.com/2022/05/13/alitos-leaked-draft-majority-opinion-and-the-medieval-history-of-abortion/. For cogent insights about gender, anger, and accountability, see Martha C. Nussbaum, *Citadels of Pride: Sexual Assault, Accountability and Reconciliation* (New York, NY, 2021).

[77] For sexual crimes unpunished, see the remarks in Dyan Elliott, *The Corrupter of Boys: Sodomy, Scandal, and the Medieval Clergy* (Philadelphia, PA, 2020). For the pervasiveness of rape in law and literature in the period, see Kathryn Gravdal, *Ravishing Maidens: Writing Rape in Medieval French Literature and Law* (Philadelphia, PA, 1991).

[78] On this process of compilation and writing, see Kuskowski, *Vernacular Law*, esp. 155–88 on the tensions among jurisdictions – royal, comital, and ecclesiastical. Indeed, notably, the *coutumiers* authors cite the *Decretals* as they shape the law and hammer out lines of jurisdiction.

judge having jurisdiction over him [*ordinaire*]; and an admission before a judge who is not his proper judge is invalid, according to written law in the *Decretals*.>[79]

Guidance from Philippe de Beaumanoir, a fellow *bailli* and compiler of another code of laws and practices for the Beauvaisis and the county of Clérmont known as the *Coutumes de Beauvaisis* (c. 1283), is even more vague. Something similar to the possible fate of Geoffroy's daughter would most likely be addressed among the examples in Chapter 30 on 'Offenses'. Here we learn of various punishments imposed upon those who seduce, or abduct, a man's wife or daughter. But the jurist notes, 'if a man kills the man and the woman [his wife or daughter] or one of them, he loses neither life nor property. And in such cases, we have seen men released three times in the king's court before we wrote this book.'[80] In other words, Beaumanoir saw exceptions for such retributive actions, examples when the angry husband was let off. Oddly, or tellingly, the paragraph that follows and concludes Chapter 30 pertains to what must have been related in Beaumanoir's mind: 'Some people believe that persons caught in the act of stealing rabbits or other big game in someone else's game preserve are not to be hanged; but [I say] they are if they do it by night, for it is obvious they are going there with the intention of stealing. … and what we have said of hunting preserves we also apply to fish in enclosed areas and fishponds [*viviers*].'[81] Might Geoffroy have counted on, or hoped for, release if he appealed his story to the king's court? Might he have realized that the treatment of his daughter was or would have been associated with the sorts of crimes he himself adjudicated, 'offenses' of poaching or seizing a man's animals or fish?[82] This flattening of the law is surely troubling, as was relying on the exceptions granted by the sovereign.

Anger and its regulation, as well as other forms of misbehavior, had become a pressing question in the thirteenth century, particularly as it pertained to governance and to justice. In theory there was very little place for anger in governance. Anger was a passion, in the Greek sense of the word, and here I

---

[79] *The* Etablissement *de Saint Louis: Thirteenth-Century Law Texts from Tours, Orléans, and Paris*, trans. F.R.P. Akehurst (Philadelphia, PA, 1996), 58–9: 'Chapter 89. On jurisdiction over clerks, and on handing over crusaders to Holy Church'. Translated from the French: *Les Etablissements de Saint Louis*, ed. Paul Viollet, Société de l'Histoire de France (4 vols, Paris, 1881–6). I have followed Akehurst's translation. See also Steiner, 'Neck Verse'.

[80] Strikingly, this is Philippe's eyewitness assessment about the exceptions to justice, witnessing events that would have taken place during Geoffroy's lifetime. See *The* Coutumes de Beauvaisis *of Philippe de Beaumanoir*, trans. F.R.P. Akehurst (Philadelphia, PA, 1992), 330: 'Chapter 30. Offenses, para. 933, translated from the French: *Philippe de Beaumanoir: Coutumes de Beauvaisis*, ed. Amédée Salmon (2 vols, Paris, 1899–1900). I again follow Akehurst's translation.

[81] Beaumanoir, *Coutumes de Beauvaisis*, 331, ch. 30, para. 935.

[82] This is an extreme example of the objectification of persons. Much more could and should be said about this in the context of medieval serfdom and freedom. My thinking has been influenced in part by the related arguments developed in Joshua Bennett, *Being Property Once Myself: Blackness and the End of Man* (Cambridge, MA, 2020).

think we are in fact better served to turn to philosophers and political theorists than to turn to the recent emotions' literature.[83] Anger was understood in both the ancient and Christian contexts as either retributive or corrective, that is, transitional and therefore capable of moving on toward a resolution. The anger that was felt and that then leads to amending behavior could be useful and could lead to reform, even political reform.[84] Anger, by contrast, that was wrathful and enacted out of vengeance was destructive. Kings were counseled, as the late Paul Hymns showed in the case of King Henry III of England, to keep vengeful anger under wraps by means of *prudentia*, prudence and wisdom.[85] So, too, *baillis,* being an extension of the king, were instructed to act in the same manner. Thus, Beaumanoir records that a *bailli* 'if he was to be an honest judge and a just one should have ten virtues'.[86] These include wisdom; the love of God; kindness without being severe; vigorous; generous; obedient to his lord's commands; skillful in management; and he should be 'indulgent and ready to listen without getting angry or upset about anything, for the *bailli* who... gets upset and angry at what he hears cannot remember [memorize] what is said before him in court. And since he cannot remember it, he cannot recall it from memory'; and he cannot perform his job.[87] Anger clouds one's judgments and obscures justice.

Although we cannot know the precise details behind Geoffroy's behavior, it must have come to the attention of the king and informed his thinking about similar issues. For anger about the exceptional status of clerics confronted Louis periodically during his reign. In the 1230s, when Queen Blanche, Louis's mother, still served as regent, the king's men had killed several clerics connected to the nascent University of Paris.[88] Similarly in 1259–60, the king would again be forced to deal with a baron, Enguerrand IV de Coucy, who had likewise

---

[83] See above, note 75. Also Martha C. Nussbaum, *The Therapy of Desire: Theory and Practice in Hellenistic Ethics* (Princeton, NJ, 1994), esp. 402–39. For the role of anger in literature as instructive morally, see Emily Katz Anhalt, *Enraged: Why Violent Times Need Ancient Greek Myths* (New Haven, CT, 2017). My thinking about anger and its role in the past has also been shaped by teaching the *Iliad* for over a decade in the context of a European/Western Civilization core course.

[84] This is essentially the point that Nussbaum (cited above) and many other thinkers who advocate for non-violence change, resistance, and anger makes clear. In this way, anger that awakes the senses, that points to a wrong done and what that means in terms of human dignity and ethics, is fundamentally instructive and useful.

[85] Paul Hyams, 'What Did Henry III of England Think in Bed and in French about Kingship and Anger?', in *Anger's Past*, 92–124.

[86] Beaumanoir, *Coutumes de Beauvaisis*, 14, Ch. 1 ('On Judges'), para. 12.

[87] Beaumanoir, *Coutumes de Beauvaisis*, 15, Ch. 1 ('On Judges'), para. 15.

[88] For some discussion of this context, see Peter R. McKeon, 'The Status of the University of Paris as *Parens Scientiarum*: An Episode in the Development of its Autonomy', *Speculum* 39 (1964), 651–75. For an overview of the major sources, see *La fondation de l'université de Paris (1200–1260)*, ed. Pascale Bermon (Paris, 2017), 139–232. I thank Pascale Bermon for directing me to this incident which loomed over Louis IX's reign, and for a wonderful conversation about these and other issues surrounding different forms of anger in the past and present.

overstepped his jurisdiction by famously hanging three adolescents caught poaching in his forests, who then turned out to be clerics. The king, much to the displeasure of his other barons, imprisoned the lord Coucy and fined him harshly as a consequence.[89] Despite the outrage of the barons, the king remained unwilling to make an exception.

As William Jordan has suggested, when 'the *enquêteurs* come into the records in 1247… a great deal of thought preceded their introduction'.[90] The king and his advisors must have engaged in 'deep speech' before creating the *enquêteurs* and unleashing them on the system of royal governance.[91] Such a move implied a deep distrust of those employed to serve the king; it undercut a system of mutual dependence and gave it a sharp moral paring that was lost on no one at the time. This reform followed on the heels of Geoffroy's denouement. It 'fulfilled the demands of the king's conscience and improved the efficiency of the local administration', while moralizing governance in preparation for the crusade, itself a profoundly penitential undertaking.[92] By means of the *enquêteurs*, Louis imposed a penance on the full range of his government, forcing a fined atonement on his officials that was then channeled to pay for the crusade. Although we cannot know the content of the king's deliberations, I submit that Geoffroy's story would have informed some of that conversation.

IV

Let me conclude by thinking about some of the silences in this case. The bishop's archive and the municipal records are unyielding when it comes to the history of Geoffroy's daughter – her story is and will remain here a spectral history, a haunting in what has gone unsaid, unaccounted for, left unwritten.[93] We hear of the clerics, although we do not learn their names; they, too, remain anonymous. We know these events took place when Mathieu Lemongnier was mayor, for that is when they are enrolled in the municipal record of Amiens,

---

[89] On this event, see Edmond Faral, 'Le Procès d'Enguerrand IV de Coucy', *Revue historique de droit français et étranger* 26 (1948), 213–58; and Dominique Barthélemy, 'L'affaire Enguerran de Coucy', in *Affaires, scandales et grandes causes: De Socrate à Pinochet*, ed. Nicolas Offenstadt and Stéphane Van Damme (Paris, 2007), 3–28. For comparable examples faced by Louis IX, see Xavier Hélary, *L'ascension et la chute de Pierre de La Broce, chambellan du roi (d. 1278): Étude sur le pouvoir royal au temps de Saint Louis et de Philippe III (v.1250–1280)* (Paris, 2021), 160 note 1; see Guillaume de Saint-Pathus, *Vie de Saint Louis*, ed. H.-François Delaborde (Paris, 1899), 136–50.

[90] Jordan, *Louis IX*, 53.

[91] Jordan, *Louis IX*, 53.

[92] Jordan, *Louis IX*, 57. And this was a moralizing regime that would continue with even greater intensity after the king returned. See the arguments in William Chester Jordan, *Men at the Center: Redemptive Governance under Louis IX* (The Natalie Zemon Davis Annual Lectures) (Budapest, 2012).

[93] See Trouillot, *Silencing the Past*; and Ethan Kleinberg, *Haunting History: For a Deconstructive Approach to the Past* (Stanford, CA, 2017).

the so-called *Livre d'or*.[94] But the events that precipitated Geoffroy's repentance inhabit a silent void. I have tried to piece together a context, a scene, a sense of precedent and pressures that I think inform a reading of the silence as one of stark abuse that precipitated retributive, uncontrolled anger that could not be tolerated by the king nor the episcopate. It is possible too that Geoffroy saw and understood, after the fact, that his behavior was morally wrong, that this was not the response befitting a judge. His submission to an elaborate punishment suggests he viewed his actions as those requiring penance and contrition.

My goal here, however, is not to make an argument from silence, but rather an argument *about* what the silence yields, where it points us, and what its effects were in the past and in our present. It could be noted that one of the methods I have employed to this end is a micro-reading, a microhistory, an approach that often works to expose the ordinary through the extraordinary.[95] The crime perpetuated against Geoffroy's daughter, it seems, was so ordinary, so much like the poaching of game or fish, that it need not be put into the written record. That crime was not the point; it was the consequences – the clash of royal and episcopal jurisdictions, the bodies hanging from the gibbets the next morning, the forced amends of a community, and a *bailli*'s extended penance – that left their mark in the records. This alone is significant, especially when that ordinary crime – one of clerics seizing someone's daughter and humiliating or worse raping her – came to stand behind extraordinary actions.

Geoffroy's story and his royal service also falls into silence after his exquisite punishment, with one exception, a kind of whisper in the archive. Indeed, fifteen years after his condemnation, in June 1259, Geoffroy flickers in and among the busied correspondence of Eudes of Châteauroux, the papal legate, friend to King Louis IX, and long-time supporter of the French Church under Pope Alexander IV (r. 1254–61).[96] As a papal auditor, Eudes heard disputes involving all manner of ecclesiastical business. In this capacity he recorded several cases involving 'absolution' relating to the bishop of Amiens and complaints over papal letters, one of which pertained to the royal *bailli* of Amiens, our own Geoffroy. In other words, Geoffroy received absolution for what remained of his punishment. A

---

[94] A. Janvier, *Livre d'or de la municipalité Amiénoise* (Paris, 1893), 8; Daire, *Historie de la ville d'Amiens*, 529–31.

[95] On the history and benefits of such a method, see Sigurdur Gylfi Magnússon, '"The Singularization of History": Social History and Microhistory within the Postmodern State of Knowledge', *Journal of Social History* 36 (2003), 701–35; and Carlo Ginzburg, 'Latitude, Slaves, and the Bible: An Experiment in Microhistory', *Critical Inquiry* 31 (2005), 665–83. I thank my colleague Michael Kwass for his insights and reflections on the possibilities of microhistory in this case.

[96] On Eudes's legatine business and whereabouts at this time, see Nicholas Vincent, 'Eudes of Châteauroux and the Holy Blood of Neuvy-Saint-Sépulchre', in *Political Ritual and Practice in Capetian France: Studies in Honour of Elizabeth A.R. Brown*, ed. M. Cecilia Gaposchkin and Jay Rubenstein (Turnhout, 2021), 143–90; on his connection to Louis IX and role in the king's first crusade expedition, see William Chester Jordan, 'Sustaining Crusader Ardor: Eudes of Châteauroux's Memorial Sermons for Count Robert of Artois', *Religions* 14: 735. https://doi.org/10.3390/rel14060735.

version of Eudes's letter survives only in a copy made by Garnier of a now lost cartulary of the bishops of Amiens.[97] Tellingly, in the grant of absolution and commutation of his sentence, Geoffroy is referred to as 'a certain Geoffroy de Milly, *bailli* of our most dear son in Christ, the illustrious king of France (*quondam Gaufridus de Mililaco ballivus karissimi in Ch[rist]o filii nostri regis Francie illustris)*', that is, *bailli* to Louis IX.[98] As the letter notes, Geoffroy, who was by that point sixty years old, was absolved from going to the Holy Land and as a redemption was to pay another 120 *lbs*.[99] Eudes charged the guardian of the Friars Minor in Paris to oversee this extension of mercy. An echo of Eudes' correspondence was also copied in an inventory of the cathedral's titles and papers made in the mid-eighteenth century. There, too, is noted a record of a 'Bull given by Pope Alexander IV, the 17th calends of January, in the fifth year of his pontificate, containing the dispensation made to Geoffroy de Milly, *bailli* of Amiens, from going to Jerusalem in the place of which he was condemned to pay a sum of 120 *livres* for pious works'.[100] It would appear that after all this time, after his elaborate penances, Geoffroy retained some connections in Paris, enough to have a hearing before the papal legate or to have someone travel to Rome on his behalf. What sort of exceptions had been extended to him in the end? Had sovereign authority in fact intervened to mollify his punishment, to allow him to remain in France? Or was this a petition to return made after having served time in Outremer? We are left to wonder with haunting suspicions.

V

Different histories come to light depending on where one looks and when and where one encounters them. This is in part a statement of methodology, but it is also the reality of historical accident and the powerful and often deliberate silencing of the written record. Objects carry histories too, evoking them in differently durable ways. Indeed, although the bishop's registers would be copied, recopied, and set aside, and the Picard *enquêtes* returns would be cut apart and reused as bindings for Greek grammar books, Geoffroy's sumptuous,

---

[97] Paris, BnF ms Picardie 97, fol. 35. I thank Nicholas Vincent for bring this document to my attention, and for sharing his transcription of the text with me. And I thank Amanda Racine for making digital photos of the text available to me.

[98] Paris, BnF ms Picardie 97, fol. 35.

[99] Paris, BnF ms Picardie 97, fol. 35: ... iam existens sexagenarius non posset commode in terre sancte subsidium proficisci, et paratus esset huiusmodi transmarinum iter eleemosynis et aliis peregrinationibus redimere ac dictas 100 libras solver pro constructione oratorii supradictit, a nobis suppliciter dudum petiit ut provideri sibi super hoc misericorditer curaremus, et licet nos, moti misericordia circa ipsum, sibi per dilectum filium gardianum fratrum minorum Parisien[sis] sub certa forma nostris inserta litteris mandaverimus provideri, dictus tamen gardianus quod in hac parte mandavimus efficere non curavit.

[100] Durand, *Inventaire sommaire: Somme*, series G, vol. 2, pt 2: 331, G 650, fol. 198. This is a modern inventory of the register of 282 folios made at the order of M. Louis-François Gabriel d'Orléans de la Motte, bishop of Amiens between 1744 and 1746.

commissioned silver basins persisted, hanging above the choir in Amiens Cathedral. At some point, according to Garnier, the basins were melted down and remade into a three-armed candelabra, for use at the altar.[101] Only in 1768, perhaps in anticipation of the anger of the Revolution to come, did that object go missing. In the intervening time, Geoffroy's story, the fate of the six clerics, and the potentially devastating abuse of his daughter, hung in the air, hauntingly, above the altar, suspending memories, anger, and authority in things, holding histories far more complex than the parchment record could reveal or encapsulate.

---

[101] Garnier, 'Inventaires du Trésor de la cathédrale d'Amiens', 261n2.

9

The C. Warren Hollister Memorial Essay 2021

The Politics of Witnessing: *Enquêtes* as a Technique of Power in Thirteenth-Century France

Richard E. Barton

By 1200, the procedure known as *inquisitio* had become so widespread in western Europe that some historians have described it as constituting 'a principle central to the entire institutional development of the period',[1] and even as 'the heart of a revolution that was not only judicial and governmental, but also, more broadly even, socio-political and cognitive'.[2] At its core, *inquisitio* referred to a process of inquiry or investigation, one that attempted to locate the truth of a matter through the questioning of witnesses.[3]

Although it was originally a procedure of Roman law, and although the Carolingians had also made use of a form of the process, *inquisitio* came into its own in the twelfth century with the revival of interest in Roman law and the general development of learned legal and intellectual culture.[4] It was a flexible concept, one that was used in many different ways across the central and later Middle Ages. Among these uses, *inquisitio* was understood to lie at the heart of estate

---

[1] Robert Bartlett, *The First European Revolution, c.970–1215* (London, 2000), 172.
[2] Julien Théry, 'Fama: l'opinion publique comme preuve judiciaire. Aperçu sur la révolution médiévale de l'inquisitoire XIIe–XIVe siècles', in *La preuve en justice de l'Antiquité à nos jours*, ed. Bruno Lemesle (Rennes, 2003), 119–47 at 121. Marie Dejoux, *Les enquêtes de Saint Louis. Gouverner et sauver son âme* (Paris, 2014), 69, accepts Théry's characterization. In the last twenty years, two colloques have been dedicated to the procedure of *inquisitio*: *L'enquête au Moyen Âge*, ed. Claude Gauvard, (Rome, 2009), and *Quand gouverner c'est enquêter. Les pratiques politiques de l'enquête princière (occident, XIIIe–XIVe siècles)*, ed. Thierry Pécout (Paris, 2010).
[3] For this definition, see Élisabeth Lalou, 'L'enquête au Moyen Âge', *Revue historique* 657 (2011), 145–54 at 146; and Alain Boureau, 'Introduction', in *L'enquête au Moyen Age*, 1–10 at 1.
[4] Bruno Lemesle, 'Premiers jalons et mise en place d'une procédure d'enquête dans la région angevine (xie–xiiie siècle)', in *La preuve en justice*, 69–93; Lemesle, 'L'enquête contre les épreuves. Les enquêtes dans la région angevine (XIIe–début XIIIe siècle)', in *L'enquête au Moyen Âge*, 41–73; and David S. Bachrach, 'Inquisitio as a Tool of Royal Governance under the Carolingian and Ottonian Kings', *Zeitschrift der Savigny-Stiftung für Rechtsgeschichte. Germanistiche Abteilung* 133 (2016), 1–80.

surveys, such as Domesday book; customary practices for setting the boundaries of particular manors and villages; efforts to determine the precise package of rights a lord possessed over his tenants; periodic attempts to impose accountability on seigneurial or royal agents; and, most obviously, formal elements of the law of proof in both ecclesiastical and secular settings. A decisive moment for the history of medieval legal procedure occurred in 1215, when Innocent III and the Fourth Lateran Council collated and centralized a series of previous canon law rulings into a new set of decrees that required ecclesiastical courts to thereafter rely solely on *inquisitio* as a mode of proof; other modes of proof, including ordeals and duels, were set aside.[5] Since the middle of the twelfth century, the Plantagenet and Capetian monarchs had begun incorporating components of *inquisitio* into their newly centralized judicial and institutional constructs,[6] and the decisive move by Innocent III accelerated the process by which secular legal systems embraced a procedure that relied on investigation and witnessing. By the end of the 1250s, *inquisitio* (or *enquête*, as it became known in France) had been so fully embraced by Louis IX in France that the king ordered that proof by witness testimony should thereafter supplant duels as the regular procedure for settling disputes within the royal domain.[7] Indeed, from this point onward the emerging appeals court known as the Parlement de Paris considered *enquête* to constitute the primary procedure by which proof was to be demonstrated before it.[8] What

---

[5] Richard M. Fraher, 'IV Lateran's Revolution in Criminal Procedure: The Birth of *Inquisitio*, the End of Ordeals, and Innocent III's Vision of Ecclesiastical Politics', in *Studia in Honorem Eminentissimi Cardinalis Alphonsi M. Stickler*, ed. R.I. Castillo Lara (Rome, 1992), 97–111.

[6] For France, see John Baldwin, *The Government of Philip Augustus: Foundations of French Royal Power in the Middle Ages* (Berkeley, CA, 1986), 141–4; and Marie Dejoux, 'Gouverner par l'enquête en France, de Philippe Auguste aux derniers Capétiens', *French Historical Studies* 37 (2014), 271–302 at 274–6.

[7] For Louis' ruling, see *Les établissements de Saint Louis*, ed. Paul Viollet (4 vols, Paris, 1881–6), i, 487–93. For commentary, see *inter alia* Paul Guilhiermoz, 'Saint Louis, les gages de bataille et la procédure civile', *BEC* 48 (1887), 111–20; Yvonne Bongert, *Recherches sur les cours laïques du Xe au XIIIe siècle* (Paris, 1949), 33–4; Ferdinand Lot and Robert Fawtier, *Histoire des institutions françaises au moyen age. Tome II: Institutions royales* (Paris, 1958), 316–18; Marguerite Boulet-Sautel, 'Aperçus sur le système des preuves dans la France coutumière du Moyen Âge', in *La preuve. Deuxième partie: Moyen Âge et Temps Modernes*, Recueils de la société Jean Bodin 17 (Brussels, 1965), 275–325 at 298–9; Dejoux, *Les enquêtes*, 70–2; and Ariella Elema, 'Trial by Battle in France and England' (PhD dissertation, University of Toronto, 2012), 301–05.

[8] See *Les olim, ou, Registres des arrêts rendus par la Cour du roi sous les règnes de Saint Louis, de Philippe le Hardi, de Philippe le Bel, de Louis le Hutin et de Philippe le Long*, ed. Arthur Auguste Beugnot (3 vols, Paris, 1839–48), i [1254–73], as well as the invaluable digital edition, *Enquêtes menées sous les derniers capétiens*, ed. Élisabeth Lalou et al. (Paris, 2007–), online at www.cn-telma.fr/enquetes/. See also Paul Guilhiermoz, *Enquêtes et procès. Étude sur la procédure et le fonctionnement du Parlement au XIVe siècle* (Paris, 1892); Dejoux, *Les enquêtes*, 71–2; Boulet-Sautel, 'Aperçus sur le système des preuves', 317; Alan Harding, *Medieval Law and the Foundations of the State* (Oxford, 2001), 162–3. Dejoux, *Les enquêtes*, 72, estimates

all of this meant was that by 1200 or so, *enquêtes* and the process of *inquisitio* could be found 'everywhere'.⁹

Since at least the seventeenth century, scholars have argued for the revolutionary significance of this new procedure of *inquisitio*, typically by emphasizing one of two interrelated approaches. The first approach is that of the history of law, in which *inquisitio* or *enquête* is understood as a particular stage in the linear progress of modes of proof from a 'primitive', 'religious', or 'irrational' mode best exemplified by ordeals and duels towards a 'modern', secular, and 'rational' mode that relied on argumentation, evidence, and witnessing.¹⁰ Montesquieu, for instance, noted that anyone who bothered to consider the issue would immediately conclude that the new procedure of *inquisitio* was 'more natural, more reasonable, and more in keeping with morality, religion, public order, and the safety of persons and things' than what came before it.¹¹ The fact that the practice of proposing and conducting ordeals was hardly irrational was either invisible or irrelevant to Montesquieu and to almost all subsequent scholars.¹² Well into the 1980s the new procedures, whether they were called juries or inquests, as in England, or *enquêtes*, as in France, were being considered as ineluctable proof of the triumph of 'reason' over the irrationality and 'mysticism' of ordeals and duels, which were said to be relics of the 'traditions of pagan and barbarian sorcery'.¹³ Even when less polemical language was used, legal historians maintained that the *enquête* represented the best possible form of proof, and was an obvious improvement over the legal 'chaos' that had existed prior to its implementation.¹⁴

The second approach applied the conclusions of the legal history approach to narratives concerning the growth of modern, or nascent modern, state structures. In these narratives concerning the so-called 'rise of the modern state',¹⁵ the

---

that 54% of the 1,500 cases extant from the records of Parlement between 1254 and 1270 involved *enquêtes*.

9   Dejoux, 'Gouverner par l'enquête', 271.
10 The classic statement remains Jean-Philippe Lévy, 'L'évolution de la preuve des origines à nos jours. Synthèse générale', in *La preuve*, 9–70.
11 Montesquieu, *Esprit des lois*, lib. xxviii, c. 38: 'Quand on vit dans ses tribunaux, quand on vit dans ceux de quelques grands seigneurs une manière de procéder plus naturelle, plus raisonnable, plus conforme à la morale, à la religion, à la tranquillité publique, à la sûreté de la personne et des biens, on abandonna l'autre.' This passage is quoted approvingly by Ferdinand Lot and Robert Fawtier, *Histoire des institutions françaises au moyen age*, 320.
12 As decisively demonstrated by Stephen D. White, 'Proposing the Ordeal and Avoiding It: Strategy and Power in Western French Litigation, 1050–1110', in *Cultures of Power: Lordship, Status and Process in Twelfth-Century Europe*, ed. Thomas N. Bisson (Philadelphia, PA, 1995), 89–123.
13 Boulet-Sautel, 'Aperçus sur le système des preuves', *passim*, but see in particular 278 and 289.
14 Bongert, *Recherches sur les cours laïques*, 33, 34, and 270 ('la meilleure preuve possible').
15 Boureau, 'Introduction', 4, notes the scholarly linkage of *enquête* with the emergence of the 'l'État moderne'. For an overview of the two recent European-wide research

emergence of *enquêtes* was a crucial step in the development of centralized legal institutions, without which state formation could not have occurred. Because *enquêtes* were, by the 1250s, a primary mechanism by which, at least in France, the new legal and political institutions such as the Parlement de Paris extended and solidified the power of the king over his domains, the legal procedure of *inquisitio* in general and the judicial *enquête* in particular could be characterized as a central, even determining, factor in state formation,[16] and perhaps even as constitutive of government itself.[17] In traditional scholarship, therefore, Louis IX regularly appears as semi-prophetic figure who by championing *enquêtes* of various sorts intuitively recognized the superiority of the sort of rational, public-oriented, accountable government that is imagined to exist in the present.[18] Scholars have made it clear that the *enquête* 'was intimately linked to the development of the apparatus of the State' and that 'royal centralization rested upon the generalization of [the process of] inquiry' in a 'synchronous' fashion.[19] Although exceptions exist,[20] it should be clear that these approaches have largely tended to produce teleologically progressive narratives of historical change in general, and instrumentalist and often triumphalist readings of constitutive elements of those narratives (such as *enquêtes*) in particular.

In this essay, I attempt to complicate scholarly understanding of the place of *enquêtes* in thirteenth-century France through a close examination of the depositions produced over the course of several adversarial or judicial *enquêtes*.[21] In a general sense, I highlight, first, the degree to which the records produced in such *enquêtes* are not merely documents which present information

---

projects devoted to the 'genesis of the modern State', see Jean-Philippe Genet, 'L'État moderne: un modèle opératoire?', in *L'État moderne: genèse, bilans et perspectives*, ed. Jean-Philippe Genet (Paris, 1990), 261–81; and Genet, 'La genèse de l'État moderne. Les enjeux d'un programme de recherche', *Actes de la recherche en sciences sociales* 118 (1997), 3–18.

[16] Olivier Guillot, Albert Rigaudière and Yves Sassier, *Pouvoirs et institutions dans la France médiévale. Vol. 2: Des temps féodaux aux temps de l'État*, 3rd edition (Paris, 2003), 55–6; André Gouron, 'Continuité et discontinuité dans l'histoire du législatif médiéval: réflexions sur une recherche collective', in *L'État moderne*, 217–26 at 218–19 and 226.

[17] Dejoux, 'Gouverner par l'enquête', 271 ('enquêter c'est gouverner').

[18] Bongert, *Recherches sur les cours laïques*, 34, 236–8, 269–70; Boulet-Sautel, 'Aperçus sur le système des preuves', 278 ('Mais, il est, cependant, symptomatique de relever que saint Louis en fut l'agent décisif'), 298–9, 315–25; Dejoux, *Les enquêtes*, 69 (the age of Louis IX was une 'étape fondamentale dans la construction étatique'); Harding, *Medieval Law*, 148–52; Gérard Sivéry, 'Le mécontentement dans le royaume de France et les *enquêtes* de saint Louis', *Revue historique* 269 (1983), 3–24 at 4 and 23–4.

[19] Claude Gauvard, 'Introduction', in *Quand gouverner c'est enquêter*, 9–19 at 13.

[20] Dejoux, *Les enquêtes*, 2–4 and 371–9; see p. 377. In acknowledging the coercive and ideological aspects of Louis' *enquêtes*, Dejoux flirts with views offered by Michel Foucault, without, however, fully embracing them: Michel Foucault, 'Truth and Juridical Forms', in Michel Foucault, *Power*, ed. James D. Faubion (New York, NY, 2000), 1–89 at 48; Michel Foucault, *Surveillir et Punir. Naissance de la prison* (Paris, 1975), 226–7.

[21] By adversarial or judicial *enquête* I mean the formal legal procedure of applying *inquisitio* as a means to help settle a dispute between two litigants. In thirteenth-century

about events and legal procedure, but also act 'as political strategies aimed at imposing a particular vision of the state'.[22] Second, I reveal the ways in which such strategies can be manipulated by both the agents of the incipient royal 'state' and the subjects who offered their testimonies. In support of these general positions, I argue two more specific points. First, I maintain that *enquêtes* – or, perhaps, the extant artifacts of *enquêtes*, whether in the form of summaries of cases or written transcriptions of witnesses' depositions – retain and demonstrate a fundamental sense of orality.[23] That orality is central to the entire process of *inquisitio*, and can be glimpsed in surprising and often powerful ways in the records of depositions. In emphasizing orality, I undercut most legal and institutional histories of this period, which instead focus on the (undoubtedly momentous) emergence of written records and on the degree to which nascent states made use of writing to expand their powers.

Second, I argue that the very orality of the procedure of *enquête*, particularly as practiced in adversarial contexts in France in the middle of the thirteenth century, permits us to identify *enquêtes* not merely as instrumentalist artifacts of a process of state formation but also as sites of contested strategies of representation and claims to power. Or to put it slightly differently, we might see the *enquêtes* as contested sites of political practice and of truth production, rather than as neutral conveyers of a single truth. As I shall show, the authorities that ordered *enquêtes* – whether the royal court or an ecclesiastical judge – could and often did shape the outcome of the matter through their choice of *enquêteurs*, of witnesses, of the questions posed to witnesses, and of the specific language used in those questions. In so doing, such an authority might use the adversarial *enquête* to attempt to discipline or constrain those who had agreed to participate in the new procedure. Yet, also because *enquêtes* relied on the oral testimony of witnesses, who were often supplied by the parties to a dispute, depositions could be used to pose counter-narratives to the centralizing narrative preferred by the 'state' authority. In other words, witnesses could – and sometimes did – shape the narrative in surprising ways, ways that were entirely unanticipated by the men charged with carrying out the *enquête*. In this sense, *enquêtes* served as contested terrain in which competing stories about what was important,

---

terms, such *enquêtes* involved the summoning and interrogation of witnesses; see below, pp. 164–70, for this process.

[22] Pierre Bourdieu, 'Rethinking the State: Genesis and Structure of the Bureaucratic Field', in Bourdieu, *Psoractical Reason. On the Theory of Action* (Stanford, CA, 1998), 35–63 at 38–9. For *inquisitio* as (merely) a 'tool' used by kings 'to acquire the information they required to make well-considered decisions', see Bachrach, *passim* and, e.g., 75.

[23] See Guilhiermoz, 'De la persistence', *passim*. Ernest Glasson, *Histoire du droit et des institutions de la France. Volume 6: La féodalité (suite). Les finances et la justice du roi* (Paris, 1895), 178 and n. 3, argued against Guilhiermoz that thirteenth-century legal procedure was not oral in character, but rather was 'à la fois orale et écrite'. Compare Sophie Peralba, 'Des coutumiers aux styles. L'isolement de la matière procédurale aux XIIIe et XIVe siècles', in *Cahiers de recherches médiévaux et humanistes* 7 (2000), paras 42–3, mis en ligne le 03 janvier 2007, consulté le 08 novembre 2022, http://journals.openedition.org/crm/887; DOI: https://doi.org/10.4000/crm.887.

and even about what was true, might be presented. This second part of my argument suggests that *enquêtes* should be seen not as logically superior signs of cognitive development, nor even as neutral tools for the implementation of putatively benign 'order' on a wildly violent countryside, but rather as sites for the strategic presentation of competing visions for how law and society should be understood.

The Oral Character of *Enquêtes*

By the middle of the thirteenth century in France, the defining feature of any judicial or adversarial *enquête* was the oral recitation of individual narratives by sworn witnesses.[24] This point is worth emphasizing, since too often scholars eager to demonstrate the progressive march of written culture at the expense of oral culture have focused on the artifacts of *enquêtes*, that is, the documents which record the depositions and/or legal judgments, instead of on the actions which those artifacts represent. To be sure, the immense proliferation of written records as famously described by Michael Clanchy is profoundly important both for historians and for the development of medieval institutions.[25] It surely matters that the new royal appeals court, the Parlement de Paris, had begun keeping records of its cases from at least the 1250s, and that a royal archiving process begun under Philip Augustus was firmly in place by the end of the century.[26] By systematizing the presentation of legal procedure, as well as the language with which that procedure was represented, these documents helped the monarchy 'produce and impose... categories of thought' that would, over time, enhance royal power over its subjects.[27] And yet, despite the very real power of writing, it is important not to forget the essential orality of the process of *enquête*. After all, the preservation of the written records of depositions taken in the process of conducting an *enquête* was not yet considered essential. Potin and Dejoux have demonstrated the haphazard and partial preservation of the famous *querimoniae* of Louis IX (the first *enquêtes* of reparation) and the circuitous, centuries-long path that brought them to the Trésor des Chartes; the depositions were 'working

---

[24] Boulet-Sautel, 'Aperçus sur le système des preuves', 303.
[25] M.T. Clanchy, *From Memory to Written Record: England, 1066–1307*, 3rd ed. (London, 2013). See also Clanchy, 'Literacy, Law and the Power of the State', in *Culture et idéologie dans la genèse de l'État moderne* (Rome, 1985), 25–34.
[26] For Philip Augustus, H.-F. Delaborde, 'Introduction: Les registres de Philippe Auguste', in *Recueil des actes de Philippe Auguste, roi de France* (6 vols, Paris, 1916–), i, v–xl; *Les registres de Philippe Auguste, tome I: Texte*, ed. John W. Baldwin (Paris, 1992), 6–7; Baldwin, *Government*, 401–03. For Parlement, A. Grün, 'Notice sur les archives du Parlement de Paris', in *Actes du Parlement de Paris. Tome Premier, 1254–1299*, ed. Edgard Boutaric (2 vols, Paris, 1863–7), i, lviii–cxxii; Olivier Guyotjeannin, 'La méthode des archivistes du roi de France (XIIIe–début XVIe siècle)', *Archiv für Diplomatik* 42 (1996), 295–373; and Yann Potin, 'Archiver l'enquête? Avatars archivistiques d'un monument historiographique: les '*enquêtes* administratives' de Louis IX (1247–1248)', in *L'enquête au Moyen Âge*, 241–67, esp. 244–7.
[27] Clanchy, 'Literacy', 25. The quotation is from Bourdieu, 'Rethinking', 35.

documents' intended to 'facilitate or support' the actions of the *enquêteurs* during their investigation, and were never intended to be preserved.[28] As Tryoen has argued, the same holds for the depositions taken in adversarial, or judicial, *enquêtes*;[29] they were practically useful during the course of the *enquête*, but were of little use once a decision had been rendered. Their survival is thus largely a product of chance and local politics. For example, there is the unlikely survival of a massive set of depositions taken in a case from 1246 that was settled prior to judgment: they survive only as a seventeenth-century antiquarian copy of a manuscript preserved by the opponent of the party that collected the depositions.[30] In this case, there is zero evidence that the depositions were ever used at the time or at any time thereafter. Preservation must be considered fortuitous rather than instrumental. What this suggests is that while Clanchy and others who highlight the significance of the rise in written records are surely correct, it is equally certain that for medieval people engaged in the process of *enquête*, the essence of the procedure was to be found in its oral forms and not in its written artifacts.[31]

What is more, medieval legal culture itself prioritized oral testimony. Indeed, one of the central principles of later medieval legal theory, one formalized in French legal procedure in 1566, observed that 'temoins passent lettres', that is, 'witnesses are superior to documents'.[32] While canonists were wrestling with questions of proof from the middle of the twelfth century, and continued to do so throughout the middle ages, Innocent III's bull of 1206–09, *Cum Johannes*

---

[28] Potin, 'Archiver l'enquête?', 244; Dejoux, *Les enquêtes*, 46–8.
[29] Lucie Tryoen Laloum, 'Le rouleau dans les procedures judiciaires au chapitre de Notre-Dame de Paris au XIIIe siècle', in *The Roll in England and France in the Late Middle Ages. Form and Content*, ed. Stefan G. Holz, Jörg Peltzer, and Maree Shirota (Berlin, 2019), 53–76 at 70 and *passim*.
[30] *Enquête de 1245 relative aux droits du chapitre Saint-Julien du Mans*, ed. Julien Chappée, Ambroise Ledru et L.-J. Denis (Paris, 1922), clv. Incredibly, the editors provide an incorrect shelf mark for the sole extant manuscript of the text: the correct shelf mark is Paris, BNF ms latin 17123, pp. 275–484.
[31] Paul Guilhiermoz, 'De la persistance du caractère oral dans la procédure civile française', *Nouvelle revue historique de droit français et étranger* 13 (1889), 21–65. Clanchy, of course, was too good a historian to insist on a binary replacement of the oral with the written; he emphasized the coexistence of both forms throughout the thirteenth century: Clanchy, *From Memory*, 265–6. See also Paul Bertrand, 'À propos de la révolution de l'écrit (Xe–XIIIe siècle). Considérations inactuelles', *Médiévales* 56 (2009), 75–92 at 86–7.
[32] See Bongert, *Recherches sur les cours laïques*, 276; Michel Petitjean, 'Quelques remarques sur les témoins et leurs témoignages d'après la doctrine médiévale', in *Les témoins devant la justice*, ed. Benoît Garnot (Rennes, 2003), 55–65 at 55; Paul Ourliac and J. de Malafosse, *Histoire du droit privé. I. Les obligations*, 2nd ed. (Paris, 1969), 120. For its influence, see *inter alia* Olivier Guerrier, 'Fortune de 'Témoins passent Lettres', de l'Italie à la France, du droit à la "littérature"', in *Quand Minerve passe les monts. Modalités littéraires de la circulation des savoirs (Italie-France, Renaissance–XVIIe siècle)*, ed. Carine Roudière-Sébastien (Pessac, 2020), 17–23, [en ligne] https://una-editions.fr/fortune-de-temoins-passent-lettres/ [accessed 15 December 2020].

eremita, and its incorporation into Gregory IX's registers,[33] ensured the principle that proof by oral testimony from more than one person was superior to proof offered by documents. At about the same time, perhaps worried that courts might take the new procedure of oral testimony too far, Innocent III also set a rough cap of forty as the number of witnesses who should, in most circumstances, be introduced into a legal hearing.[34] Adversarial *enquêtes* certainly bear witness to the notion that witnesses were better than documents, even if they sometimes failed to adhere to the forty-witness cap.[35] For one, as Dejoux has noted in general terms, it is very rare to find written texts introduced in *enquêtes* as part of a deposition.[36] This fact in itself suggests the preference for oral narratives offered by legitimate witnesses; had procurators and judges been interested in viewing documents, then we would find more in the records. At least before 1250 or so, this is simply not regular practice. The few cases in which written evidence is mentioned in a deposition, moreover, typically serve as the proverbial exceptions to the rule. For example, in the context of a war that Count Guy of Forez had recently fought against his neighbor, Guillaume, lord of Baffie, the royal court commanded that that an *enquête* be held to investigate the matter. Count Guy appeared before the *enquêteurs* with a prepared written statement (*quemdam cedulam*), apparently hoping to present it instead of speaking in his own voice.[37] But the *enquêteurs* forced him to read it out loud to them and then required that he take an oath in their presence that what was found in the statement was true. Only then did they copy the cedula into the record of the *enquête*. So, while this is evidence of written evidence being offered in an *enquête*, it also shows the entirely grudging acceptance of such evidence by the *enquêteurs*. They had required Guy to make an oral narration, even if that narration simply consisted of him reading out his prepared statement. Other anecdotal evidence from this period shows that written proof was often discounted or only accepted when read aloud.[38]

---

33 X, 2.22.10 (*Corpus iuris canonici*, ed. E. Friedberg (2 vols, Graz, 1959), ii, cols 350–352). Lemesle, 'L'enquête contre les epreuves', para. 7, notes earlier papal preferences for oral over written proofs.

34 X, 2.20.37. See Charles Donahue, Jr, 'Proof by Witnesses in the Church Courts of Medieval England: An Imperfect Reception of the Learned Law', in *On the Laws and Customs of England. Essays in Honor of Samuel E. Thorne*, ed. Morris Arnold et al. (Chapel Hill, NC, 1981), 127–58 at 149; and Yves Mausen, *Veritatis adiutor: la procédure du témoignage dans le droit savant et la pratique française (XIIe–XIVe siècles)* (Milan, 2006), 89–95.

35 For an *enquête* with ninety-nine witnesses, see *Enquête de 1245*, passim.

36 Dejoux, *Les enquêtes*, 82.

37 Only some extracts of the *enquête* have been published, in *Actes du Parlement de Paris*, i, cccvi; a summary is also found in *Layettes du Trésor des chartes*, ed. H.-F. Delaborde (5 vols, Paris, 1863–1909), v, no. 406. The *enquête* opens with this statement: *Dictus Guido Forenensis nobis tradidit quamdam cedulam, quam coram nobis legere fecimus, et, lecta cedula, dictus comes dixit coram nobis per suum sacramentum a nobis receptum, quod totum illud quod insertum in dicta cedula verum erat, que talis est.*

38 Cases from 1247: *Recueil des historiens des gaules et de la France*, ed. Martin Bouquet et al. (24 vols, Paris, 1738–1904) (hereafter *RHGF*), xxiv, 82, no. 119; 85–6, no.

An *enquête* conducted in Le Mans in 1246 offers more nuanced, but still compelling evidence concerning the preference for oral proof over written proof. This *enquête* aimed to resolve a dispute between the cathedral chapter of Le Mans and the suburban monastery of la Couture over the chapter's claim to be able to impose ecclesiastical censure on the monks.[39] The chapter's claim rested on its assertion that Bishop Hamelin of Le Mans (d. 1214) had granted them full powers of ecclesiastical jurisdiction at a specific moment in the recent past. To that end, the procurator for the chapter deposed the most senior canons of the chapter, men who had actual memories of the grant in question. When asked to respond to the question 'did the dean and chapter of Le Mans possess the right of ecclesiastical jurisdiction?', then, a series of canons responded 'yes'. When asked how they knew this to be true, at least eight replied that it was because they had seen and read, many times, charters issued both by Bishop Hamelin and the papal legate, Octavian, which made and confirmed the grant of ecclesiastical jurisdiction to the chapter, as well as a confirmation letter issued by Pope Innocent III.[40] These and other witnesses also noted that the documents had been read out in diocesan synods on a regular basis over the years, both in Latin and in French.[41] Beyond simply citing the existence of the charters in question, the first witness, Robert, dean of the chapter, actually produced the charters, displayed them to the *enquêteurs*, and offered an oral description of the diplomatic features of the texts and seals. In one sense, at least, the witnesses were claiming authority from written instruments.

Yet is clear that the procurators felt that the mentioning and displaying the charters was not enough. Indeed, Dean Robert, who was deposed first, who presented and described the charters, and who had them copied into his deposition, was forced to admit that he had not been present when the grant was made, since he only came to Le Mans many years later. He was thus only familiar with the grant *because* he had read the charters in the chapter archive.[42] Since it was known that charters could be forged, this was clearly an issue. Other witnesses faced the same problem. The brothers Renaud and

---

158. A case from 1230: *Actes du Parlement de Paris*, i, ccciii–ccciv. In another case from 1230, a judgment was made after specific documents were read out in the *curia regis*, thus showing that while documents were used and prepared, it was the hearing of them that led to the judgment: *RHGF*, v. 24, 295*.

39 *Enquête de 1245*, 1. The dispute was settled out of court, albeit after witnesses had been deposed: *Cartulaire des abbayes de Saint-Pierre de la Couture et Saint-Pierre de Solesmes*, ed. les Bénédictins de Solesmes (Le Mans, 1881), no. 338 (18 February 1246, o.s.).

40 *Enquête de 1245*, 15–16, 29, 55, 85. The charters in question were copied by the cathedral chapter into its thirteenth-century cartulary: *Liber albus*, nos 201, 202, 204 and 205.

41 *Enquête de 1245*, 77, 96–97, and 118. One witness had been a secretary (*clericus episcopi*) to Bishop Hamelin and had himself read the charters out in open synod. The advocate Nicolas de Capella, however, knew of the privileges but said 'he never saw them nor heard them read': *ibid.*, 121.

42 *Enquête de 1245*, 1 and 2.

Aimery Clarel, who came from a family closely connected to the chapter and who had themselves grown up in the chapter, also admitted that although they remembered Bishop Hamelin fondly (since he had bestowed their prebends on them), they only knew about the grant of ecclesiastical sanction either because they had heard their elders talking about it or because, many years later, they had read the charters.[43] Much of their testimony was spent attempting to confirm that the grant of sanction had occurred by citing (and dating) episodes that they had personally witnessed. Renaud, for instance, claimed that he had received his prebend forty-eight years ago on All Saints Day; moreover, on the feast of St Nicholas of that first year after he became a canon, he heard the deacon who read the gospel publicly excommunicate Guy de Laval by the authority of the chapter. Renaud concluded, logically, that Bishop Hamelin's grant of censure had to have occurred before that date, probably, he thought, forty-nine years ago (i.e., in 1197). His brother Aimery performed a similar intellectual juggling act; because he thought that Guy de Laval had been excommunicated forty-two years ago, he estimated that, from his reading of the charters, the grant of censure must have occurred forty-five years ago (i.e., in 1200).[44] Several older canons, such as Eudes the archdeacon, Étienne the Burgundian, Denis the clerk, Master Raherius, and the priest Guillaume Buisson also admitted they had not witnessed the grant of this crucial power, and knew about it only through writing or through specific incidents of sanction which they, too, attempted to date by memory of events (with somewhat comic results). It is perhaps telling that the procurator dug up, at last, someone who *had* actually witnessed Bishop Hamelin publicly grant the right of sanction to his chapter, namely Guillaume Meigret, a townsman in his sixties. Guillaume affirmed that:

he had been present in that chamber of the bishop's palace which leads into the smaller, interior chamber, when he heard Nicolas, who was dean at that time, and Eudes, who is now archdeacon, begging Bishop Hamelin to give them the power of exercising ecclesiastical justice over those who wronged them [*malefactores*], since the bishop was often absent was thus unable to offer justice to them as often as was necessary. And then he heard in person the bishop confirm this [power] to them, but he does not recall in what words. And he heard it said that the bishop also issued documents concerning this [grant], but he doesn't recall [seeing] that [happen], nor does he recall ever having seen the documents.[45]

Guillaume's testimony is remarkable, particularly when paired with the testimonies of the learned clergy. Where the clergy tried hard to overcome their own lack of eyewitness evidence – they literally had neither seen nor heard the all-important grant of authority being made – by citing the charters, Guillaume Meigret's testimony takes the opposite approach: his testimony is fully sensory in the way that medieval legal opinion preferred, for he had seen the crucial

---

[43] *Enquête de 1245*, 29, 54.
[44] *Enquête de 1245*, 28 (Renaud), 55 (Aimery).
[45] *Enquête de 1245*, 137.

moment and heard the participants as the power of sanction was requested and conveyed.[46] It is thus clear that even when they were taking written documents seriously, as they were in Le Mans in 1246,[47] oral narratives and witnesses' memories played a determinative role in what would be accepted as truth.

Given medieval preference for oral testimony, it is perhaps unsurprising to discover that what marked an adversarial *enquête* as an *enquête* was the basic act of using oral testimony of two or more witnesses to help decide the truth (and thus to help shape a judgment) in a dispute over rights or property (but rarely crime).[48] Such testimony differed from that provided by witnesses and oath-helpers in previous centuries because the deponents were asked to respond with specific factual information to a set slate of questions produced by the procurator, rather than merely attesting to the moral character of one of the parties to the dispute; also unlike earlier witnesses or oath-helpers, those witnesses gathered for an *enquête* were not themselves liable for any legal penalty, unless, of course, they perjured themselves.[49] A sense of the oral context of these *enquêtes* is easily gained by even a cursory survey of the procedure.[50] *Enquêtes* were not, of course, automatically triggered by a particular sort of dispute or offense, but rather were ordered by courts on an *ad hoc* basis, when it was hoped that the testimony collected by the *enquête* would provide sufficient proof for the court to render a judgment. By the 1240s in France, both secular and ecclesiastical courts were ordering *enquêtes*. For instance, a papal legate ordered witnesses to be deposed in Le Mans in 1246, in the context of an ecclesiastical dispute between the cathedral chapter of Le Mans and the suburban monastery of Saint-Pierre de la Couture over the chapter's right to correct the monks.[51] In about 1240, it was the king, or rather his court, who ordered an *enquête* to be conducted in the Auvergne into the actions of outlaws operating within the lands of the lord of Bourbon.[52] In an unusual case, the archbishop of Reims

---

46 On the medieval preference for witnesses who had seen and heard, and/or for their sensory appreciation of what they were describing, see Petitjean, 'Quelques remarques sur les témoins', 61–2. Note, however, that Aimery's claim that he had heard his seniors in the chapter discussing the grant might also have counted as having 'seen' the event: *ibid.*, 62. On medieval legists' discussion of the relative value of various means by which a witness might 'know' or 'believe' what he said, Mausen, *Veritatis adiutor*, 610–49.
47 Several depositions describe the inspection of other charters: *Enquête de 1245*, 90, 141–2, 143, 149–50.
48 Boulet-Sautel, 'Aperçus sur le système des preuves', 303. By the thirteenth century, the principle that at least two witnesses were necessary for a legal procedure of *inquisitio* (*testis unus, testis nullus*) was firmly ensconced: Lévy, 'L'évolution de la preuve', 37–9; Boulet-Sautel, 'Aperçus sur le système des preuves', 306; Petitjean, 'Quelques remarques sur les témoins', 56; Dejoux, *Les enquêtes*, 79.
49 Bongert, *Recherches sur les cours laïques*, 213–14, 254–5; Boulet-Sautel, 'Aperçus sur le système des preuves', 305–08.
50 Lot and Fawtier, *Histoire des institutions françaises au moyen age*, 387–9, provide a description of the process from later prescriptive texts.
51 *Enquête de 1245*, 1.
52 *Olim*, i, 1016: *Inquesta facta... mandato domini* regis. The case is calendared in *Layettes*, v, no. 414.

preemptively ordered an *enquête* to be conducted concerning his own rights over the monastery of Saint-Rémi and its suburb so that he might present the results to the king; sparked by this act, the archbishop's opponent, the abbot of Saint-Rémi, also ordered depositions to be taken.[53]

The ordering of *enquêtes* by a judicial authority came in response to initial oral arguments presented to the court by the parties or their procurators (lawyers). Sometimes we can get a glimpse of such oral argumentation, even if it is usually transformed into declarative third-person prose. For example, a papal letter of 1223 from Honorius III to judges-delegate investigating the dispute between the cathedral chapter of Le Mans, on one side, and Queen Berengaria and the canons of Saint-Pierre-de-la-Cour, on the other, distinguished the arguments of the two parties at length before commanding the judges to settle the matter.[54] The records of the Parlement de Paris are typically more succinct but regularly convey the gist of the oral arguments that the court had heard. For instance, in 1258 the Parlement records related how the count of Sancerre claimed, orally, that he and his men had the right to seize any open sacks of grain being offered for sale in the villa of Saint-Satur; his opponent, the abbot of Saint-Satur, spoke 'ex adverso', saying that it had been the ancient custom that anyone coming to Saint-Satur to sell grain was free from exaction.[55] In this case, the court ordered an inquest (whose depositions are lost) that proved the justice of the abbot's claim. Infrequently, the accounts of the initial arguments also represent fragments of direct speech, such as the case in which the royal sub-bailli of Arras was said to have called Robert, a chaplain of the cathedral of Arras, 'a lecherous priest', or the case in which Roger, lord of Huriel, was said to have entered the lands of the prior of Chapelaude with his men, shouting 'Are you a man of the prior? If so, you will pay!'[56] It is clear that the even in the highly formulaic world of mid-thirteenth-century legal pleading, the role of oral argumentation was central to the business of law.[57]

When a judicial authority commanded an *enquête* to be made, it typically delegated the actual conduct of the inquiry to a pair of men known to scholars as *enquêteurs*. The *enquêteurs* were literate, trained in law, familiar with the pro-

[53] Guilhiermoz, *Enquêtes et procès*, 311–29, at 311–12 and 326–7.
[54] *Cartulaire du chapitre royal de Saint-Pierre-de-la-Cour, du Mans*, ed. Samuel Menjot d'Elbenne and L.-J. Denis (Le Mans, 1907), no. 213 (1225). The chapter presented its petition, but then the canons answered 'ex adverso'.
[55] *Olim*, i, 63–4, no. i: *Cum comes Sacri-Cesaris diceret quod... Diceret etiam... [etc.] Cum etiam abbas et conventus Sancti Satiri dicerent ex adverso... Per inquestam inde factam melius probatum est a apercius pro abbate Sancti Satiri quam pro comite Sacri-Cesaris.*
[56] *Olim*, i, 38, no. iii (Arras, 1266), and 341–3, no. xiii (Chapelaude, 1270).
[57] Contemporary manuals for those negotiating the royal courts acknowledged the importance of oral pleading: Sophie Peralba, 'Des coutumiers aux styles. L'isolement de la matière procédurale aux XIIIe et XIVe siècles', in *Cahiers de recherches médiévaux et humanistes* 7 (2000), paragraphs 42–3, mis en ligne le 03 janvier 2007, consulté le 08 novembre 2022, http://journals.openedition.org/crm/887; DOI: https://doi.org/10.4000/crm.887.

cedure, and expected to show no partiality towards either party.[58] Unfortunately, the surviving records do not always name the *enquêteurs*, as is the case with the Le Mans inquiry of 1246. When they are named, it is possible to infer data about how and perhaps why they were chosen. In the case of *enquêtes* ordered by a secular court, the team was often, as with the *missi* of the Carolingian empire, composed of one layman and one clerk. Ecclesiastical courts, however, deputed two churchmen to perform the inquiry. Sometimes the *enquêteurs* were local, or semi-local, and thus presumably familiar with the region, the parties, or even the case; other times they appear to have been outsiders sent by a centralized court into a local dispute. In the Arras dispute mentioned above, the *enquêteurs* were Guillaume de Chevry, a knight from suburban Paris, and Henri de Champrépus, a royal clerk originally from Normandy; neither of them can be presumed to have had any local contacts in Arras.[59] In an Angevin *enquête* from *c*. 1240, the royal bailli for the region, Geoffroy Payen, conducted the *enquête*.[60] Geoffroy knew both parties and probably many of the deponents, at least those who identified as knights. In an Auvergne *enquête* from *c*. 1240, however, the royal court named as *enquêteurs* the (unnamed) dean of the collegial church of Monter-Moyer in Bourges, and Raoul Gandelus, the royal bailli in Bourges;[61] since Bourges was only 80–120 km distant from the seats of the disputing parties, the *enquêteurs* might have been chosen partly for their relatively local knowledge, and also, in the case of Raoul, for his presumed fidelity to the king's interests. In another *enquête* conducted at about the same date, also in the Auvergne, the identity of the team of *enquêteurs* was more mixed.[62] One of the two, Guillaume of Chantelle, took his name from the lord of Bourbon's castle of Chantelle, and may have been a minor landholder in the region; as such, he would have had extensive local knowledge of the subject of the *enquête*, which addressed events that had occurred in and around Chantelle itself.[63] On the other hand, the second *enquêteur*, Jocelin de Ardena, seems to have been sent to the region from Paris.[64] In the case of the ecclesiastical *enquête* conducted in Reims in 1254,

---

[58] Mausen, *Veritatis adiutor*, 284–95.
[59] *Olim*, i, 238, no. iii.
[60] *Layettes*, v, 143–44, no. 418: the identity of the *enquêteur* is known only from a dorsal indication on the ms.
[61] *Olim*, i, 1016–19.
[62] Martial Alphonse Chazaud, *Quelques traits de moeurs féodales en Bourbonnais (XIIIe–XIVe siècles)* (Moulins, 1875), 13–23; an excerpt is printed in *Layettes*, v, no. 421, at 144–5.
[63] A Guillaume de Chantelle, knight, son of another Guillaume de Chantelle, quitclaimed vines to the church of Chantelle in 1225: *Chartes du Bourbonnais, 918–1522*, ed. J. Monicat and B. de Fournoux (Moulins, 1952) no. 84.
[64] Rémy Roques, 'Le gouvernement d'Alphonse de Poitiers en Auvergne', *Annales du Midi* 127 (2015), 325–48, at 342 and n. 127, discovered a royal balance sheet for 1239 that includes payments to a Jacquelin d'Ardena and a Master Eudes of Saint-Denis for a journey to the Auvergne *pro quadam inquesta facienda* (citing *RHGF*, xxii, 600). Jocelin and Jacquelin de Ardena are certainly the same person.

however, all three *enquêteurs* were strictly local: Abbot Everard of Igny, Abbot Gérard of Cuissy, and Eudes, the prior of the Dominicans of Reims.[65]

The task of the *enquêteurs* was to pose a set of pre-arranged questions (*articuli*) to the witnesses gathered for this task, and then to record their responses. Although learned law had clear guidelines for drawing up the questions, it is not always clear from the extant records whether the presiding authority or the *enquêteurs* themselves constructed the list of questions.[66] Nor, in most cases, is it possible to reconstruct the list.[67] A few rare exceptions exist. For example, the transcript of a set of depositions conducted *c.* 1246 in the context of a dispute between the Parisian abbey of Saint-German-des-Prés and the men of its villa of Esmans commences with a list of the eight questions that were posed to the witnesses.[68] While the Le Mans *enquête* of 1246 did not properly list the articles, many of the depositions referred to the various articles by number. From this evidence it is possible to identify at least thirty-five questions that were posed to at least some of the witnesses: the list ranges from simple background questions (#2: 'What are the boundaries of the city of Le Mans'), to more pointed ones (#12: 'Does the cathedral chapter have the power of imposing ecclesiastical censure?').[69]

In most *enquêtes*, however, the questions asked of the witnesses must be inferred from context, typically from the appearance of the word *requisitus de* ['having been asked about...'] within a deposition. For instance, in an *enquête* conducted in 1240 in the Orléannais, Pierre de Rillé, the first witness for Richard de Beaumont, offered information concerning 1) the status of assarted lands at Chaumont; 2) the status of some hedges at Villers, 3) the status of land held by the monks of Pontlevoy (who were not a party in the case), and 4) the nature of legal jurisdiction in the lands of Matthieu le Jai of Candé.[70] Subsequent witnesses spoke to the same matters, at least so long as they had something to

---

[65] Guilhiermoz, *Enquêtes et procès*, 311. The abbeys of Igny and Cuissy were within 35 km of Reims.
[66] On these 'questionnaires', see Jean-Pierre Delumeau, 'La mémoire des gens d'Arezzo et de Sienne à travers des dépositions de témoins (VIIIe–XIIe s.)', in *Temps, mémoire, tradition au Moyen Age* (Aix-en-Provence, 1983), 43–67 at 46; and Lemesle, 'L'enquête contre les épreuves', 12.
[67] Dejoux, *Les enquêtes*, 33, found only one set of articles for all of the *querimoniae* of Louis IX. The records of important fourteenth-century 'show trials' tell a different story, though. For one such trial, see Alain Provost, 'Déposer, c'est faire croire? À propos du discours des témoins dans le procès de Guichard, évêque de Troyes (1308–1314)', in *La preuve en justice*, 98–118. Web. http://books.openedition.org/pur/15837, paragraphs 7–9.
[68] Guilhiermoz, *Enquêtes et procès*, 293–311 at 293–4.
[69] *Enquête de 1245*, 110–11, which lists by number questions #4 to #20. Other questions can be inferred elsewhere in the *enquête*: ibid., 117, 120–1, and 126–7. Since the scribe who recorded the testimonies often abbreviated the question, some of the articles must be reconstructed from context: e.g. question #19 (p. 111): *Item de XIX°: si Octavianus auctoritate sue legationis etc.*
[70] See *Layettes*, v, no. 418: *Petrus de Rilleio, miles, requisitus de exemplatis Calvimontis, dixit quod... Requisitus de haiis de Vilariis, dixit quod...*

say about them.⁷¹ The same questions were asked of the witnesses for Count Hugues de Blois, the other party in the case. Inevitably, their responses differed in important ways. For example, Guillaume de Rillé, witness for Richard, said concerning the rights of justice in the lands of Matthieu of Candé, '[all] justice [there] was Richard's, and Matthieu held jurisdiction from him', whereas Geoffroy de Aguizon, witness for the count, countered with 'the said Richard held no justice there, at least none concerning the shedding of blood'.⁷² To take another example, one of the Auvergne *enquêtes* from *c.* 1240 focused on whether known outlaws were being tolerated within the lands of Lord Archambaud de Bourbon. From the responses of the witnesses, it is clear that the witnesses were asked several simple questions: 1) have you seen any of the men who had been outlawed? 2) if so, where? 3) were they within the lands of the lord of Bourbon when you saw them? All of the depositions address these issues, albeit in different ways. For example, Pierre Bobius responded in this way: 'he said that after the said outlaws had burned the monks' cloister at Bayet, he saw them in the marketplace of Charroux, which is a castle of the lord of Bourbon'. Amicus of Port-Paluel was more forthcoming. He said that 'he saw three of the outlaws at Belcaire, one of the lord of Bourbon's villas; and Amicus ate with them around Shrovetide, in the house of the lord of Bourbon's prévôt for Belcaire. And the men stayed in the prévôt's house for the entire day.'⁷³ The articles, whether stated or inferred, clearly provided a structure and regularity to the procedure while also permitting the *enquêteurs* to build towards a desired outcome through their choice of questions and language. In this, they participated in the project of disciplining the king's subjects through the structure and language of their questions. But, as the varying responses to the questions indicate, the open-ended nature of witnesses' responses to the questions allowed room for personal knowledge and experience, individual expression, and alternative narratives; as we shall see, the flexibility afforded by soliciting (and recording) open-ended testimony could undercut the *enquêteurs'* desired or intended goals.

The crux of the *enquête* was, of course, the oral testimony provided by some number of witnesses. Witnesses were summoned to give testimony at a specific place and a specific time. While learned law of the thirteenth century specifies that summons might be made in writing or orally, and while Clanchy describes

---

⁷¹ The scribes sometimes noted that a witness had said 'exactly the same as' one of the previous witnesses: e.g. *Layettes*, v, no. 418. If a witness had nothing to say, the scribe said so: *Odo de Monteyanno... de justicia terre de Candeio, nichil scit*. On scribal use of the phrase *nichil scit*, see Daniel Lord Smail, 'Témoins et témoignages dans les causes civiles à Marseille, du XIIIe au XVe siècle', in *Pratiques sociales et politiques judiciaires dans les villes de l'Occident à la fin du Moyen Âge*, ed. Jacques Chiffoleau, Claude Gauvard and Andrea Zorzi (Rome, 2007), 423–37 at para. 9, http://books.openedition.org/efr/1831, DOI: https://doi.org/10.4000/books.efr.1831.

⁷² *Layettes*, v, no. 418. Lemesle, 'L'enquête contre les épreuves', 65, notices this stark contradiction.

⁷³ *Olim*, i, 1018.

for England in the thirteenth century the replacement of the practice of oral summoning with summons by writ,[74] I have found no positive evidence in French *enquêtes* prior to 1250 concerning the methods by which witnesses were summoned in secular cases. It is tempting to infer from other legal situations, such as evidence from Le Mans that shows how those who injured the rights of the cathedral chapter were summonsed orally by the chapter's bellringers,[75] or the ample evidence from southern France showing how secular sergeants delivered summons in person,[76] that witnesses to *enquêtes* in France were summoned orally, by subsidiary agents of the convening authority. Since witnesses could not be compelled to give testimony, however, the concept of the summons must not be pushed too far;[77] their appearance was at least superficially voluntary, even if it might be complicated by lordship, friendship, or regional identity.

In many adversarial *enquêtes*, and especially those convened by ecclesiastical courts, each party in a dispute was expected to produce its own slate of witnesses. Thus, in an *enquête* held in Le Mans in 1246, the record clearly indicates that all ninety-nine witnesses had been summoned on behalf of the cathedral chapter of Le Mans.[78] While we can safely assume that the other party, the monastery of Saint-Pierre de la Couture, had also deposed witnesses, no record of such depositions survives. In a case from Reims in 1254, both parties produced a slate of witnesses, but only the full transcript of the depositions from one side survives; we must be content with a later summary of those from the other side.[79] In a highly unusual ecclesiastical case from 1246, not only did both parties produce a set of witnesses, the *enquêteurs* called their own, third set of (distinct) witnesses, and also deposed the parties themselves.[80] The evidence from secular *enquêtes* is more mixed. In at least some cases, the procedure worked in ways similar to those found in the church courts. For example, in the *enquête* conducted in Anjou by the royal bailli, Geoffroy Payen, the surviving record clearly distinguishes the 'witnesses produced on the side of Lord Richard de Beaumont' from the 'witnesses on the side of the count of

---

[74] Clanchy, *From Memory*, 274–5.

[75] *Enquête of 1245*, 35 and many other locations. The word used for these figures was *sonitor* (bell-ringer), but in practice they also served as messengers or criers for the chapter.

[76] On sergeants, see Michel Hebert, 'Les sergents-messagers de Provence aux XIIIe et XIVe siecles', in *Le petit peuple dans l'occident médiéval: terminologies, perceptions, réalités*, ed. Pierre Boglioni, Robert Delort et Claude Gauvard (Paris, 2002), 293–310; and Sébastien Hamel, 'Être sergent du roi dans la prévôté de Saint-Quentin à la fin du Moyen Âge', in *Entre justice et justiciables: les auxiliaires de la justice du Moyen Âge au XXe siècle*, ed. Claire Dolan (Laval, 2005), 55–68.

[77] Bongert, *Recherches sur les cours laïques*, 254.

[78] *Enquête de 1245*, 1: *Primus testis ex parte decani et capituli Cenomannensis contra abbatem et conventum de Cultura Cenomanensi*.

[79] Guilhiermoz, *Enquêtes et procès*, 311–29.

[80] Guilhiermoz, *Enquêtes et procès*, 293–311. Guilhiermoz comments on the unusual quality of this *enquête* at *ibid.*, 53–4, 66–7 and 294 n. 1.

Blois'.⁸¹ More commonly, though, the extant form of a secular *enquête* does not state explicitly who had summoned the witnesses, nor on behalf of which party they were testifying. Such is the case in an *enquête* held in Le Mans in 1223x1226 concerning contested rights to woodland,⁸² and in the pair of Auvergnat *enquêtes* from *c*. 1240 mentioned above.⁸³ In these examples, and most others, a slate of depositions is presented without framing apparatus at all.

Once summoned or gathered, witnesses were required to swear an oath to tell the truth.⁸⁴ Many records of depositions note this fact by including the word 'juratus' after the name of each deponent: hence the ubiquitous formula '*N., juratus, dixit...*'⁸⁵ Their words were then recorded by scribes working for the *enquêteurs*, and the depositions were returned to the authority that ordered them made for discussion and analysis. It is of course necessary to acknowledge that the scribes were engaged in works of translation. Even though the deponents almost invariably offered their testimony in the vernacular, that is in one of the dialects of French, most *enquêtes* were recorded in Latin through the 1250s, and even when they start to be recorded in French, it is in the Parisian dialect, which was not necessarily that of the speakers. The degree to which ecclesiastical Latin, or the Parisian French of the court, truly captured the vernacular dialects of the witnesses remains an open and valid question.⁸⁶ Beyond the fact of literal translation, we must also acknowledge that the scribes did not present a literal transcript of everything a witness said; instead, the scribes distilled, condensed, and even shaped the form in which a witness's testimony might be preserved.⁸⁷ Despite these caveats, though, the depositions often reflect not only the individuation of witnesses concerning factual knowledge, but also differences

---

⁸¹ *Layettes*, v, no. 418: *Testes producti ex parte domini Richardi de Bellimonte... Testes ex parte comitis Blesensis.*
⁸² *Les registres de Philippe Auguste*, 174–6.
⁸³ *Olim*, i, 1016–19, and Chazaud, *Quelques traits*, 13–23. The *enquêtes* are difficult to date. The one found in the *Olim* opens with the following rubric: *Inquesta facta... anno domini MCCXL, mense aprili*. Since the calendar year began at Easter in medieval France, and since Easter fell on 27 March in 1239, on 15 April in 1240 and on 31 March in in 1241, a medieval date of 'April 1240' could refer only to the period 16–31 April 1240. But since the deponents recall events that happened on specific feast days, including 22 April, 25 April, and 8 May, it is impossible for the witnesses to have provided depositions in an *enquête* held 16–31 April 1240 about events that occurred as late as 8 May of the same year. It is likely, then, that the *enquête* of April 1240 actually concerned events that had transpired the previous year, that is in April and May 1239. Since King Louis gave the Auvergne in appanage to his brother, Alphonse of Poitiers, in the spring of 1241, and since the *enquêtes* were either conducted or concerned royal baillis (and not Alphonse's men), both *enquêtes* must have been conducted prior to Alphonse's assumption of his appanage in June 1241.
⁸⁴ Petitjean, 'Quelques remarques sur les témoins', 56.
⁸⁵ *Actes du Parlement de Paris*, i, cccvii–cccviii (with summary in *Layettes*, v, no. 479).
⁸⁶ Leonard Boyle, 'Montaillou Revisited: Mentalité and Methodology', in *Pathways to Medieval Peasants*, ed. J.A. Raftis (Toronto, 1981), 119–40 at 120–3; Charles Donahue Jr, *Why the History of Canon Law is not Written* (London, 1986), 7–8.
⁸⁷ See Mausen, *Veritatis adiutor*, 350–63.

in motivation and personality. Indeed, every once in a while, a scribe shifts into first person speech[88] in ways that carry the whiff of authenticity and reveal the emotions and patterns of oral argumentation that undoubtedly accompanied such depositions.

The moments of (filtered) direct speech allow analysis to shift from the realm of fact (what happened) to contemporary attitudes and mentalities concerning those facts (what the facts meant). Consider two examples taken from the non-adversarial *enquêtes* of reparation ordered by Louis IX in 1247. In the first, a deponent named Odinus Brichet complained to the *enquêteurs* that after he had been fully cleared in the royal court of a slanderous accusation, the royal bailli Joscius nevertheless said to him 'You may be free from [your accuser], but you are not, however, free from me.' The bailli then proceeded to demand 100s. from Odinus in return for his freedom.[89] In the second, the widow Jeanne la Bigote complained that the royal bailli Geoffroy Payen had unjustly used the death of a local lord to disseise Jeanne of her goods. Although she successfully proved her rights to the goods in court, the bailli told her 'whatever you might say, it is fitting that I should get something of yours before I release your goods, since your late husband, Jean le Bigot, had been very rich'. According to Jeanne, the bailli extorted 25 livres worth of goods.[90] These two representations of direct speech, however filtered, offer evidence of the lived experience of predatory exaction that I have described elsewhere; they show the reflexive sense of power and arrogance with which agents of lordship, whether royal (as in this case) or seigneurial (as in many others), operated.[91]

The Auvergnat *enquêtes* of 1240 offer moments of direct speech that also reveal deeper social meanings. One of the *enquêtes* sought to gather evidence concerning the killing of a tenant of Prior Renaud of Saint-Pourçain by the castellan of Chantelle and his men. The *enquêteurs* were anxious to know which of the castellan's men were present at the killing, and, more specifically, who had struck the killing blow. In his testimony, Geoffroy de Lapa first addressed those questions, but then added that he had 'heard Chalamel and Guillaume d'Ussel [two of the castellan's men] saying that they had made fresh meat of someone, who will now fertilize the vineyards'.[92] Another witness, Beatrix, the daughter of Blanchart of Tercac, noted in her testimony that 'on the day in

---

[88] E.g. Chazaud, *Quelques traits*, 13–14: *Guillelmus de Meceron, juratus, ...dixit eidem castellano quod retro iret, quia prior Sancti Porciani et homines sui erant in gregio et asseguragio domini Borbonii, et quod dominus meus Borbonii propter hoc miserat me cum dicto priore.*

[89] *RHGF*, xxiv, 76, no. 41.

[90] *RHGF*, xxiv, 85–6, no. 158.

[91] Richard E. Barton, '*Enquête*, Exaction and Excommunication: Experiencing Power in Western France, c.1190–1245', *ANS* 43 (2021 for 2020), 177–96. See also Robert Bartlett, 'The Impact of Royal Government in the French Ardennes: The Evidence of the 1247 *enquête*', *JMH* 7 (1981), 83–96.

[92] Chazaud, *Quelques traits*, 19: *audivit dicere Chalemel et Willelmo d'Ussel, quod fecerant de quodam carnem recentem, qui servabit a modo vineas.*

which the prior's man was killed, she heard lord Aymonin [one of the castellan's men] admitting that he had satisfied his need to avenge the death of his brother by killing a man of the prior of Saint-Pourçain'.[93] Here nested layers of speech, with the spoken words of two witnesses reproducing a man's bloodthirsty 'joke', on the one hand, and another man's satisfied boast, on the other – offer much deeper insight into the social world of these actors than can a bare recitation of fact. The joke about the body fertilizing the vineyards again reflects the sense of casual ruthlessness with which seigneurial agents might treat local tenants. But it also echoes Gadi Algazi's point that aristocratic society may have depended upon a certain degree of what might today be called terror tactics, by which violent action taken against peasants and townsmen served to maintain the proper social order.[94] The boast by Aymonin is perhaps even more telling, since it offers a possible explanation for the killing. Where the *enquêteurs* wished only to know who did the deed, Aymonin's comment attempts to explain, and even justify, that deed. By boasting that the killing had finally allowed him to assuage his wounded honor, which had been injured when either the victim, his friends, or his neighbors had killed Aymonin's brother, the meaning of the killing is transformed. It is no longer an apparently senseless act of violence, but becomes a cognitive act, a strategic move in a vengeance game that has been going on for some time. Aymonin thus cloaks the killing with the familiar aristocratic logic of honor, vengeance, and feud.[95] In so doing, his callous boast transforms our understanding of the event, since it suggests a wider context of traditional – and strategic – action within which the killing must be considered.

The oral accounts of witnesses like Odinus, Jeanne, Geoffroy (relating the 'joke'), and Beatrix (relating Aymonin's 'boast') do more than merely provide some color to dry legal accounts. They transform the meaning of the events in important, and surprising, ways. The speeches of Odinus and Jeanne reveal not only their specific complaints, but speak to the vast gulf that lay between the objects of seigneurial predation, that is, people like Odinus and Jeanne, and the agents of seigneurial power. For, as the *enquêtes* of reparation make clear, the baillis Joscius and Geoffroy Pagan, who threatened to deprive Odinus and Jeanne of their goods regardless of what the courts had ruled, were not simply bad apples. They were the norm, both in 1247 when these cases were recorded, and across the rest of the thirteenth century (as subsequent *enquêtes* de reparation make clear). Whatever the pious intentions of Louis IX, however much the royal legists vowed to bring peace and order to the newly enlarged kingdom, many subjects of the incipient 'État moderne' experienced royal power, that

---

[93] Chazaud, *Quelques traits*, 22: *Dixit etiam quod audivit dominum Aymonem, die illa qua homo dicti prioris mortuus fuit, recognoscentem, quod ultionem acceperat de morte fratris sui, quia hominem prioris sancti Porciani occiderat.*
[94] Gadi Algazi, 'Pruning Peasants: Private War and Maintaining the Lords' Peace in Late Medieval Germany', in *Medieval Transformations: Texts, Power and Gifts in Context*, ed. Esther Cohen and Mayke de Jong (Leiden, 2000), 245–74.
[95] Howard Kaminsky, 'The Noble Feud in the Later Middle Ages', *PP* 177 (2002), 55–83.

is, royal justice, as 'high-handed, arbitrary, tenacious, [and] violent'.[96] In this, the *enquêtes* of reparation, no more than contemporary adversarial *enquêtes*, did nothing to bring progress or 'reason' to the procedures of state; instead, they merely revealed, through the oral nature of the process, the lived reality of royal power. Similarly, the statements of Geoffroy and Beatrix concerning the 'joke' made by Chalemel and Guillaume and the boast made by Aymonin also undercut neat teleological narratives by which new, rational procedures helped bring order to a violent countryside. While it might be possible to read the Auvergne *enquête* as engaging in such disciplining or pacification, to do so is to embrace the statist mentality so effectively described by Bourdieu and to overlook the competing narratives of social order that aristocratic conceptions of honor and vengeance maintained, even into the middle of the thirteenth century.

The Politics of Witnessing, or *Enquêtes* as Sites of Political Confrontation

The oral character of thirteenth-century French *enquêtes* made them the ideal sites for the interplay of competing strategies of political practice. Even though first canon law and later secular law attempted to provide a standardized set of guidelines for how *enquêtes* should be conducted, the majority of adversarial *enquêtes* in the thirteenth century offered plenty of space for subjective manipulation of the process. In this, the belief of some legal and institutional historians[97] that *enquêtes* contributed to an imagined progress towards a more modern, administrative 'State' because they are inherently rational and administered by nascent bureaucrats whose only loyalty is to the law and its centralizing royal guarantor seems to overlook both the degree to which the 'State' as an ideological concept is largely a 'mask which prevents our seeing political practice as it is', and the degree to which the 'State' functions to 'mis-represent

---

[96] Bartlett, 'The Impact of Royal Power', 95.
[97] Boulet-Sautel, 'Aperçus sur le système des preuves', 316–18, esp. 318, where Louis IX's shift to *enquête* marked the 'radiation absolue de l'irrationel' and the 'consécration parfaite de la vérité objective'. Bongert, *Recherches sur les cours laïques*, 34, suggested that the rise of *enquêtes* had to have reflected the sincere desires of the subjects, since 'la loi ne change donc jamais radicalement les moeurs d'une societe'. R. Howard Bloch, *Medieval French Literature and the Law* (Berkeley, CA, 1977), 131–8, saw the procedure as producing truth: 'The information collected by the king's *enquêteurs* was, first and foremost, a truthful account of infraction' (132). See also Gérard Giordanengo, 'Le pouvoir législatif du roi de France (XIe–XIIIe siècles): travaux récents et hypothèses de recherche', *BEC* 147 (1989), 283–310 at 296 (on French legists' belief, from *c.* 1100 onward, in the public good) and 303 (on Louis' eventually successful good intentions to create a better world); C. Warren Hollister and John Baldwin, 'The Rise of Administrative Kingship: Henry I and Philip Augustus', *AHR* 83 (1978), 867–905 at 887 and 893 (for centralizing through 'elite curiales', prévôts and baillis); Harding, *Medieval Law*, 117–19 (on the professionalization of French baillis and prévôts); and Guillot, Rigaudière and Sassier, *Pouvoirs et institutions*, 5, on the new administrative monarchy that allowed the construction of 'l'État moderne.'

political domination in ways that legitimate subjection'.[98] *Enquêtes* cannot thus be understood merely or even primarily as instruments used by a tangible 'object' (the 'State') to obtain or maintain a universally recognized state of 'peace' or 'order'. Instead, *enquêtes* must be understood at least partly as tools of legitimation deployed by an 'ideological project' (the 'State') in order to obtain and enforce subjection; that is, they are sites, occasions, or practices within which subjective political agendas can be advanced and contested. To recognize the subjective and often nakedly partisan ways by which various parties, including the king but also including litigants and witnesses, might seek to use *enquêtes* to further their own strategic advantage in the field of political practice is to accept what medieval society already knew: law was a strategy and a means to press advantage, as the famous saying 'law goeth as lordship biddeth him' acknowledged.[99] After all, the royal judges in thirteenth- and fourteenth-century England – a country much more centrally administered than France – were simultaneously judges *and* the paid retainers of the political elites who argued cases before them.[100] To dismiss and delegitimize such ubiquitous practice as 'corrupt' deviation from the judicial ideal, as modern historians have routinely done,[101] is unhelpful, for it is merely to accept the normalizing discourse of the agents of a 'State' seeking to assert their own subjective claims over and against those of other interested parties, and to label one subjective discourse among many as 'normal' and 'correct'. One thus need not even adopt a fully cynical view that rejects the possibility of more 'absolute standards of justice' to recognize that subjectivity and 'favor' were essential elements of the late medieval legal universe.[102]

Largely because they have focused on institutions as abstractions, and hence on *enquêtes* as existential processes, and because they have much less frequently examined the circumstances surrounding individual *enquêtes*, modern historians have typically been too willing to accept at face value the claims made by interested parties in the Middle Ages, including both jurists and the clerks and other officers of the growing Capetian monarchy, about the theoretical superiority of *inquisitio* as a procedure of law, superior, that is, because it was (allegedly)

---

[98] Philip Abrams, 'Notes on the Difficulty of Studying the State (1977)', *Journal of Historical Sociology* 1 (1988), 58–89 at 58 and 75–6.
[99] Jonathan Rose, *Maintenance in Medieval England* (Cambridge, 2017), 319. Sir John Fastolf quoted a variant of this maxim, 'law goeth as it is favored': *Paston Letters and Papers of the Fifteenth Century*, ed. Norman Davis, Richard Beadle and Colin Richmond, Early English Text Society, Supplementary Series 20–2 (Oxford, 2004–5), part II, no. 520, 115. See also Christine Carpenter, 'Law, Justice and Landowners in Late Medieval England', *Law and History Review* 1 (1983), 205–37 at 209.
[100] J.R. Maddicott, *Law and Lordship: Royal Justices as Retainers in Thirteenth- and Fourteenth-Century England* (Oxford, 1978).
[101] Maddicott, *Law and Lordship*, 1, 2, 25; Jonathan R. Lyon, *Corruption, Protection and Justice in Medieval Europe: A Thousand-Year History* (Cambridge, 2022), 4 and *passim*.
[102] Carpenter, 'Law, Justice and Landowners', 209. Maddicott, *Law and Lordship*, 1, admits that it might be 'inadequate' to label as 'corrupt' 'practices so normal and pervasive' [as judges retained by those arguing cases before them].

more fair and less subjective. Yet to accept such a narrative is, as just noted, to accept uncritically the ideology of the state itself, which argues for its own superiority, its own neutrality, its own objectivity, and its own rationality, usually by contrasting these principles against the allegedly inferior, personally motivated, subjective, and irrational character of the non-state entities with which it clashed.[103] The claims of the State or of learned law to be impartial, claims which were partly made through the imposition of the procedure of *enquête*, thus themselves constitute a technique of power; that is, they embody ways of using a particular system of knowledge (law) and of particular modes of knowledge acquisition (*inquisitio*) to reinforce particular power relationships.[104] Again, to admit this fact does not require fully rejecting the classic narrative of the rise of administrative kingship or of *la genèse de l'État moderne*; it is possible to appreciate the process by which the king, aided by legists, built institutions and power structures while simultaneously acknowledging that the claims of impartiality and uniform access to justice that (partly) accompanied emerging concepts of royal sovereignty were themselves partial and self-interested, and that they worked to obscure other relationships of power.

Medieval thinkers were fully aware of the potential subjectivity represented by oral testimony. Yves Mausen has demonstrated that even as they constantly reiterated the principle that a true witness was by definition impartial, the jurists of the thirteenth and fourteenth centuries routinely wrestled with the possibility that witnesses might actually be partial.[105] In particular, they worried that a witness's kinship or lordship relations might lead them to utter testimony that was colored by partiality and thus not fully true. The legists eventually decided that certain categories of person were inherently partial and should thus be barred from providing testimony in circumstances were that partiality might be brought to bear; judges and *enquêteurs* were supposed to ensure that such witnesses were not allowed to provide testimony.[106] While there is a wide gap between such legal theory and the actual conduct of *enquêtes* in the thirteenth century, some evidence of these nascent principles can already be glimpsed in an Auvergne *enquête* of 1240. Since this *enquête* aimed to uncover information about the killing of a tenant of the prior of Saint-Pourçain, the *enquêteurs* asked many of the witnesses 'whether they were of the kindred of the prior, or were his vassal/man, or his servant'.[107] All the deponents who were asked such a question responded 'no'. The *enquêteurs* in this case clearly wished to present an image of impartiality, at least according to accepted legal doctrine, by ruling out anyone who fell into recognized categories of partiality. As we shall see, other relatively obvious vectors of potential partiality (acquaintance with the

---

[103] Bourdieu, 'Rethinking', 36–8.
[104] Foucault, *Surveillir et Punir*, 226–7, used *enquêtes* as a classic example of his notion of power/knowledge.
[105] Mausen, *Veritatis adiutor*, 32–3 and *passim*.
[106] Mausen, *Veritatis adiutor*, 175–83.
[107] Chazaud, *Quelques traits*, 19–20: *Requisitus utrum erat de parentela prioris, vel ejus homo, vel serviens, dixit quod non.*

dead man, residence in the villas owned by the prior) were not considered. It is difficult to not see such efforts as representing a classic distinction between theoretical ideals (neutrality of testimony) and the reality of practice; indeed, the legists' concerns seemed largely ineffective in fully eliminating testimony that might be partial.

I maintain that the orality which underlay the *enquêtes* permitted and perhaps even encouraged the articulation of these types of political interventions and strategic contestations. At every stage – the choice of *enquêteurs*, the framing of articles, the selection of witnesses, and the recording of testimony – the play of power relations and the fundamentally oral nature of the process meant that human subjectivities had an opportunity to intervene and thus that *enquêtes* would become the locations in which competing narratives could hope to structure notions of legitimacy, rightful authority, and local identity. As a way of demonstrating these points, I offer two extended case studies.

The first case study involves the remarkable *enquête* conducted in Le Mans in early 1246.[108] The dispute centered on the capacity of the cathedral chapter of Le Mans, as distinct from the bishop, to impose full ecclesiastical censure on the monasteries and other ecclesiastical institutions of the city and diocese; the two parties in the case were thus the cathedral chapter itself and the powerful Benedictine monastery of Saint-Pierre de la Couture located in the suburbs of Le Mans. As an ecclesiastical matter, the dispute had reached the papal curia through means invisible to us. Pope Innocent IV assigned the case to the papal legate for France, Cardinal Pietro Capocci, for judgment.[109] Cardinal Capocci, following the procedure of *inquisitio*, ordered the preparation of articles that touched on the central legal matters of the dispute, and then commanded the parties to depose witnesses. Here it is important to recall that especially in canon law cases it was customary for the lawyers of each party to locate and depose their own witnesses; it was not, at least in the thirteenth century, the responsibility of the judge to do so. The record of ninety-nine witnesses gathered and deposed by the procurators for the cathedral chapter survives, and constitutes perhaps the single longest and most detailed *enquête* from the period.

The number and depth of the depositions permits identification of several competing narrative strategies which were accomplished through the oral processes of question and answer. The first strategy is the obvious one effected by the procurator for the chapter; we might call it the master narrative. It attempted to prove through a combination both of the status of the witnesses and the specifics of their answers that the chapter did indeed possess the general right to impose censure over 'every type of malefactor, lay and cleric, secular and regular, men and women, and [over] all types of injuries, in the broad sense of the word, namely, "injury", [meaning] anything that is not done by

---

[108] See above, note 30.
[109] *Enquête de 1245*, 1. For Cardinal Pietro Capoccio, see *Fasti Ecclesiae Gallicanae, 1200–1500* (Turnhout, 1996–), xviii, *Diocèse du Mans*, ed. Jean-Michel Matz, (Turnhout, 2018), 139.

right'.[110] To prove this sweeping claim, the procurator first sought the judge's permission to depose the dean of the chapter, Robert de Domfront, and several of the oldest canons from the chapter.[111] Since the dean and other canons were one of the parties to the case, it was an unusual request to allow him to stand as a witness; after all, canon law defined a 'true witness' as one who was impartial, and the party to a case could not be said to be impartial. Dean Robert, along with the canons Renaud Clarel, Aimery Clarel (Renaud's brother), Eudes, and Étienne the Burgundian were deposed first. Their responses were long and obviously scripted, since, as parties to the case, they were aware of the articles and undoubtedly prepared their strategy in advance alongside the procurator who would depose them.[112] All five based their testimony on several things: familiarity with still-extant written documents which seemed to prove the existence of the grant, their own memories of events which had transpired over the previous fifty years, and, although it was unsaid, their own status as prominent churchmen in Le Mans. The harmony with which these testimonies concurred sent a powerful message to the other witnesses: after all, all five had seen and could describe and date the documents; all five could describe in sometimes vivid details specific moments in which censure had been applied; and all five were instantly recognizable members of the local ecclesiastical elite, men who exercised lordship and jurisdiction over many of the other witnesses who were waiting to offer their depositions. What tenant of the chapter would offer testimony that obviously contradicted the dean or the other canons, who were their temporal lords?[113] What townsmen, whose livelihoods depended in part on the economic motor of church business and who themselves had to navigate the web of ecclesiastical jurisdictions that lay over the city, would naysay such men?[114] Even if the procurator followed the procedure prescribed by canon law and by many local coutumiers and deposed each witness separately and in private,[115] the 'official narrative' articulated by the important men of the

---

[110] *Enquête de 1245*, 4: *in omnes injuriatores, laicos et clericos, seculares et regulares, viros et mulieres, super omnibus injuriis large sumpto vocabulo, scilicet: injuria, quod non jure fit.*

[111] *Enquête de 1245*, 1: *et voluit procurator eorumdem decani et capituli quod dictus decanus in testem productus ad presens examinaretur a XVI° articulo ipso... usque ad XXXII^{um}.*

[112] *Enquête de 1245*, 1–96. These five depositions comprise 40% of the entire dossier.

[113] For testimony by tenants of the chapter, see *Enquête de 1245*, 194 (Eremburga la Seurisse), 208 (Ameline), 209 (Aubri the bachelor), 230 (Jean carpenter). Many others who are not explicitly named as 'man' or 'woman of the chapter' were undoubtedly tenants of the chapter.

[114] *Enquête de 1245*, 125 (Nicolas the advocate estimated he participated in 1500 legal cases brought over twenty-five years by the chapter against townsmen), 130 (Pierre Boju notes that as voyer he was summoned 'many times' over fifteen years to answer for his actions), 132–4 (Hubert Bérard the voyer admits he was excommunicated at least once and summonsed many times by the chapter).

[115] For learned law concerning private deposition, Mausen, *Veritatis adiutor*, 299–311. For the customs of Paris, *Établissements*, 5 [translated as *The Etablissements de Saint*

chapter would have been widely known and articulated prior to the depositions; this narrative would thus have stood not only as a legal truth, uttered by 'true witnesses' in a formal *enquête*, but also as the public transcript, one to which the other witnesses would need to adhere in their own testimonies.[116] It is hardly surprising that the testimonies of the persons of lesser status were significantly shorter, and focused simply on recitation of remembered moments in which the witness had seen the chapter impose sanctions on various people. In this sense, relations of power within the community that produced the witnesses, as well as the procurator's strategic ordering of those witnesses, ensured that the formal transcript of depositions would act as what Alain Provost has called 'une véritable opération de transformation', by which even truthful statements uttered by individual witnesses were shaped or transformed – subtly and overtly – by the power relations that surrounded them.[117]

If the master narrative offered by the dean and his fellow canons clearly served to justify and reinforce the authority of the hierarchical church against challenges to its supremacy, the oral nature of the proceedings allows us to identify other narratives which sometimes support and sometimes undercut that of the official one. Three are worth a brief analysis: two broadly uphold the canons' master narrative, while nevertheless subtly challenging the authority of competing secular and ecclesiastical powers in the city, while the third undercuts it. In each case, it is possible to see a political intervention at work, one only possible given the oral nature of the procedure of *enquête*. The first narrative to demonstrate the strategic use of witnessing to make political points concerns the way in which numerous depositions represent the collegiate church of Saint-Pierre-de-la-Cour. Recall that the legal case that spawned the *enquête* was argued between the chapter of Le Mans and the Benedictine monastery of Saint-Pierre de la Couture. The church of Saint-Pierre-de-la-Cour was never a party to the lawsuit at all. Whereas la Couture was an ancient monastery located in the suburbs of the city, with widespread estates in the diocese and a long tradition of proudly independent regular life, la Cour was the small church located within the comital palace of Le Mans whose authority and influence came not from its antiquity or its wealth, but from its tight association with the count of Le Mans.[118] Even though la Cour was not a party to the lawsuit, many deponents used the opportunity afforded by the case against the monks to represent the canons of la Cour as equally disobedient and resistant to the legitimate exercise of the cathedral chapter's rights.

Louis: Thirteenth-Century Law Texts from Tours, Orléans, and Paris, tr. F.R.P. Akehurst (Philadelphia, PA, 1996), 9].
[116] James C. Scott, *Domination and the Arts of Resistance* (New Haven, CT, 1990), 1–16.
[117] Provost, 'Déposer, c'est faire croire?', paragraphs 37–9.
[118] See Richard Barton, 'Remembering Female Lordship: the Case of Queen Berengaria of Navarre, Lord of Le Mans (1204/1205–1230)', in *Gender, Memory and Documentary Culture, 900–1300*, ed. Laura Gathagan and Charles Insley (Woodbridge, forthcoming); and Samuel Menjot d'Elbenne, *Le chapitre royal de l'église collégiale de Saint-Pierre-de-la-Cour* (Le Mans, 1909).

The opportunity to do so was provided by the cathedral chapter's legal strategy, which as we have seen entailed producing as many remembered examples as possible of the chapter censuring its foes. Some of the most notorious of those moments were the several occasions on which the chapter had placed the city of Le Mans under interdict in response to financial exactions imposed by the 'count', Queen Berengaria of Navarre. As a result of the interdict, all churches were required to close their doors and cease celebrating the sacraments and other liturgical rites. The witnesses who recalled these moments almost uniformly supplemented the official narrative of the lawsuit, which saw the interdict as an example of the use of exactly that type of censure over which the lawsuit was fought, by describing how the church of la Cour had brazenly ignored the interdict by continuing to ring its bells and celebrate divine services. Dean Robert was the first to make this point. When asked if the authority of Octavian, the papal legate who had confirmed the initial grant of ecclesiastical censure to the cathedral chapter, extended over the entire diocese, Robert replied:

Yes, and he [Robert] knows this because he [Octavian] calls himself in his charter *legatum*, and the lord pope similarly in his charter calls him 'legate' and confirms that which the said Octavian gave, as has been said. The same pope also confirms the sentence which the same legate offered concerning the observation of the interdict which the dean and chapter of Le Mans had levied, and which the canons of Saint-Pierre-de-la-Cour did not want to observe, as will be discussed more fully later on.[119]

At this moment the official question concerned the scope of legatine powers, but Robert chose to shift his response to a depiction of the disobedience of the canons of la Cour; his comments were unnecessary in an evidentiary sense, but they served to build a narrative that would cast la Cour as rebellious and disobedient. Renaud Clarel developed the story, stating that because the canons of la Cour refused to obey the interdict, 'he believes that on account of this they were excommunicated'. He went on to state that 'he heard it said' that la Cour entered into a lawsuit with the cathedral chapter in the presence of the same legate Octavian, and that first Octavian and then Pope Innocent III had ordered the canons to obey the interdict; he knew this not because he was present, but because he had read documents of Octavian and Innocent that stated it all clearly.[120] The same story was told, generally with less detail, by Aimery Clarel, Eudes, Guillaume Buisson and several others.[121] Even Scholastica, the widow of Julien Laurent, one of Berengaria's fiscal agents whose actions had sparked one of the interdicts, chose to speak about la Cour:

She says also that at that time [of the interdict] the bells were ringing in the church of Saint-Pierre-de-la-Cour and the divine offices were being celebrated. Concerning

[119] *Enquête de 1245*, 16.
[120] *Enquête de 1245*, 34–5. See above, pp. 161–3.
[121] *Enquête de 1245*, 56, 77–8, 119, 123, 129, 207, 226.

the church of la Couture she doesn't know, except that there [the office] was being chanted, such that she could easily hear it at the door of the church which was closed; but she does not know if there was ringing anywhere except at Saint-Pierre-de-la-Cour. Concerning the date, she says 20 years have passed, or so she believes. Concerning the other things asked, she knows nothing more.[122]

The story that began with the dean, was filled out by Renaud Clarel, and then was repeated by men and women of varying status was remarkably similar: the canons of la Cour refused to adhere to church law and might, if Renaud's hearsay could be trusted, even have been excommunicated for it. This sub-narrative clearly served as a warning in the present to the current canons of la Cour; their disobedience was not only remembered, it was repeated and performed orally before a papal legate, before the senior clergy of the diocese, and likely before a crowd of townswomen and townsmen. The opportunity afforded by the depositions thus allowed the chapter simultaneously to assert its claims to ecclesiastical supremacy over all (except the bishop) and to discipline (or so it was hoped) the future behavior of its ecclesiastical rivals.

The forceful reminder of la Cour's past misdeeds with its implied threat concerning the canons' future behavior was, however, deeply ironic, since the careful narrative offered by Dean Robert, Renaud Clarel and all the others is utterly garbled. If it isn't exactly false, the details that the memories of the cathedral canons produced for the depositions bear little resemblance to what modern historians can piece together of the genuine chronology of the ecclesiastical discord that wracked Le Mans in the first decades of the thirteenth century. What is more, the slipperiness of the cathedral canons' chronology, despite its reliance on written evidence, helped produce the second sub-narrative found in the *enquête*: namely, the representation of Queen Berengaria's arrival in Le Mans as the ultimate source of the discord that prompted the interdicts and, consequently, la Cour's disobedience. The connection between these two strands – Berengaria's assumption of comital power over the city and the disobedience of the comital chapel of la Cour, whose members typically served as the count's chancery and ecclesiastical advisors – cannot be underestimated. By conflating several interdicts into one in order to demonstrate la Cour's intransigence, the cathedral chapter could simultaneously shape a narrative about the nature of Berengaria's rule. One need not even imagine a dark conspiracy on the part of Dean Robert and his companions, one designed to malign la Cour and the memory of Berengaria (who had died in 1230); it is perfectly possible that the senior members of the cathedral chapter had, over the more than forty years since the chapter had received the grant of censure, simply come to believe the (mis)information that they presented in the *enquête*, since their version of events accorded with their generalized understanding of ecclesiastical order. Of course, to modern eyes their misrepresentation of the charters and of the dates of the

---

[122] *Enquête de 1245*, 188–9.

various interdicts can also stand as an example of truth production, one designed to assert a reality that the chapter simply desired to be true.

The senior cathedral canons seem to have agreed (in advance) on a script concerning the chronology of events. Three of them – Renaud Clarel, Aimery Clarel, and Eudes – offered a remarkably uniform account of the first significant examples of the chapter's actual deployment of censure: they recalled in detail the chapter's actions against the important baron Guy de Laval, as well as other cases directed against Brisegault de Coesmes and against King John's constable for Le Mans.[123] In their telling, these episodes occurred before Berengaria arrived in Le Mans; their memory, at least in this instance, was correct, as Guy's case probably occurred in 1203x1204, and that of John's constable before 1203.[124] These canons all agreed, moreover, that the first interdict laid by the chapter across the entire city followed shortly after these early cases and was intimately connected to Queen Berengaria's arrival in the city. The details offered by their accounts were remarkably consistent and mutually supporting. All three noted that the interdict was sparked by the actions of Berengaria's *voyers* in seizing *costuma* or taille from André of la Chapelle-Saint-Aubin; all three implied that this was the first time that the chapter had laid an interdict on the city; all three stated that every church in the city and Quinte had obeyed the interdict except the comital chapel of Saint-Pierre-de-la-Cour; and all three noted that the papal legate, Octavian, had ruled against the canons of la Cour for refusing to obey the interdict.[125] Eudes's reference to this last point carried particular weight since, as he admitted, he had been at the time of the interdict both a canon of the cathedral chapter of Le Mans and the dean of la Cour. He recalled that although the canons of la Cour had asked him to intervene with the cathedral chapter on their behalf, he had declined, citing, firstly, the fact that he owed loyalty to both institutions, and secondly, the fact that the canons of la Cour possessed no charters granting them specific exemption from interdicts.[126] Although only Renaud articulated the point explicitly, explaining that the interdict had occurred just after Berengaria had taken up her office,[127] in their internal sequencing the other two accounts

---

[123] All three discussed the excommunication and interdiction of Guy de Laval (*Enquête de 1245*, 9, 29, 55, 76–7) and the excommunication of Brisegault de Coesmes (*ibid.*, 31–2, 56, 77). Only Renaud recalled Geoffroy de Hongrie, King John's constable (*ibid.*, 30–1).
[124] Since Guy appealed the chapter's actions to King Philip, the excommunication could only have occurred after the barons of Maine had abandoned John for Philip, that is, after December 1202; for the appeal, *Enquête de 1245*, 50, 76; for the date, Daniel Power, *The Norman Frontier in the Twelfth and Thirteenth Centuries* (Cambridge, 2004), 348. Geoffroy de Hongrie was in Le Mans in August 1202 when he received 20 l. from the royal treasury: *Grands rôles des échiquiers de Normandie*, ed. Amédée Léchaudé d'Anisy (Paris, 1845), 111. Geoffroy's excommunication probably occurred in 1202, and at the latest prior to Philip's seizure of Le Mans in spring 1203.
[125] *Enquête de 1245*, 32–5, 56, 77–8.
[126] *Enquête de 1245*, 78.
[127] *Enquête de 1245*, 32: *in novitate regine Berengarie, quando primo venit Cenomanni causa morandi*. For the association of *novitas* with the assumption of office, see R.E. Latham, *Revised Medieval Latin Word-List* (London, 1965; repr. 1989), 315, sub 'novus'.

support the notion that this interdict occurred early in Berengaria's reign. What is more, all three firmly distinguished this first interdict from a second, later interdict that had also been sparked by Berengaria's agents.[128] The official line, supported by the unimpeachable memories of senior canons who had been alive and in office at the time the events were thought to have occurred, was thus that the cathedral chapter had never had to lay an interdict on the city *until* Berengaria arrived and imposed a fiscal administration that was too aggressive in trampling ecclesiastical rights. What is more, the legate Octavian had intervened in this first interdict, by forcing the church of la Cour to submit to the chapter's rightful authority.

The problem is that Berengaria's arrival in Le Mans occurred at least four years after Octavian had departed forever from France. Berengaria, widow of Richard I of England from 1199, acquired Le Mans from King Philip II of France in August 1204 through adroit negotiation. She may well not have arrived in the city until the spring of 1205.[129] Yet Octavian, the papal legate who confirmed Bishop Hamelin's original grant of censure, and who had apparently ordered the church of la Cour to obey an interdict laid on the city by the cathedral chapter, had exercised his office as legate only between summer 1200 and summer 1201, that is, at least three and possibly four years before Berengaria's arrival in the city.[130] It was thus literally impossible for the interdict sparked by Berengaria's arrival to be the same as the one whose terms the legate Octavian had enforced on the church of la Cour. Since Octavian's letter enjoining la Cour to obey the interdict is still extant,[131] we must conclude that three interdicts, and not just the two sparked by Berengaria's men, were laid on the city between 1200 and 1230. By erasing memory of the first interdict, and by conflating it with the interdict that followed Berengaria's assumption of lordship, the testimonies rewrote the recent past. Their new 'truth' served to link the disobedience of the church of la Cour to the financial extortion of the queen, thereby reinforcing the chapters' obvious contention that the two institutions – the secular lord of the city and that lord's personal chapel – had always been, and might continue to be, threats to proper religious discipline and order. Never mind that la Cour's 'disobedience' predated the queen's aggressive collection of taille; a better truth could be obtained by joining them together, regardless of the damage it did to the reputations of la Cour and of Berengaria. After all, in the new telling, the interdict associated with Berengaria's arrival – which did occur, but was the second such event – was transformed from one episode among several, into an event uniquely connected to the queen's grasping nature. The gendered readings of this transformation are worth exploring elsewhere.

[128] For the later interdict of 1216x1217, *Enquête de 1245*, 40–2, 59–61, 78.
[129] Barton, 'Remembering Female Lordship', forthcoming.
[130] For the dates of Octavian's legatine activity, see Werner Maleczek, *Papst und Kardinalskolleg von 1191 bis 1216. Die Kardinäle unter Coelestin III. und Innocenz III.* (Vienna, 1984), 80–3 and tables at 375–85.
[131] *Liber Albus*, no. 103. The act must date to Octavian's legateship, that is, between summer 1200 and summer 1201.

A third example of the ways in which the depositions in the Le Mans *enquête* reflect the ability of witnesses to inject political strategies of their own beneath the master narratives of the *enquêteurs* may be found in the lapidary depositions of two townswomen of Le Mans. Ameline, widow of Aubri Ernaud, essentially spent her entire deposition boasting about how she had taken advantage of her status as one living under the jurisdiction of the cathedral chapter to have the chapter discipline her personal enemies. Ameline explained how a certain Gervais Houdebert had stopped her carts and seized six pennies in *pedagium* (a toll) from her. So, as a '*femina capituli*', she marched into the chapter, registered a legal accusation against Gervais, and watched as he was excommunicated and then forced to perform humiliating penance dressed only in his britches. While there are plenty of examples of the chapter punishing similar acts of exaction, it is rare to find testimonies in which non-elite secular persons exercise agency in pursuing their own justice. Ameline proceeded to describe several more instances in which 'she caused to be summoned' or 'caused to be excommunicated' another person who had wronged her. For instance,

She says that she caused Foulques de Nemore, who was not a man of the chapter, to be excommunicated by the authority of the chapter, on account of the 20 shillings that he owed to her. And Foulques endured the excommunication for 3 years, and later made satisfaction to her and was absolved by the authority of the chapter. Concerning the date, she says 20 years or more have elapsed, as she believes.[132]

Ameline concluded, rather smugly it seems, by asserting that 'she caused many other persons to be cited to the chapter at her instigation over diverse dates and on many occasions that she does not recall, but over a thirty-year period'.[133] Her message was clear: she had figured out how to use the chapter, with its grandiose claims to exercise jurisdiction over 'anyone' who offended 'any member of the chapter or any of its (wo)men', to prosecute her own vengeance against her enemies. While her testimony served in a general sense to support the chapter's claims, the way in which she inserted herself at the center of the action changed the hero of the story. To Ameline, the deposition was an opportunity to demonstrate that she was not a woman to be trifled with.

The deposition of Scolastica, widow of Julien Laurent, offers a similar sort of hidden transcript. Julien's actions in seizing *costuma* for Queen Berengaria had led to the second interdict laid on Le Mans during her reign. As the senior canons all noted, Julien had extorted five pennies as sales tax from men who should have been immune; when he and the queen were asked to return the pennies, Berengaria refused, Julien was personally excommunicated, and eventually the city was laid under interdict.[134] Only after many months in which the churches remained closed and only after a settlement between the queen and

---

[132] *Enquête de 1245*, 208.
[133] *Enquête de 1245*, 208–09.
[134] Five witnesses mention Julien by name (although others refer to his actions without naming him): *Enquête de 1245*, 40–1, 61, 160, 201, 207.

the chapter did Berengaria return the pennies; it was only at this point that Julien was permitted to perform penance and have the excommunication lifted. None of the five (male) witnesses who cited Julien's deeds by name, nor any of the many others who describe the interdict without naming him, mention Julien's wife or household at all. Scolastica's deposition reveals another side to the story:

> Scolastica... said first that she who is speaking and the said Julien were excommunicated, and their entire household was interdicted by the authority of the chapter, because the said Julien took 5 pennies of *costuma* belonging to the chapter, as it was said. And they were interdicted for a long time in such a way that they could not enter any church. Also, since Queen Berengaria, despite having been warned, as it was said, did not want to return the said *costuma*, the chapter interdicted the city of Le Mans, and it lay for a long time under interdict. She was asked how she knows that her husband had been excommunicated on account of this by the authority of the chapter. She responded that he conducted himself as one excommunicated and did not enter the church, as she said above; and it was commonly said that this was done by the authority of the chapter, and that it had imposed the interdict. But she didn't know whether this was true. She says also that later she heard it said by the said Julien that he had been absolved by the authority of the chapter, but she was not present for the absolution.[135]

In other words, the chapter had first excommunicated not just Julien, but Scolastica and their entire household as well, before eventually turning to the more serious measure of a city-wide interdict. Yet no one except Scolastica found the chapter's excommunication of her and her family and servants to be noteworthy. In her testimony, Scolastica thus simultaneously fulfilled her obligation to confirm the chapter's ability to impose spiritual penalties, while asserting her own victimization. In this sense she momentarily subverts the main narrative of the *enquête* to assert her own agency. She had committed neither crime nor sin; indeed, as she somewhat bitterly observed, she didn't even know if it was true that her husband had done what he had been accused of doing. And yet she herself had been punished by the chapter for his alleged misdeeds. It must have seemed a grave injustice. The deposition thus allowed Scolastica the opportunity to clearly identify that injustice even as she perhaps grudgingly confirmed the 'justice' of the chapter's claim to possess the right of censure. Her testimony offered her own individual narrative concerning the great affair of the interdict, one that reasserted her own agency and sought, perhaps, to carve out a little justice for herself.

The second case study involves a pair of related *enquêtes* conducted in the Auvergne in 1240. Unlike the Le Mans *enquête*, these two *enquêtes* – which I will refer to as the homicide *enquête* and the outlawry *enquête* – were secular;[136] at least one, and probably both, were ordered by the royal court in Paris. Since

---

[135] *Enquête de 1245*, 188–9.
[136] Outlawry *enquête*: *Olim*, i, 1016–19. Homicide *enquête*: Chazaud, *Quelques traits*, 13–23. See above, note 83, for dating.

the pair predate the beginning of the archiving of the records of the Parlement de Paris, it is impossible to link the depositions to a specific lawsuit, even though it is clear that one or more lawsuits must have been initiated in order for the *enquêtes* to have been mandated in the first place. Since the homicide *enquête* concerned the killing of one of the tenants of Prior Renaud of the Benedictine priory of Saint-Pourçain at the hands of Bernard Blanc, castellan of Lord Archambaud VIII of Bourbon's castle of Chantelle, and his men, it is likely that the *enquête* stemmed from a suit brought by the prior against Archambaud. As for the outlawry *enquête*, it is difficult to guess at the specific nature of the suit, since the rubric attached to the list of depositions merely states that the *enquêtes* concerned 'the behavior of the men who had wronged the prior of Saint-Pourçain'. Because the depositions respond to this basic question, 'Were the men whom Archambaud de Bourbon had publicly outlawed for crimes against Saint-Pourçain still to be found dwelling in Archambaud's lands?', we might imagine that the prior had appealed Archambaud to Paris for failure to perform justice (by not actually expelling the outlaws from his lands).

Regardless of the precise nature of the lawsuits that had engendered the *enquêtes*, it is clear that both concern a seigneurial conflict being waged in the region of the Haut-Auvergne, along the Sioule and Allier rivers in the northern portion of the diocese of Clermont, and particularly around the town and Benedictine priory of Saint-Pourçain.[137] It is equally clear that the two *enquêtes* are directly connected to each other, because each concerns the same two disputants – Lord Archambaud de Bourbon and Prior Renaud of Saint-Pourçain – and because the outlaws named in the outlawry *enquête* as 'les Garinens'[138] are obviously the same men whose actions led to the killing described in the homicide *enquête*.[139] Finally, even a superficial reading of the *enquêtes* reveals that in both cases, Archambaud de Bourbon was the defendant. It was his seigneurial agents who were alleged to have killed the prior's tenant, and it was his regard for public order that was being questioned by his refusal to expel the

---

[137] Despite its prominence as an important priory of Saint-Philibert de Tournus since the late ninth century, Saint-Pourçain has been little studied: see *Gallia Christiana, in provincias ecclesiasticas distributa*, ed. Denis de Sainte-Marthe (16 vols, Paris, 1715–1865), ii, cols 371–4; Fazy, *Les origines du Bourbonnais* (2 vols, Moulins, 1924), ii [*Formation territoriale du Bourbonnais*], 110–14; Anne Prache, 'Le prieuré de Saint-Pourçain', in *Saint-Philibert de Tournus. Histoire, archéologie, art*, ed. Jacques Thirion (Tournus, 1995), 497–505; Isabelle Cartron, *Les pérégrinations de Saint-Philibert: Genèse d'un réseau monastique dans la société carolingienne* (Rennes, 2010), 147–63. No comprehensive study of its tenurial holdings is known to me.

[138] Chazaud, *Quelques traits*, 14, where the Garinens are named. Several witnesses refer to the 'brothers' (*fratres*) that composed the band, but it is clear that they were not a kindred; rather, the implication is that they were a sworn band, possibly of mercenaries. Some are named: Bartholomé, Amblart, G. de Valle.

[139] Even though no witness in the outlawry *enquête* (*Olim*, i, 1016–19) uses the name of 'Les Garinens', the fact that several witnesses described that the 'malefactors' had burned Prior Renaud's villa of Nuillec and the monks' cloister at Bayet, we can safely conclude that they were the same men as Les Garinens.

outlaws from his lands. The fact that the royal court had chosen to take up the prior's evident complaints and to subject Archambaud's justice and lordship to royal scrutiny was itself momentous. The king had used his claim to be the special protector of churches anywhere in France, and especially in those areas where he did not enjoy direct seigneurial authority, as a means of exerting royal power where previously it had been absent. Given this policy, it is perhaps not surprising that the royal court would support the prior of Saint-Pourçain against a local lord.[140] It was also true that over the course of the twelfth and early thirteenth centuries, the lords of Bourbon had pushed their influence southward into the Auvergne. By 1200 they held lordship over a semi-circle of castles and other estates that ringed Saint-Pourçain in an arc from Bessay and Verneuil in the north, through farmlands to the west, and then to the castles and market towns of Chantelle, Charroux and Gannat in the south.[141]

What made the king's support of Saint-Pourçain against Archambaud de Bourbon significant was the fact that royal expansion and Bourbon expansion in the Auvergne had been symbiotic until just a few years prior to the *enquêtes*. Indeed, in 1196 Mathilde, heiress to the lordship of Bourbon, had married Guy de Dampierre, one of King Philip Augustus' closest advisors; for the next two decades Guy, as lord of Bourbon, both pursued Capetian interests and benefitted from Capetian largesse.[142] Lord Guy's son, Archambaud VIII of Bourbon, enjoyed the same cozy relationship with the king, at least until the early 1230s. Archambaud served, for instance, as royal constable for the Auvergne from 1216 to at least 1233 and, as such, fought wars in the region in the king's name.[143]

---

[140] Rémy Roques, 'Résister au pouvoir royal dans l'Auvergne du XIIIe siècle', *Questes* [En ligne] 39 (2018), 43–56, http://journals.openedition.org/questes/4996. René Germain, 'Les sires de Bourbon et le pouvoir: de la seigneurie à la principauté', in *Les princes et le pouvoir au moyen age, XXIIIe Congrès de la SHMES (Brest, mai 1992)* (Paris, 1993), 195–210, para. 21, notes that the priory of Saint-Pourçain is conspicuously absent from the list of religious establishments patronized by the twelfth- and thirteenth-century lords of Bourbon.

[141] The castle and town of Chantelle were the lord of Bourbon's by at least 1214: Max Fazy, *Les origines du* Bourbonnais, i [*Catalogue des actes*], no. 529. Archambaud VI of Bourbon (1216–42) issued charters from Chantelle: *ibid.*, nos 582 (1219), 609 (1221), 675–6 (1227). Chantelle was one of the traditional seventeen castellanies of the lordship of Bourbon: Chazaud, *Étude sur la chronologie des sires de Bourbon (Xe–XIIIe siècle)* (Moulins, 1865), 112. Germain, para. 14, calls Chantelle the fortress that guarded the route between the Berry and the Auvergne.

[142] Chazaud, *Étude*, 188. For example, Philip allowed Guy to assume the lordship of Montluçon in 1202/1203: Fazy, *Les origines du Bourbonnais. Tome 2*, 212, who rejects the earlier findings of Chazaud, *Étude*, 189–91.

[143] Archambaud fought in the king's name against Robert I Dauphin, count of the Auvergne: Roques, 'Résister', paragraph 13. For Archambaud as constable, see Fazy, *Les origines du Bourbonnais*, i, nos 623, 624, and 626 (1222); 644 (1223); and Delisle, 'Baillis d'Auvergne', in *RHGF*, xxiv, 205* and 205* n. 9 (1221). In 1227, 1229, and 1237, the royal constable for the Auvergne was Beraud de Mercoeur, but Beraud was simultaneously acting as Archambaud's marshal, so it is clear that Archambaud retained his influence to this date: Fazy, *Les origines du Bourbonnais*, i, 669, 692, 774. Archambaud

Yet shortly before 1240, Archambaud's privileged status as the chief royal agent in the region evaporated: a new royal constable for the Auvergne is found by 1238, and, famously, in 1241 King Louis IX granted all of the royal lands in the region – lands that the lords of Bourbon had until that point held in custody for the king – to his brother Alphonse as part of Alphonse's great appanage.[144] By 1238, then, the days in which the interests of lords of Bourbon were synonymous with those of the kings of France were over; the two *enquêtes* of 1240 thus merely confirm the king's about-face with regard to Archambaud.

The choice of *enquêteurs* in the outlawry *enquête* was straightforward. The men chosen to supervise the proceedings were the dean of the collegial church of Monter-Moyer in Bourges, and Raoul Gandelus, the royal *bailli* in Bourges.[145] Neither was an obvious friend to either Archambaud or Prior Renaud. Naming the closest *bailli* to Archambaud's lands as *enquêteur* may have represented an effort to ensure that a powerful lord like Archambaud could not intimidate a lesser clerk; after all, Raoul would have been expected to promote the king's agenda in the region as much as possible, and he possessed the judicial and enforcement resources of his bailliage to help him achieve it. For the homicide *enquête*, however, the choice of *enquêteurs* is more difficult to parse.[146] Of the two, Jocelin of Ardena, who was sent from Paris, may also have been a clear representative of royal interests, one who would have both ensured the letter of the law and the shaping of the proceedings according to the king's interests. The other, however, was Guillaume de Chantelle, who was presumably a local man and one who may well have known Lord Archambaud personally. If, moreover, the *enquêteur* Guillaume de Chantelle can be identified with the future castellan of Chantelle named Guillaume Ogier, then an even deeper connection to the lord of Bourbon may be presumed.[147] Perhaps the selection of Guillaume represented a compromise effected by Archambaud's lawyers in Paris; the *enquête* would go forward only if a man suitable to Archmbaud was one of the *enquêteurs*. This possibility seems strengthened by the fact that although the *enquête* mentions a royal 'bailli' for the Auvergne, who ultimately sought to apprehend the men responsible for the homicide, he was not selected as one of the *enquêteurs*.[148]

The facts of the matter in the homicide *enquête* do not appear in doubt. Eighteen witnesses present an almost entirely synchronous account of a series of deadly encounters: first, enemies (*inimicos*) of the prior known colloquially as

---

is called *procurator Arverniae ex parte domini regis Francorum* in 1233: *ibid.*, i, no. 747 (November 1233).

[144] For Amauri de Courcelles, bailli and constable of the Auvergne, in 1238–40: Fazy, *Les origines du Bourbonnais*, i, no. 812; and *RHGF*, xxiv, 205*–06*. For Henri de Ponceaux as bailli and constable for the Auvergne, a role that he continued to fill for Count Alphonse after 1241: *RHGF*, xxiv, 206*.

[145] *Olim*, i, 1016. See above, p. 165.

[146] Chazaud, *Quelques traits*, 13. See above, p. 165.

[147] A Guillaume Ougier was castellan of Chantelle in 1245, but it is not clear that this is the same man: Fazy, *Les origines du Bourbonnais*, i, no. 881.

[148] Chazaud, *Quelques traits*, 23.

'Les Garinens' invaded the lands of Saint-Pourçain and seized plunder, including three horses. As a result, the prior's tenants took up arms and began to pursue these enemies. When the pursuit neared Archambaud's castle of Chantelle, only a few kilometers away, the castellan – a certain Bernard Blanc – burst forth from the castle with a band of mounted and dismounted men and rode down the tenants of Saint-Pourçain. After the dust cleared, one of the prior's men lay dead, and ten more languished in captivity in Chantelle. When representatives from the royal bailli of the Auvergne arrived to summon Bernard, the castellan, to answer for the killing and the seizures, he flatly refused.

The eighteen witnesses deposed in the outlawry *enquête* also present a uniformly consistent account. When asked about the 'behavior' of a band of men who had been publicly 'outlawed from the lord of Bourbon's lands at the king's command',[149] all agreed that a band of men (i.e., les Garinens) had previously entered the lands of Prior Renaud and burned his villas and plundered his tenants' goods; as a result, they had been publicly outlawed. All of the depositions agreed that the outlaws had indeed been spotted within Archambaud's domain, even after the proclamation of outlawry; what is more, they were living like kings, enjoying the hospitality of Archambaud's tenants and the protection of his seigneurial officers.

Each *enquête* deposed eighteen witnesses, the majority of whom were persons of low status from the villages of the region. In the outlawry *enquête*, for instance, witnesses included a widow of a local knight, a vassal of one of Lord Archambaud's most important vassals, several men subject to the Hospitallers of Buxières, three 'men of the lord king', several servants of Lord Archambaud, three merchants from the town of Saint-Pourçain, and the widow of the prévôt of Montor. Aside from the three merchants, all were from villages and castles in the arc of Bourbon lands that lay just west of Saint-Pourçain. No obvious patterns of subjectivity emerge from the identities of the witnesses, since all, whether king's man, man of lord Archambaud, or merchant of Saint-Pourçain, agreed about the continued presence of the outlaws.

It is much harder to place the witnesses from the homicide *enquête*, since the scribes did not routinely provide toponyms for them, nor did they reveal to whose lordships the deponents belonged. Still, from the narratives of the witnesses some tidbits can be gleaned. One of the witnesses was the knight in whose house, at Chareil, the prior's tenants took refuge from the castellan and his men, and from which house the ten men were dragged off to captivity in Chantelle. Several, including the chaplain of Chareil, noted that although they hadn't witnessed the killing themselves, they had learned the identity of the killer from conversation with 'friends of the dead man'.[150] A larger group were actually victims of the attack; they had been among the tenants of Prior Renaud who were pursuing the outlaws when Bernard Blanc and his men fell upon

---

[149] *Olim*, i, 1016: *dixit quod vidit… malefactores ecclesie Beati Porciani qui forbanniti erant de terra domini Borbonensis, de mandato domini regis.*
[150] Chazaud, *Quelques traits*, 15–16.

them; one described the actual killing, and several more were among the ten led into captivity. The final witness was a knight sent by the unnamed royal bailli of the Auvergne to bring Bernard Blanc and another of his men in to answer at justice. The selection of witnesses was thus entirely detrimental to the castellan of Chantelle; all of the witnesses deposed in the case were among those directly harmed by his actions, or those involved in attempting to bring him to the royal court for justice.

By virtue of the content of their testimony, moreover, the depositions from both *enquêtes* provided a master narrative that neatly upheld Prior Renaud's contention about the bad behavior of Lord Archambaud while simultaneously appearing to reinforce the centralizing, order-producing function of royal law. In this sense the *enquêtes* ordered by the royal court could be seen to be confirming the existential purpose of royal law. By curbing the 'violent' and 'anarchic' impulses of aristocrats such as Archambaud de Bourbon, the *enquêtes* might have been said to have demonstrated the clear superiority of 'rational' procedures like *inquisitio* and of the royal promise of peace and social order. By intimating that Archambaud's actions would be disciplined through law, the king's *enquêteurs* and *baillis* could argue that they, and not Archambaud, were the superior authority for the people of the Auvergne.

Yet if the familiar state-building narrative seems easy to apply to these *enquêtes*, it is important to heed Bourdieu's warning about doubting the state,[151] since it also seems clear that the royal actions glimpsed in these two *enquêtes* were themselves strategies, strategies of self-representation and misrepresentation designed to advance particular political positions. By posing carefully worded articles to carefully chosen witnesses, the *enquêteurs* could almost be assured of achieving twin goals: the production of 'truth' alongside the advancement of the royalist agenda for asserting royal sovereignty over lords like Archambaud. By careful examination of both the text and the context of the depositions made by these 'little people' from the Auvergne, it is possible to identify competing narratives that, at least rhetorically, undercut that master narrative.

Consider the homicide *enquête*: it presents several unusual features, at least if one presumes that the point of the *enquête* was to determine the truth behind a horrible crime and, ideally, to bring justice for the crime. First, it is clear both from the questions posed and the answers received, that the *enquêteurs'* interest in the matter was in the rights of lords, not the killing of a man. After all, even though thirteen of the witnesses were present at the killing and could describe it to some degree of detail, the victim was never named. This fact is particularly striking since at least seven of the thirteen were companions to the victim; those seven, along with the victim, had been part of the group of the prior's men who were chasing les Garinens, and all seven had been forcibly removed from the house in which they had taken refuge and had been led into captivity by the castellan's men. It is certain that some, if not all, of these seven, and possibly

---

[151] Bourdieu, 'Rethinking', 36: 'For, when it comes to the State, one never doubts enough.'

others of the thirteen eyewitnesses, knew the victim by name. Yet his identity remains a mystery. Why? Because the *enquête* was not intended to procure justice for this poor, nameless victim; rather, it was intended to provide a legal justification for royal action against Lord Archambaud de Bourbon.[152] After all, even though the witnesses agreed that the castellan, Bernard Blanc, had not personally participated in the killing – it was done by Aymonin de Vallières and Bergoinz the sergeant[153] – the royal *bailli* stated clearly that Bernard, and by extension Bernard's lord, Archambaud, would be held responsible both for the seizure of Prior Renaud's men and for the killing.[154] Law goeth as lordship biddeth him, indeed.

The language used by the witnesses reinforces the sense that either they, or the procurators who questioned them, or the scribes who recorded their testimony, or, what is most likely, all of the above, were painting an image that was as detrimental to Archambaud as possible. This becomes clear when we consider for a moment what sparked the event. The Garinens were found in the lands of the prior, having seized some amount of plunder.[155] Every single one of the witnesses describes les Garinens as *inimicos prioris*, as 'enemies of the prior'.[156] But *inimicus*, as Robert Bartlett has shown, meant more than 'opponent'; it connotated deep, personal, and long-standing feelings. Enmity was, according to Bartlett, an institution, and as such medieval law acknowledged that violence done to an enemy was 'in a quite different category from harm done to anyone else, and has different legal consequences'.[157] Even Roman law recognized enmity as a formal legal category.[158] So, by labeling les Garinens as 'enemies', the witnesses were making a legal and moral argument, one that – if accepted – would have justified, or at least placed in a different legal framework, any response that the prior's men might take against them. And what was that response? The witnesses describe how 'the men of the prior' took up arms and 'pursued' (*persequebant*) Les Garinens. In other words, they responded by taking up the hue and cry. Faced with notorious enemies, the proper response was to drop one's tools, equip one's weapons, and pursue or follow those enemies. Just as labeling Les Garinens was a strategy, then, so too was describing the response

---

[152] Smail suggests that the facts of most cases were well known to all participants, and that the purpose of holding an *enquête* lay in the pursuit of fiscal or political advantage: Smail, 'Témoins et témoignages', para. 1.

[153] Chazaud, *Quelques traits*, 14, 15, 16, 22.

[154] Chazaud, *Quelques traits*, 23. Guillaume de Uçone, whom the bailli had sent to Chantelle, reported *quod ipse et alii nuncii culparent dictum castellanum de predictis morte et capcione*.

[155] Chazaud, *Quelques traits*, 16.

[156] Chazaud, *Quelques traits*, 13–22. Fifteen of the eighteen witnesses use the word '*inimicus*'. It is significant that the outlawry *enquête* never uses the word, preferring instead '*malefactor*'.

[157] Robert Bartlett, '"Mortal Enmities": the Legal Aspect of Hostility in the Middle Ages', in *Feud, Violence and Practice: Essays in Medieval Studies in Honor of Stephen D. White*, ed. Belle S. Tuten and Tracey L. Billado (Farnham, 2010), 197–212 at 198–200.

[158] Bartlett, 'Mortal Enemies', 204.

of the prior's men as 'pursuit', for this was an appropriate verb to use when taking up the hue. Thus, even though the *enquête* wasn't concerned prima facie with the actions of the prior's men, but rather with the actions of the castellan, the depositions of the 'victims' – that is, the prior's men – assert a legal and moral justification for their actions.

In contrast, the witnesses, as prompted by the articles posed by the *enquêteurs*, used equally charged language to describe Bernard Blanc and his men. The verb that nearly all of the witnesses used to describe the castellan's action was *chacare*, that is, to hunt, or at least to chase in the context of a hunt.[159] The voice of Simon de Bayet can stand for the others:

[Simon] 'said that the said castellan and André and all the others [of the castellan's men], just as have been named in the preceding testimony, hunted he who is speaking, and the other men of the prior... and he saw the castellan and the other named men chase down a certain man of the said prior while the man was still alive, and he saw them come to a stop around that man, and when they left, the man lay dead on the ground.'[160]

One of the witnesses also used a nominative form of the same word, *chacia*. Like Simon, Bardinaz noted how the castellan and his men 'hunted [*chacaverunt*] the men of the prior', but added that 'in that hunt [*chacia*], a certain of the prior's men was killed with swords'.[161] The deployment of the language of the hunt was undoubtedly intentional and strategic, for it served to delegitimize the actions of the castellan in exactly the same way that calling Les Garinens 'enemies' had legitimized the pursuit of the prior's tenants. Simon, Bardinaz and the others were claiming that Bernard and his men had treated them like animals, and certainly not like men who were pursuing a legitimate, public enemy.

Perhaps this is actually how it happened. Perhaps Bernard and his men were indeed the proverbial bad lords, whose inherent capacity for unrestrained violence overflowed into a terrible hunt for the most dangerous game. Some hints in two of the testimonies indicate, however, that other readings are possible. When asked 'who was with the castellan when the killing occurred?',

---

[159] Chazaud, *Quelques traits*, 13–23. The text uses *chacare*, a variant of the more common *caciare*; see J.F. Niermeyer, *Mediae Latinitatis Lexicon Minus* (Leiden, 1976), 113. *Caciare* is the obvious root of the French *chasser*. Only three of the eighteen depositions do not use *chaciare*; one of those three substituted '*fugaverunt*', which might carry similar implications.

[160] Chazaud, *Quelques traits*, 18–19: dixit quod dicti capellanus et Andreas et omnes alii, prout nominantur in precedenti teste, chacaverunt ipsum qui loquitur, et homines prioris... et vidit castellanum et ceteros nominatos chacare quemdam hominem dicti prioris vivum, et vidit eos super eum arretare, et quando recesserunt dictus homo mortuus remansit.

[161] Chazaud, *Quelques traits*, 22–3: Bardinaz, juratus, dixit quod vidit et interfuit, quando homines prioris persequebantur inimicos prioris, et quod castellanus Cantelle, et Andreas de Montelucio, et Bergoinz, Durandus clericus, Bergoinz [*sic*], Aymonins de Valeris, et multi alii venerunt contra eos, et chacaverunt homines prioris, et in illa chacia quidam hominum priorum [*sic*] cum gladiis mortuus fuit, sed non vidit eum interficere.

the first witness, Guillaume de Mecenon, gave a long and complicated account: at first, Guillaume thought, it was just Bernard, his sergeant Bergoinz, and the knight Aymonin, who hunted the prior's men. Then, he said, two of the horsemen pulled ahead – Aymonin and Bergoinz – and it was that pair that would eventually perform the killing. But, Guillaume added, 'shortly after [seeing only the three of them], he saw a great many men join the castellan, some with and some without weapons, some mounted and some not, just as is the custom when answering the hue and cry'.[162] In other words, Guillaume interpreted Bernard's response as customary and normalized, and as part of the legal obligation for all free men to follow the hue and cry when it was made. Even if the other witnesses do not mention it, Guillaume's account thus offers a different reading of events: when his lands were invaded by an armed band, Bernard and many others did what was proper and necessary: they raised the hue and cry, and charged in pursuit of the alleged malefactors, *just as* the tenants of Saint-Pourçain had justified their pursuit of Les Garinens within the framework of the hue. Such a reading is supported, moreover, by the testimony of the knight who came to summon Bernard before the royal *bailli* to answer for the killing and the captivity of the prior's men. According to the knight's testimony, Bernard responded that he would do none of the things the bailli commanded without the advice of Lord Franco d'Avenières, who was not then present. When the knight said that Franco's presence was unnecessary, since the summons did not name him, Bernard noted that Lord Archambaud himself had commanded Bernard to seize any armed men whom he found in Archambaud's lands.[163] Other charters identify this Franco d'Avenières as a knightly companion and close advisor of

---

[162] Chazaud, *Quelques traits*, 14: Requisitus utrum vidisset occidere hominem prioris qui fuit occisus, dicit quod vidit ire longe ante dictum castellanum duos eques [sic] quorum nomen unius erat Aymonins de Valeris qui occidit dictum hominem, prout idem Aymonins eidem Willelmo recognovit. Nomen autem alterius ignorabat. Requisitus iterum idem Willelmus qui erant cum dicto castellano, dixit quod Bergoinz, serviens ejusdem castellani, erat tantum dicto castellano tunc: sed postea vidit quamplurimos venire ad dictum castellanum cum armis et sine armis sic[ut] mos est venire ad cri, sine equis et cum equis. Interrogatus qui erant illi cum armis, dixit quod vidit Hugonem Challamel, eques [sic], habentem arcum et sagittas, et dictum Aymonem armatum super quodam equo, et Regnerium lo Pechior similiter armatum; et vidit Brunum et Durandum, clericos de Chantella, super equos, sed non armatos, ut ipse credit, et quamplurimos alios pedes.

[163] Chazaud, *Quelques traits*, 23: Guillelmus de Uçone, miles, juratus dixit quod ballivus Arvernie misit ipsum qui loquitur et unum alium militem et clericum suum ad Bernardum Blanc, castellanum Cantelle, ut diceret dicto castellano ut homines prioris Sancti Porciani, quos ceperat, deliberaret sive redderet, et quod coram ipso ballivo compararet juri pariturus super dicta capcione et super homine prioris qui mortuus fuerat, qui erat de consocietate captorum, et dictus capellanus respondidit [sic] eis quod nichil de premissis faceret sine domino Francone de Faveneriis qui non erat presens, et ipse qui loquitur et alii nuncii replicaverunt quod non expectarent dominum Franconem, quia non erant missi ad eum, et quod ipse et alii nuncii culparent dictum castellanum de predictis morte et capcione. Idem castellanus dixit quod dominus Borbonii preceperat ei ut homines quoslibet quos inveniret in terram [sic] dicti domini Borbonii cum armis, caperet.

Archambaud de Bourbon.[164] Bernard was thus citing his responsibility to his superiors, both Archambaud's close advisor, Franco, and the lord of Bourbon himself, as justifications for his actions; whatever might have transpired, it was legitimate because Archambaud was loyally fulfilling his obligations to his lords by defending their lands from armed invaders. While we might consider this a species of tendentious pleading, it was also plausible tendentious pleading. That is, it would have been fully comprehensible that Bernard was obliged, as the vassal of Archambaud de Bourbon, to raise the hue against and to repel with force any armed men who invaded Archambaud's lands. That Bernard's actions resulted in a killing might have been unfortunate, but, as he seems to have been doing here, Bernard could plausibly shift the blame onto the victim, whose aggressive actions necessitated hue and, eventually, the armed response. Here the oral nature of the *enquête* allowed Guillaume Mecenon (and others) to undercut the master narrative that was being pushed by the *enquêteurs* – that Bernard and company were savage hunters of men – by reframing the killing as a necessary act of public order, connected to the hue and cry.

If we have seen the witnesses adopt language to legitimize their actions and delegitimize Bernard's, and if I have also argued that the testimonies suggest how Bernard might have justified his actions through his obligation to defend Archambaud's lands from armed invaders, there is also room for a third reading. If it is true that many of the witnesses describe Bernard admitting, in a form of filtered direct speech, that 'We have killed a man', it is also clear from the testimonies that Bernard, and indeed the majority of his men, struck no blows at all and were thus not legally culpable for the killing. Instead, as all the accounts make clear, the killing was entirely encompassed by the knight Aymonin de Vallières and the sergent Bergoinz. As Jean Daire attested, he saw

that the said Aymo de Vallières struck the prior's man on the head with his sword, so that the man collapsed. Then Bergoinz ran the man through the body with his lance, and then Aymo repeatedly slashed him in the guts with a knife and then struck him again with his sword, such that the man died immediately.[165]

We have also already heard from Beatrix, the witness who overheard this same Aymonin, as he was leading away two of the prior's horses, boast that he had now 'satisfied his need for vengeance for the death of his brother by killing one of the prior's men'.[166] The combination of Aymonin's apparent eagerness

---

[164] See Archambaud's charter for Charroux (1245x1246): Fazy, *Les origines du Bourbonnais*, i, no. 881. In addition to Franco d'Avenières, Archambaud's entourage on this occasion also included Blain le Loup, who made homage to Archambaud's father in 1209 (Chazaud, *Étude*, 189), and whose man provides testimony in the other *enquête* of 1240: *Olim*, i, 1017 (testimony of Geoffroy l'Espau).
[165] Chazaud, *Quelques traits*, 16: et vidit quod dictus Aymo de Valeris percussit hominem prioris de ense per capud ita quod dictus homo cecidit, et postea dictus Bergoinz percussit dictum hominem per corpus de lancea, et iterato dictus Aymo percussit dictum hominem de cultro per intestina, et de ense suo iterum percussit eum, ita quod incontinenti obiit.
[166] See above, pp. 170–1.

to ride ahead of the pack and his later claim to have sated his need to avenge his brother shifts the episode – at least the killing part of it – into a different register, that of a vengeance killing. Rather than seeing the killing as a naked act of dehumanizing aggression, as the *enquêteurs* made it out to be, or as an unfortunate consequence of the castellan's need to defend his lord's lands, as other testimonies hint, these fragments suggest that the killing was the product of a social logic that was entirely comprehensible to thirteenth-century knightly society, namely the need to take vengeance for the killing of a kinsman. What is more, since vengeance could not be sated by random killing, the fact that Aymonin 'satisfied' his need for vengeance by killing a tenant of Prior Renaud meant that he blamed the men of Saint-Pourçain for his brother's death. The killing which the *enquête* describes, in its official register, as a savage hunt against largely defenseless men, was seen by Aymonin, Bergoinz and probably other members of the household of Chantelle, as justifiable retaliation for a previous killing, one which Aymonin squarely laid at the feet of Prior Renaud and his men; it is only Beatriz's little fragment of voluntary speech about Aymonin's boast, moreover, that allows the entire character of the episode to be seen in this new light.

Of course, the fact that bad blood already existed between Aymonin and the prior might have implied that feud-like conditions *also* existed between Aymonin's superiors (Bernard of Chantelle and Archambaud de Bourbon), on the one hand, and Prior Renaud, on the other. And yet, again, the depositions seem consciously to skirt this possibility; the public narrative, as elicited by the lawyers who questioned the victims, was that the killing was the product of brutal savagery inflicted by the 'hunters' on their prey. Thanks to these fragments of speech, though, it seems entirely possible that a rather different story might have been told, one that explained (but did not excuse) the killing as the product either of individual vengeance or of regional feuding. But the truth presented by the witnesses (or, as we might prefer, the narratives they presented) was carefully shaped by the *enquêteurs* and the procurators who posed the articles to them. The master question that necessitated the *enquête*, and the requirement to respond clearly to only those specific questions posed by the procurators, resulted in a very particular representation of events. In this representation, the ripples and eddies of local politics are effaced, such that Bernard, and ultimately Archambaud, appear merely as villains. To acknowledge the possibility that the *enquête*'s rhetoric of simple crime concealed a deeper fissure of regional feud does not mean, of course, that we must dismiss or relativize the human tragedy that accompanied Aymonin's brutal slaying. The point is simply this: even though vengeance killings were perfectly comprehensible within the logic of medieval aristocratic norms, and might thus have provided a framework for representing the events outside Chantelle, it is meaningful that only one of the depositions even hints at the possibility that the killing was retaliatory. Only thanks to Beatrix's extraordinary relation of Aymonin's boast are we permitted a glimpse of the underlying circumstances of feud that seemed to operate between Chantelle and Saint-Pourçain. Her deposition thus offers a foot into the door of a competing narrative, one that only becomes visible thanks to the orality of the *enquête* procedure.

The outlawry *enquête* sheds further light on the play of competing narratives presented in the depositions. All told, the eighteen witnesses reported seeing one or more of the 'outlaws' in fourteen named locations scattered throughout Archambaud's domain, with multiple sightings at Bransat (5 km west of Saint-Pourçain), Neris (53 km west of Saint-Pourçain), Chantelle (14 km southwest of Saint-Pourçain), and Charroux (19 km southwest of Saint-Pourçain). For instance, one witness saw the men hanging about Archambaud's castle of Bessay; he knew this because he was personally ordered to provide them with food and drink from the castle stores.[167] Another encountered them at Archambaud's villa of Belcaire, where they were dwelling in the house of the lord of Bourbon's *prévôt*; the witness in fact shared a meal with them.[168] A third reported that the entire band had been dwelling for more than six days in three houses that lay between Vanassor and Villefranche.[169] The depositions present an image of the malefactors living an unfettered, untroubled existence within Archambaud's lands: they moved around at will, and they received food and shelter both from Archambaud's tenants and from his *prévôts* and castellans.

These depositions can again be read on two or more levels. The first is the surface, legal one, in which the depositions offer an apparently simple answer to the question: their testimonies demonstrate that despite having been outlawed by both the king and by Archambaud himself, Les Garinens moved freely and easily through Archambaud's lands for many weeks after being outlawed. The implication, of course, was that Archambaud had failed to uphold his or the royal justice; he might even be understood to have been in default of justice himself. In this reading, the depositions' medieval status as putatively objective procedures for the identification of truth would have helped to demonstrate the stark contrast between truthful and good Capetian justice, and the deceptive but false justice of Archambaud de Bourbon. In one sense, then, this top-level reading of the depositions might be seen as supporting the traditional view of the expansion of royal power over the seigneuries of thirteenth-century France. After all, the depositions' indictment of Archambaud provides obvious justifications for the intrusion of superior, fairer, more rational royal justice. Yet we must recall that such an indictment was not, as the royal baillis and scribes might have wished it to be, uninterested. Royal justice, and the new modes of knowledge acquisition and truth production that supported it, was itself a technique of power, one that initially competed with other, older, more local modes of power before eventually coming to underpin and justify the concept of royal sovereignty.[170]

---

[167] *Olim*, i, 1017.
[168] *Olim*, i, 1018.
[169] *Olim*, i, 1017.
[170] Fredric L. Cheyette, 'The Sovereign and the Pirates, 1332', *Speculum* 45 (1970), 40–68 at 43–6, notes that royal claims to sovereignty were a means of suppressing the violence (and only that violence) that the king opposed.

In other words, what this top-level reading of the depositions concerning Les Garinens reveals is an episode in the use of the new techniques of royal power to undermine and supplant other forms of power relationships in the Bourbonnais.

And yet another, competing reading seems possible, thanks to the very orality of the depositions. By reading closely, and against the grain of the official narrative, we can glimpse the shadows of other ways in which the inhabitants of the region may have understood the presence of Les Garinens, and the complex relationships that existed between Bourbon and Saint-Pourçain; that is, they suggest other senses of community and relationships of power that the royal claims to justice and sovereignty worked to ignore and suppress. Consider that nearly without exception, the deponents exhibit no fear of les Garinens.[171] This is so despite the fact that the only term used to describe them is *malefactor*, that is 'wrong-doer' or possibly 'criminal'.[172] By labeling them *malefactores*, the depositions – or, as is more likely, the procurators who framed the questions to which the witnesses responded – asserted their guilt as fact, not as something to be proven. And yet, as the content of the deponents' answers revealed, the inhabitants of the Bourbonnais did not seem to see or treat Les Garinens as criminals, as public outlaws whom custom might have required those inhabitants to detain or impede. Instead, the witnesses generally represent the outlaws neutrally and even positively. As noted above, the witnesses met them on the roads, saw them in the markets, ate meals with them, drank with them in taverns, and in one case, actually joined them in a raid against the lands of Saint-Pourçain.[173] Here is the testimony of Jean Constantine, a self-identified 'man of the king':

On the feast of St Mark, Jean was at Bransat, and there he came across one of the malefactors, who is called Amblart. Jean conversed with him, and then told Amblart, 'I am going to join you willingly, since I have a grudge against the prior of Saint-Pourçain.' And so Amblart set a day on which Amblart would come to Jean in his sister's house at Voussac in order to finalize their partnership; that day was the following sabbath day, a Sunday. That villa was in the land of the lord of Bourbon. And they would leave from Voussac to do damage to the lands of the prior of Saint-Pourçain.[174]

---

[171] *Olim*, i, 1017–18 (a hostel-keeper kicked the witness out of his tavern at midnight out of fear of Bartholomé) and 1018 (Bartholomé tried to steal the witness's salmon).
[172] By the fourteenth century, *malefactor* was a synonym for criminal: Claude Gauvard, '*De grace especial.' Crime, État et société en France à la fin du Moyen Âge* (1991; reprint, Paris, 2010), 120.
[173] The one witness who reported 'criminal' behavior on the part of the 'outlaws' (the attempted theft of a salmon) was a merchant based in Saint-Pourçain, and not an inhabitant of the lands of Bourbon: *Olim*, i, 1018.
[174] *Olim*, i, 1017: Dixit insuper quod in die Beati Marci fuit apud Bransac, villam domini Borbonensis, et illic invenit quemdam de malefactoribus qui vocatur Amblart, et locutus fuit cum ipso et dixit ei, 'Ego libenter essem de societate tua, quia discordiam habeo cum priore Sancti Porciani;' et predictus Amblart posuit eidem diem quod ad se veniret, die sabbati subsequenti, vel die dominica, pro societate confirmanda inter ipsos, apud

In other words, Les Garinens were an accepted feature in the communities that comprised the Bourbonnais, and their task – to harass the prior of Saint-Pourçain – was at the least tolerated, and sometimes even embraced by other inhabitants of the region. The notion that support for the outlaws ran deep is confirmed, moreover, by two other witnesses. Geoffroy de Lespau described how the outlaws were guided one night to Nuillec, a villa of Saint-Pourçain, by two of Lord Archambaud's foresters, Clavelet and André Guitum. Once at Nuillec, they burned it to the ground.[175] Isabelle, the widow of another of Archambaud's *prévôts*, offers an even more telling tale:

> She said that she saw one of the malefactors... in the week after the Apparition [8 May] at Chantelle, a town of the lord of Bourbon. Namely, she saw Bartholomé, and he was in the house of Bernard Blanc, who was then castellan of Chantelle. And Bartholomé had dwelled in Bernard's house for eight days, and he received all his necessities from that house. She also says that on many occasions she saw all the outlaws gathering in the house of the said castellan, and they all received all their sustenance there.[176]

If there were any doubt that Archambaud was continuing to support the Garinens, their presence at Chantelle alongside Bernard Blanc, the very man whose actions would also be scrutinized in the homicide *enquête*, should put that to rest. Taken together these three snippets of testimony describe a high level of popular and official support from the inhabitants of the Bourbonnais for Les Garinens, and of a comparable level of popular and official hostility towards the priory of Saint-Pourçain. Men such as Jean Constantine harbored grudges against the prior, just like Aymonin the knight blamed the prior's men for the death of his brother; such grudges were enough to bring presumably ordinary men, like Jean, to join burning expeditions. What is more, Archambaud's seigneurial agents, including the *prévôts* who administered his villas and the castellans who managed his castles, actively provided food, shelter, and presumably all other supplies to Les Garinens.

These depositions thus suggest a different narrative, and a different set of social facts, one that cuts across the grain of the neat legal claim that Archambaud

---

Vonsac, in domo sororis sue; et ipsa villa est in terra domini Borbonensis, et inde irent forisfacere in terra prioris Sancti-Porciani.

[175] *Olim*, i, 1017: et quum recesserunt ab ipso castello nocte illa, duo forestarii domini Borbonensis, videlicet Claveletus et Andreas Guitum eos duxerunt ad quamdam villam comburendam, que vocatur Nuillec, villam Sancti-Porciani, et ipsam villam nocte illa combuxerunt.

[176] *Olim*, i, 1018–19: Isabellis, relicta prepositi de Montor, jurata, dixit quod vidit, in ebdomada post Aparicionem, unum de malefactoribus ecclesie Beati Porciani apud Chantelle, villam domini Borbonensis, videlicet Bartholomeum, in domo Bernardi Albi, qui tunc temporis castellanus erat de Chantelle, et in domo predicti castellani mansit per octo dies, et capiebat in ipsa domo omnia sibi necessaria. Dixit insuper quod vidit multociens omnes forbannitos venientes in domo predicti castellani, et ibi capiebant omnia sibi necessaria.

was in default of justice. Beneath the scripted questions of the *enquêteurs*, the witnesses' words offer glimpses of a very different social reality, one that in other circumstances and in other texts might simply have been labeled as a war or feud (*guerra*), instead of crime and default of justice. As both *enquêtes* reveal, feelings of hostility, even vengeance, ran through the social strata of the two lordships; those feelings can be identified in the interstices of the official narrative and assembled, like a jigsaw puzzle, to form a picture utterly distinct from the centralizing narrative about crime. The story told by these puzzle pieces went something like this: bad blood had existed between the inhabitants of Archambaud's lands and the tenants of Prior Renaud for some time. At some point, the prior's men had killed the brother of Aymonin de Vallières, whose thirst for vengeance eventually led him to kill one of the prior's men. Other inhabitants of the Bourbonnais also harbored 'grudges' against the prior, such that they were willing to join outlaws to prosecute war against the prior's lands. At the same time, Lord Archambaud employed, or at least aided, abetted, and supported, a force of men – Les Garinens – who pursued the basic tactics of thirteenth-century warfare between 'mortal enemies' by burning and plundering the lands of Saint-Pourçain. And finally, the castellan of Chantelle, ultimately followed his lord's orders to the letter and came to the defense of Les Garinens when they were pursued as 'mortal enemies' by the prior's tenants.

But, of course, the *enquêtes* did not choose to view Bernard Blanc and Les Garinens as actors in a war or feud, and therefore as participating in a kind of recognized medieval institution with its own internal logic. Instead, first by summoning the victims of Bernard Blanc (and none of his own men) in the homicide *enquête*, and then by posing brief, contextless questions in which the legal status of the Garinens was already predetermined in the outlawry *enquête*, the *enquêtes* used the testimonies to impose a different kind of logic, the logic of royal sovereignty and royal justice. To succeed, moreover, that logic needed to frame itself not merely as a competing logic, but as a logic that was superior to and more legitimate than whatever social logic Archambaud might have claimed to have been following. Perhaps Archambaud's apparent devotion to the older logic of local war, one that possessed internal mechanisms for limiting and ultimately ending violence, deserved to be critiqued.[177] We cannot say for sure. But we can, however, note that the structure of the *enquêtes*, and the content of the depositions, work clearly in the favor of Prior Renaud and, ultimately of King Louis IX. Is this because the truth, as we might say, is ecclesiastical, or royal? Perhaps. The orality of the *enquêtes* reminds us, however, that law is itself an idiom of power, one that in the hands of royal *enquêteurs* and in the form of putatively 'objective' inquiries into 'truth' such as *enquêtes*, competed with and ultimately silenced other idioms. The very orality of those *enquêtes*, through which witnesses may be seen to tell several tales at once and throwaway anecdotes can be seen to carry hidden meaning,

---

[177] Stephen D. White, 'Feuding and Peace-making in the Touraine around the Year 1100', *Traditio* 42 (1986), 195–263.

also allows us a glimpse behind the curtain, a glimpse into the struggle between those idioms for acceptance and dominance.

Conclusion

In this essay I have suggested new approaches to using adversarial *enquêtes* as objects of historical analysis. On one level, I argue simply that the hundreds of extant records of adversarial *enquêtes* surviving from France from the 1180s and onward represent an overlooked source for the analysis of social and political action. The *enquêtes* offer a mass of engaging detail concerning medieval legal, social, economic, and political practice. Elsewhere, for instance, I have used *enquêtes* to highlight the degree to which forcible exaction remained a, or perhaps *the*, core principle of both royal and seigneurial power well into the thirteenth century.[178] What is more, the Auvergne *enquêtes* have a lot to teach us about competing notions of public order, feuding, and violence, while the Le Mans *enquête* stands as a rich source for ecclesiastical competition and for analyzing the socio-economic strata of a thriving thirteenth-century city. The list of topics could be expanded.

I have also highlighted the dual character of *enquêtes*, which exist simultaneously as artifacts of a new written culture and as testaments to the important role that oral argument and testimony played in medieval legal and political culture. If I have emphasized the oral elements of *enquêtes*, it is mostly because they have previously been treated primarily as evidence of 'revolutions' in writing, administration, and abstract 'cognitive' development. It is of course only proper to highlight such radical changes in the ways in which medieval society organized itself and remembered itself. Yet in emphasizing 'la révolution de l'écrit', especially in legal procedure and administration,[179] we risk overlooking the relentless orality of legal culture in general, and of *enquêtes* in particular; after all, the essence of the procedure of *enquête* comprised oral statements made by witnesses to questions posed orally by the *enquêteurs*. As we have seen, while the *enquêteurs* could and did shape the responses by how they chose and ordered the questions, as well as by the potentially leading language (e.g., *inimicus*, or *chacare*) they used to frame the questions, witnesses also could and did inject the proceedings with their own ideas and agendas. Sometimes that subjectivity can be glimpsed in fragments of direct speech, such as Chalamel's cruel joke or Aymonin's vengeful boast, and sometimes by the ways in which witnesses like Ameline framed the events that they had experienced. The very recourse to spoken testimony ensured that depositions, and thus the trials that they fueled, would remain sites in which ideas and ideologies could be contested.

The final element of my argument concerns the larger historiographical interpretation of *enquêtes*. The procedure of *enquête* has been understood

---

[178] Barton, '*Enquête*, Exaction, and Excommunication.'
[179] Bertrand, 'À propos de la révolution de l'écrit', *passim*; Clanchy, *From Memory*, *passim*.

teleologically, both by legal historians who represent it as the triumph of rational procedure over subjective, irrational practice, and by historians of state formation who represent it as a central, instrumentalist plank in the creation of a 'modern' monarchical state in which the needs of the res publica were prioritized over private interests. It would foolish, of course, to overlook the undeniable increase in the power and bureaucratic capacity of both ecclesiastical and royal structures of government in the thirteenth century. After all, it is obvious that *enquêtes* conducted by royal *baillis* and ecclesiastical procurators did, at least partially, accomplish what the medieval legists and modern state-formation historians assumed they would do; that is, they assisted in the royal penetration of the Auvergne, and they helped to affirm the hierarchy of ecclesiastical power in Le Mans. Yet it would also be foolish to accept uncritically the rhetorical claims of royal and papal legists and administrators to be acting solely in the name of justice and the common good. After all, the claims made by royal theoreticians of sovereignty that *enquêtes* represented a more rational and more just mode of resolving disputes can also be seen as an 'ideological device in terms of which the political institutionalization of power is legitimated'.[180] The implicit arguments of the king and his ministers, that by implementing *enquêtes* (as well as other tools of the State, such as taxation) they were offering the only alternative to 'chaos' or 'anarchy', and therefore that opposition to their new institutions could be construed as illegitimate or disordering behavior, were reflexive; they asserted as objective fact the very subjective point they wished to impose. Other modes of social organization, of legal proceeding, and of dispute resolution than those offered by the nascent monarchical 'national' state were clearly possible at the turn of the thirteenth century.[181] I contend that the oral character of the *enquêtes* allow us a glimpse of some of these alternatives. By focusing on the ways in which small details presented orally by witnesses of varying social condition might offer interpretations of the political and social reality that directly competed with, or even contradicted, the master narrative, I have shown not merely that the speech of witnesses is inherently subjective; I have also suggested that the procedure of *enquête* provided a locus classicus within which competing strategies of social organization and power relations could be presented and contested. To accept the State's characterization of the *enquête* alone (or of the political and legal order that the *enquêtes* claimed to support), as historians of state formation have done, therefore, is ignore the rich contestations that depositions revealed. By emphasizing the play of competing strategies that can be teased out of the depositions, I have sought to remedy this singular focus and to suggest that the master narrative that argued for the progressive, rational, and objective nature of *enquêtes* was nothing more than a

---

[180] Abrams, 'Notes on the Difficulty of Studying the State', 82, who notes that this 'ideological device' is 'the claimed reality of the State'.
[181] Charles Tilly, 'Foreword to Princeton Classic Edition: Joseph Strayer Revisited', in Joseph Strayer, *On the Medieval Origins of the Modern State* (1970; Princeton, NJ, 2005), xiv.

technique de pouvoir, that is, a means by which the authorities that favored their use could assert their own emerging ideas about the superiority of centralized justice and construct the subjection of those whom they wished to dominate.[182] At the same time, I have argued that the same play of competing political strategies and narratives allowed for resistance to those *techniques de pouvoir*, since witnesses in Le Mans, the Auvergne and elsewhere, could and did use the opportunity to shape reality in their own words to present narratives that explicitly and implicitly undercut the dominant narrative. In this play between master and hidden narratives, I have argued that rather than seeing the *enquêtes* as inert objects in a functionalist march towards the modern state, the *enquêtes* should be seen as dynamic fields within which competing narratives of social and political organization were articulated and debated.

---

[182] Dejoux, *Les enquêtes*, 3: 'L'enquête permet de construire la sujétion, faite tour à tour de contrainte et de consentement à la domination. Le fait d'organiser une enquête permet à la fois au monarque de se renseigner, de se faire reconnaître, voire aimer, lorsqu'il s'agit pour les sujets de dénoncer les abus de l'administration, comme dans les enquêtes de réparation.'

The C. Warren Hollister Memorial Essay 2022

Taking It on Trust? Writing about Officials in the Medieval Italian Communes[1]

Frances Andrews

The starting point for this essay is the repeated, painted representation of professed men of religion employed as counters of coin on the wooden covers of ledgers produced for the communal treasuries of Siena from the 1250s onwards (figure 10.1).[2] The images are attractive and familiar enough to be regularly reproduced, part of the unquestioned portrayal of medieval Italian urban life, evoking in idealized terms the notarial culture and burgeoning offices of communal Italy. For present purposes, instead, they raise a single, critical question which has long fascinated me.[3] In a period when ascetic poverty was an influential ideal and some professed religious deemed handling money deeply problematic, what

---

[1] I am very grateful to the organizers and particularly to Joanna Drell and Bill North for the kind invitation to deliver the lecture on which this essay is based. It was a delight to spend a few days in Richmond together. All translations are my own unless otherwise indicated.

[2] *Le Biccherne. Tavole dipinte delle magistrature senesi (secoli XIII–XVIII)*, ed. L. Borgia, E. Carli, M.A Ceppari, U. Morandi, P. Sinibaldi and C. Zarrilli (Rome, 1984). For the Cistercians appointed between 1257 and 1375, see Andrea Canestrelli, *L'Abbazia di San Galgano* (Florence, 1896), 20 and 126–7, doc. 20. The opening image of this article offers a rich example of the genre. Under the patronage of the Cistercian treasurer Don Simone di Ser Vanni, a monk of San Galgano, for the July–December 1343 accounts, an anonymous painter has depicted the collaboration between the religious and secular officials (Metropolitan Museum of Art, New York, NY; Item no. 10.203.3).

[3] Frances Andrews, 'Regular Observance and Communal Life: Siena and the Employment of Religious', in *Pope, Church and City. Essays in Honour of Brenda M. Bolton*, ed. Frances Andrews, Christoph Egger and Constance Rousseau (Leiden, 2004), 357–83; Frances Andrews, 'Living like the Laity? The Negotiation of Religious Status in the Cities of late Medieval Italy', *TRHS* 20 (2010), 27–55; *Churchmen and Urban Government in Late Medieval Italy, c. 1200–c. 1450: Cases and Contexts*, ed. Frances Andrews with Maria Agata Pincelli (Cambridge, 2013), with case-studies of Bergamo, Cremona, Lucca, Modena, Parma, Perugia, Piacenza, Pistoia, Venice, Verona and Viterbo/Tuscia, and comparative essays on Sardinia, the *Regno* and the English Crown; Frances Andrews, 'Como and Padua', in *Italy and Medieval Europe. Papers for*

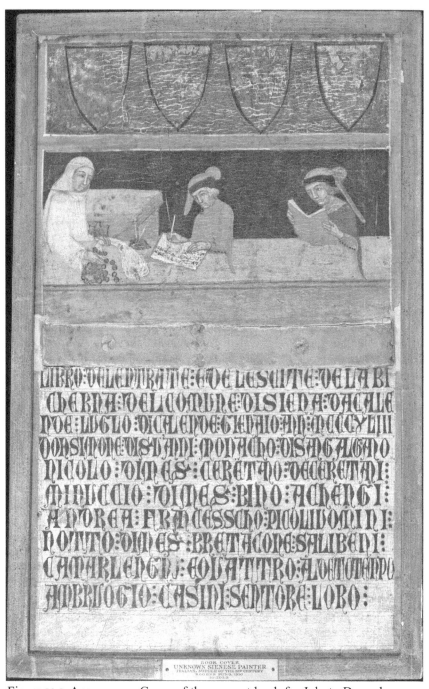

Figure 10.1. Anonymous, Cover of the account book for July to December 1343 produced by the Cistercian treasurer, Don Simone di Ser Vanni, monacho di San Galgano, Siena, Treasury of the Biccherna (Metropolitan Museum of Art, New York, NY; Item no. 10.203.3).

do the activities of these and other monks and religious, documented in a large number of communes and in multiple different offices, signify for conventional understandings of the place of churchmen in Italian communal life?[4] Why and how far did secular governments trust the Humiliati brothers and Cistercian or Vallombrosan monks portrayed on the ledgers in Siena, or the many different religious in other communes assigned such roles, and why did they take them on? There are parallels with practice in other parts of Western Europe: with the employment of Templars and Mendicants by thirteenth-century French and Iberian royals, for example, or of secular clergy and abbots by the English.[5] Men of religion handling communal funds and assuming other responsibilities of the *reipublica*, were not unique to Italian communes. These practices were, however, uniquely configured there, and so is the historiography, embedded in the history of communes and of religious orders, and as we will see, often engaging with histories of trust.

This essay explores some of the writing about religious in office, starting upstream and following the currents of ideas to track two main features down to the end of the twentieth century: how perceptions of men of the Church employed by the Italian communes changed alongside shifts in the writing of history and what interpretations of this one theme can tell us about those doing the explaining. This is mostly history-writing in a minor key since before the 2000s the practice was only rarely a focus of attention. Yet this approach exposes something of historians' assumptions about critical relationships for understanding the medieval communes: those between the laity, faith, and power. Following the interconnecting streams of commentary on officeholding by religious over the *longue durée* opens a bird's-eye view onto history-writing in, and about, communal Italy, while also encompassing larger concerns, the social and institutional changes shaping, as it were, the banks of those streams.[6]

Three interrelated, preliminary points are needed to contextualize and elucidate the approach adopted here (and to keep in mind in what follows). First, the idea that trust works differently in different societies may now be a given, but it was not always so. In the late 1990s most historians, including medievalists, were not writing about subjects like 'trust'. In 2006, in a lecture for the

---

Chris Wickham, ed. Ross Balzaretti, Julia Barrow and Patricia Skinner (Oxford, 2018), 525–38.
4 One brief demonstration: Roberto Lambertini, '*Denarii et pecunia* : la riflessione francescana sulla moneta nei commenti alla *Regola*', *Mélanges de l'École française de Rome. Moyen Age* 128.2 (2016), 10–20.
5 Three examples among many: Philippe Josserand, 'Les ordres militaires et le service curial dans le royaume de Castille (1252–1369)', in *Les serviteurs de l'état au moyen âge* (Paris, 1999), 75–83; Martin Heale, 'The Abbot and Public Life in Late Medieval England', in *Churchmen and Urban Government in Late Medieval Italy, c. 1200–c. 1450: Cases and Contexts* (Cambridge, 2013), 331–47; Marie Dejoux, *Les enquêtes de saint Louis: gouverner et sauver son âme* (Paris, 2014).
6 On debates about the autonomy or otherwise of history as a discipline, see G.E. Aylmer, 'Introductory Survey: From the Renaissance to the Eighteenth Century', in *Companion to Historiography*, ed. Michael Bentley (London, 1997), 249–80 at 249.

Royal Historical Society in London, Geoffrey Hosking, a historian of Russia and the Soviet Union, asked whether 'Trust and Distrust' were a suitable subject for historians.[7] He shaped his analysis as a question but, drawing on the work of sociologists, the answer was of course affirmative, introducing a convincing case that 'trust is crucially involved in fundamental social phenomena', by which he meant anything from daily routines or the working of government, to religion or community solidarity.[8] Understanding the way trust works is essential to the work of historians.

Through his lecture and a later monograph Hosking did much to move trust to center stage in historical investigation.[9] For medievalists however, his work has since been superseded by the research of another anglophone historian, Ian Forrest, who has set out to reconstruct the personal identity, status and reputation of the 'Trustworthy Men' chosen as lay collaborators of bishops in the late medieval English church, men who contributed, among other things, to the management of financial transactions. Forrest provided an extensive discussion of the meanings of 'trust' or *fides* and how it worked, before examining how laymen came to be defined as trustworthy, as *viri fidedigni*. Economic standing, *fama*, patriarchy, social ties: all played a role in constructing social power and trustworthy status, proving among other things that 'people did not need the church to define trustworthiness on their behalf'.[10] Forrest's subjects were laymen but he briefly noted the way bishops appointed monks as collectors of clerical dues for the Crown, arguing that this was because '[t]he wealthier religious houses [...] had extensive lands that could be seized as collateral if necessary [so] the question was not "who is honest" but "who has something to lose"'. At the same time, he suggested, the heads of religious houses were 'deemed suitable for this role because they could inspire confidence in kings and overawe the diocesan clergy'.[11] Both approaches fit the critical insight that 'power is a relationship', and that in the pre-modern world, the 'power of the state' depended heavily on the 'direct relationship established between subjects and public officers'.[12]

A second introductory perspective comes from a slightly earlier historiographical pillar. Thirty years ago, in another brilliant lecture for the Royal Historical Society, Susan Reynolds (1929–2021) set out to challenge the blanket adoption of Annaliste-style *mentalités*, or what she termed 'Social Mentalities'

---

[7] Geoffrey Hosking, 'Trust and Distrust: A Suitable Theme for Historians?', *TRHS* 16 (2006), 95–115.
[8] Hosking, 'Trust and Distrust', 113.
[9] See Geoffrey Hosking, *Trust: A History* (Oxford, 2014).
[10] Ian Forrest, *Trustworthy Men. How Inequality and Faith Made the Medieval Church* (Princeton, NJ, 2018), 14, 35, 61.
[11] Forrest, *Trustworthy Men*, 270.
[12] An approach succinctly summarized by María Ángeles Martín Romera and Hannes Ziegler, 'Local Communities and Central Officers: The Rise of Public Accountability', in *The Officer and the People. Accountability and Authority in Pre-Modern Europe*, ed. María Ángeles Martín Romera and Hannes Ziegler (Oxford, 2021), 1–23 at 2.

as a methodology for understanding how previous societies work, and inveighed with a lightness of touch as only she could against those who viewed the Middle Ages as full of unreasoned piety or credulity. Her attack on the idea of this period as an 'Age of Faith' may not seem so necessary now, but Reynolds wisely pointed out that 'it has been more often assumed than argued that people in different societies think differently'.[13] She argued that it was the 'content' rather than the 'process' of thought that diverged, the result of changing societal opportunities. As she suggested, '[if] you lived in the eighth century you could not become a physicist, though if you were lucky enough to be a monk with a good library, you might exercise your mathematical talents on calculations of Easter'.[14]

Reynolds' insights retain their relevance both as a warning not to patronize the past, and as a tool for examining the assumptions of some of the writers whose work is outlined below. It will, however, sometimes become useful to turn Reynolds' logic back to front, to ask instead whether 'it has been more often assumed than argued that people in different societies think like us'. As we will see, for generations, quite a number of historians, often but not always themselves clerics, saw the employment of religious as a reflection of the standing of (individual) churchmen, and expressed this by marking either the similarity or the difference with their own society. They 'took it on trust', without interrogating the logic driving their assumptions.

Caution is needed in this kind of analysis: as Peter Biller pointed out in another essay with a question mark in the title, on the recent historiography of Waldensianism[s], there are risks, 'for considering [confessional] sympathies may lead to oversimplification of a historian's outlook, and the investigation and delineation of the precise bearing of such sympathies are very difficult'.[15] Biller's interest was in conflicting assessments of the organizational coherence of a medieval heretical community, a research field where the influence of post-medieval confessional understandings on the writing of history has long been recognized. The spotlight here is on the relations between communes and churchmen as officeholders, interactions that for post-medievals involved differently divided sympathies, no less in need of self-aware investigation, particularly when sampling fragments across centuries of historical writing and multiple centers. The risks of offending by omission are not small.

The Middle Ages

Accounts looking back at professed religious in communal offices began to appear already in the late Middle Ages. Brief mentions in two texts from the flourishing tradition of urban chronicle-writing, one acquiring renown, the other

---

[13] Susan Reynolds, 'Social Mentalities and the Case of Medieval Scepticism', *TRHS*, 4th series, 1 (1991), 21–41 at 21–2.
[14] Reynolds, 'Social Mentalities', 23–4.
[15] Peter Biller, 'Goodbye to Waldensianism?', *PP* 192 (2006), 3–33 at 10.

largely forgotten in later centuries, provide implicit and sometimes explicit explanations that can be taken as a base line for what follows. Of these, the most famous and extensive (but still not very long) is from the mid-fourteenth-century *Nuova Cronica* of the Florentine Giovanni Villani (d. 1348) who recorded the appointment of Cistercian monks from Settimo and Humiliati brothers of Ognissanti in the communal treasuries of Florence in the previous century. This he linked, without comment, to the return to power of the Guelf faction:

> In this way were ordered the condition and direction of the Commune and of the *Popolo* of Florence at the return of the Guelfs; and the religious of the Badia di Settimo and of those of Ognissanti were treasurers of the money, alternating every six months.[16]

Villani went on to explain the further use of *conversi*, lay brothers attached to a Cistercian monastic house, holders of the communal seal in the early fourteenth century, as a response to an attempted theft by an errant podestà who, guilty of corruption, had hoped to avoid end-of-term audit:

> How the podestà of Florence fled with the seal of the commune: Messer Carlo d'Amelia… having performed many acts of corruption, made profits and performed very bad deeds in Florence… took with him the seal of the commune… and from then on, it was ordered that neither podestà nor priors should keep the seal of the Commune, but the brother *conversi* of Settimo, who reside in the Arsenal in the palace of the priors were made its chancellors and guardians.[17]

As a communal magistrate Villani would have known some of the men occupying these roles in his own lifetime. He had himself been accused of corruption in office (*baratteria*) in 1331 and had been successful in proving his innocence.[18] His account sits between record (he had access to government archives) and historiography. Yet his earlier sequence was slightly out. Monastic treasurers are first documented in Florence from the rise of the Guelfs in the 1250s, not their later return.[19] Whether this was a failure of documentation, of shared 'memoria de' nostri fatti passati', or of organization of the body of information at his

---

[16] Giovanni Villani, *Nuova Cronica*, ed. Giuseppe Porta (3 vols, Parma, 1990–1), i, 439–40: 'In questo modo s'ordino lo stato e corso del comune e del popolo di Firençe ala tornata de guelfi. E camerlinghi della pecunia feciono i religiosi dela badia di Settimo e di que d'ognesanti di sei in sei mesi.' See also Andrews, 'Living like the Laity?', 36.
[17] Villani, *Nuova Cronica*, ed. Porta, ii, 186: Come la podesta di Firençe si fuggio col suggello del commune: Messer karlo damelia … auendo elli … fatto in firençe molte baratterie e guadagnerie et pessime opera… sinne porto secho il suggello del commune… e d'allora innançi s'ordino che podesta ne priori tenessono suggello di comune, ma fecionne cancellieri e guardiani i frati conversi di Settimo, che stanno nela cammera dell'arme del palagio de' priori.
[18] Marino Zabba, 'Villani, Giovanni', in *Dizionario biografico degli Italiani* 99 (2020), online.
[19] See Daniela De Rosa, *Alle origini della repubblica fiorentina: dai consoli al "primo popolo" (1172–1260)* (Florence, 1995), 206–07.

disposal, Villani nonetheless provides us with two clear explanations.[20] He rationalized the selection of men of religion for the offices of the commune either as a consequence of changing political alliance, or as a reaction to corruption. He may have understood the choice of Cistercian *conversi* as custodians of the Florentine seal as a pragmatic one because they were already securing the communal armory, but trust in the religious was implicit in this framing of the decision as countering fraud.

Villani's account introduced Cistercians and Humiliati as key players but is unusual in the level of explanation and elaboration at least on Messer Carlo d'Amelia's misbehavior. A more typical chronicle which makes mention of monastics in communal offices comes from Parma, where an anonymous writer recorded, matter-of-factly, that in 1292 the commune ordered that Cistercian brothers of the neighboring monastery of Chiaravalle della Colomba 'must be treasurers of the commune and overseers of the salt tax and mines' for the next five years, in return for which they were to be paid 200 *lire imperiali* a year and receive a quarter of the lands that a *dominus* Giacomo Tavernarii had left to the commune in his will.[21] Almost certainly a notary or lawyer, like Villani the anonymous Parma chronicler was close to the context he described but writing a long time later. His text continues to 1338 and fills out in later years, whereas the 1292 entry belongs to a section apparently still heavily dependent on checking through the registers of the commune.[22] He made no mention of the activity of the Humiliati, the other religious heavily involved in communal offices in Parma, who merited naming in his Chronicle only for exceptional crises, such as a lightning strike in July 1293 setting fire to one of their houses when it was full of hay, despite rain.[23] The Humiliati's activities on behalf of the commune were less newsworthy, and this lack of interest is confirmed by the silence of most other chroniclers and diarists.[24] In his *Istorie di Firenze* (covering 1380–1405), for example, Goro Dati enumerated the multiple treasury roles, including the *Cassiere di Camera* and nine different *Camarlinghi* (treasurers) employed by the Florentine commune of his day, contributing to a proud description of his city. He itemized the length of their offices and pay but did not mention that key roles

---

[20] Quote from Villani, *Nuova Cronica*, ed. Porta, iii, 268.
[21] *Chronicon Parmense, ab anno MXXXVIII usque ad annum MCCCXXXVIII*, ed. Giuliano Bonazzi, *RIS*, ix/9 (Città di Castello, 1902–04), 64: Item eo anno per commune Parme fuit ordinatum quod fratres de Claravale debent esse massarij, et masaroli laboreriorum communis, et superstantes, tam in civitate quam extra, ad doanam salis et saline communis, et ad puteos, et ad faciendum fieri salinam communis usque ad quinque annos, com [sic] salario cc librarum imperialium pro quolibet anno; et etiam ob hoc per commune Parme fuit eis largita quarta pars poderis condam domini Jacobi Tavernerij, quam sibi reliquerat in testamento suo.
[22] As suggested by Bonazzi, in *Chronicon Parmense*, ed. Bonazzi, vii.
[23] *Chronicon Parmense*, ed. Bonazzi, 65, 102, 176.
[24] For the Humiliati in Parma offices, see Frances Andrews, '*Ut inde melius fiat*: the Commune of Parma and its Religious Personnel', in *Churchmen and Urban Government* ed. Andrews with Pincelli, 45–66.

were occupied by men of religion.[25] In the next generation, the humanist scholar Leonardo Bruni, Chancellor of the Florentine Signoria from 1427 until his death in 1444, was critical of previous writers, including Villani, in his classicizing (and modernizing) *History of the Florentine People*, but also deeply interested in 'domestic conditions' and the workings of government. He made frequent use of public records and included a description of the mid-thirteenth-century administrative shifts introduced by the government of the *popolo*.[26] These had brought the introduction of Cistercians and Humiliati into the city's treasuries, so we might expect some mention, but, as James Hankins observed, Bruni viewed the state as 'the font of honor', in which citizens should be 'allowed to compete freely for honor and offices'.[27] Appointing religious on the grounds of their ecclesiastical standing would not fit this model. It is perhaps unsurprising that Bruni made no mention of the employment of religious in the Florentine treasuries, even though the practice only ended in 1436, during his own years in office.[28] The involvement of religious did not belong.

Whereas urban chroniclers might record religious officeholders in passing, or ignore them altogether, a more celebratory view is to be found in the account of a member of the Humiliati, the order from which much of the best evidence and discussion emerges, as we will see. A Milanese brother, Fra Giovanni di Brera, wrote two histories of his order. The first, inward-looking account of its origins and functioning, produced in 1419, made no mention of the brothers' urban officeholding, a reminder of its peripheral importance to religious life.[29] Two years later, however, Fra Giovanni (or a collaborator) produced an illustrated, abbreviated version of his 1419 chronicle including a pen and wash sketch portraying Humiliati as officials holding the keys of four walled towns.[30] Intent on celebrating their importance, he captioned the image with an explanation of

---

[25] Goro Dati, 'Istorie di Firenze', ed. Antonio Lanza, *Firenze contro Milano. Gli intellettuali fiorentini nelle guerre con i Visconti (1390–1440)* (Florence, 1991), 211–300 at 288. As it survives, this section of the chronicle has both omissions and later interpolations. Lanza, *Firenze contro Milano*, 96.

[26] Leonardo Bruni, *History of the Florentine People*, ed. and trans. Jim Hankins (3 vols, Cambridge, MA, 2001, 2004), i, book 2, 108–11. For Bruni's interest in the workings of government see, for example, i, book 3, 294–7 (on the reforms of 1282); i, book 4, 348–53 (on the Standard-Bearer of Justice); or ii, book 5, 72–3, 150–1 on sortition of magistrates (of which he disapproved) replacing voting in 1323 and then later adjustments.

[27] Hankins, 'Introduction', in Bruni, *History of the Florentine People*, ed. Hankins, i, xix.

[28] Florence, Archivio di Stato, provvisioni, registro 127, fol. 152v (17 August 1436).

[29] Transcribed in Girolamo Tiraboschi, *Vetera Humiliatorum Monumenta* (3 vols, Milan, 1776–8), iii, 229–86. See also Luigi Zanoni, *Gli Umiliati nei loro rapporti con l'eresia, l'industria della lana ed i Comuni nei secoli XII e XII* (Milan, 1911), 248–9.

[30] Milan, Biblioteca Ambrosiana, MS G 301 inf., *Chronica fratris Iohannis Braidensis*, fol. 30. For 'canevari/us', see below, note 33. On Fra Giovanni, see Giovanni Mercati, 'Due ricerche per la storia degli Umiliati', *Rivista di storia della chiesa in Italia* ii (1957), 168–94 at 177–8; Frances Andrews, *The Early Humiliati* (Cambridge, 1999), 12 and Lucia dell'Asta, 'Documenti e antichi archivi degli Umiliati a Milano', *Aevum* 87 (2013), 441–513.

how the brothers had been employed in urban communes in Lombardy. While finalizing the text, however, either he or a rubricator crossed out a few words, changing the interpretation:

How the Humiliati brothers in several cities of Lombardy carried out the office of treasurer for the supplies of cities, and they did not enter office by the means of tribute but were given the keys of stores because of ~~the goodwill and~~ trust ~~with which they were regarded~~.[31]

Fra Giovanni chose to underscore two features: that his brothers had not carried out these tasks for a reward and had been assigned them out of trust (*confidentia*). He went on to add that the superiors of four houses had been involved in these tasks over a long period, in Bergamo, Como, Tortona and Milan itself, communes he perhaps selected 'among the many other cities' he could have named not just because they were all in *Lombardia* but also because all were within fifty miles of the Brera.[32]

By the time fra Giovanni was writing, his order was shrinking and no longer regularly committed to communal offices; indeed, he described their activities using the past tense. In naming only superiors (prelates and provosts) he overstated the standing of most of the men directly engaged as officeholders and seems to have had only a vague idea about the positions they held. Treasurers did much more than hold the key to the stores, which is the more narrowly monastic meaning of *canevarius* (or *caneparius*).[33] Although other names were also used (*camerarius, clavarius, massarius*), the *officium canevarie* designated the communal treasury in various northern towns, including Milan, as fra Giovanni must have known. When these brothers held keys, it was more often to money chests. The mismatch again suggests that memories were fading, and that fra Giovanni was beginning to shape practice to match what he 'knew' of his order, assuming earlier brothers thought like him. What mattered primarily to fra Giovanni was the expression of trust (*confidentia*) in the Humiliati. The crossing out of *benivolentia* is intriguing, but it was hardly a generous act to assign the work to the brothers. Renunciation of personal property was central

---

[31] Milan, Biblioteca Ambrosiana, MS G 301 inf., fol. 30: Capitulum xxxvi. Qualiter fratres humiliati in quam pluribus ciuitatibus lumbardie exercebant officium caneuarie circa moniciones ciuitatum, et hoc non per vadum tributi ad officium accedebant sed ex ~~beniuolentia et~~ confidentia ~~quam erga habebatur~~ claues monicionem dabantur. Also transcribed in Zanoni, *Gli Umiliati*, 336–45 at 344. For *vadum tributi* as *modum tributi*, see Girolamo Tiraboschi, *Vetera Humiliatorum Monumenta*, i, 171.

[32] Milan, Biblioteca Ambrosiana, MS G 301 inf., fol. 30: Scilicet prelato Brere per commune Mediolani, atque domus communis per commune Pergami, proposito de Rondenario per commune de Cumis et sancti Marci Tertone per eiusdem commune et sic [diu?] pluribus aliis ciuit[atibus]. Zanoni, *Gli Umiliati*, 344. 'diu' appears to be a non-scribal intervention.

[33] Charles Du Cange, *et al.*, *Glossarium mediae et infimae latinitatis*, édition augmentée (10 vols, Niort, 1883–7), ii, col. 72.

to the Humiliati, as to most monastic ideals.[34] Paying 'tribute' to acquire offices and earn from them, such as by farming taxes, was common for laymen but would not have suited our brother's model of his order, nor, arguably, that of those who may have commissioned his chronicle. He saw being worthy of trust (*confidentia*) on the other hand, as an entirely appropriate ambition for a religious and his community.

By the end of the Middle Ages, historical explanations of the employment of religious in communal office thus included factional change, prevention of fraud, and trust. Accounts might offer only rudimentary causes and explanation, and details had begun to fade, but their analyses are worth bearing in mind as we paddle downstream, when the practice itself largely disappeared along with communal forms of government and those writing necessarily became less personally implicated.

1450–1800

In the early modern period, the continuing tradition of writing patriotic histories of urban centers slowly extended the interpretations of the role of religious in office. The prevention of fraud was certainly uppermost in the understanding of the notary, humanist historian and collector Benedetto Giovio (1471–1545). In his document-based history celebrating his hometown of Como, long-since absorbed into the duchy of Milan, Giovio wrote approvingly of the Humiliati of their leading house in Rondineto playing a crucial role in its commune's smooth workings:

During the times of the commune of Como, regular brothers and above all [the Humiliati] took care of the weights and of their offices, by which the frauds of artisans were curbed, and property that creditors confiscated from debtors that could not safely be settled was deposited with the brothers of Rondineto.[35]

Giovio, writing in the early sixteenth century, took for granted the status of the Humiliati of Como as a safe pair of hands in the face of transactional risks. Within forty years, however, the male order of the Humiliati had been suppressed by Cardinal Carlo Borromeo, not only because their numbers had dwindled almost to nothing, but also following a scandalous attempt on the cardinal's life by one of their number. This disastrous end did not affect accounts of their earlier involvement in urban offices, but it is striking that fuller justifications began to appear in the following century.

By the seventeenth century, it was 'esteem' that emerged as an explanatory key. In his 'Annals of Alessandria' published in the 1660s, the patrician and historian Girolamo Ghilini (1589–1668) made several references to the appointment of

---

[34] Andrews, *Early Humiliati*, 178–9.
[35] Benedetto Giovio, *Historiae patriae libri duo: storia di Como dalle origini al 1532* (Venice, 1629, repr. Como, 1982), 221.

Humiliati to offices in this medieval city. He first interpreted the commune's reliance on the local provost of the order to provide a brother to serve as the 'Ragionato del Comune', allowed to be present at council meetings, as a 'sign of honourable status (*onorevolezza*) and recognition' towards them and added that because of the 'great esteem' of the commune they handed the key to each of their fortresses to the same provost, 'so that without his consent they could not be opened'. There is an obvious parallel here with Fra Giovanni's account of the Humiliati holding the keys of supplies in several communes. Ghilini then added that the Alessandria commune conceded the 'privilege' that those collecting tolls on the public gates of the city and on the bridge over the river Tanaro should be Humiliati, chosen by the provost, a privilege that had since been removed with changes in the 'stato di essa città'.[36] Ghilini's use of 'privilege' suggests that he saw officials as men of status, or viewed these tasks as a beneficial source of income through farming the tolls. In either case, conditions were now different. Ghilini placed all three activities under 1189, however, which is improbably early both for the history of communal officialdom, and for the history of the Humiliati, who had been condemned as heretics just five years earlier and were not readmitted by the papacy until 1201. It is unlikely that the citizens of Alessandria, refounded in 1168 by an alliance closely aligned with the popes, would have ignored the brothers' excommunicate status. There is, though, later evidence for Alessandria selecting its treasurers and other officials through the Humiliati provost.[37]

Ghilini presumably misread the dates on his first sources, but he pursued a similar interpretation in his description of a decision of the communal council in 1492 assigning responsibility for selecting the wardens of the river Bormida to the provost of the Humiliati. The religious superior was to identify men who would regulate the distribution of water to the benefit of the commune and its citizens and ensure the 'equal' irrigation of fields. Ghilini accounted for this choice by reference to the individual merits of the local provost and the good opinion that the Alessandrini 'had always had for the order'.[38] Strong personal and collective relationships combined to explain the decision.

Giovio and Ghilini are typical of a cohort of urban historians writing in the sixteenth and seventeenth centuries (and later): locally engaged, keen to document the history of their own communities and their virtues and assuming that office was a matter of high status.[39] The same period also saw large, documentary histories of the religious orders, including a calendar of papal bulls issued to the Augustinian Hermit friars prepared by friar Lorenzo Empoli,

---

[36] Girolamo Ghilini, *Annali di Alessandria overo le Cose accadute in essa città... dall'anno dell'origine sua sino al 1659* (Milan, 1666), 13 (1189).
[37] *Statuta communitatis Novariae anno mcclxxvii lata*, ed. Antonio Ceruti, *Historiae Patriae Monumenta* (22 vols, Turin, 1876), 16/i, Leges municipales i, 549–50.
[38] Ghilini, *Annali di Alessandria*, 114 (1492).
[39] See below, notes 49–50, and, for a much later example, the work of the Pavian nobleman Giuseppe Robolini (1768–1840), *Notizie appartenenti alla storia della sua patria* (6 vols in 5, Pavia, 1823–38).

or the eight-volume *Annales Minorum* of the Irish Franciscan, Luke Wadding (1588–1657), re-edited and published in the early eighteenth century. Wadding's calendar of papal documents included bulls such as *Pia desideria*, issued by Alexander IV in 1255 protecting penitents from being required to 'accept public or private secular offices' ('recipere publica vel privata officia secularia').[40] Empoli and Wadding were early practitioners of a type of document collecting that still continues, including by members of the other main orders whose medieval brethren had been implicated in communal offices, whether or not directly in the treasury or in stipendiary positions. The first half of the eighteenth century, for example, saw the publication of systematic calendars of papal bulls for both the Dominicans and the Franciscans, giving direct access to papal decisions on questions of engagement with the world beyond the cloister.[41] These did not, however, add to the cases of interest here.

The accumulation of evidence and shifts towards more expert history writing in the eighteenth century built on the findings of previous writers but began variously to modify their accounts. In his famously extensive collection of sources and dissertations on medieval Italy Ludovico Muratori (1672–1750), parish priest and librarian of the Este dukes of Modena, included brief mention of the employment of religious which moved beyond a single urban context and raised both the quality of the information and the sophistication of the analysis.[42] He first noted the political interventions of medieval religious and then specified those he had found engaged in communal urban offices in thirteenth- and fourteenth-century Modena and Ferrara. These were Mendicants and Humiliati involved in collecting taxes, supervising commercial measures, overseeing elections, serving as treasurers or proctors, collecting tolls, or selecting the laymen to take responsibility for food supply. Muratori accounted for this by referring once again, if in generic terms, to admiration for the religious involved, but he also seems to have been the first post-medieval writer to articulate the gap between religious profession and urban officeholding:

So great was also the esteem for these pious men, that their counsel, authority, and energy were very often introduced in political affairs, and especially in settling the public discords of citizens, in establishing treaties and peace. Indeed, what is

---

[40] *Bullarium ordinis eremitarum S. Augustini*, ed. Lorenzo Empoli (Rome, 1628); Luke Wadding, *Annales Minorum* (25 vols, 2nd ed., Rome, 1731–1886), i, 393, 550 (*Pia Desideria*, 27 April 1255).

[41] *Bullarium Carmelitanum*, ed. Eliseo Monsignano (2 vols, Rome, 1715–18) (vols 3–4 added by Ioseph Alberto Ximenez [Rome, 1768]); *Bullarium ordinis f[ratrum] praedicatorum*, ed. Thomas Ripoll (8 vols, Rome, 1729–40); *Bullarium Franciscanum*, ed. Giovanni Giacinto Sbaraglia et al. (4 vols, Rome, 1759–68). Calendars for the Augustinian Hermit Friars and the Servites were completed much later: see *Bullarium ordinis eremitarum sancti Augustini. Periodus formationis (1187–1256)*, ed. B. van Luijk (Würzburg, 1964) and *Bullarium ordinis servorum sanctae Mariae*, ed. Andrea Dal Pino (Rome, 1974).

[42] Ludovico Antonio Muratori, *RIS* (23 vols, 1723–51), and Ludovico Antonio Muratori, *Antiquitates italicae medii aevi sive Dissertationes [...]* (6 vols, Milan, 1738–42; new edition, 17 vols, Arezzo, 1777–80).

surprising is that communes used their efforts even in those offices of the state which seem foreign to the profession of a religious man. In the commune of Mantua... [list of examples]. Behold what faith was to be had in the probity of religious men of that time.[43]

Muratori conveyed amazement at both the levels of trust involved and the probity of medieval religious. He thought religious had acted and been assessed 'differently' in the Middle Ages. His surprise either that 'offices of the state' were occupied by religious men or that religious could be relied upon (or both) appears as much as a comment on his own period as on the medieval evidence he had uncovered. It bears comparison with later assumptions about a medieval 'Age of Faith'. Other writers were engaging with these topics in these years, but as a key figure in the emergence of modern Italian history writing, Muratori's decades-long project, publication of uncountable records and discursively critical approach in his dissertations ensured his multi-volume works circulated widely and long enjoyed a reputation as examples of rigor.[44] The *Antiquitates* became the reference point for this subject as for many others.

A near contemporary to Muratori who offered an illuminatingly alternative approach, though in a work with much smaller circulation, was Abbot Giovanni Ludovico Lucchi, author of a documentary history of the Benedictine Badia Leonense, south of Brescia, published in 1759. Lucchi also adopted esteem and trust as his twin explanatory frames but with different implications. He reported on the dismal circumstances of the Badia in 1351 by quoting a charter documenting an imposition of eighty lire which the monks had left unpaid, because either they could not raise the funds, or they did not think payment was legal. As a result, Humiliati brothers, acting as 'exactors of communal property', had seized food, furnishings, and other moveable property, leaving the monks feeling 'exiled from their own house'. Lucchi linked this to thirteenth-century statutes of Brescia requiring two brothers of the Humiliati to be sent with the armies of the commune to handle all payments and keep written records. He concluded, 'from this it is clear that the administrators of Brescian affairs had not only a great opinion of the faith (or trust, *fides*) of the Humiliati, but also the conviction that it was permissible for the Humiliati to lend their service to the state in such matters'.[45] Abbot Lucchi does not appear to have shared this

---

[43] Muratori, *Antiquitates Italicae medii aevi*, xiii, 219–20: Tanta etiam fuit ejusmodi piorum hominum existimatio, ut in politicis negotiis, ac praesertim in civium publicis discordiis sedandis, in foederibus & pacibus statuendis, illorum consilium, auctoritas, & industria saepissime interponeretur. Immo quod mirere, eorum opera utebantur in iis etiam Reipublicae muneribus, quae a religiosi hominis professione aliena videantur. In *Mutinensis* Republica... En quanta fides haberetur probitati religiosorum hominum temporis illius.

[44] In the same years Giovanni Benedetto Mittarelli and Anselmo Costadoni documented all references to officeholding Camaldolese brothers they came across, without comment, in *Annales Camaldulenses* (7 vols, Venice, 1755–73), see for example, v, 338, 373.

[45] *Monumenta Monasterii Leonensis Brevi Commentario Illustrata* (Rome, 1759), 83: 'ex quo constat, curatoribus rerum Brixianarum non solum magnum fuisse opinionem de

assessment, whether out of partisan interest in the fate of the Badia Leonense, or as an early modern Benedictine reading the rules of the religious life.

By contrast to Lucchi, the Florentine Jesuit Giuseppe Richa (1693–1761), author of a richly illustrated history of the churches of his city, provided documentation which presented a *quid pro quo* between the Humiliati of Ognissanti and the commune (not unlike the Chronicle of Parma's account of the deal with local Cistercians), one which in Richa's view demonstrated 'that our republic always held the Humiliati in consideration'. He based this assessment on the settlement of a dispute between the Badia di Settimo and Ognissanti over rainwater runoff across their lands, resolved by a decision that the commune would build an underground drain at its own expense, because 'the monks of Settimo and the Humiliati [...] served the commune on all those occasions that were needed and for this they suffered many inconveniences and hardships'. Richa linked this in turn to the honors paid to the Humiliati (*onori fatti dalla Repubblica ai nostri Umiliati*), notably as treasurers of the commune, culling examples from 1320 and 1329 before adding a much later case of a Humiliati serving as ambassador for Florence in 1406.[46] Although 'onor/honor' might also imply 'office', the phrasing suggests Richa, like Ghilini, understood urban officeholding as a privilege.

In the decade after Richa and Lucchi, another Jesuit, Girolamo Tiraboschi (1731–94), now best known for his multi-volume history of Italian literature, began a more systematic pursuit of the records of the Humiliati, prompted by his appointment in 1755 as professor of rhetoric at the Brera, the most prominent of the Milanese houses of the suppressed male order, which still held their archives. The success of his three-volume documentary history, published between 1766 and 1768, contributed to his appointment in 1770 as prefect of the Este Library in Modena, the position earlier occupied by Muratori.[47] By the nature of his project Tiraboschi was particularly concerned to identify who the religious involved were and how their employment by communes fit into their religious ethos. He linked the employment of Humiliati brothers in communal governments with the benefits of the brothers' fame as wool workers and, like Muratori and Richa, took for granted that this choice was based on esteem, while also, like Ghilini, assuming their interest in the common good:

For while the art of wool-making and cloth-weaving were celebrated for the Humiliati and were perceived to be of great benefit to the Republic, it was thought that it would be advantageous if other tasks were also entrusted to them that would require men of integrity and faith, and who were concerned only for the public interest.[48]

---

fide humiliatorum, sed etiam persuasionem, licere humiliatis commodare operam suam civitati in huiusmodi negotiis'.

[46] Giuseppe Richa, *Notizie istoriche delle chiese Fiorentine: divise ne' suoi quartieri* (10 vols, Florence, 1754–62), iv: *Del quartiere di S. Maria Novella*, ii, 256–7.

[47] Enrico Zucchi, 'Tiraboschi, Girolamo', *Dizionario Biografico degli Italiani* 95 (2019), online.

[48] Girolamo Tiraboschi, *Vetera Humiliatorum Monumenta*, i, 168–9: Cum enim hac

Tiraboschi did not leave it at this, but sought direct evidence of the tasks the Humiliati took on, gathering together the accounts of earlier writers, and turning to contemporaries such as Giorgio Giulini (1714–80), from whose letters and unpublished work he also frequently quoted.[49] He thus documented members of the order active on behalf of communes both large and small, from Milan to Casale Monferrato, Siena to Paganico (in the Sienese countryside).[50] From Casale Monferrato, he recorded the 1276 appointment, by the podestà, of Fra Guglielmo di Leventino as overseer of the works on the cathedral of Sant'Evasio, replacing a Fra Alberico, and himself then renewed in office in 1305, a situation that apparently provoked a dispute between the chapter of the cathedral and the commune.[51] Tiraboschi was an acute historian of the order. He recognized that this Alessandria evidence was unclear about whether the Humiliati undertaking these tasks belonged to their First, Second, or Third orders but argued that in another case, reported to him by the director of the Strozzi library in Florence, Domenico Maria Manni (1690–1788), the overseers of the works on the walls in early fourteenth-century Florence were from the Second, and sometimes the First order. He also looked back to the Florentine chronicler Villani on the treasurers in Florence, the anonymous Chronicle of Parma on the employment of Cistercians and to Fra Giovanni di Brera on Humiliati *canevari*, checking Du Cange's dictionary of late medieval Latin to clarify the meaning of this terminology.[52]

In his second volume Tiraboschi published an important sequence of papal letters, including several issued in response to Humiliati complaints about being assigned or forced into secular offices.[53] This led him to observe that there was nothing in their rule that required them to take on these tasks and indeed that 'they denied that it was lawful for them to perform this kind of work'. Yet they were 'compelled by force', a view he linked in particular to offices he did not consider suitable for religious, such as staffing city gates.[54] His own sense of ecclesiastical propriety was clearly in play. Tiraboschi was nothing if not thorough and he outlined all the evidence at his disposal, including records sent to him by colleagues. He thus set out what could be known about this one

---

lanae faciendae, pannorumque contexendorum arte Humiliati celebrarentur, ac plurimum viderentur prodesse Reipublicae, visum est e re fore, si alia etiam munera iis committerentur, quae integros spectaeque fidei homines, ac de publica tantum utilitate sollicitos requirerent.

[49] Giorgio Giulini, *Memorie spettanti alla storia, al governo ed alla descrizione della città e della campagna di Milano ne' secoli bassi* (7 vols, Milan, 1760–5).

[50] Tiraboschi, *Vetera Humiliatorum Monumenta*, i, 169–71, thus quoted urban historians who had reported religious officeholding without commentary, including Bernardino Corio (1459–1519), *L'historia di Milano volgarmente scritta* (Padua, 1646), 209 and Girolamo Gigli (1660–1722), *Diario Sanese* (2 vols, 2nd ed., Siena, 1854), ii, 268–9, 798.

[51] Tiraboschi, *Vetera Humiliatorum Monumenta*, i, 169–71 citing an unpublished manuscript history by the provost Benedetto Collio.

[52] Tiraboschi, *Vetera Humiliatorum Monumenta*, i, 172.

[53] Published in Tiraboschi, *Vetera Humiliatorum Monumenta*, ii; discussed in Tiraboschi, *Vetera Humiliatorum Monumenta*, i, 174–7.

[54] Tiraboschi, *Vetera Humiliatorum Monumenta*, i, 174–5.

order's role in communal offices in the late eighteenth century, whether recorded by later writers, reported to him by his wide circle of correspondents, or quoted from primary sources. He also offered a first catalogue of the different tasks undertaken by the Humiliati, one that applies to most, but not all, of the orders involved: as well as providing secure storage, staffing the treasury, overseeing building works, or following the army as treasurers, this included supervising food supply and communal weights and measures and, as he put it, the 'more lowly tasks' (*vilioribus muneribus*) of collecting tolls, entrusted to them 'lest there should be any fraud in bringing in crops'.[55] Tiraboschi also repeated the implausible claims made by Ghilini, that the Humiliati had already been active in communal offices in Alessandria in 1189.[56] Despite his painstaking approach, Tiraboschi's accumulation of sources thus included some of dubious reliability, as in practice did Muratori's, but the breadth of his research allowed him to affirm that trusting the Humiliati was expected to reduce fraud.

Like Muratori, Lucchi, and many of those he quoted, Tiraboschi was working in the erudite tradition of men of the Church: a man of religion, he was interested in the history of a religious institution, not the supposed medieval obscurantism identified by contemporary Enlightenment scholars. His volumes remain a critically important source collection, well supplied with footnotes and references but in keeping with contemporary practice, he was often satisfied with secondary authority, whether men with whom he corresponded or whose books sat in the library where he worked. Perhaps the main contribution of his ten-page discussion of the subject of officeholding was to put the brothers of this order firmly on the map as communal officials, documented not just by evidence for their activities in over a dozen cities, but also through the papal letters which allowed him a greater understanding of their attitudes to urban office.[57]

1800–1950

Tiraboschi's publication was to provide the standard account for later writers, even as interpretations changed in tone. Cesare Cantù (1804–95), for example, novelist, historian, archivist and political agitator, included an almost verbatim copy of Tiraboschi's examples in an appendix to his history of Milan, noting the shared role of Cistercians and Humiliati in Siena, and arguing that these two orders' 'reputation for integrity and ability led them to be chosen by communes... for delicate offices'. He also, like Tiraboschi, pointed out their resistance and emphasized the inflicting of 'unwelcome offices' such as tax-collection and other 'burdens which were often imposed on the Humiliati' by secular authorities, frequently using violence to coerce them (a reference to communal threats

---

[55] Tiraboschi, *Vetera Humiliatorum Monumenta*, i, 176, 177.
[56] Tiraboschi, *Vetera Humiliatorum Monumenta*, i, 174.
[57] Tiraboschi, *Vetera Humiliatorum Monumenta*, I, 171–8.

to stop purchasing their goods or using their mills, as recorded in the papal privileges published by Tiraboschi, though not footnoted by Cantù).[58]

During Cantù's lifetime 'history' was emerging as a professional discipline in Italy, taught in universities, and, after unification, publicly funded. At the same time vast new collaborative projects continued to make ever more primary sources available in print, most obviously in the editions of urban statutes of the *Historiae Patriae Monumenta* published from 1838 by the 'Regia deputazione sopra gli studi di storia patria', founded by King Carlo Alberto in Sardinia in 1833, and soon followed by other regional *Deputazioni* which promoted the study of their histories and edition of sources.[59] The close of the nineteenth century also saw the foundation of the *Istituto storico Italiano per il Medio Evo* in Rome and of other learned associations designed to produce source editions and local histories, one of the most prolific being the *Società storica subalpina* founded by Ferdinando Gabotto in 1896. In the twentieth century many of these continued as either learned academies at least partially funded by the government or as associations of amateur enthusiasts. One outcome was to encourage history writing with a strong regional character (a reflection too of continuing cultural, linguistic, and political realities).

The effect of the historiographical shifts accompanying the institutional changes of the nineteenth century on perceptions of History as a subject were of course substantial, with added understanding of source criticism and the need to test the truth of claims about the past. The move towards original sources produced abundant new evidence for religious as treasurers – across all orders and communes – and led to plenty of other commentary in line with Cantù's binary approach. Amadio Ronchini (1812–90), Director of the Parma *Archivio di Stato* and editor of the city's communal statutes, chose to focus, for example, on secular hostility to the clergy in Parma and attempts to diminish their privileges and influence, which led to their exclusion from office, removal of the previously monastic treasurer and of other religious officials (with a few exceptions: religious continued as superintendents of public works and penitents were treasurers for *cercatori* and staffed communal weighing scales).[60]

A second example instead reflects the range of 'learned' opinion. In 1871, the painter Luigi Mussini, Director of the *Istituto delle Belle Arti* of Siena (from 1850), gave a lecture on the treasury book covers held in Siena with which this essay began and which were only to be reunited and catalogued in 1878.[61] His lecture was – as it happens – delivered to the members of *L'Accademia dei Rozzi*, founded in the early sixteenth century, one of the literary academies that

---

[58] Cesare Cantù, 'Gli Umiliati', in *Storie Minori* (2 vols, Turin, 1864), 2, 212–27 at 214–15.
[59] *Historiae Patriae Monumenta*, ii (Turin, 1838) was the first of four volumes of 'Leges Municipales', the last published in 1955.
[60] Amadio Ronchini, 'Preface', in *Statuta communis Parmae ab anno mcclxvi ad annum circiter mccciv* (Parma, 1857), iii–xxxiv at xxii–xxiii.
[61] See Auguste Geffroy (1820–1895), 'Tablettes inédites de la Biccherna et de la Gabella de Sienne', *Mélanges d'Archéologie et d'Histoire* 2 (1882), 403–34.

were also important fora in the development of historical writing. Considering the employment of Cistercians as treasurers in Siena, Mussini first suggested that 'at that time administrative arrangements were extremely simple', that good faith was a valid guarantee of integrity, and no one had yet dreamed of 'separating offices fatally weakening individual responsibility'. So it should not be a surprise that monks, Cistercian or Vallombrosan (he did not mention the Humiliati on the covers), were so employed since 'every type of science, even that of numbers', was almost exclusively cultivated in the cloister.[62] Mussini was an amateur historian, making a political point for his own time, but his Middle Ages were full of people thinking 'differently' about life and faith and dominated by men of the church.

As sub-disciplines of history acquired ever more stringent contours, so different approaches to the employment of religious as treasurers emerged. Three are worth touching on here: histories of law and accountancy, of communal offices (emerging out of the long tradition of urban history), and as always, of religious orders. In the 1870s and 1880s, Antonio Pertile (1830–95), professor of law at the University of Padua, produced an oft-reprinted, multi-volume history of the law in Italy compiling and synthesizing innumerable cases (and drawing extensively on the newly published editions of communal statutes). This led him to the employment of *frati* to oversee elections to communal offices, one of a number of measures 'to ensure good government', alongside exercise of the most protected offices ('gli uffici più gelosi') of custody of the public seal, the communal purse and the public archives (citing Villani) and the verification of votes, entrusted to religious 'when partisanship had destroyed all public trust'.[63] Pertile thus substantially expanded the repertoire of examples in play while also bringing the analysis back to 'trust' rather than hostility (and assuming religious were not partisan). In the 1890s a teacher of accountancy, Pietro Rigobon, produced a study of the public accounting practices of Florence in which he cited Pertile, summarized previous work but also added an alternative viewpoint. For Rigobon, the Florentine system of entrusting the custody of the treasury to religious was a sign of lively religious sentiment and 'intimate' relations between monastic orders and the commune, the slow increase in the numbers of laymen involved in part due, instead, to the gradual diminishing of both sentiment and intimacy.[64] This he supported by reference to the sixteenth-century writer Scipione Ammirato (1531–1600), 'who dated impiety in Florence to 1348' and to the simultaneity of events in 1378, when the number of secular

---

[62] Luigi Mussini, 'Le tavole della biccherna e della gabella della repubblica di Siena. Lettura. Adunanza del dì 17 luglio 1877', *Atti e Memorie della sezione letteraria e di storia patria della regia Accademia dei Rozzi*, n.s. 3 (1878), 25–36 at 28–9.

[63] Antonio Pertile, *Storia del diritto Italiano dalla caduta dell'Impero Romano alla codificazione* (8 vols, Padua, 1873–87), ii.1, *Storia del diritto pubblico e delle fonti*, 153–4, with reference to offices in Verona, Chieri, Alessandria, Casale, Lucca, Parma, Florence, and Brescia and to storage of records and valuables in Chieri, Treviso, Turin, Moncalieri, Mantua, and Ravenna.

[64] Pietro Rigobon, *La contabilità di stato della repubblica di Firenze e nel granducato di Toscana* (Girgenti, 1892), 46, 50.

treasurers increased in line with the Ciompi revolt, 'during which not even convents were spared'. 'Ideas of the renaissance were already beginning to fill the air in Florentine Society.'[65] Employment of religious in office was evidently a medieval practice, driven by proximity and faith and driven out by increasing, laudable secularism.

Twenty-five years later, another historian of accountancy, Vittorio Alfieri (1863–1930), writing about the financial offices of medieval Perugia, quoted Robolini, but stuck to the Middle Ages without hazarding opinions about post-medieval change. He suggested that Perugia, unlike other communes, did not generally use 'religious' in the treasury, preferring penitents, beguines, *pinzocheri* or Franciscan tertiaries (evoking a strictly canon-legal definition of 'religious'). Nonetheless those other cities, he argued, entrusted the treasury to religious 'out of conviction that the custody of money was safer and its handling more honest'.[66]

A year after Alfieri's book was published, Lodovico Zdekauer (1855–1924), a professor of law in Macerata, indefatigable editor of archival sources, and one of the founders of the *Commissione di storia patria di Siena*, delivered a lecture to *L'Accademia dei Rozzi* on public life in thirteenth-century Siena, based closely on his work on the *Constituto* of the commune of 1262. His account of the reasons for choosing religious as treasurers repeated familiar ideas but also introduced new features. A Cistercian monk would be chosen (he did not notice the other religious involved), he argued,

trusting that he would better resist the always seductive temptation to spend other people's money, which seems to be nobody's when it is called public; perhaps even more because they [the commune] considered the brothers smarter (*più furbi*) and more experienced in business, as they may well have been, given the grandiose and multiple business of their abbeys. The shrewd and refined faces of the treasurers, whose portraits have been preserved in the Biccherna tablets, are proof of this; nor during the course of the thirteenth century was a voice ever raised contrary to the treasurer friar.[67]

Zdekauer's reading of the *tavolette* images, while over-optimistic in identifying shared moods (let alone portraits) in the serial images of treasurers painted over generations, was nonetheless remarkable for its recognition of a political message in the visual language chosen; his allusion to the problem of 'public property' was also acute. Moreover, his authoritative status in Sienese history-writing was such that his lecture set a standard for other writers, reprinted as late as the 1960s.

In the early twentieth century, from the ever more professionalized world of archive studies came the account of the Florentine archivist and historian

---

[65] Rigobon, *La contabilità*, 50–1.
[66] Vittorio Alfieri, 'L'amministrazione economica dell'antico comune di Perugia', *Bollettino della società Umbra di storia patria* 2 (1896), 379–472 at 398.
[67] Lodovico Zdekauer, *La vita pubblica dei Senesi nel dugento. Conferenza tenuta il 10 Aprile 1897* (Siena, 1897, anastatic reprint Bologna, 1967), 18–19.

Demetrio Marzi (d. 1920), who undertook a history of the Florentine chancery that began life as his archival studies thesis. In the vast tome he ultimately published in 1910, Marzi described the close ties that then existed 'between church and learning' and the 'vigilance and protection that the Church provided for all forms of knowledge', so that almost all men of learning and authority were clergy, an approach echoing Mussini's. This led him to admire the constancy with which the chancery remained a secular institution (specifically its *laicità*).[68] In Florence, the wondrous *laicità* of the chancery was however broken, Marzi argued, when the communal seal was stolen by a podestà, the episode narrated by Villani. Only then, according to the Florentine archivist, did the inadequacy of the endless substitution of lay officials become evident. For Marzi the laymen had been too closely dependent on the power of the *Signori*, not constrained by any other powerful bond and unable to provide the necessary guarantees. This, he argued, made it necessary to turn to *frati conversi*. Thus, the employment of an occasional religious in the admirably lay world of the Florentine chancery was not to be explained in terms of esteem or learning but of social ties, or rather, the lack of them. Bound by religious bonds while required to live in the palace of government, *conversi* would, he surmised, '*not have been able to commit abuses* [and] would *know how to resist* the demands of men and officials, protected by their habit, their convents and the ecclesiastical hierarchy' [my italics].[69] For Marzi, it was the obligation of these *conversi* towards their superiors and their physical presence in the Palazzo that prevented abuse, as also their ecclesiastical status. The stringency of their incorruptibility (they were able to resist) was safeguarded by their personal and organizational identity as religious, while the ecclesiastical hierarchy would act as a deterrent to anyone daring to disagree with them. This thereby introduced new currents of interpretation based on organizational structures but remained tied to assumptions about a world where ecclesiastical authority was paramount (and the Church a watertight corporation, in which ideal and action were synonymous).

Whereas earlier historians signaled the esteem and trust invested in religious, Marzi, writing when the relations of the Vatican with the Kingdom of Italy remained unresolved, focused his admiration on lay institutions while yet attributing great power to clerical status. He drew a clear category distinction between laymen and *conversi* and between lay and ecclesiastical hierarchies (as, implicitly, had Muratori and other earlier writers). In doing so Marzi articulated much early twentieth-century thinking about the need for (and roots of) separation between Church and State, with the commune read as the 'state'. It was a long-lived model. By the 1980s, Julius Kirshner (one of many) would allude lightly to the 'perennial conflict between Church and state' of the fourteenth century.[70]

---

[68] Demetrio Marzi, *La cancelleria della repubblica fiorentina* (Rocca S. Casciano, 1910), 383.
[69] Marzi, *La cancelleria della repubblica fiorentina*, 384.
[70] Julius Kirshner, 'Storm Over the "Monte Comune": Genesis of the Moral Controversy

Marzi's approach was deeply (and appropriately) hierarchical. The mechanisms that forged secular compliance or its absence, were determined by social chains of dependence just as ecclesiastics were protected by their bonds within the church. But his energy was directed at explaining what he considered the anomalous employment of religious. His more famous contemporary, the German journalist and historian Robert Davidsohn (1853–1937), whose project embraced the full scope of Florentine history, necessarily observed a wider range of activities involving religious, including not just their role in the treasury and arsenal but also, from the fourteenth century, in the coordination of spying.[71] Davidsohn concluded that in the treasury at least, the employment of religious 'was a measure that must have proven itself at least with regard to the personal honesty of the religious... seeing that both the Ghibellines, lords of Florence after Montaperti (1260), and the Guelfs, when they returned to power [in 1282 with the *secondo popolo* and the creation of the priorate of the Guilds], continued for more than twenty years to employ monks of the same two monasteries'. Setting aside the fact that such activities were, à la Muratori, 'remote from the spiritual duties of these men', Davidsohn suggested, in contrast to Marzi, that the religious in the treasury ended up by provoking the criticisms of the Florentines, 'apparently because they lacked sufficient determination in the face of the influence and arbitrariness of magnates and the rich'. This assessment was based on a shift in practice in 1289 which in fact led to the continued employment of religious, so his logic was weak.[72] It was nonetheless a substantial breach in the wall surrounding historians' assumptions that clergy were necessarily suited to the task and always trusted.[73]

Meanwhile, just a year after Marzi's life's work was printed and while Davidsohn was in the process of publishing his volumes on Florence, Luigi Zanoni, a Milanese student of Gioacchino Volpe, produced the book of his thesis on the early Humiliati that included an extended discussion of their employment in communes.[74] Explicitly starting from but vastly expanding Tiraboschi's account of the order, and aiming to offer 'new conclusions', Zanoni identified generic categories of activity based mostly on statutes from cities in the Po valley and fleeting reference to Florence, Orvieto, Perugia and Siena.[75] He identified the 'completely contrasting behaviour of the Commune in relation

---

Over the Public Debt of Florence', *Archivum Fratrum Praedicatorum* 53 (1983), 219–76 at 222.

[71] Robert Davidsohn, *Geschichte von Florenz* (4 vols, Berlin, 1922), iv.1, 114–15.
[72] Andrews, 'Living Like the Laity?', 38–9.
[73] Robert Davidsohn, *Geschichte von Florenz*, iv.1, 110.
[74] For Volpe on heresy as a factor of 'modernization', see Enrico Artifoni, 'Medioevo come periodo e come problema: il ruolo della dimensione religiosa nella prima metà del secolo XX', *Quaderni di Storia Religiosa Medioevale* 22.1 (2019), 11–34 at 26.
[75] Zanoni, *Gli Umiliati*, x, 216–43 and appendix 3, 327–35, transcriptions of a dozen documents on the Humiliati as *massari* in Cremona. The Po valley cities Zanoni mentioned were Brescia, Como, Cremona, Milan, Novara, Parma, Pavia and Reggio Emilia.

to clerics and religious, of diffident antipathy towards the former, of trust and veneration towards the latter...'[76] He further argued that the employment of religious depended on the 'special probity' of religious, their detachment comparable to that required of a podestà, but suggested too that communes might be requiring public service in return for exemptions from taxes.[77] Zanoni also pointed out that financial offices often required wealth, so as to be able to advance large sums and refund any losses, which meant that the holder must be either a rich layman, or a religious with a convent's wealth behind him. So his reliance on notions of 'special probity' and detachment stretched only so far. Zanoni suggested, however, that from the end of the thirteenth century communes that did not move to perennial signorial rule still increasingly sought to have 'their own men' administering the vital interests of the city (except for archives and election scrutinies). His was a brilliant undertaking, despite a flawed conclusion based on what he thought was a lack of sources after 1300. It was also an 'othering' of churchmen as not belonging comparable to that adopted by Marzi (and characteristic of the period).[78]

Zanoni himself acknowledged that his considerations might apply to all religious. One effect, nonetheless, of his work, published by Hoepli in paperback in a series that could be relatively easily obtained, was eventually to confirm the Humiliati as the go-to placeholder for historians encountering religious in urban office even though most work on the order in the following decades focused on either their heretical origins, or their industrial activity.[79]

In the five hundred years from the end of the Middle Ages to the middle of the twentieth century the arguments that had been proposed by those interested in describing the 'anomalous' appointment of religious to public offices can be condensed as follows (though no one ever compiled it on paper in this way). There was exceptional esteem for and trust in the probity of religious (for Muratori, particularly Mendicants). This was matched by a need for men of respected integrity, interested only in public utility, in whose hands public money would be secure, its handling more honest, a medieval model based on faith. Such ideas further entailed the special capacity of religious, who would know how to resist, protected by their habit, convent, and hierarchy. Repetition

---

[76] Zanoni, *Gli Umiliati*, 216.
[77] Zanoni, *Gli Umiliati*, 219–20.
[78] Zanoni, *Gli Umiliati*, 242.
[79] Of the many, see Romolo Caggese, *Roberto d'Angio e i suoi tempi* (2 vols, Florence 1922), i, 77; Ellen Scott Davison, *Forerunners of St Francis and Other Studies* (Boston, MA, 1927), 168–200; Antonino de Stefano, 'Delle origini e della natura del primitivo movimento degli Umiliati', *Archivum Romanicum* 11 (1927), 31–75; Filippo Carli, *Storia del commercio Italiano*, ii: *Il mercato nell'età del comune* (Padua, 1936), 76; Robert S. Lopez, *Studi sull'economia genovese nel medio evo* (Genova, 1936), 86, 107; Gino Barbieri, *Economia e politica nel ducato di Milano: 1386–1535* (Milan, 1938), 46; Alcantara Mens, *Oorsprong en betekenis van de Nederlandse begijnenen- en begardenbeweging: Vergelijkende studie: XII^{de}–XIII^{de} eeuw* (Antwerp, 1947), 48. For a brief exception, see Pietro Torelli, *Studi e ricerche di diplomatica comunale* (Mantua, 1915), 34, 161, 247.

indicated that it worked, despite being alien to religious profession, and this was in large part because of the veneration for professed religious, not secular clergy, and the mutual distrust of the laity. The wealth of monastic houses provided collateral but after 1300 they were replaced by communes' 'own men'.

1950–2000

There was of course a substantial shift in emphasis in the second half of the twentieth century. Historians increasingly acknowledged that characterizing relations between clergy and government elites in the late Middle Ages as an encounter of extraneous men of the 'Church' with the 'State' does not reflect the evidence.[80] In Italy, these categories took shape in the nineteenth century, not the thirteenth. Nevertheless, as historians themselves worked to realize the (fundamentally Enlightenment) ambition of becoming ever more detached observers, analyzing the past on its own terms, the idea that medieval religious were employed because they too were separated from the lay mass, perhaps inevitably retained a central place in explanations.

In the second half of the twentieth century, the most in-depth work was undertaken by Italian historians of religious and monastic orders, usually exploring individual cases or contexts, sometimes renewing familiar arguments about esteem for the religious involved.[81] Two exceptions from the 1960s are worthy of note. In 1963 the German medievalist Norbert Kamp (1927–99), observing that in Viterbo in the second half of the thirteenth century, Cistercian monks from the nearby abbey of San Martino al Cimino were repeatedly elected as communal *camerari*, argued that this was 'in order above all to have experts in the administration of municipal finances who were unrelated to the internal struggles of faction and [significantly] social class'.[82] The other exception, from 1964, was a brief contribution by Paolo Brezzi (1910–98) a medieval historian who was later to be elected as a communist senator in the Italian Parliament (1976–83), provoking strong disagreements among colleagues about who should be writing ecclesiastical history and how.[83] Considering relations between monasteries and communes in Piedmont, Brezzi outlined some general patterns in interactions between monastic patrimonial lordships and neighboring

---

[80] See for example, Mario Sbriccoli, 'Conclusioni', in *Gli statuti delle città: l'esempio di Ascoli nel secolo XIV*, ed. Enrico Menestò (Spoleto, 1999), 165–79 at 178.
[81] Enzo Salvini, 'I Cistercensi e il Comune di Firenze nel Trecento', *Notizie Cistercensi* 1 (1968), 179–83 at 180 on particular admiration for the Cistercians.
[82] Norbert Kamp, *Istituzioni comunali in Viterbo nel medioevo* (Viterbo, 1963), 24. Cited by Eleonora Rava, 'On the Trail of Religious in the Medieval Communes of Viterbo and Tuscia', in *Churchmen and Urban Government*, ed. Andrews with Pincelli, 201–18 at 206.
[83] See Antonio Rigon, 'Paolo Sambin e la 'Rivista di Storia della Chiesa in Italia', *Rivista di Storia della Chiesa in Italia* 58 (2004), 381–89 at 388. Cited in Agostino Paravicini Bagliani and Neslihan Şenocak, 'A View of the Historiography', in *A People's Church. Medieval Italy and Christianity 1050–1300*, ed. Agostino Paravicini Bagliani and Neslihan Şenocak (Ithaca, NY, 2023), 1–20 at 9.

communities, such as the erosion of monastic lands and rights by expanding urban claims. At the close of his paper, he proposed that another study might be made of the 'well-known' custom of giving monks the communal treasury, or having urban archives held in monastic houses, a case that 'still has a connection with politics, even though it starts and ends with ethical ideals'. For Brezzi, this arose because there was 'faith in the honesty and impartiality of those people dedicated to God, even though there was no intention, with that gesture, to include them in daily activities or give them direct responsibility in civil administration'. Brezzi went on to suggest research was needed to identify personal origins (urban or rural), familial circumstances and how far individual monks maintained ties with family or co-citizens, a necessary element for understanding the nature of the interactions of monastery and city.[84] He thus set an agenda for research which recognized the importance of personal relations in constructing power.

In the 1970s, no doubt in part inspired by the interest in the laity of Vatican II, but also by the valiant labors of the Belgian historian and theologian Gilles Gérard Meersseman (1903–08) in publishing the critical sources, major new studies focused on lay piety and penitents, several of which made mention of communal office holding by religious.[85] Already in 1968, a Capuchin friar and historian of the Church, Stanislao da Campagnola (1929–2012) writing on Perugia (where he taught at the university), viewed it as an 'interesting case of socio-religious collaboration with the new Mendicant orders', one that he believed was otherwise found only in a few communes of *Lombardia*, where 'the administrations used another religious institution with quite a few affinities with the Mendicant orders: the Humiliati', a clue to the continuing influence of Zanoni's (and Tiraboschi's) work.[86] For da Campagnola, officeholding was a by-product of Mendicant mentalities (those of his own order). In the same years, Raoul Manselli (1917–84), whose work ranged very widely but included major contributions to the histories of Christianity and religiosity, briefly summarized the activity of the Humiliati as treasurers and noted their engagement in the delicate handling of the goods of the banished, or organizing *estimi* and *catasti*,

---

[84] Paolo Brezzi, 'Il contributo dei Monasteri piemontesi alla vita dei Comuni della Regione', in *Monasteri in Alta Italia dopo le invasioni saracene e magiare (sec. X–XII)* (Turin, 1966), 315–26 at 326.

[85] Gilles Gérard Meersseman, *Dossier de l'ordre de la pénitence au xiiie siècle* (Fribourg, 1961). See also, among multiple later contributions, Lino Temperini, 'Il penitente francescano nella società e nella chiesa, nei secoli XIII–XIV', in *La 'Supra montem' di Niccolò IV (1289). Genesi e diffusione di una regola. Atti del 5º convegno di studi Francescani*, ed. Raffaele Pazzelli and Lino Temperini (Ascoli Piceno, 1987), 325–80; Antonio Rigon, 'Frati minori e società locali', in *Francesco d'Assisi e il primo secolo di storia francecana*, ed. Attilio Bartoli Langeli and Emanuela Prinzivalli (Turin, 1997), 259–81 at 273–5.

[86] Stanislao da Campagnola, 'Gli ordini religiosi e la civiltà comunale in Umbria', in *Storia e arte in Umbria nell'età comunale* (2 vols, Perugia, 1971), ii, 469–532; See also, *I frati penitenti di san Francesco nella società del due e trecento*, ed. Mariano d'Alatri (Rome, 1977).

the new forms of taxation developed in the thirteenth century. Manselli's short paper endorsed (without space for references), the arguments of previous historians: the importance of technical expertise, the possibility of claiming any losses against the holdings of the convent, 'which must have been at least partially used as a guarantee', and the personal honesty of religious, 'rightly considered greater than that of the laity'. He also suggested, perhaps picking up where Kamp had left off, that the Humiliati were employed by communes because of their humble social origins, from 'modest or middling backgrounds' occupying what he described as a position of 'autonomy from those in power', free of favor by any faction and disengaged from ruling groups.[87] This notion set aside Villani's direct association of officeholding with faction in Florence, and fell by the wayside once renewed research into the order underscored the bourgeois origins of many of its members.[88] It has perhaps most to tell us about Manselli's own idealizing assumptions about the status of the clergy. As a professor in the University of Rome and Director of the Centro Studi sull'Alto Medio Evo in Spoleto, his was, however, a powerful voice and his prioritizing of ideas of detachment was to remain influential.

Manselli's approach to the subject, published in 1970, shared some assumptions with the work of an American social historian, William Bowsky, whose first Sienese study, of the commune's public finances, came out in that year, though his attitude was more cautious. Considering the position of the treasurer, Bowsky both drew on conventional explanations and, knowingly or not, echoed Paolo Brezzi's recent intuition about personal ties:

It was perhaps because he served as a check over the activities of the Four [lay *provisores*] themselves, that statute required the *camerarius* to be religious, hence, hopefully, less subject to the temptations of peculation, and perhaps distant from any direct relations with the important Sienese families that held high Biccherna offices. This last is but a conjecture, however, for although the treasurers ordinarily were selected from among the Cistercian monks of San Galgano in the diocese of Volterra or from among the Umiliati, many Sienese joined those orders.[89]

Bowsky's use of 'hopefully' here indicates he was less inclined to take religious probity on trust. He did not pursue his insight about the recruitment of local men into religious orders. Nor did he make any connection with specific political contexts.

---

[87] Raoul Manselli, 'Gli Umiliati, lavoratori di lana', in *Produzione, Commercio e Consumo dei Panni di Lana (nei secoli xii–xviii)*, ed. Marco Spallanzani (Florence, 1976), 231–6 at 234–5. For the new research, see Andrews, *Early Humiliati*, 31 and *Sulle tracce degli Umiliati*, ed. Maria Pia Alberzoni, Annamaria Ambrosioni and Alfredo Lucioni (Milan, 1997).

[88] See especially, Giuseppina de Sandre Gasparini, 'Movimenti evangelici a Verona all'epoca di Francesco d'Assisi', *Le Venezie francescane*, n.s. 1 (1984), 151–62 at 154. First published in *Note mazziane* 17.2 (1982), 53–7.

[89] William M. Bowsky, *The Finance of the Commune of Siena, 1287–1355* (Oxford, 1970), 7.

The relations between urban contexts and the new religious orders of the twelfth and thirteenth centuries were a lively subject of discussion in the 1970s, stimulated in part by the work of Jacques Le Goff (1924–2014) and his students.[90] This was marked in particular, for our theme, by the collaborative project dedicated to the Mendicant orders and the towns of central Italy (c. 1220–c. 1350), led by André Vauchez at the Ecole Française in Rome, culminating in a collective volume published in 1977. Vauchez included a questionnaire drawn up by participants to structure their research, including a request for consideration of 'the role of Mendicants in local political life'. Research was to cover whether the friars' churches were used for meetings by civic powers, whether their convents received regular or occasional subventions, whether they had any influence in communal councils, participated in factional conflicts, intervened to modify statutes, and whether there were signs of hostility towards the friars.[91] It was a first serious attempt at mapping these practices across multiple centers.

Among the responses, Mauro Ronzani, a Pisan medievalist, sketched the scarce evidence for this commune in the thirteenth century, identifying not mendicants but penitents employed in collecting a tax on behalf of the commune, already in 1247, and another penitent and a Pulsanese monk of S. Michele degli Scalzi serving as communal ambassadors in 1276. He observed only that this was 'a phenomenon well known to historians of communal societies'.[92] It was instead Brigitte Szabò-Bechstein whose brief, schematic summary of relations between the commune of Siena and its religious encompassed enough evidence to redirect the focus of research. She pointed on one hand to the 'services' rendered by Mendicants for the commune, as ambassadors, treating peace, freeing prisoners, supervising transport of grain, recruiting new podestà and negotiating *cose secrete*, activities which allowed the commune to exploit the 'general esteem awakened by the new orders and their external connections'. On the other hand, she presented several reasons why the 'real services' of the Mendicants to the administration of the Siena commune never reached particularly high levels: the nature of the orders, focused on other ideals; repeated papal bulls opposed to their involvement; and the political context, which, she suggested, 'did not always allow the commune to trust the orders and their ties with the pope'. Instead, numerically much more significant in communal administration were penitents, a category of 'partial religious', 'more suited to performing communal functions' who 'enjoy[ed] particular trust from the communal authorities even if, probably for social reasons, they never accessed the prestigious role of treasurer'.[93]

---

[90] See Jacques Le Goff, 'Ordres mendiants et urbanisation dans la France médiévale', *Annales. Economies, Sociétés, Civilisations* 25 (1970), 924–65.

[91] André Vauchez, 'Introduction', to journal subsection: 'Les ordres mendiants et la ville en Italie centrale (v. 1220–v. 1350)', *Mélanges de l'École Française de Rome. Moyen Age* 89 (1977), 557–60, questionnaire at 561–2.

[92] Mauro Ronzani, 'Penitenti e ordini mendicanti a Pisa sino all'inizio del Trecento', *Mélanges de l'École Française de Rome. Moyen Age* 89 (1977), 734–41 at 734.

[93] Brigitte Szabò-Bechstein, 'Sul carattere dei legami tra gli ordini mendicanti, la

Szabò-Bechstein's foregrounding of lay penitents was repeatedly picked up in many later works. Martina Wehrli-Johns, for example, writing in the 1990s suggested that in the case of penitents, communes eventually substituted demands for taxes and military service with service in hospitals or poor-relief, care for prisoners and church buildings, or repair of bridges and walls that 'as meritorious tasks were compatible with their penitent status'.[94] For Wehrli-Johns, penitents embodied the social conscience of the commune, and it was the core ideals to which they were vowed that determined their urban activities.

We have come a long way down stream and the possible currents of discussion we might follow are multiplying fast. Instead of getting lost in the reeds of many possible new directions let us close in on a last few contributions. A conference on monasticism in communal Italy held at the Abbey of San Giacomo Maggiore in Pontida in 1995 typifies the state of play for most historians of monasticism or the religious life at the close of the twentieth century. Gregorio Penco simply observed that '*conversi* were adapted by the communes to various roles'.[95] Maria Pia Alberzoni reviewed the *locus classicus* of Humiliati engagement with the communes.[96] Most of the other papers dealt with an earlier period, but the conference is a snapshot of perceptions at this date: most historians of Italian monasticism and the religious life were aware of the role of the Humiliati in urban life in Lombardy; most were probably conscious of the comparable employment of *conversi* (if only through Villani), and most associated engagement in the communes above all with either the Humiliati or the Mendicant friars whose urban apostolate transformed the meaning of the religious life. Few had pursued the question, preferring to rely on the important studies of lay piety and penitents published in the 1970s. One exception was Giovanna Casagrande (another Perugia academic), not a participant at the Pontida conference, but whose studies of the lay penitents of Umbria collected and published in the same year fleshed out examples of their engagement in office in central Italy. Casagrande's approach was pragmatic: penitents were simply trustworthy and credible, used as needed, and benefited in turn from being deemed worthy of such roles, not to mention salaries, protection and support.[97] Another exception was Reinhard Schneider (1934–2020), whose case for the Europe-wide role

---

confraternita dei penitenti ed il comune di Siena nel Duecento', *Mélanges de l'École Française de Rome. Moyen Age* 89 (1977), 743–7.
94 Martina Wehrli-Johns, 'Voraussetzungen und Perspektiven mittelalterlicher Laienfrömmigkeit seit Innozenz III. Eine Auseinandersetzung mit Herbert Grundmanns "Religiöse Bewegungen"', *Mitteilungen des Instituts für Österreichische Geschichtsforschung* 104 (1996), 286–309 at 300.
95 Gregorio Penco, 'Monasteri e comuni cittadini: un tema storiografico', in *Il monachesimo italiano nell'età comunale. Atti del IV convegno di studi storici sull'Italia Benedettina. Abbazia di S. Giacomo Maggiore, Pontida (Bergamo), 3–6 settembre 1995*, ed. Francesco G.B. Trolese (Cesena, 1998), 5–19 at 16.
96 Maria Pia Alberzoni, 'Umiliati e monachesimo', in *Il monachesimo italiano*, ed. Trolese, 219–51 at 243–6.
97 *Religiosità penitenziale e città al tempo dei Comuni* (Rome, 1995), 166–75. See also Giovanna Casagrande, 'Religious in the Service of the Commune: The Case of

of Cistercian monks and *conversi* in the development of financial budgeting techniques included an outline of this order's gradual acceptance of the need to lend personnel to lay elites and a brief summary of Cistercian officeholding in Siena and Florence.[98] For Schneider, in the communes as elsewhere, the key was the expertise of Cistercian monks, sought-after as proficient financiers and project managers.

Alongside historians whose central concern was the religious life, the last quarter of the twentieth century also witnessed the publication of several key contributions by historians more directly engaged in communal history. Among these Richard Trexler, writing in 1978, stands out, followed (on this issue) by Philip Jones.

Richard Trexler exploited his capacious knowledge of the Florentine archives to argue for the trust function of religious in a lay world where suspicion was rife.[99] He underscored the importance of the charisma that a clerical presence brought into government. What mattered was not personal holiness (nor esteem as earlier writers might have put it) but official charisma: 'in the absence of personal charisma and noble honor in the representative elements of the regime, clerical participation acted as a guarantee. The individual religious did not need to be particularly holy or charismatic but was a functionary incorporating the official charisma of the Church.' Like Kamp, Manselli and others, Trexler saw clerical officials as 'uncompromised outsiders' but identified them with particular social roles, binding the community together and preserving its records. Like Marzi, he identified the importance of the abbot (or other superior) as the authority behind the religious official appointed. Trexler also sought to categorize the different ways religious in public life were involved as 'direct representatives of the principal of ethical objectivity' (faintly echoing Brezzi): they either handled the wealth of the community (as treasurers, tax assessors and so on) or were called upon when secrecy was particularly required (in electoral procedures, scrutinies, et al.). For Trexler, like Marzi and Davidsohn, the religious status of the official provided a guarantee for the secular society in which they operated: they made possible 'honor among thieves'.[100]

Trexler's explicit engagement with how and why religious fit into the administrative structures of the communes was picked up two decades later by Philip Jones in a short paragraph of his major account of the Italian cities. This was nonetheless a significant staging-post in the historiography of religious officeholding because (like Brezzi and Trexler) he again opened up its wider

---

Thirteenth- and Fourteenth-Century Perugia', in *Churchmen and Urban Government*, ed. Andrews, 181–200 at 185.
[98] Reinhard Schneider, *Vom Klosterhaushalt zum Stadt- und Staatshaushalt. Der Zisterziensische Beitrag* (Stuttgart, 1994), 80–5.
[99] See also Andrews, 'Introduction', in *Churchmen and Urban Government*, ed. Andrews, at 2–7.
[100] Richard Trexler, '"Honor Among Thieves". The Trust Function of the Urban Clergy in the Florentine Republic', in *Essays Presented to Myron P. Gilmore*, ed. Sergio Bertelli and Gloria Ramakus (Florence, 1978), 317–34.

significance for practices of government but did so in a book intended as a comprehensive guide to the period:

> By contrast [to a ban on usurers in office in Pisa, or lawyers in Savona], in all places clergy and religious [...] were increasingly charged with positions of trust and drawn into elections. Various typical practices and constitutional devices originated partly as checks to corruption or private interest: the growing recourse by governments and guilds to 'foreign' officials sequestered from local contacts or the custom of syndication, the democratic expedients of election by lot, rotations of offices, and *divieto* [the ban on returning to office for a fixed period]...[101]

Like Trexler, Jones juxtaposed the 'positions of trust' assigned to clergy with other attempts to limit malpractice. But in an earlier paragraph of his densely argued volume Jones had instead concluded that from the late 1100s urban governments and smaller bodies such as neighborhood associations (*contrade*) were entirely in the hands of lay citizens (*cives*):

> From the later twelfth century, bishops and other clerical magnates, dispossessed of formal dominion and the greater part of their *districtus*, withdrew or were pushed aside from government... while clerics of all ranks, though occasionally described still as *cives* (for example in a Sienese statute of 1207/8), were excluded from effective citizenship and, with some few exceptions, denied all place in communal councils and offices, notariate and bureaucracy, even general assemblies and meetings of *contrade* (unless ecclesiastical affairs were for discussion). In the communes before all states in Europe government and politics were altogether secularized – in Dino Compagni's chronicle clergy as a class do not figure.[102]

This was a deft reminder of the point made long before by Zanoni (and further articulated by others in the meantime): it was not religious who were increasingly detached, but secular clergy under the bishop, pushed out of offices they had once dominated. Jones was writing about the shrinking jurisdiction of prelates, and the absence of secular clergy, not about regulars or religious whose presence in office long remained sought-after. Forty years earlier he had himself undertaken an extended study of the finances of the Cistercian Badia di Settimo, one of the two houses to supply officials to Florence. In his 1956 essay he had proposed that entrusting positions of public responsibility to monks and *conversi* was a 'a frequent practice in the communes, where public morality was poor'.[103] He also noted that the monks of Settimo were granted somewhat precarious exemption from taxes, alongside other benefits: in 1317, the monks were promised the construction, at the expense of the commune, of an underground drain, on the urban land where their racks for drying wool

---

[101] Jones, *The Italian City State. From Commune to Signoria* (Oxford, 1997), 532.
[102] Jones, *The Italian City State*, 425.
[103] Philip Jones, 'Le finanze della Badia cistercense di Settimo nel XIV secolo', *Rivista di storia della Chiesa in Italia* 10 (1956), 91.

cloth stood (reiterating the episode identified by Richa, with the correct date).[104] Religious were not so detached after all.

After the brief mentions in Philip Jones' *magnum opus* the close of the century saw other contributions from urban historians. In 1999, Paolo Pirillo writing – like Trexler – on Florence, provided a little more context when he argued that the reasons for choosing religious as treasurers were 'evident', given that the religious replacing laymen, 'at least on a theoretical level, seemed to be able to offer an impartiality it had not previously been possible to obtain, even by entrusting the position of treasurer to an individual outside the city'.[105] In the same journal issue Paolo Grillo, writing about the Cistercians of Chiaravalle Milanese and the fragmentary evidence for men chosen to hold urban offices in mid-thirteenth-century Milan, tracked down the presence of monks in that city's treasury whose families belonged to the *popolo* and were aligned with the Della Torre (thereby opening a way to answer Brezzi).[106] A couple of years later Grillo further noted the difference in status between monks and Humiliati. Thus, he wrote, the Cistercians carved out for themselves 'a leading part in Milanese political life', based on their 'great prestige and role *super partes*' as communal treasurers and tax collectors, offices in which the monastery placed men tied to the families of the *Popolo* (who also dominated the monastic chapter in these years). Although the Humiliati did not reach these heights, they too had important responsibilities, not only storing registers but also collecting taxes and probably verifying tax declarations made to the *catasto*.[107] The Milanese Humiliati too, were closely implicated in factional politics, as both Maria Pia Alberzoni and Gabriele Archetti had earlier pointed out.[108]

In sum, by c. 2000 the arguments deployed to explain the employment of regular religious, *conversi*, tertiaries and penitents in urban offices – men some of whose images are so prominently displayed on the Siena ledgers – depended first of all on ideas about their special qualities. A further compilation of the arguments circulating might run something like this. Religious were employed as officials because they were experts in administration (people trusted the Cistercians because of their economic success), and as 'uncompromised outsiders', unrelated to faction and distant in social terms from the communal elites. This also had something to do with ethics: they expressed ethical objectivity, a check to corruption or private interest. This was, however, no longer so confidently affirmed: they were 'hopefully' less subject to temptations, and 'seemed' to

---

[104] Jones, 'Le finanze', 90–122 at 91n. For Richa, see above, note 46.
[105] Paolo Pirillo, 'I cistercensi e il comune di Firenze (secoli XIII–XIV)', *Studi storici* 40.2 (1999), 395–405 at 396.
[106] Paolo Grillo, 'Cistercensi e società cittadina in età comunale: il monastero di Chiaravalle Milanese (1180–1276)', *Studi storici* 40.2 (1999), 357–94.
[107] Paolo Grillo, *Milano in età comunale (1183–1276)* (Spoleto, 2001), 586.
[108] Maria Pia Alberzoni, 'L'esperienza caritativa presso gli umiliati: il caso di Brera (secolo XIII)', in *La carità a Milano nei secoli XII–XV*, ed. Maria Pia Alberzoni and Onorato Grassi (Milan, 1989), 201–23 at 204–5; Gabriele Archetti, 'Gli umiliati e i vescovi alla fine del duecento. Il caso bresciano', in *Sulle tracce*, 267–314 at 308.

be able to offer impartiality. Among those more interested in an ecclesiastical perspective this was understood as a collaborative activity, religious occupying fiduciary positions not necessarily on grounds of individual, personal probity but ecclesiastical charisma, needed because communal elites lacked personal charisma. The argument for distance from key families was however beginning to crack under the weight of evidence that citizens joined those same monastic houses and of family links between religious officials and particular factional identities. There was, thus, also beginning to be some practical awareness of political ties, a return to the insights of Giovanni Villani with which we began.

Conclusions

I have chosen to follow some currents and have ignored others. A different history might be written if we focused more on historians of administration in the Italian communes, though as far as I can tell, these were, like Leonardo Bruni, not much interested in the presence of religious.[109] In 1998, French medievalists held a conference asking whether there was such a thing as 'servants of the state' in the Middle Ages. The resulting papers ranged across the whole period, from bishops serving the Lotharingian crown in the ninth century to canons of Angers serving the dukes of King René in the fifteenth. Two dealt with the Italian peninsula, both by authorities on Italian communes based in French Universities: Pierre Racine (1925–2021), covering communal notaries in Piacenza in the twelfth and thirteenth centuries, and Guido Castelnuovo, on the 'social, economic and professional capital' of the corps of officials of the Savoia lands in the fourteenth and fifteenth centuries.[110] Although both Piacenza and the Savoia made use of them, neither writer made mention of religious in office. It was not what they found interesting or pertinent.

The nature of Italian historiography before c. 2000, frequently determined as it was in its resistance to wider synthesis, makes a comprehensive account impossible here too. Many of those mentioned are, moreover, much better known for other work. Vice versa, other historians not mentioned made parallel contributions. Nor were all the connections I have identified intended by those writing. This is, as I wrote at the outset, 'History in a minor key' but the implications are not minor. Following the currents of writing about religious in communal officialdom reveals local pieties and replication, but also increasingly innovative thinking. As individual writers encountered the same evidence, with or without awareness of previous historians' work, familiar ideas were revisited

---

[109] See for example, Victor Crescenzi, 'Il sindacato degli ufficiali nei comuni medievali Italiani', in *L'educazione giuridica*, iv/i, *Il pubblico funzionario: modelli storici e comparativi* (Perugia, 1981), 384–529 at 397–8.
[110] Pierre Racine, 'Le notaire au service de l'état communal italien (XIIe–XIIIe siècles)', in *Les serviteurs de l'État au moyen âge* (Paris, 1999), 63–74; Guido Castelnuovo, 'Physionomie administrative et statut social des officiers savoyards au bas Moyen Âge: entre le prince, la ville et la seigneurie (XIVe–XVe siècle)', in *Les serviteurs de l'État au moyen âge*, 181–92.

but new interpretation also emerged, and the amount of information available, including in scientifically produced new editions, increased exponentially, in turn generating more writing and new thinking. Growing institutional support, whether through library and archive positions, literary academies, *Deputazioni di storia patria* or university history departments (and the many conferences and journals these generate), as well as the publishing demands of career-building, shaped the nature of investigation. Taking it on trust, the apparently conflicting (and simplified) assumptions that people in the past either processed ideas differently (on matters not just of faith, but also propriety, the clergy and where social power and prestige lay) or thought about these things in the same way as the historians doing the writing, turn out to have been intertwined currents, variously (and confidently) adopted, not necessarily consciously, and only slowly discarded.

'Taking it on trust' had largely disappeared by 2000 and in the years since some arguments have found strength while others have withered. There is a new sensitivity to the bi-directionality of trust (from the institution to the individual and vice versa) as Forrest's work made clear.[111] The capacity for personal charisma of political leaders such as podestà and communal elites, understood not as spiritual gifts but as their ability to move others to action, to drum up support and mobilize crowds, *pace* Trexler, was already recognized in the twentieth century and its applicability to non-religious in the communes has become ever more plausible.[112]

Whereas Trexler's focus on charisma suggested that we should expect to find clerical involvement in government, this did not appear everywhere, nor were his reasons why it did, or did not, made clear (those were not the questions he was asking). As I wrote in 2004, echoing Tiraboschi, 'At no point were the ideals of the religious orders conveyed as an undertaking to engage in the daily business of secular administration.' In 2010 I suggested that religious status might be an 'object of negotiation' between city and churchmen, a fluid and contingent 'tool in the repertoire of power relations' and one that often led to churchmen living like the laity. In more recent work I have sought to understand the reasons for the presence or absence of religious in different communal contexts, dealing with the much more difficult business of arguing from silences.[113]

A few historians have continued to write on this subject. At the close of a collective volume published over a decade ago, the result of a conference which involved several of them, I wrote a brief epilogue summing up our findings and setting out the areas in need of further investigation. Having established that the employment of religious 'may never have been the result of a conscious decision,

---

[111] See above, p. 204.
[112] See Stephen J. Milner, 'Rhetorics of Transcendence: Conflict and Intercession in Communal Italy, 1300–1500', in *Charisma and Religious Authority: Jewish, Christian, and Muslim Preaching, 1200–1500*, ed. Katherine Ludwig Jansen and Miri Rubin (Turnhout, 2010), 235–50. See also the essays in *Tecniche di potere nel tardo medioevo. Regimi comunali e signorie in Italia*, ed. Massimo Vallerani (Rome, 2010).
[113] Andrews, 'Como and Padua'.

but emerged piecemeal', I suggested, building on the insights of Brezzi,[114] and Bowsky,[115] as well as the contributors to the volume, that 'what determined the difference was membership of a particular religious community: in other words, the social, familial and political ties of the [men] employed'. I also repeated my earlier observation that 'the institutional identities of religious orders were not coterminous with those of urban communities. In the gap between the two, negotiation, collaboration and tension are all evident.'[116]

Returning finally to the Sienese book covers, it is clear that some of the previous answers to the questions they raise require further elaboration, and although the evidence for such individual cases is compelling, there remain some questions that can only be answered by adopting a perspective covering the whole of communal Italy, which I plan to attempt in forthcoming work. The first of these is simply the chronology and mapping: where can this practice first be documented, why, and how did it travel? Was it channeled through religious orders, through urban officials, or by other means? At what point did a community become large enough to employ religious as officials? What role did bishops play and what was it that determined the choice of one order or another? How did different religious superiors respond? And finally, what are the dynamics that explain its disappearance? Increasing secularism cannot answer for the great variety across communal Italy, so was it the emergence of signorial rule? These are some of the questions now needing an answer.

---

[114] Brezzi, 'Il contributo dei Monasteri piemontesi alla vita dei Comuni della Regione.'
[115] Bowsky, *The Finance of the Commune of Siena*.
[116] Frances Andrews, 'Epilogue', in *Churchmen and Urban Government*, ed. Andrews with Pincelli, 348–57. Another useful summary of the conference is in Paolo Grillo, '*I religiosi al servizio dello stato (comuni e signorie, secoli XIII–inizio XIV)*', in *La mobilità sociale nel Medioevo italiano*, iii, *Il mondo ecclesiastico (secoli XII–XV)*, ed. Sandro Carocci and Amedeo De Vincentiis (Rome, 2017), 313–35 at 321–8.

II

Following Her Star: Evelyn Faye Wilson, *The Stella Maris of John of Garland*, and Making a Career in Medieval Studies in America[1]

William Chester Jordan

Louis John Paetow, professor of history at the University of California at Berkeley, died on 22 December 1928 at the age of forty-eight. Professional medievalists in the United States would long remember him as having had the potential to become the most distinguished intellectual disciple of the author of *The Renaissance of the Twelfth Century*, the legendary Charles Homer Haskins of the University of Wisconsin and subsequently Harvard.[2] When Paetow died, he orphaned his newest PhD student, Evelyn Faye Wilson. This essay addresses some singular aspects of her career in the long aftermath of her mentor's loss and the genesis of one of the seminal studies of Marian devotion in the Middle Ages, Wilson's *Stella Maris of John of Garland*.[3]

Educational Background

Evelyn or, as she preferred, E. Faye or Faye Wilson came to Berkeley indirectly from Beloit College in Wisconsin.[4] Born on 29 September 1899,[5] she graduated from Beloit in 1921 with high honors in English and with strong Latin. She

---

[1] A number of people (administrative staff, archivists, curators and librarians) facilitated my 'virtual' access to their special collections during the pandemic of 2020–2, when I was carrying out research for this essay. My thanks to them all.
[2] Edward Kennard Rand, 'The Classics in the Thirteenth Century', *Speculum* 4 (1929), 249–69 at 249–50. Paetow himself refers to Haskins as his inspiration, when the latter taught at the University of Wisconsin, before leaving for Harvard; see the 'Preface' to his dissertation 'The Arts Course at Medieval Universities with Special Reference to Grammar and Rhetoric', later published as no. 7 in *University Studies of the University of Illinois* 3 (1910), iii.
[3] *The Stella Maris of John of Garland. Edited together with a Study of Certain Collections of Mary Legends Made in Northern France in the Twelfth and Thirteenth Centuries*, ed. E. Faye Wilson (Cambridge, MA, 1946).
[4] For the biographical details that follow and supporting references, see William Chester Jordan, 'Evelyn Faye Wilson, John of Garland, and the "Invisible" Jews', forthcoming, in the festschrift for Professor Jeremy Cohen, tentatively titled *The Hermeneutical Jew*.
[5] I wish to thank Professor Cord Whitaker of Wellesley College for verifying this date

soon headed west for a job teaching high school in Portland, Oregon, but her entry-level classroom experience was unsatisfying, and over the next several years, she looked for a Masters or PhD program for training in medieval history. After overcoming some obstacles, including her father's doubts, she gained admission to Berkeley, intending to work with Paetow.[6] A year and a half after entering the program, however, Paetow died. Yet, Faye Wilson's training did not end there. Instead, for a number of reasons the two senior medievalists at Harvard, Edward Kennard Rand (E.K. Rand) and Charles Homer Haskins, both of whom had greatly admired Paetow, brought her to Cambridge, managed to get her enrolled at Radcliffe College, and mentored her, Haskins probably in his 'Mediaeval History' course, History 20c. It was at Radcliffe that she finished writing her dissertation, though the University of California-Berkeley formally granted her the PhD degree in 1930.[7]

E.K. Rand was a founder of the Medieval Academy of America (1925) and the journal *Speculum* (1926). He was also the first President of the Academy. In his 1929 Presidential Address at the Annual Meeting, he lauded the then recently deceased Paetow, deeming one of his works, *Two Medieval Satires on the University of Paris*, the winner of the Academy's aptly named Rand Prize, a 'masterpiece'.[8] He also expressed the hope that 'some younger scholar [might] arise competent to push on in the path that [Paetow] had blazed!' Here, Rand was urging a continuation of Paetow's own successes, for, as a eulogist noted, 'One of his [Paetow's] great achievements was in training and arousing the enthusiasm of students who are carrying on his work in the study of the Medieval universities.'[9] This meant that they were editing and translating difficult medieval Latin texts written in the scholastic tradition, recovering the extent of the classical legacy in the Middle Ages, and rescuing from scholarly

---

through the good offices of the faculty records archivist of Wellesley where Wilson later taught; personal email communication, 21 February 2022.

[6] She reflected on her father's attitude in an interview for the 'Centennial Historian', a collection of oral history transcripts documenting Wellesley College's history, 2; accessed online 9 April 2021 at: https://drive.google.com/drive/folders/1OOxQ9g4mh-7nEiLG7QT55I-yLSGaVKDRz.

[7] Radcliffe College, *Alumnae Directory, 1934*, 279, which indicates her status as a graduate student at the college in the academic year 1929–30 by a lower-case g, while also noting her PhD degree from Berkeley; accessed online 12 March 2021 at Harvard Mirador Viewer (https://iiif.lib.harvard.edu/manifests/view/drs:427981533$396i). See also on the professional relations among Paetow, Haskins, and Rand, the dedication page in Louis John Paetow, *Two Medieval Satires on the University of Paris*, volume 4 of the *Memoirs of the University of California* 4 (1927); Radcliffe College, *Courses of Instruction for the Year 1929–1930*, 76; accessed online 12 March 2021 at Harvard Mirador Viewer (https://iiif.lib.harvard.edu/manifests/view/drs:427992293$17i); Radcliffe College, *Catalogue of Names, 1929–1930*, 22, also accessed online 12 March 2021 at Harvard Mirador Viewer (https://iiif.lib.harvard.edu/manifests/view/drs:428016197$26i).

[8] 'The Classics in the Thirteenth Century', 250. See also the rapturous review of *Two Medieval Satires* by Anson Phelps Stokes in *American Historical Review* 34 (1929), 573–5.

[9] 'Historical News', *American Historical Review* 34 (1929), 672.

obscurity many medieval virtuoso writers of Latin prose and verse, like the university master, John of Garland.[10] It was on part of John of Garland's oeuvre, namely, his *Epithalamium* or allegorical nuptial poem on the Virgin Mary, that Wilson wrote her dissertation.[11]

Faye Wilson rose to Rand's challenge by choosing to expand her work on John of Garland in the years to come. In so doing, she proved herself loyal to Paetow's memory and unswervingly faithful to his scholarly perspectives. She was also single minded in her pursuit of a professorship that would give her the opportunity to continue her scholarly work. Wilson never married. In her own words, 'you had to make a decision as to whether you were going to get married or have a career'.[12] In the beginning, however, the prospects of a professorship for her were grim. Indeed, with the Crash and the Great Depression the times could scarcely have been worse for finding a permanent job in academia; yet, difficult as these years were, her 'persistence', according to a later assessment, paid off.[13] Temporarily, she returned from Massachusetts to the West Coast and taught briefly at an Indian school serving the Yakima tribe in Toppenish, Washington.[14]

Toppenish was an economically depressed town in a distressed region of Washington State. Economic growth, in the words of Jim Kershner, 'would not continue through the 1920s. A large sugar beet processing factory, built in 1917, closed down in 1920 when the Yakima Valley's sugar beet crop was damaged by blight. Toppenish was also hurt by the more general farming slump of the 1920s.'[15] Faculty who taught at Indian schools, like the one on the reservation,

[10] Rand, 'The Classics in the Thirteenth Century', 250.
[11] Evelyn Faye Wilson, 'A Study of the Epithalamium in the Middle Ages: An Introduction to the *Epithalamium beate Marie virginis* of John of Garland' (PhD dissertation, Department of History, University of California-Berkeley, 1930).
[12] While many female faculty identified themselves as 'Mrs", Wilson always appeared as Miss in the Wellesley College catalogues; see for example *Bulletin of Wellesley College, 1960–1961*, 74, accessed online 16 November 2020 at https://archive.org/details/cataloguenumber01960well/mode/2up?q=Wilson. I have not discovered Wilson's personal papers, if they survive, and have therefore had to piece together my portrait of her career from documentary evidence, including official institutional records, other people's reminiscences of her and the like.
[13] *Bulletin of Beloit College*, July 1956, 2, refers to her 'persistence' in its report of her receiving a distinguished alumna award that year; accessed online 16 November 2020 at https://archive.org/details/cataloguenumber01956well/mode/2up?q=Wilson. Much of the evidence on Wilson's career after receiving her PhD comes from the *Annual Reports Number of the Wellesley College Bulletin* 31.1 (1941), 34, but the report of her Beloit award also appeared in *Maine Alumnus*, which celebrated her earlier service on the University of Maine faculty; *Maine Alumnus* 38 (November 1956), 7, accessed online 12 March 2021 at Maine Alumnus, Volume 38, Number 2, November' 1956 (umaine.edu) (https://digitalcommons.library.umaine.edu/cgi/viewcontent.cgi?article=1462&context=alumni_magazines), and the *Wellesley Townsman*, 21 June 1956, 12, accessed online 12 March 2021 at http://digital.olivesoftware.com/Olive/APA/Wellesley/default.aspx#panel=browse.
[14] Helen Schuster, *The Yakima* (New York and Philadelphia, PA, 1990).
[15] Jim Kershner, 'Toppenish – Thumbnail History', accessed online 1 November 2022

and indigenous students who attended them endured excruciatingly difficult conditions.[16] Although settled in Toppenish, Wilson was still eager for a career in higher education and gambled that a prestigious fellowship might aid her in doing so. She applied for a residency at the distinguished School of Classical Studies of the American Academy in Rome in pursuit of her goal.[17] Yet, she also hedged her bets, for the School existed to help expand the knowledge base of *high school teachers* of Latin, a career path that she also knew she might have to resume.[18] She was accepted, and managed to meet cost requirements because she was a graduate alumna of the University of California, which along with a few other institutions made financial contributions to the Academy in return for a reduction of residency fees for those of its graduates who attended the School of Classical Studies.[19]

The greatest benefit to Wilson's future scholarly career may not have been residency at the Academy per se, where a kind of risqué culture flourished, even if it did not prevail.[20] The singular benefit was the required travel, 'designed', as the descriptive materials explained, 'to give American high school Latin teachers direct experience with places in Italy associated with antiquity and return with a renewed enthusiasm for and greater understanding of their subjects. [Over a period of eight months] participants… visited sites associated with Caesar, Cicero, Ovid, and Virgil in the morning, followed by an afternoon lecture on Roman history or literature as well as instruction in modern Italian.'[21]

Wilson, however, had to cut her travels short when she received word of a temporary job offer to fill in for the medieval historian, James Field Willard, on the faculty of the University of Colorado at Boulder. An expert on English institutions, Willard had taken his PhD at the University of Pennsylvania, where he was a student of Dana C. Munro, which gave him a Louis John Paetow connection as well. Paetow had edited a volume of essays in Munro's honor

---

at Toppenish – Thumbnail History – HistoryLink.org (www.historylink.org/File/10400).
[16] David Adams, *Education for Extinction: American Indians and the Boarding School Experience, 1875–1928* (Lawrence, KS, 1995), 89–90.
[17] Microfilm reel 5785, of the archives of the American Academy in Rome (scanned for me by Sebastian Hierl, Drue Heinz Librarian; personal email, 27 May 2021).
[18] 'From the Archives: Classical Summer School', *American Academy in Rome Magazine* (Fall/Winter 2021), 6.
[19] See the Academy's *Annual Report* covering the years 1918–31, 62, 64, 75 and 82, accessed online 27 May 2021 at https://babel.hathitrust.org/cgi/pt?id=ien.35556008853590&view=1up&seq=568&q1=Evelyn.
[20] On the culture of the Academy at the time, including the 'problem with fellows [of the Academy] sneaking women into Villa Aurelia [its exhibition palazzo] during the night', and attempts to curb such behavior, see the American Academy in Rome records, 1855–2012, Series 4.1, Box 33, Folder 27, description accessed online 27 May 2021 at Series 4 | A Finding Aid to the American Academy in Rome records, 1855–2012 | Archives of American Art, Smithsonian Institution (si.edu) (www.aaa.si.edu/collections/american-academy-rome-records-6320/series-4. Women, it has been noted, 'outnumbered men by three or four to one' in the Classical School; 'From the Archives: Classical Summer School', 6.
[21] 'From the Archives: Classical Summer School', 6.

that appeared in 1928 to which Willard, as a fellow student, contributed.[22] I infer that knowledge of Faye Wilson's quality had probably come to Willard from Paetow (or indirectly from Haskins or Rand). Preparing, as Willard was doing, for a two-year combined sabbatical and fellowship leave to conduct archival research in Europe (1930–2), a word to his Colorado colleagues in favor of hiring Wilson as a temporary replacement probably sufficed.[23] Nothing to my knowledge, however, has survived on the content or quality of her teaching at the university.

Not too long after Willard's return to Colorado and the consequent termination of her contract, Wilson landed on her feet when the University of Maine at Orono offered her a tenure-track position. This was partly owing to an article Wilson published in *Speculum* in 1933 on the early thirteenth-century text known as the *Georgica spiritualia*, an allegorical reading of Virgil. In the article, she made a conclusive identification of John of Garland as the author of the text.[24] As far as one can tell, European scholars, at the time the gold standard for approval, accepted Wilson's findings.[25]

The University of Maine's capacity to make an appointment at all during the economic depression was due to one man, its president, Harold Sherburne Boardman. 'Despite drastic cuts in funding from the state and other sources', Boardman demonstrated creative leadership and continued to make money available for hires and for other positive undertakings by 'improving efficiencies and coordination between programs and colleges.'[26] One of these hires was Faye Wilson, and she fit in well. All-Maine-Women, the honor society of college women in the state, recognized her as a rising star in 1936 by 'elect[ing her] an honorary member', the same year as she was promoted to Associate Professor.[27]

---

[22] *The Crusades, and Other Historical Essays: Presented to Dana C. Munro by his Former Students*, ed. Louis John Paetow (New York, NY, 1928).

[23] The first printed notice of Wilson's affiliation with the University of Colorado appears in the ascription of her early article, 'The *Georgica Spiritualia* of John of Garland', *Speculum* 8 (1933), 358–77 at 377. For notice of Willard's extended leave abroad in 1930–2, see the 'Preface' to *The English Government at Work, 1327–1336*, I: *Central and Prerogative Administration*, ed. James F. Willard and William A. Morris (Cambridge, MA, 1940), vi–vii, and the 'Inventory of Biographical Material' on him in the University of Colorado's Special Collections calendared online at Biographical Material, 1891-1935 | Special Collections & Archives (colorado.edu) accessed online March 2021 at https://archives.colorado.edu/repositories/2/archival_objects/35184212. He kept diaries of his itinerary in these years in London, Italy, and Holland; Travel Materials, 1912-1937 | Special Collections & Archives (colorado.edu), accessed online 16 March 2021 at https://archives.colorado.edu/repositories/2/archival_objects/351843).

[24] 'The *Georgica Spiritualia*', 358–77.

[25] See, for example, 'Recueils périodiques et sociétés savantes', *Revue historique* 172 (1933), 390.

[26] 'Past UMaine Presidents', accessed online 26 May 2021 at Harold Sherburne Boardman – Office of the President – University of Maine (umaine.edu) (https://umaine.edu/president/umaine-presidents/harold-sherburne-boardman/).

[27] *The Maine Campus*, 30 April 1936, 1, and 1 October 1936, 3; accessed online 12 March 2021 at Maine Campus April 30 1936 (umaine.edu) and at Maine Campus October 01

In May 1937, Phi Kappa Phi, the national scholastic honorary society founded years before on the University of Maine campus, named her a fellow.[28] Wilson was long remembered as 'a fine teacher and well-trained medievalist', in the words of an undergraduate advisee who went on to a career as a professor of history also at Maine.[29] Another word used to describe her was 'inspiring'.[30] Wilson remained on the faculty at Maine from 1933 until 1941. During most of this period, she was one of only two female instructors of professorial rank in the university.[31]

Wilson nevertheless gave up her associate professorship and left the University of Maine in 1941. She did so for the more prestigious as well as private, all women's, and increasingly well-endowed, Wellesley College. On the one hand, as she explained much later, her decision reflected her apprehension that Maine's predominantly male student body, whose enthusiasm for medieval history was actually quite high, would drain away into the armed forces if the United States entered World War II.[32] On the other, the position she accepted at her new institution was that of assistant professor.[33] Nonetheless, she again persisted, rising in the ranks at Wellesley to become associate professor once more in 1944 and occupying from 1956 on, one of only four endowed chairs at the college.[34] It was the chair that carried the most status at the time, for it honored the 'revered' Alice Freeman Palmer, the second President of Wellesley (1881–7), who later served as Dean of Women at the then recently established

---

1936 (umaine.edu) (https://digitalcommons.library.umaine.edu/cgi/viewcontent.cgi?article=4033&context=mainecampus).

[28] *Maine Alumnus*, May 1937, 10, accessed online 12 March 2021 at Maine Alumnus, Volume 18, Number 8, May 1937 (umaine.edu) (https://digitalcommons.library.umaine.edu/cgi/viewcontent.cgi?article=1414&context=alumni_magazines).

[29] *Minerva: The Honors College at the University of Maine* (2017–18), 5, accessed online 12 April 2021 at Minerva 2018 | University of Maine by University of Maine - issuu (https://issuu.com/umaine/docs/minerva_single_pages_jan2018).

[30] 1021 *Maine Alumnus* 53 (April–May 1972), 3, accessed online 12 March 2021 at Maine Alumnus, Volume 53, Number 4, April–May 1972 (umaine.edu) (https://digitalcommons.library.umaine.edu/cgi/viewcontent.cgi?article=1472&context=alumni_magazines). Other words used to describe her were 'inspiring', 'the kindest and the best', and 'electrifying'; see the Wellesley *History Newsletter* accessed online 25 July 2023 at www.wellesley.edu/sites/default/files/assets/departments/history/files/history_newsletter_spring_2022.pdf (see p. 15, 'Student and Alumnae News').

[31] 'Centennial Historian' project, p. 1 of the introductory summary of the interview; accessed online 9 April 2021 at https://drive.google.com/drive/folders/1OOxQ9g4mh-7nEiLG7QT55I-yLSGaVKDRz.

[32] 'Centennial Historian' project interview, p. 2; accessed online 9 April 2021 at https://drive.google.com/drive/folders/1OOxQ9g4mh7nEiLG7QT55I-yLSGaVKDRz.

[33] *Wellesley College Bulletin* 31 (1941), 13; accessed online 26 March 2021 at Full text of 'Catalogue number [of the Bulletin]' (archive.org).

[34] *Wellesley College News*, 25 March 1944, 1, accessed online 9 April 2021 at 217023248.pdf (core.ac.uk); and Nannerl Keohane (personal email communication, 13 October 2020). According to Keohane, a Wellesley alumna and former President of the College, Wilson was 'an active and highly respected member of the faculty' throughout her teaching career.

University of Chicago.³⁵ Wilson also helped found the Medieval Studies Honors Program at the college, and it bore a characteristic mark of her fascination with the encounter with the classics in the Middle Ages. Six credit hours of Medieval Latin were required for this undergraduate program.³⁶

In the course of her research career, Wilson came to know John of Garland's extensive oeuvre extremely well. Her dissertation, which she never published, had already done more than merely explicate the *Epithalamium*. Rather, she compared John's allegory to other works in the genre – classical, late antique and medieval – and included long Latin passages of the 6,000-line poem with full or partial translations based on manuscript transcriptions. My comparisons of her work with that of the now available critical edition of the ten-book (or ten-canto) text of the *Epithalamium* confirms that Wilson, aided, as she acknowledged, by Paetow with the first two books of the poem, was a remarkably adept paleographer.³⁷

Wilson did publish one book, and it was devoted to the Marian literature of the High Middle Ages, which included John's *Epithalamium* as well as his *Stella Maris* (Star of the Sea), the commonly used metonym for the Virgin Mary. It appeared after much travail in 1946 under the title, *The Stella Maris of John of Garland*, Number 45 in the still ongoing series known as Medieval Academy of America Books.³⁸ It comes perhaps as no surprise that she chose to publish with the Academy. Her first article, noted above, appeared in its journal, *Speculum*, and E.K. Rand as a founder of both, along with Charles Homer Haskins, must have urged her to submit the brilliant piece to their publication brainchild. Unlike the article, however, the manuscript of the book did not sail through the Academy approval process. The remainder of this essay explores the unexpected difficulties of bringing the book project to fruition.

---

35 I quote Keohane on the reverence for Alice Freeman Palmer's memory (personal email communication, 13 October 2020). There is a considerable bibliography on Freeman Palmer; the standard biography is Ruth Bordin's *Alice Freeman Palmer: The Evolution of a New Woman* (Ann Arbor, MI, 1993).
36 'Centennial Historian' project interview, p. 8; accessed online 9 April 2021 at https://drive.google.com/drive/folders/1OOxQ9g4mh7nEiLG7QT55I-yLSGaVKDRz.
37 The critical edition is Giovanni di Garlandia (John of Garland), *Epithalamium beate virginis Marie*, ed. and tr., Antonio Saiani (Firenze, 1995). For a not very damning critique of this edition, see Gregory Hays, 'Notes on John of Garland's *Epithalamium Beatae Virginis Mariae*', *Journal of Medieval Latin* 24 (2014), 53–8. For Wilson's acknowledgement of Paetow's early help, see her *Study of the Epithalamium in the Middle Ages*, iii.
38 Commending the thoughtfulness and technical quality of her work were, for example, Archer Taylor in *Speculum* 22 (1947), 272–5, and F.J.E. Raby in *Medium Aevum* 15 (1946), 70–1. See also *Wellesley College, 1875–1975: A Century of Women*, ed. Jean Glasscock (Wellesley, MA, 1975), 106, accessed online 18 October 2020 at https://archive.org/details/wellesleycollege1975well/page/n7/mode/2up?q=wilson.

A Publication History

When I first began to pursue research on Faye Wilson, I was seeking an answer to a troubling question. Why did her work on John of Garland, superb as far as it goes and as of this date still widely cited (much of it was reissued in 2012), never explore in depth one of the strongest motifs in his writings, namely, its anti-Judaism?[39] I have tried to explain this elsewhere with reference to the conventions of the scholarly tradition within which she wrote at the time, conventions that defined the topics deemed appropriate or inappropriate for coverage by scholars who studied the reception of the classics in the Middle Ages.[40]

However, even though this argument seemed and still seems plausible to me, the thought also occurred that Wilson's one major published book, *The Stella Maris of John of Garland*, might have had discussions of John's anti-Judaism in its original draft. Moreover, it was conceivable that she revised her manuscript in response to referees' reports and excised these discussions. Ultimately, I discovered that she had indeed made extensive cuts on the way to publication and made detailed notes about these cuts, but there was no indication that any of the material she jettisoned dealt with John of Garland's representation of Jews. The Marian tales he told or, rather, retold in the *Stella Maris* and his other works had negative portraits of Jews, but though she faithfully related them, she did not concern herself with their specifically social or cultural implications.

After some false starts leading me to believe that the referees' reports and associated materials related to the publication of her monograph were lost, the staff of the Medieval Academy located them in an off-site repository and kindly photographed them for my use.[41] It is a fascinating archive.[42] The initial report and a follow-up note on Wilson's submission, dated 3 January [1941] and 9 January 1941, were slash-and-burn. They used words like 'confusing', 'pedantic', 'clumsy', 'infelicities of phrase', 'errors of grammar', 'carelessness', 'prolix', and 'repetitious' to describe her manuscript. 'I greatly doubt', wrote the referee, Princeton Professor of English, G.H. Gerould, a protégé of another (unrelated) Wilson, Woodrow, and one of the original Fellows of the Medieval Academy,[43] 'whether the revision could be made by Professor Wilson

---

[39] See Jordan, 'John of Garland on the Jews', *JMH* 48 (2022), 478–95.
[40] Jordan, 'Evelyn Faye Wilson, John of Garland, and the "Invisible" Jews'.
[41] In the next several paragraphs, I refer to these materials by their individual dates. I wish to thank Lisa Fagin Davis of the Academy for permitting access and Sheryl Mullane-Corvi for taking the photographs.
[42] This section of the present essay greatly expands on the discussion of Wilson's publication experiences in Jordan, 'Evelyn Faye Wilson, John of Garland, and the "Invisible" Jews.'
[43] Gordon Hall Gerould (1877–1954) was not only a distinguished medievalist; he was also a talented folklorist who was brought to Princeton by University President Woodrow Wilson to help staff the new preceptorial system the latter had introduced; 'Memoirs of Fellows of the Mediaeval Academy of America', *Speculum* 29 (1954), 649. He was elected a Fellow of the Academy in the initial class in 1926, along with Charles Homer Haskins, Louis John Paetow, and Edward Kennard Rand; see Fellows of the Medieval

without an amount of help that an editorial board could scarcely be expected to give.' In the face of this damning criticism, especially Gerould's refusal in a follow-up note to endorse a revise-and-resubmit recommendation, the Medieval Academy's Secretary of Publication, Paul Ward, acknowledged the referee's evaluation and his follow-up note with thanks in two separate letters (8 and 22 January 1941). In the second one of these, however, he willfully misled Gerould into believing that the manuscript would not go forward. For on the same day as the second letter to Gerould went out (22 January), Ward wrote to Faye Wilson, explaining to her that though the referee, whose report he did *not* share with her, desired certain clarifications, some updating of bibliography and considerable shortening, the Academy would be receptive to considering a revised version of the manuscript for publication.

There is no doubt that E.K. Rand contributed crucially to this outcome; indeed, one might well say labored behind the scenes to effect the result. His informal assessment (there was no written report) trumped G.H. Gerould's formal evaluation at the meeting of the Academy's Executive Committee, according to a memorandum dated 16 January 1941. This was six days *before* Paul Ward misled the referee into thinking the Committee had not yet met but would follow his negative recommendation when it did. The memorandum also noted that Ward invoked and endorsed Rand's favorable assessment of Wilson's work. Ward was a Harvard-trained medievalist, but as a constitutional historian, he had no particular expertise unlike the two Academy Fellows, Rand and Gerould, in the transmission of the classical tradition.[44] It was only Rand's opinion that could have carried the day.

To put the matter another way, E.K. Rand was still looking after Louis John Paetow's student twelve years after the latter's death. Why? No doubt he thought well of her struggle to succeed in academe, but he was also a fierce enemy of what scholars now term the 'publish or perish' mentality in research colleges and universities. In 1935 Rand had bemoaned this unforgiving practice, at the time commonly labelled 'up or out', to the man who instituted it at Harvard, its famous president, James Bryant Conant.[45] Contrary to Conant, Rand maintained that '[a]s for publication we should cease to regard it as a major criterion of scholarship... If a scholar never publishes at all, that is not necessarily

---

Academy – The Medieval Academy of America, accessed online 2 September 2021 at https://www.medievalacademy.org/page/CompleteFellows.

44 On Paul Langdon Ward's distinguished career as a medieval and early modern constitutional historian and educational administrator (he went on to become President of Sarah Lawrence College), see his obituaries in the *New York Times*, 18 November 2005, and *Amherst Magazine*; both accessed online 21 July 2021 at Paul L. Ward, 94, Historian and College President, Dies – The New York Times (nytimes.com) (www.nytimes.com/2005/11/18/nyregion/paul-l-ward-94-historian-and-college-president-dies.html) and Paul L. Ward '33 | 1933 | Amherst College (www.amherst.edu/news/magazine/in_memory/1933/paulward).

45 Paul Bartlett, 'James Bryant Conant 1893–1978: A Biographical Memoir', in *Biographical Memoirs* (Washington, DC: National Academy of Sciences, 1983), 98.

against him.'[46] Yet, it is also clear that he foresaw no success for his view, which reflected his nostalgia for the rapidly fading presence of the 'gentleman scholar'. Where Harvard led, others followed. Men and the increasing number of women scholars in the academy soon had to meet a new publication standard. As anyone realizes – anyone who reads the annual reports of Mildred McAfee Horton, the president of Wellesley from 1936 to 1949 – the college under her leadership certainly accepted the new paradigm and zealously and generously poured resources into supporting faculty publication and did so with remarkably productive consequences.[47] Rand's determination that Faye Wilson *not* perish meant helping to insure that her manuscript appear as a printed book, despite his manifest distaste for the pressure that compelled her to publish. Perhaps Charles Homer Haskins would have acted in the same manner, but he had passed away in 1937.

Even summarized in the supportive way Paul Ward did, his comments on Wilson's manuscript convinced her that she had considerable work ahead of her. It would turn out to be uncomfortably slow. When she received Ward's letter, she was in process of giving up her position at the University of Maine and was teaching full time her last semester there before moving to Wellesley College and reverting to an assistant professorship. Yet, Wilson believed that she would need the book out or in press for promotion again. She took up the task as best she could. Over the next three years, she exhaustively refashioned the manuscript, but when the time finally came for the promotion decision, it remained unpublished. Fortunately for her, those who assessed cases for promotion at the college in academic year 1943–4 clearly thought that the typescript passed muster and approved Wilson's advancement to the rank of associate professor for 1944.

Wilson was in direct contact with Rand in the years leading up to this decision, reassuring him strongly and listing in detail (a good example is a letter of 3 February 1943) what she had cut. She also explained how she had taken account of everything that he and others had suggested while also requesting confirmation of his satisfaction with her revisions and/or additional feedback from him. He meanwhile added his name as he had earlier done to those of her supporters, but this time not informally requesting the Executive Committee of the Medieval Academy to offer her an opportunity for resubmission, but rather offering written assessment of her manuscript arguing for outright acceptance. He also mentioned as an aside in a letter to a correspondent on 17 February 1943, that he had 'had a very high opinion of the scholarship' of the unrevised manuscript, an obvious though unnamed dig at the intemperate original referee's

---

[46] Quoted in the 'Database of Classical Scholars', accessed online 21 July 2021 at RAND, Edward Kennard (rutgers.edu) (https://dbcs.rutgers.edu/all-scholars/9045-rand-edward-kennard).

[47] See, for example, the 'Report of the President 1940', *Annual Reports Number of the Wellesley College Bulletin* (October 1940), 18 and 44–50; accessed online 27 July 2021 at WCA_1A_PresidentReport_1940.pdf (https://dbcs.rutgers.edu/all-scholars/9045-rand-edward-kennard).

report tendered by G.H. Gerould. Rand's support notwithstanding, the timing, alas, was inauspicious for publication. Between Wilson's initial submission of her manuscript in December 1940 and Rand's recommendation for acceptance made to the Academy's Executive Secretary, Charles R.D. Miller, in February 1943, the war had brought a hiatus to the Academy's publication program, except for authors who could muster substantial subsidies. Could Wellesley College help? A flurry of letters and notes stretching from February 1943 well into 1944 among Wilson, Rand, the American Council of Learned Societies, the Wellesley Dean Ella Keats Whiting, who was a professor of medieval English literature and in charge of approving subventions of publication at the College and Executive Secretary Miller finally worked matters out.[48] These materials confirm that Rand was instrumental at every stage, but dying in late 1945, he was not a witness to the denouement of this long drawn-out process.

Most important, cost estimates were out of date by the time physical book production was to commence in 1946.[49] The Wellesley contribution came by check, but Dean Whiting (a great-niece of the poet John Keats) expressed her regret on 14 August 1946 that her absence from the college delayed her in signing it and thus further endangered the production schedule. There was still a shortfall after all the contributions arrived, but no sponsor was willing to go back to his or her subsidy committee to seek additional funds. Worse yet, Wilson made so many changes in the page proofs that the Harvard Printing Office wanted a 'shock[ing]' surcharge of $496 (over $7,000 in today's prices). This was 'about five times what it should normally be!', Executive Secretary Miller noted in a letter of 27 July 1946 to Dean Whiting. He knew what he was talking about: though a medievalist, Miller had an extraordinary experiential level of knowledge of printing and book production in general and a reputation for utmost vigilance in keeping costs under control.[50]

In the same letter, Miller referred to himself as having faced down the Harvard Printing Office by demanding a tedious labor accounting it would not have welcomed, 'an explanation and a break-down of the charge to indicate number of lines re-set, hours of labor, and charge per hour'. This may have worked. No invoice appears to survive in the Academy archives documenting a payment of the surcharge. However, in an imploring note to Faye Wilson dated 19 November 1946, the Academy staff was still asking her to broach with Wellesley the possibility of further helping to defray the charges for the proof edits, conceding, however, that '[o]ur natural tendency of course is not to press the point' by insisting that the author pay. I think it likely that the Academy

---

[48] See letters and memoranda of 1943, dated 15, 17, 19 and 26 February, 2, 5 and 9 March, 12 April, 13 May, 21 and 23 June, 14 July, 22 September, 11 October, and 15, 17 and 24 November. Relevant materials during 1944 date from 25 and 29 March, 4 April and 3 May.
[49] See letters and memoranda and invoices, dated 12 April, 15 and 22 June, 25 and 29 July 14 and 17 August, and 18 November 1946.
[50] See the Memoir devoted to 'Charles Roger Donohue Miller' in *Speculum* 40 (1965), 585.

bore the brunt of what remained of the cost overrun, though in the end (the date was 3 January 1947) Wilson agreed to contribute a remaining $50 (not less than $600 in today's currency) from her own funds, and *The Stella Maris of John of Garland* finally saw the light of day. As she acknowledged in the Preface, she was 'particularly indebted to Professor E.K. Rand for aid and encouragement all along the way'.[51] One need only add that the expensive last-minute edits she made did not hurt the end product. Quite the contrary, the book appeared to stunning reviews, which the Academy staff dutifully archived.[52]

Perhaps understandably, Faye Wilson published no further books, but despite the frustrations of the 1940s, she came to play an active role in politics and had a long and esteemed scholarly career. She read widely and deeply about the war, becoming an invited speaker on many topics related to it, including its impact on women.[53] She worked hard to inform her students and the lay community about the meaning and lessons to take away from the struggle.[54] Then after the war, she became an ardent supporter of Adlai Stevenson, for whom she was an active fundraiser in the Democrat's 1952 campaign for the United States presidency. She also organized events in the Wellesley area in the fall of that year on his behalf.[55]

She served the history profession conscientiously, garnering honors before and subsequent to her retirement from Wellesley in 1965.[56] For two years

---

[51] *Stella Maris of John of Garland*, xii.

[52] Commending the thoughtfulness and technical quality of her work were, for example, Archer Taylor in *Speculum* 22 (1947), 272–5, and F.J.E. Raby in *Medium Aevum* 15 (1946), 70–1. See also *Wellesley College, 1875–1975: A Century of Women*, ed. Jean Glasscock (Wellesley, MA, 1975), 106, accessed online 18 October 2020 at https://archive.org/details/wellesleycollege1975well/page/n7/mode/2up?q=wilson. The Medieval Academy archived reviews from the *Revista di Teologia Mariana*, *Catholic Historical Review*, *English Historical Review*, and *Modern Language Review*.

[53] *The Maine Campus*, 8 May 1941, accessed online 12 March 2021 at Maine Campus May 08 1941 (umaine.edu). (https://digitalcommons.library.umaine.edu/cgi/viewcontent.cgi?article=3610&context=mainecampus).

[54] *Maine Alumnus*, April 1941, accessed online 21 March 2021 at Maine Alumnus, Volume 22, Number 7, April 1941 (umaine.edu). *The Maine Campus*, 17 February 1944, accessed online 12 March 2012 at Maine Campus February 17 1944 (umaine.edu) (https://digitalcommons.library.umaine.edu/cgi/viewcontent.cgi?article=3691&context=maine-campus); *Maine Alumnus*, March 1944, accessed online 1 April 2021 at Maine Alumnus, Volume 25, Number 6, March 1944 (umaine.edu) (https://digitalcommons.library.umaine.edu/cgi/viewcontent.cgi?article=1348&context=alumni_magazines).

[55] *The Wellesley Townsman*, 9 October 1952, 14; 16 October 1952, 10; and 30 October 1952, 11, January 1959, accessed online 13 October 2020 at http://digital.olivesoftware.com/Olive/APA/Wellesley/default.aspx#panel=browse.

[56] Wilson received recognition from Beloit College (above note 12) and the University of Maine (above notes 26 and 27). She also served as a Councillor of the Medieval Academy, which Beloit deemed an honor; 'Proceedings of the Annual Meeting of the Mediaeval Academy of America', *Speculum* 32 (1957), 626; *Bulletin of Beloit College*, July 1956, 2; accessed online 16 November 2020 at https://archive.org/details/catalogue-number01956well/mode/2up?q=Wilson. See, too, the *Wellesley Townsman*, 22 January

thereafter she taught at the Radcliffe Institute,[57] an act that may be understood as a gesture to the institution that nurtured her when, more than thirty years earlier, she was finishing her dissertation. Wilson subsequently moved to the La Jolla area of San Diego.[58] There faculty members at a new branch of the University of California (UCSD) were developing a Western Civilization (Great Books) curricular track for the mostly science-oriented types and mostly men who were its first students.[59] The track stressed the culture of Europe from Antiquity through the Middle Ages.[60] To secure the siting of the university in the La Jolla neighborhood, which was anticipating a likely influx of Jewish academics, residents had to disavow their 'infamous' reputation for 'genteel anti-Semitism'.[61] Whether Wilson cultivated friendships with the faculty or assiduously exploited the resources of the new University, which began taking students only two years after she finished teaching at Radcliffe, is uncertain. Yet, even if she did, her loyalty remained to the institution to which she owed the most in getting her book published, Wellesley College, rather than to UCSD, UC-Berkeley, Radcliffe, Maine or even her undergraduate alma mater, Beloit. She long maintained an active relationship with the college and was named to an

---

1959, 17 and 10 October 1963, 3, accessed online 13 October 2020 at http://digital.olivesoftware.com/Olive/APA/Wellesley/default.aspx#panel=browse.

[57] 'Centennial Historian' project, p. 1 of the introductory summary of the interview; accessed online 9 April 2021 at https://drive.google.com/drive/folders/1OOxQ9g4mh7nEi LG7QT55I-yLSGaVKDRz.

[58] 'Centennial Historian' project, p. 1 of the introductory summary of the interview, accessed online 9 April 2021 at https://drive.google.com/drive/folders/1OOxQ9g4mh 7nEiLG7QT55I-yLSGaVKDRz.

[59] Christine Clark, 'Trailblazing Class of 68' Celebrates 50th Anniversary', *thisweek@ucsandiego*, 9 October 2014, accessed online 5 May 2021 at Trailblazing Class of '68 Celebrates 50th Anniversary (ucsd.edu) (https://today.ucsd.edu/story/trailblazing_class_of_68_celebrates_50th_anniversary?utm_campaign=thisweek&utm_medium=e-mail&utm_source=tw-2014-10-09).

[60] On the early history of UCSD (there was initially some debate as to 'whether [it] should be named for La Jolla or San Diego'), see Abraham Shragge, 'Growing Up Together: The University of California's One Hundred-Year Partnership with the San Diego Region', *Journal of San Diego History* 47 (2001), accessed online 5 May 2021 at Fall 2001 - San Diego History Center | San Diego, CA | Our City, Our Story (https://sandiegohistory.org/journal/2001/october/index-htm-128/).

[61] Mary Ellen Stratthaus, 'Flaw in the Jewel: Housing Discrimination Against Jews in La Jolla, California', *American Jewish History* 84 (1996), 189–219, accessed online 5 May 2021 at https://webcitation.org/5quH6gLRG?url=http://www.fairhousingforall.org/sites/default/files/files/Stratthaus.pdf, and Will Carless, 'A Specter from our Past: Longtime Residents Will Always Remember the Stain Left on the Jewel by an Era of Housing Discrimination', *La Jolla Light*, 7 April 2005, accessed online 5 May 2021 at LaJollaLight.com | A specter from our past: Longtime residents will always remember the stain left on the Jewel by an era of housing discrimination (https://web.archive.org/web/20100913084414/http://www.lajollalight.com/printer/article.asp?c=223555). The words quoted are from Sue Garson, 'The End of Covenant', *San Diego Jewish Journal*, 21 July 2008, accessed online 5 May 2021 at La Jolla Covenant- San Diego Jewish Journal (https://web.archive.org/web/20080723060708/http:/www.sdjewishjournal.com/stories/jewishnewsstory.html).

exclusive group of honorary graduates 'who have made a life-long connection to Wellesley alumnae through their dedicated commitment to Wellesley College and the Association [of Graduates]'.[62] She continued in emeritus status until her death in 1993.[63] Unlike her mentors, Paetow, Haskins and Rand, and her chief adversary, Gerould, she was never elected a Fellow of the Medieval Academy.

One last point: by retiring to La Jolla, Faye Wilson took up residence in a community that, by chance, boasted one of the most charming monuments ever dedicated to *Stella Maris*. It was also 'one of La Jolla's most photographed and treasured buildings… the white Spanish Mission-style Mary, Star of the Sea Catholic Church'.[64] A coincidence no doubt, but quite fitting as a constant reminder to Wilson of her own academic interests, considerable perseverance and substantial accomplishments.

---

[62] See www.wellesley.edu/alumnae/awards/honorarymembers, accessed online 10 October 2020.
[63] Wellesley *Catalogue*, accessed online 13 October 2020 at https://archive.org/details/cataloguenumber01993well/mode/2up?q=wilson), in the 'Faculty' section, p. 265.
[64] Linda Hutchison, 'Mary, Star of the Sea: Daily Mass and Ministries for All', *La Jolla Light*, 20 November 2014, accessed online 5 May 2021 at Mary, Star of the Sea: Daily Mass and ministries for all - La Jolla Light (www.lajollalight.com/sdljl-mary-star-of-the-sea-church-2014nov20-story.html).

12

The Life, Scholarship and Legacy of Bennett David Hill, 1934–2005[1]

Randall Todd Pippenger

On 8 October 1971, Bennett David Hill wrote,

I have had the advantage of studying with what was probably the most distinguished group of medievalists assembled in one place (Princeton) in the twentieth century: Theodor Mommsen, Ernst Kantorowicz, and Joseph Strayer in History, Kurt Weitzmann and Erwin Panofsky in Art History, and D.W. Robertson in English Literature. If not to myself, I believe that I owe it to them to produce a book that will stand the test of time, a work that fifty years from now students will be told they must consult.[2]

Fifty-three years after that statement and nineteen years after his death in 2005, this essay seeks to acknowledge the life and scholarship of Bennett David Hill, one of the very first individuals to break the color barrier in the professional study of medieval history, and of European history more broadly, in the United States.[3] What follows will not quite capture the witty, charming, and genteel man of some readers' memories. After all, Bennett Hill was a man who – as a junior professor without tenure – wrote a formal letter to his department resigning from the Faculty Senate at the University of Illinois because, 'I find

---

[1] I would like to thank the organizers of the 41st Annual Haskins Society Conference at the University of Richmond, the leadership of the American Academy in Rome, and the Institute for Research in the Humanities at the University of Wisconsin-Madison, who provided the platform and financial resources for completing this essay. I would also like to thank the archival staffs at the libraries of the University of Illinois and Princeton University for their remote assistance in the fall of 2021. Finally, I am deeply grateful and indebted to William Chester Jordan, Jaroslav Folda, and the late Terrence Deneen for their conversation and insights. Without their encouragement and enthusiasm, this project would not have come to fruition.
[2] Urbana, University of Illinois Archives, Series 15/13/2, History Staff Appointments File, 1916–2000, Box 5, Folder 'Hill, Bennett D., 1963–1981' (hereafter University of Illinois Archives, 15/13/2), Bennett D. Hill to Winton Solberg (October 8, 1971).
[3] Robert Fikes, Jr, 'Surprise: There Are Black History Professors Who Don't Teach Black History', *The Journal of Blacks in Higher Education* 31 (2001), 124–8, esp. 125.

the toga uncomfortable and am constantly tripping over it.'[4] But while this essay may not always capture the humor and vitality that characterized Bennett as a person, it seeks to do justice to Professor's Hill legacy as a scholar, teacher, and medievalist.

Bennett Hill was born in Baltimore, Maryland on 27 September 1934 to Muriel Clarke and David Hill. Muriel had attended some college at Morgan State University in Baltimore, while David graduated from Coppin Teachers College, later Coppin State, in 1931. As a child, Hill's family moved from Baltimore to Philadelphia where his father worked as a mail clerk for the railroad.[5] Hill grew up attending public schools in urban Philadelphia and graduated from Central High School, an early integrated, but still all-boys, school.[6] Admission to Central High allowed Hill to take four years of Latin and two years of French as a teenager, languages which formed the foundation of his later life and career.[7] In subsequent curriculum vitae, resumés, and forms until his retirement in the 1980s Hill proudly listed 'public schools of Philadelphia' first, a possible indication of how he felt about his varied institutional experiences.[8]

In the spring of 1952, Hill was admitted as an undergraduate student on scholarship to Princeton University – one year following the graduation of the first regularly and purposefully admitted African-American undergraduate student, Joseph Moss.[9] His first-year faculty advisor was the renowned medievalist, Theodor Mommsen, the grandson of the more famous nineteenth-century German historian of the same name.[10] After a difficult first year, a year in which Hill was forced to supplement his scholarship by working as a waiter, he ultimately

---

[4] University of Illinois Archives, 15/13/2, Bennett D. Hill to Clark Spence (April 29, 1969).

[5] Princeton, Princeton University Archives, Undergraduate Academic Files, Series 4, AC198-04, 'Hill, Bennett D.' (hereafter Princeton University Archives, AC198-04), Application for Admission to the Freshman Class (February 4, 1952), 1.

[6] Central remained an all-boys institution until 1983. See 'Our History', Central High School, School District of Philadelphia, accessed 23 May 2023, https://centralhs.philasd.org/about-central-high-school/about-us/.

[7] Princeton University Archives, AC198-04, Principal's Report on Applicant (February 14, 1952), 3.

[8] University of Illinois Archives, 15/13/2, for numerous examples.

[9] Princeton University Archives, AC198-04, Student Record Summary of Hill, Bennett D. (June 12, 1956), 2; and Athletic Eligibility Record (September 17, 1952), 2. For Princeton University's history with race and its earliest African-American students, see Stefan M. Bradley, 'The Southern-Most Ivy: Princeton University from Jim Crow Admissions to Anti-Apartheid Protests, 1794–1969', *American Studies* 51 (2010), 109–30; Stefan M. Bradley, *Upending the Ivory Tower: Civil Rights, Black Power, and the Ivy League* (New York, NY, 2018), 46–91; and April C. Armstrong, 'Erased Pasts and Altered Legacies: Princeton's First African American Students', *Princeton & Slavery Project*, accessed 23 May 2023, https://slavery.princeton.edu/stories/erased-pasts-and-altered-legacies-princetons-first-african-american-students. For Moss in particular, see Mark F. Bernstein, 'A Princeton Pioneer: When Joseph Ralph Moss '51 Broke Through the Color Line', *Princeton Alumni Weekly*, 7 June 2006.

[10] Princeton University Archives, AC198-04, Dean Albert Elsasser to Muriel Clarke (May 19, 1953). Theodor Mommsen died prematurely in 1958. For the posthumous

flourished at Princeton.[11] Studying medieval history with Mommsen and Joseph Strayer, Hill graduated with honors in 1956, and his senior thesis on Innocent III and the Fourth Crusade, directed by Strayer, received honorable mention for the Walter Phelps Hall Prize in European History.[12] Following graduation, Hill enrolled in graduate school at Harvard University to study medieval history with Charles Alan Taylor, completing an ambition that he had expressed to his teachers as early as his sophomore year of college.[13] He received a master's degree from Harvard in 1958, and after a year teaching at the Putney School in Vermont and another year residing and teaching in Princeton as an instructor, Hill began the PhD program at the university in 1960 as a late enrollee under the direction of his undergraduate advisor, Joseph Strayer.[14]

Throughout his early life and into his college years, Hill was a deeply religious and committed Catholic, a fact that was even remarked upon by his teachers on several occasions in his official record.[15] From the 1960s onward, Hill also demonstrated a deep appreciation for the monastic life, past and present, which, as he wrote in his first book on the Cistercians in England, 'is only the Christian life lived extraordinarily'.[16] Hill's first work to appear in print was a 1965 editorial evaluating the performance of the American bishops at the Second Vatican Council, a performance which he believed confirmed the European view that American bishops were a 'hardworking, ingenuous, unsophisticated and theologically deficient lot'.[17] Hill argued that 'with very rare exceptions, the *inspiration* for liturgical reform and for intellectual growth within the Church has and probably will continue to come from the members of the religious orders and those ancient sources of spiritual change, the monasteries', and that furthermore, 'Monasticism is *not* exclusively a medieval institution, and

---

collection of his papers, see his *Medieval and Renaissance Studies*, ed. Eugene F. Rice, Jr (Ithaca, NY, 1959).

[11] Princeton University Archives, AC198–04, Athletic Eligibility Record (September 17, 1952), 2. We will return to this year in the second half of the essay.

[12] Bennett D. Hill, 'Innocent III and the Fourth Crusade' (BA thesis, Princeton University, 1956). On Joseph Strayer's legacy as a medievalist and mentor, see William Chester Jordan and Teofilo F. Ruiz, 'Joseph Reese Strayer, Department of History', in *Luminaries: Princeton Faculty Remembered*, ed. Patricia H. Marks (Princeton, NJ, 1996), 297–304.

[13] Princeton University Archives, AC198–04, Charles Gillispie, 'Board of Advisers Memorandum concerning Hill, Bennett D.' (May 1954).

[14] Princeton, Princeton University Archives, Graduate Alumni Records, AC105–04 (hereafter Princeton University Archives, AC105–04), Application for Admission to the Graduate School (March 1, 1960).

[15] Princeton University Archives, AC198–04, Jeremiah S. Finch to Theodor Mommsen (February 24, 1956); Princeton University Archives, AC105'–04, Norman Cantor to Robert Palmer (March 17, 1960); and University of Illinois Archives, 15/13/2, Norman Cantor to Maurice Lee (January 18, 1964).

[16] Bennett D. Hill, *English Cistercian Monasteries and their Patrons in the Twelfth Century* (Urbana, IL, 1968), 154.

[17] Bennett D. Hill, 'The North American Bishops and the Second Vatican Council', *Colloquium* 4 (1965), 23–35 at 24.

the American hierarchy [of the Catholic Church] would do well to look to the great abbeys of this country – St. John's, St. Vincent's and St. Anselm's for new theological direction.'[18] Hill's study of the Middle Ages only deepened his early faith and interest in monastic institutions, and throughout his career, Hill's scholarly interests in many ways reflected his lifelong spiritual journey, which would eventually lead him to the priesthood and to join St Anselm's Benedictine monastery in Washington, DC himself in 1985.[19]

During his graduate school years at Princeton, Hill began studying what would become the twin pillars of his scholarly life and contributions: the Cistercian Order in England and the Congregation of Savigny, a group of several dozen reform-minded Benedictine houses based in Normandy, which was eventually placed under the authority of the Cistercian General Chapter during preparations for the Second Crusade in 1147.[20] Hill published one book and four articles on the Cistercians and Savigniacs from the late 1960s to the early 1980s. He also published almost two dozen entries in the *New Catholic Encyclopedia*, Strayer's *Dictionary of the Middle Ages*, and (much later) in E. Michael Gerli's *Medieval Iberia: An Encyclopedia*, which addressed broader aspects of monastic life, practice, and history.[21]

His 1968 book, *English Cistercian Monasteries and their Patrons in the Twelfth Century*, a lightly revised version of his Princeton dissertation, set the agenda of his future scholarship. Organized in four parts, the book analyzed the early history of the Cistercians in England by foregrounding the relationship between, and the interdependence of, the spiritual life of the monks and the secular world of their benefactors. The first half of the book considered the great wave of Cistercian foundations that occurred, surprisingly, during the period of the Anarchy from 1135 to 1154 and analyzed the interrelationship of the Cistercians and their patrons. With primary benefactors including the earls of Leicester and Chester, Hill argued persuasively that the chaotic and unsettled conditions of the Anarchy encouraged the exponential growth of the Cistercians, who more than their monastic competitors, were willing to take on less productive properties in economically marginal and legally disputed areas. Hill maintained that the motivations for 'giving' varied widely among laity, that most donations do not appear to have been moved by the Spirit, haphazard, or anarchic as it were, and that many patrons expected concrete material and spiritual benefits in return for their 'donations'. Similarly, by accepting these gifts which often included annual duties and fees, the Cistercians became embroiled in local society economically, legally, socially, and politically, in contradiction and to the detriment of the Order's austere, original ideals. The second half of *English*

---

[18] Hill, 'The North American Bishops and the Second Vatican Council', 33.
[19] Jo Ann Hoeppner Moran Cruz, 'Dom Bennett D. Hill, O.S.B.', *Catholic Historical Review* 91 (2005), 571–2.
[20] Bennett D. Hill, 'English Cistercian Monasteries and their Patrons in the Twelfth Century: A Study in the Decline of an Ideal' (PhD dissertation, Princeton University, 1963).
[21] See the appended publication list for bibliographic references.

Cistercian Monasteries contained one of the first analyses of the Congregation of Savigny in England, its eventual merger with the Cistercian Order in 1147, and the institutional and spiritual issues that merger caused within the monastic community on the island. Hill concluded his monograph by examining the role of English Cistercians in the reform movement, and specifically, their institutional involvement with and support of the reformed papacy of the twelfth century.

In the sixteen years following his monograph's appearance, Hill published follow-up articles examining the Congregation of Savigny in greater detail, often for the first time in English-language scholarship. Successive articles addressed Savigny's origins in early twelfth-century Normandy, the lay patrons behind its first wave of expansion and the earliest French foundations of the Congregation, as well as the lay contribution to the Congregation's early architectural programs.[22] Complementing his work on the Savigniacs and the Cistercian Order in England, Hill also penned an important contribution in Becket studies, addressing the archbishop's close relationship and association with the Cistercian Order, especially while he was exiled from Canterbury in France during the late 1160s.[23] Likely because of the enduring popularity of the subject, 'Thomas Becket and the Cistercian Order' remains Hill's most commonly cited work today.[24]

In many ways, Hill's overall body of work was a product of its time and environment. Even today, Cistercian studies, much like studies of the Crusades, remains a discrete subfield within the broader umbrella of medieval studies with its own conventions, questions, and research agenda.[25] Women as patrons and the experience of female religious – important subjects in twenty-first-century Cistercian studies – are both largely absent from his work.[26] And as the abandoned subtitle of his dissertation 'A Study in the Decline of an Ideal'

---

[22] Bennett D. Hill, 'The Counts of Mortain and the Origins of the Congregation of Savigny', in *Order and Innovation in the Middle Ages: Essays in Honor of Joseph R. Strayer*, ed. William Chester Jordan, Brian McNab, and Teofilo Ruiz (Princeton, NJ, 1975), 237–53; 'The First French Foundations of the Norman Abbey of Savigny', *American Benedictine Review* 31 (1980), 130–52; and 'Lay Patronage and Monastic Architecture: The Case of Savigny', in *Monasticism in the Arts*, ed. Timothy Gregory Verdon (Syracuse, NY, 1984), 173–87.
[23] Bennett D. Hill, 'Thomas Becket and the Cistercian Order', *Analecta Sacri Ordinis Cisterciensia* 26 (1970), 64–80.
[24] Both anecdotally and according to the inscrutable metrics of Google Scholar.
[25] For a good and recent treatment of historiographic trends in Cistercian studies, see Anne E. Lester, 'The Cistercians', in *The Oxford Handbook of Christian Monasticism*, ed. Bernice M. Kaczynski (Oxford, 2020), 232–47.
[26] See, for example, *Cîteaux et les femmes*, ed. Bernadette Barrière (Paris, 2001); Constance Berman, *Women and Monasticism in Medieval Europe: Sisters and Patrons of the Cistercian Reform* (Kalamazoo, MI, 2002); Constance Berman, *The White Nuns: Cistercian Abbeys for Women in Medieval France* (Philadelphia, PA, 2018); Elizabeth Freeman, 'Cistercian Nuns in Medieval England: Unofficial Meets Official', *Studies in Church History* 42 (2006), 110–19; Erin Jordan, 'Gender Concerns: Monks, Nuns, and Patronage of the Cistercian Order in Thirteenth-Century Flanders and Hainault', *Speculum* 87 (2012), 62–94; and Anne E. Lester, *Creating Cistercian Nuns: The Women's*

indicates, Hill was also unafraid to cast Cistercian history in the twelfth century as one of 'rise and fall', 'decline' and 'corruption'. One of the main arguments of *English Cistercian Monasteries and their Patrons* in its final published form is that Cistercian involvement in the secular world, their willingness to carry out diplomatic and legal missions for the reformed papacy, as well as their willingness to accept disputed properties, 'gifts' from laypersons that involved encumbering duties and fees, and other religious congregations with different traditions all violated the '*original* Cistercian ideal' of detachment from the world and had a 'damaging effect on the original spirit and ideals of the Order'.[27] Although he would ease off such claims in subsequent publications, Hill thought the Congregation of Savigny had a particularly corrupting influence on the spiritual life and organizational cohesion of the Cistercians in England. To be fair, this 'Garden of Eden' narrative of pristine original ideals giving way to the corrupting influence of the world is present in the medieval sources and narratives of the Cistercian Order.[28] It also characterized most other professional scholarship from the early to mid-twentieth century, which was an era when several of the leading scholars of monastic and Cistercian history, such as David Knowles, Jean Leclercq, and Louis Lekai, were also monks themselves.[29]

In many other ways, however, Hill's work was very forward-looking. His insistence that the history of monasteries and religious orders should not be 'compartmentalized', that the economic, social, constitutional, and artistic histories of the orders should be written and understood in the context of their spiritual and religious purposes – and vice versa – anticipated the evolution of Cistercian studies over the next generation.[30] His exploitation of the charter evidence, efforts to draw connections between donors and benefactors, and his interest in how a monastery's association with the lay world around it affected its architectural program and built environment, the daily life of its monks, and their very beliefs are all precursors to recent and current studies of monastic

---

Religious Movement and Its Reform in Thirteenth Century Champagne (Ithaca, NY, 2011).
[27] Hill, *English Cistercian Monasteries*, 147–56, quotations from 151 and 153.
[28] See the dual Latin–English edition of the Order's early texts in *Narrative and Legislative Texts from Early Cîteaux*, ed. Chyrsogonus Waddell (Brecht, 1999).
[29] The best historiographic treatment of the study of monastic history during this period, remains Giles Constable, 'The Study of Monastic History Today', in *Essays on the Reconstruction of Medieval History*, ed. Vaclav Mudroch and G.S. Couse (Montreal, 1974), 21–51. But now see John Van Engen, 'Historiographical Approaches to Monasticism in the Long Twelfth Century', in *The Cambridge History of Medieval Monasticism in the Latin West*, ed. Alison I. Beach and Isabelle Cochelin (2 vols, Cambridge, 2020), ii, 649–66. See also Louis J. Lekai, *The Cistercians: Ideals and Reality* (Kent, OH, 1977).
[30] Relevant examples abound, but see Martha G. Newman, *The Boundaries of Charity: Cistercian Culture and Ecclesiastical Reform, 1098–1180* (Stanford, CA, 1996); Constance Hoffman Berman, *The Cistercian Evolution: The Invention of a Religious Order in Twelfth-Century Europe* (Philadelphia, PA, 2000); Janet Burton and Julie Kerr, *The Cistercians in the Middle Ages* (Woodbridge, 2011); Emilia Jamroziak, *The Cistercian Order in Medieval Europe, 1090–1500* (London, 2013).

orders based on the liturgy, social network analysis, and material culture.[31] The 'tensions between Cistercian "ideals" and the "realities" of monastic life' remain an issue that interests followers of twenty-first-century Cistercian studies, even if nowadays the rhetoric surrounding the question is less pejorative and scholars prefer words like 'adaptation' and 'transformation' to 'corruption' and 'decline'.[32]

The second pillar of Hill's published work demonstrates similar forward-thinking. In addition to his scholarly work on the Cistercians and Savigniacs, Hill devoted much of his energy to teaching and producing publications designed for students. Hill had a distinguished and decorated record as a teacher at the University of Illinois. His medieval surveys and English Constitutional History course were particularly popular, maintaining enrollments of more than ninety students, and he was listed as one of the 'twenty best undergraduate teachers' at the university by the graduating senior class on numerous occasions over his nineteen-year tenure.[33] Even as a graduate student at Princeton, Hill was exceptionally allowed to advise senior theses. His first senior advisee, Jaroslav Folda, would become one of the most significant and influential art historians of the medieval Mediterranean.[34] In addition, two of Hill's students at the University of Illinois, Francis Swietek and Terrence Deneen, made important contributions to monastic history. Their decades-long collaboration propelled Savigniac studies forward for a generation following Hill's retirement.[35]

---

[31] Among others, see Joan Wardrop, *Fountains Abbey and its Benefactors, 1132–1300* (Kalamazoo, MI, 1987); Megan Cassidy-Welch, *Monastic Spaces and Their Meanings: Thirteenth-Century English Cistercian Monasteries* (Turnhout, 2001); Terryl N. Kinder, *Cistercian Europe: Architecture of Contemplation* (Kalamazoo, MI, 2002); as well as the contributions in *The Cambridge Companion to the Cistercian Order*, ed. Mette Birkedal Bruun (Cambridge, 2013) and *The Cambridge History of Medieval Monasticism in the Latin West*, ed. Beach and Cochelin.
[32] Lester, 'The Cistercians', 233.
[33] University of Illinois Archives, 15/13/2, Curriculum Vitae (1977); and idem, Walter L. Arnstein, 'Obituary of Bennett David Hill' (March 7, 2005).
[34] See Folda's profile on *Resources for the Study of the Crusades*, accessed 25 May 2023, www.crusaderstudies.org.uk/resources/historians/profiles/folda/index.html. Professor Folda also kindly shared his memories of working with Hill at Princeton: Jaroslav Folda, email message to the author (8 October 2021). For Folda's scholarship, see his two fundamental works of synthesis: Jaroslav Folda, *The Art of the Crusaders in the Holy Land: 1098–1187* (Cambridge, 1995); and idem, *Crusader Art in the Holy Land: from the Third Crusade to the Fall of Acre, 1187–1291* (Cambridge, 2005).
[35] Beyond their single-authored work, especially see their joint collaborations on the Congregation of Savigny: Francis R. Swietek and Terrence M. Deneen, 'The Episcopal Exemption of Savigny, 1112–1184', *Church History* 52 (1983), 285–98; 'Pope Lucius II and Savigny', *Analecta Cisterciensia* 39 (1983), 3–25; '"Ab antiquo alterius ordinis fuerit": Alexander III on the Reception of Savigny into the Cistercian Order', *Revue d'histoire ecclésiastique* 89 (1994), 5–28; 'The Roman Curia and the Merger of Savigny with Cîteaux: The Import of the Papal Documents', *Revue bénédictine* 112 (2002), 323–55; '"Et inter abbates de majoribus unus": The Abbot of Savigny in the Cistercian Constitution, 1147–1243', in *Truth as Gift: Studies in Medieval Cistercian History in Honor of John R. Sommerfeldt*, ed. Marsha L. Dutton (Kalamazoo, MI, 2004), 89–118;

In addition to a collection of texts designed for teaching, *The Church and State in the Middle Ages*, which examined the constitutional history of the question for students, and paired translations of medieval authors such as Augustine of Hippo and Pope Boniface VIII with studies from leading scholars like Karl Morrison, Brian Tierney, Gaines Post, and of course, Joseph Strayer, Hill's most influential teaching work was 1979's *A History of Western Society*.[36] A collaboration with two of his University of Illinois colleagues, John P. McKay and John Buckler, *A History of Western Society* was designed to be used in western civilization courses, which Hill also taught at Illinois. An early attempt to decenter narratives of 'great men' and to focus on ordinary men and women, *A History of Western Society* is still in print and now in its thirteenth edition. It has been one of the most widely taught – and read – works of European history for the last half century.[37] However, again anticipating the turn toward a more inclusive and representative Global History by several decades, the three historians followed their western civilization textbook with *A History of World Societies* in 1984, which is in its twelfth edition.[38]

Hill's publication history was not without difficulty. In the early 1970s he wrote a general history of monasticism of more than 400 manuscript pages to be titled *Medieval Monasticism: Life in a Medieval Monastery*.[39] Focused on the daily lives of monks and the social interactions of monasteries across fifteen centuries, the book was designed for undergraduate students and a general audience. Despite positive internal reviews from colleagues at the University of Illinois (which Hill never read), including Paul Bernard and Donald Queller, who praised the manuscript's 'breadth of vision', 'high level of urbanity', and Hill's 'wide and thorough knowledge of monasticism', and despite the commercial success of his textbook on the Church and State, Hill could not find a publisher.[40] The new editor for history at John Wiley & Sons attempted to soften the blow of rejection by highlighting the recent paperback sales of

---

and 'The Date of the Merger of Savigny and Cîteaux Reconsidered', *Revue d'histoire ecclésiastique* 101 (2006), 547–74.

[36] Bennett D. Hill, *Church and State in the Middle Ages* (New York, NY, 1970); and John P. McKay, Bennett D. Hill, and John Buckler, *A History of Western Society* (1st ed., Boston, MA, 1979).

[37] University of Illinois Archives, 15/13/2, Walter L. Arnstein, 'Obituary of Bennett D. Hill' (March 7, 2005).

[38] John P. McKay, Bennett D. Hill, and John Buckler, *A History of World Societies* (1st ed., Boston, MA, 1984).

[39] For the title, see University of Illinois Archives, 15/13/2, Bennett D. Hill to Winton Solberg (October 8, 1971). For the length of the manuscript, see Urbana, University of Illinois Archives, Series 15/1/41, Liberal Arts and Sciences, Dean's Office, Faculty and Academic Professional Personnel File, 1959–1998, Box 9, Folder 'Hill, Bennett D., 1964–1983, History' (hereafter University of Illinois Archives, Series 15/1/41), Paul P. Bernard to Robert W. Rogers (December 9, 1974).

[40] University of Illinois Archives, Series 15/1/41, Paul P. Bernard to Robert W. Rogers (December 9, 1974); and idem, Donald Queller to Robert W. Rogers (December 10, 1974).

Church and State in the Middle Ages, trusting 'that my decision to decline your latest proposal will not cause any ill feelings and that you'll continue to think of Wiley when other writing plans evolve'.[41] After a few years, Hill dropped the project entirely and the fate of the manuscript is unknown.

It is unclear why Hill could not find a publisher for his monograph on monasticism, especially when so many similar books were appearing at the same time.[42] It is possible that it had something to do with the reviews of his first book, *English Cistercian Monasteries and their Patrons*. Although most of the reviews were positive, there was a notable exception. Susan Wood, who in 1955 had published the similarly named *English Monasteries and their Patrons in the Thirteenth Century*, wrote a critical assessment of the work which appeared in the *English Historical Review*.[43] Although not mentioned in Wood's review, Hill had criticized her assertion that several English monasteries had been founded in the twelfth century with little forethought and 'in an enthusiastic fit', comparing her claim to the notion that the British Empire 'grew on a wave of absentmindedness'.[44] Wood closed her own review of Hill's work by claiming that 'the book is attractively written, but plagiaristic'. She gave a specific example of 'six lines of unmarked verbatim quotation'.[45]

Although 'plagiaristic' is not quite 'plagiarizing', as Hill did not yet have tenure, Wood's accusation still triggered an internal investigation at the University of Illinois by his senior colleagues within the department of history. Two of those colleagues, Waldo H. Heinrichs, Jr and Walter L. Arnstein, cleared Hill of any wrongdoing other than a bit of 'carelessness'.[46] The 'unmarked verbatim quotation' referenced by Wood was an extension of a quotation in the same paragraph that Hill had cited and attributed properly to V.H. Galbraith's 'Monastic Foundation Charters of the Eleventh and Twelfth Centuries'. Missing or misplaced quotation marks to one side, Hill had also cited the lines in question to the correct pages of Galbraith in a footnote of the same paragraph, two sentences later.[47] The issue never again appeared in his official record and

---

[41] University of Illinois Archives, 15/13/2, Wayne Anderson to Bennett D. Hill (January 9, 1973).
[42] Although Donald Queller expressed some concern that 'the field is already pretty well occupied'. University of Illinois Archives, 15/1/41, Donald Queller to Robert W. Rogers (December 10, 1974).
[43] For the monograph, see Susan Wood, *English Monasteries and their Patrons in the Thirteenth Century* (London, 1955). For the review, see Susan Wood, 'Review of *English Cistercian Monasteries and their Patrons in the Twelfth Century* by Bennett D. Hill', *English Historical Review* 84 (1969), 824–5.
[44] Hill, *English Cistercian Monasteries*, 54. For the quotation, see Wood, *English Monasteries and their Patrons*, 4.
[45] Wood, 'Review of *English Cistercian Monasteries*', 824–5.
[46] University of Illinois Archives, 15/13/2, Memorandum for the file of Professor Bennett Hill (February 20, 1974).
[47] See Hill, *English Cistercian Monasteries*, 43–4 and notes 3–4. Also, see V.H. Galbraith, 'Monastic Foundation Charters of the Eleventh and Twelfth Centuries', *The Cambridge Historical Journal* 4 (1934), 214–15.

although one suspects the sting of such an investigation must have lingered, it was far from the only challenge in Hill's professional life.

On several occasions Hill expressed regret or disappointment at not having published in the quantity or quality that he believed he should have. For example, when Hill wrote to the chair of his department at the University of Illinois on 8 October 1971 that he believed he owed it to his teachers (and himself) 'to produce a book that will stand the test of time, a work that fifty years from now students will be told they must consult', he finished his letter by also asserting that 'while I expect to continue to publish articles or monographs, I am not going to be brow-beaten into publishing my study on Savigny; it will appear when I am thoroughly, or at least reasonably, satisfied with it'.[48] Of course, like his broader study of monasticism, Hill never published a monograph on the Congregation. While significant work on the Savigniacs has been done by Swiatek, Deneen, Christopher Holdsworth, and Richard Allen, and the proceedings of a conference held in Cerisy-la-Salle in celebration of the abbey appeared in 2019, no coherent monograph on medieval Savigny or its Congregation has ever been published.[49]

Based on the public memoranda and private correspondence which survive in the archival record, his published work, as well as the testimony of his friends, colleagues, and students, it is unlikely that Hill would have attributed any of his scholarship and intellectual interests, or even his professional struggles, to race. Hill always, and consistently, preferred to attribute his scholarly interests to his Christian faith and found refuge from his professional struggles in that same faith. But even so, the issue of race and examples of institutional and structural racism, often benign, sometimes malignant, were present throughout and at every step of his professional life. Explaining the quantity, much less the 'quality', of Hill's work by questioning his ability or determination, as his colleagues occasionally did in internal evaluations and deliberations for promotion, does a severe disservice to Hill as a person and to the historical context within which he labored. Hill faced strains, pressures, and expectations that his white contemporaries simply did not.[50]

---

[48] University of Illinois Archives, 15/13/2, Bennett D. Hill to Winton Solberg (October 8, 1971).
[49] Christopher Holdsworth, 'The Affiliation of Savigny', in *Truth as Gift*, ed. Dutton, 43–88; Richard Allen, 'À la recherche d'un atelier d'ecriture de la Noramandie cistercienne: le scriptorium de l'abbaye de Savigny (XIIe–XIIIe siècle), in *Les pratiques de l'écrit dans les abbayes cisterciennes (XIIe–milieu du XVIe siècle)*, ed. Arnaud Baudin and Laurent Morelle (Paris, 2016), 31–54; Richard Allen, 'The Annals and History of the Abbots of Savigny: A New Edition of the So-Called *Chronicon Savigniacense* (12th–14th c.)', *Cîteaux* 68 (2017), 9–73; Richard Allen, 'The Abbey of Savigny (Manche) in Britain and Ireland in the 12th Century: Three Overlooked Documents', *Annales de Normandie* 68 (2018), 9–33; and Brigitte Galbrun and Véronique Gazeau, ed., *L'abbaye de Savigny (1112–2012): un chef d'ordre anglo-normand: actes du colloque international de Cerisy-la-Salle, 3–6 octobre 2012* (Rennes, 2019). For Swietek and Deneen, see note 35 above.
[50] For an illustrative, if anonymous, example see University of Illinois Archives, 15/13/2,

Hill's role as a pioneer and trailblazer, as the only black medievalist – one of the only black historians – any of his white American or European peers had ever met in the 1960s and early 1970s, altered the trajectory of his career, and fundamentally shaped it, sometimes in very negative ways. Even as an undergraduate, Hill struggled in his first year at Princeton, which in 1952 was an all-male and still virtually all-white institution. He finished that year ranked 506 out of 727 students.[51] His experience was so negative that Hill's mother was moved to write to the dean of the college, expressing concern for her son and wondering why he was doing so poorly after having done so well at Central High in Philadelphia.[52] After all, Hill was not the only graduate of the integrated Central High at Princeton – there were points of comparison, if 'white' points of comparison – and as Dean Albert Elsasser's response to Mrs Hill admitted, based on his standing at Central, Hill should have performed better that first year.[53]

Throughout their correspondence Hill's race was never mentioned, although euphemisms, such as his 'adjustment', were used. When the administrator of the Helen D. Groomes Beatty Fund, which had given a scholarship to Hill, requested his transcripts from Dean Francis Godolphin in the spring of 1953 and asked about Hill's 'adjustments', an unknown person in the dean's office scribbled along the bottom margin of the letter, 'Ask Mommsen about his "adjustment".' The word, 'adjustment', was bracketed in scare quotes. Underneath, the same person continued the handwritten remarks, 'Colored. M[ommsen] has seen [him] 6 times. Quite well adjusted. Doing creditable work – think he will do better.'[54] In the event, Hill did do better in his second year, although he would be reprimanded for 'disorderly conduct' on Halloween 1953 when his white roommate – not Hill himself – hosted a party in their dorm room and the drunken guests threw beer bottles from his window in Little Hall onto the roadway below.[55]

After Halloween, Hill rose 250 places between his first and second years, and under the tutelage of Mommsen and Strayer, he found his footing. He rose higher in his class each year and in 1956 he graduated with honors and finished

---

Report on Promotion to Full Professor, Paul P. Bernard to Lynn Altenbernd (November 25, 1974).
[51] Princeton University Archives, AC198–04, Selective Service System, College Student Certificate (September 15, 1953).
[52] Princeton University Archives, AC198–04, Muriel C[larke] Hill to Dean Francis R.B. Godolphin (May 10, 1953).
[53] Princeton University Archives, AC198–04, Albert Elsasser to Mrs. David B. Hill (Muriel Clarke) (May 19, 1953).
[54] Princeton University Archives, AC198–04, Beatrice M. Baker to Dean of Men, Francis R.B. Godolphin (March 5, 1953).
[55] Princeton University Archives, AC198–04, Sweeney and Cuomo, Proctors, to Dean Francis R.B. Godolphin (October 31, 1953). The reprimand remained a part of Hill's official record at Princeton. See idem, Student Record Summary of Hill, Bennett D. (June 12, 1956), 2.

159th overall.⁵⁶ But even as his career and ambitions advanced, at Princeton and in the profession more generally, Bennet's race remained a remarked-upon issue. When he applied for admission to Princeton's graduate school in 1960, Norman Cantor, who was in the final, contentious year of his teaching career at Princeton, wrote 'on' Hill's behalf:

His undergraduate work at Princeton resulted in a good record (graduation with honors) but not an exceptionally outstanding one. He must, however, have won the attention of his teachers because he acted as a research assistant for Professor Goldman and Professor Harbison and was well liked by Professor Strayer and Professor Mommsen. How much this favorable treatment was due to the fact that Mr Hill is a Negro, I cannot say. His intense devotion to the Roman Catholic faith led him (perhaps mistakenly) towards medieval history.⁵⁷

As a PhD candidate at Princeton, Hill applied for a Fulbright in 1961 to carry out archival work on the Cistercians in England and France. He was interviewed, internally, by Dean Hamilton Cottier, himself a double graduate of Princeton, a lecturer in the English Department, and a former Rhodes scholar.⁵⁸ Cottier recorded his 'personal impression' of Hill on the application form in pencil:

Slightly odd-looking – in no way objectionable. Quiet, reserved, serious, poised. Should get along well with people and make a good impression. His maturity augurs well for his work and attitude abroad. He is a colored man, very light – hardly discernible.⁵⁹

After his interview, Hill chose not to pursue the application further.⁶⁰

In 1962, Hill left Princeton to become a lecturer at Western Ontario University in London, Canada. Following the successful defense of his dissertation in 1963, he was promoted to assistant professor there before leaving for the University of Illinois one year later, in 1964. As one might expect, after the passage of the Civil Rights Act in 1964, the Voting Rights Acts in 1965, and in the aftermath of the Civil Rights Movement of the 1960s, Hill's race and racial appearance stopped being remarked upon in marginal comments of official documents. In

---

⁵⁶ Princeton University Archives, AC198–04, Student Record Summary of Hill, Bennett D. (June 12, 1956), 1.
⁵⁷ Princeton University Archives, AC105–04, Norman Cantor to R.R. (Robert) Palmer (March 16, 1960). In the same letter, Cantor went on to describe Charles Alan Taylor's seminar at Harvard as 'dull and narrow'. For a notion of how Cantor viewed other medieval historians and himself, see his *Inventing the Middle Ages: The Lives, Works, and Ideas of the Great Medievalists of the Twentieth Century* (New York, NY, 1991); and *Inventing Norman Cantor: Confessions of a Medievalist* (Tempe, AZ, 2002).
⁵⁸ 'Obituary of Hamilton Cottier', *Princeton Weekly Bulletin* 69 (September 24, 1979), 6.
⁵⁹ Princeton University Archives, AC198–04, Fulbright Applicant-Princeton (October 2, 1961).
⁶⁰ Princeton University Archives, AC198–04, Bennett D. Hill to Dean (Hamilton) Cottier (November 8, 1961).

fact, in the surviving official record of his nineteen-year tenure as a professor in the History Department of the University of Illinois between 1964 and 1983, his race is explicitly mentioned once, again by Norman Cantor, who wrote to the chair of the search committee which hired Hill on 18 January 1964, 'I hope that you are also going to consider Bennett Hill, at Western Ontario, a Princeton product. Appointing him would be good public relations since he is both a Negro and a Catholic, but that is not the reason I support (him).'[61]

While explicit mentions of race and explicit examples of racism disappear from the official record, it continued to trouble Hill in other ways, as he was subjected to tokenism, if sometimes well-meaning or at least not ill-intentioned, throughout this period of his life as the first, and for long stretches of time, the only African-American professor in the history department at Illinois.[62] In May 1971, while Hill was in England on his first sabbatical as a junior professor, the chair of his department, Winton Solberg, wrote to him complaining of the 'recent machinations in the Department, one of which involves stirring up the BGSA (Black Graduate Student Association) to insist upon appointing black students with voting rights to our search committee for an Afro-American historian.'[63]

Hill's direct reply does not survive, if there ever was one. However, he wrote to the department's administrator, Mrs Sandy Lewis, four days later on 8 May 1971, observing: 'Letters from Solberg and others recently give the impression that all is not peace and love on the third and fourth floors of Gregory Hall. Well, I suppose the school year is almost over, and everyone can go off and get refreshed or fortified for the next round.'[64] An outwardly laconic and non-committal, yet pointed and already resigned response to the recurring battles of racial equity that would play out at the University of Illinois and across the country during his tenure, as well as to the role he would be asked to play in those struggles. Years later, on the same day in August 1975, Hill was appointed as the history department's affirmative action officer and, despite being a historian of medieval Europe in a faculty of well over a dozen American historians, he was made chair of the search committee for Afro-American History (following the departure of the eventual 1972 appointee, Robert L. Harris).[65]

By August 1975, Hill had already been promoted to full professor and had served as the acting chair of the department. In 1978, he formally became the first African-American chair of the history department at the University of Illinois. For two years, Hill fought university budget cuts amid an inflation

---

[61] University of Illinois Archives, 15/13/2, Norman Cantor to Maurice Lee (January 18, 1964).
[62] Paul Wood, 'Colleagues Recall UI's First Black History Professor', *The News-Gazette*, Urbana, Illinois, 22 March 2005.
[63] University of Illinois Archives, 15/13/2, Winton Solberg to Bennett Hill (May 4, 1971).
[64] Bennett Hill to Mrs. [Sandy] Lewis, 8 May 1971. University of Illinois Archives.
[65] University of Illinois Archives, 15/13/2, Walter L. Arnstein to Bennett D. Hill (August 29, 1975). It should be noted that Arnstein remained a good friend of Hill's throughout his life and wrote a moving obituary for him following his death in 2005.

crisis, but also struggled to change the department's curriculum. In his first departmental newsletter, written from the 'not-so-easy chair', Hill explicitly centered the need for those changes in the 'social challenges' and transformations that had occurred in the 1960s, cautioning however, 'it is easier to move a graveyard than to revise a university curriculum'.[66] In his second and final newsletter, published a year later, he admitted that 'only modest changes were made in the undergraduate program', noted that some of the changes which had occurred were for the worse, and cautioned that the 'quality of undergraduate education remains a very serious concern'. Hill ended his message by writing that 'the ancient concept of universities providing a liberal education which introduces the student to many aspects of culture, which broadens the mind and expands the options disappears. *Tempus edax rerum.*'[67]

Hill held the chairmanship for two years before abruptly resigning the chairmanship in the fall of 1980. He took a leave of absence, at first a paid sabbatical, then an unpaid one, journeyed to Washington, DC, and found refuge in Saint Anselm's Benedictine monastery. He resigned from the university, without ever returning, in the summer of 1983 at the age of forty-eight.[68] His chairmanship, and his professional experiences more generally, had taken a toll.

Although Hill's race was never mentioned in his official record at the University of Illinois, it was highlighted, in a negative context, in the student newspaper: *The Daily Illini*. On 14 February 1970 Hill became embroiled in a controversy over the appointment of a new dean of students. The student newspaper published an exposé on the search committee's deliberations, on which Hill served alongside other faculty members and students. Under the subheading 'Black dean under pressure?' a student reporter wrote that 'The racial issue raised some uncomfortable moments in the committee meetings firstly when Hill, who is black, reportedly suggested that the next dean should not be black because of the pressures it would place him under.'[69] Hill was furious. Two days later, alleging that the 'article is easily the most irresponsible and distasteful piece of undergraduate journalism that I have seen' and that his comments had been taken 'out of context' and 'distorted', he wrote a memorandum to the chancellor of the university resigning from all university committees. Despite the fact that Hill had been, and would continue to be, an inspiring teacher who advocated on behalf of undergraduate students, he refused

---

[66] Bennett D. Hill, *History at Illinois* (1978–9), 1. Incidentally, this quotation is sometimes attributed to Princeton and US President, Woodrow Wilson. A recent example: Frank H.T. Rhodes, 'The University and Its Critics', in *Universities and their Leadership*, ed. William G. Bowen and Harold T. Shapiro (Princeton, NJ, 1998), 10.
[67] Bennett D. Hill, *History at Illinois* (1979–80), 1.
[68] University of Illinois Archives, 15/1/41, Bennett D. Hill to William C. Widener (July 9, 1983).
[69] 'Those Who Would Be Dean: The Confidential Committee Report and How It Came About', *The Daily Illini*, 14 February 1970, 14.

to be placed on any future committees that involved students.[70] His resignation was accepted by the chancellor on the same day.[71] Context and distortion to one side, it is hard not to view Hill's reported comments in that committee meeting as self-referential. Few people, in 1970, understood the pressures a black academic and university official would be placed under better than Bennett Hill.

Despite these challenges and pressures, and the substantive effect they had on the trajectory of his career, throughout his life Hill remained deeply enthusiastic about medieval studies and the study of history, the promise of the university, and about his own studies at Princeton as an undergraduate and graduate student, and especially, about his direct teachers and advisors. Following his retirement from St Anselm's in the 1990s, Hill continued writing reviews, primarily for the *Library Journal*, and editing his influential series of textbooks. He served as an executive in the American Catholic Historical Association and once again became a regular presence at Medieval Studies' events in Princeton, then guided by William Chester Jordan.[72] In 1993, he endowed the Joseph R. Strayer Prize, named in honor of his undergraduate and graduate advisor who had passed away a few years prior, but which recognized the best senior thesis in medieval studies, broadly defined, acknowledging the debts he had long felt he owed to his teachers across the humanities.[73] Although it is unacknowledged by the university, Hill was the first African-American alumnus in Princeton's history to endow an academic prize.

Bennett Hill remained a trailblazer to the very end of his life. Every year in August when a student opens *A History of World Societies* for the first time and in May when the Joseph R. Strayer Prize is awarded to another student who has a written an exemplary senior thesis addressing some aspect of medieval society and culture, his legacy lives on.

---

[70] University of Illinois Archives, 15/13/2, Bennett Hill to Chancellor J.W. Peltason (February 16, 1970).
[71] University of Illinois Archives, 15/13/2, Chancellor J.W. Peltason to Bennett Hill (February 16, 1970).
[72] John Bilinkoff, Thomas R. Greene, and Sandra Horvath-Peterson, 'Report of the Committee on Nominations', *Catholic Historical Review* 81 (1995), 232.
[73] William Chester Jordan, email message to author (30 April 2021).

Figure 12.1. Bennett David Hill, 1960.
(Princeton, Princeton University Archives, Graduate Alumni Records, AC105–04)

Publications of Bennett D. Hill

Books

English Monasteries and Their Patrons in the Twelfth Century (Urbana, IL, 1968).
Church and State in the Middle Ages (New York, NY, 1970).
with John P. McKay and John Buckler. *A History of Western Society* (1st ed., Boston, MA, 1979).
with John P. McKay and John Buckler, *A History of World Societies* (1st ed., Boston, MA, 1984)

Articles

'The North American Bishops and the Second Vatican Council'. *Colloquium* 4 (1965), 23–35.
Entries on 'Alphanus of Salerno', 'St. Bertherius', 'Charles of Villers', 'Abbey of Lorsch', 'St. Lull of Mainz', 'St. Marius of Avenches', 'St. Mainrad of Einsiedeln', 'Bl. Merbot', 'Bl. Oderisius', 'St. Othmar', and 'St. Peter Pappacharbano' in *The New Catholic Encyclopedia*. New York, 1967.
'Thomas Becket and the Cistercian Order'. *Analecta Sacri Ordinis Cisterciensia* 26 (1970), 64–80.
'The Counts of Mortain and the Origins of the Congregation of Savigny'. In *Order and Innovation in the Middle Ages: Essays in Honor of Joseph R. Strayer*, ed. William Chester Jordan, Brian McNab, and Teofilo Ruiz, 237–53. Princeton, NJ, 1975.
'The First French Foundations of the Norman Abbey of Savigny'. *American Benedictine Review* 31 (1980), 130–52.
'Lay Patronage and Monastic Architecture: The Case of Savigny'. In *Monasticism in the Arts*, ed. Timothy Gregory Verdon, 173–87. Syracuse, NY, 1984.
Entries on 'Aelred of Rievaulx', 'The Benedictines', 'The Camaldolese', 'The Carthusians', 'The Celestines', 'The Cistercians', and 'Savigny, abbey and congregation of'. In *Dictionary of the Middle Ages*, ed. Joseph R. Strayer, 13 vols. New York, 1982–9.
Entries on 'Abbey of Poblet', 'Abbeys, Royal', and 'Asceticism'. In *Medieval Iberia: An Encyclopedia*, ed. E. Michael Gerli. New York, 2003.

Printed and bound by CPI Group (UK) Ltd, Croydon, CR0 4YY
01/12/2024
14602691-0001